PANTHEISM

AND

CHRISTIANITY

PANTHEISM

AND

CHRISTIANITY

By JOHN HUNT, D.D.

VICAR OF OTFORD, KENT

'Ο Θεὸς τὰ πάντα ἐν πᾶσιν.
ST. PAUL.

Γέγονεν ἄνθρωπος, ἵνα ἡμᾶς θεοποιήσῃ
Θεοὶ διὰ τὸν ἐν ἡμῖν Λόγον.
ST. ATHANASIUS.

KENNIKAT PRESS
Port Washington, N. Y./London

PANTHEISM AND CHRISTIANITY

First published in 1884
Reissued in 1970 by Kennikat Press
Library of Congress Catalog Card No: 78-102573
SBN 8046-0733-8

Manufactured by Taylor Publishing Company   Dallas, Texas

PREFACE.

It is now seventeen years since I published a book called 'An Essay on Pantheism.' That book has been for a long time out of print. Though often asked to issue another edition, I always hesitated because the magnitude of the subject seemed to increase the more I looked at it. Moreover, on the special subjects of some of the chapters, as Buddhism and Spinozism, much had in the meantime been written which required to be read and considered. I at length determined on another edition, but after re-writing and printing the first chapter I found it was necessary to make a new book. A large portion of the original matter has been retained but revised, retrenched, or enlarged, while several chapters have been added in which the argument is brought to a more definite issue.

'Christianity and Pantheism must be reconciled, otherwise it will be the worse for Christianity,' are the words of one of the reviewers of the 'Essay on Pantheism.' The object of this book is to show not only that they can be reconciled, but that Christianity will be a great gainer by the reconciliation. Something which is called Pantheism is found invariably to be the ultimate utterance of reason on God and his relation to nature. Christianity, properly understood, will meet at the same goal. Objections to many Christian doctrines will be found to have no validity when these doctrines are considered apart from anthropomorphic conceptions of the Deity. Many controversies that have distracted the Christian Church will cease when it is clearly seen that though we may speak of God as if he were a man, yet that the Bible fully justifies us in speaking of him as if he were not a man. The dogmas or definitions of the Churches are not to be regarded as absolute truth, but as merely provisional expressions to be superseded by others as the human mind advances in its conception of what God is and how he reveals himself to man. This was seen by Peter Lombard, who wisely said that 'the determinations of the Church were rather designed to exclude from the simplicity of the divine Essence than to put anything into it.' It will be seen from the following pages that not only schoolmen and fathers of the Church, but even Bible writers, have spoken of the super-personality of God and of his immanency in the world in words often as startling as the words of those who are called Pantheists. They are all efforts to speak of God as he is, and their failing is the negative one of imperfection rather than of positive error. So far as they are genuine expressions of reason, at whatever stage of development and however varied their external forms, they will all be found to verge to a common meaning.

In the revision of what is retained of the 'Essay on Pantheism,' I have used largely Ueberweg's 'History of Philosophy,' translated by Professor Morris, with additions by Dr. Noah Porter. Had this valuable work existed twenty years ago, I should have been saved much labour. Many of the passages which I had translated from Greek or Latin authors, or other passages with the same meaning, are there given in the original.

Among the eminent men with whom the former book brought me into correspondence or acquaintance, two, now no more, are never to be forgotten. One of them was Dr. John Muir of Edinburgh, who revised the chapter on the Indian religions, and took a special interest in the whole subject. The other was Dean Stanley, who honoured me with his friendship, and when he had an opportunity helped me by his patronage. Before I knew him personally, he wrote these characteristic words, 'I like your book, because it is *inclusive* not *exclusive.*'

OTFORD VICARAGE, SEVENOAKS,
19th *October*, 1883.

In the former book the impersonal deity of the Brahmans was written Brahm. In accordance with the recent custom of Sanscrit scholars, it is here written Brahmă (neu.), while the personal God is Brahmā (mas.).

CONTENTS.

CHAPTER I.
INDIAN RELIGIONS.

CHAPTER II.
PERSIAN, EGYPTIAN, AND GREEK RELIGIONS.

CHAPTER III.
GREEK PHILOSOPHY.

CHAPTER IV.
PHILOSOPHY OF THE JEWS.

CHAPTER V.
NEO-PLATONISM.

CHAPTER VI.
The Church.

CHAPTER VII.
Heresy.

CHAPTER VIII.
Scholasticism.

CHAPTER IX.
The Italian Revival.

CHAPTER X.
Mystics.

CHAPTER XI.

SUFEYISM.

CHAPTER XII.

MODERN IDEALISM.

CHAPTER XIII.

TRANSCENDENTALISM.

CHAPTER XIV.

POETRY.

CHAPTER XV.

MODERN THEOLOGIES.

CHAPTER XVI.

REFUTERS OF PANTHEISM.

CHAPTER XVII.

PHILOSOPHY.

CHAPTER XVIII.

NATURE.

CHAPTER XIX.

CHRISTIAN THEOLOGY.

PANTHEISM.

INTRODUCTION.

OF the word Pantheism we have no fixed definition. The most opposite beliefs are sometimes called by this name; and systems which in the judgment of some are notoriously Pantheistic, are defended by others as compatible with the received doctrines of Christianity. The popular definition does not go beyond the etymology of the word,* God is all, or the all is God; but this defines nothing until we know either what God is, or what the all is. If the universe is material, taking matter in its ordinary sense, then according to this definition God is matter, or, what is the same thing, there is no God; if, on the other hand, the universe is spirit, then God is spirit and matter is only an illusion. There is, then, no material universe, and what we call matter is only appearance, the image or shadow of Being. Hence two classes of Pantheists wholly distinct from each other, the material and the spiritual. The one is without a real God, the other has only a phenomenal world. To call the first by any name which implies that they are Theists, is a contradiction in terms. The second is the class which is chiefly intended when we speak of Pantheists. Since we neither know what matter is, nor what spirit is, it being impossible to demonstrate the existence of the one apart from the other, the indefinite meaning of Pantheism necessarily remains. Between the Pantheism of these two kinds of Pantheists, that which denies a real God and that which denies a material universe, there is a multitude of intermediary views approaching more or less to one or other of these. It is conceivable that mind may be eternally associated with matter,

* Πᾶν, all; θεός, God.

A

and thus the relation between God and the universe may correspond to that of the human soul with the human body. It is again conceivable that matter may be the mere external manifestation of mind having reality only from its connection with mind; or there may be a reality of which mind and matter are both but manifestations, and the reality may be that all which is identical with God. The question of Pantheism will be best discussed after we have examined the beliefs that have been called Pantheistic.

CHAPTER I.

INDIAN RELIGIONS.

NEARLY all writers on Pantheism trace its origin to India. M. Maret reaches the climax of his argument against the French philosophers, by showing that their doctrines came from India, 'the mother of superstitions.' Pierre Leroux, one of Maret's ablest opponents, admitted the fact of his agreement on many subjects with the Indian sages, and added, with an air of triumph, that 'all religions and all philosophies have their root in India, and that had Pantheism not been found in India that would have been a strong argument against its truth, for then humanity would have erred in its beginning.'

In India the creed of modern intellect is combined with the worship of an infinity of gods. This is the problem of the Indian religion; this is the puzzle on every Hindu temple. When this problem is solved for Hinduism, there will be light shed on a similar problem that presents itself in nearly all religions. M. Leroux again truly says, 'The religion of India does not concern India alone; it concerns humanity.'

The history of men's thoughts on the greatest questions on which they can be exercised, God and creation, is everywhere substantially the same. There may be different stages of progress, the development may be checked or stunted, there may be abnormal growth; but however great the phenomenal variety, there is always a real identity.

It is in India that we can trace the fullest development of religious thought. The continuity is less broken. We seem here at the fountain-head of natural religion, and can follow the stream flowing onward with but little interruption to where we now stand. In other countries, the succession has passed from one nation to another, and its course cannot always be traced; but in India the connection is visible between the first men capable of worship, and the latest and best thoughts of the furthest-reaching philosophies, as well as the worst developments of the popular religion.

THE VEDIC HYMNS.

The oldest books of the Hindus are the Vedas, which are four in number. Of these the most important is the Rig Veda. The Atharva is of much later origin than the other three. The Sama, which is the second, and the Yajur, or third, were written in imitation of the first. The knowledge of the Vedas was called the three-fold knowledge, or, literally, 'the three-fold Veda.' At first the Vedas consisted only of mantras or verses. To these were added Brahmanas, or ceremonial prescriptions, and Upanishads, or reflections.

The date of the Vedas is unknown, but the same legends are connected with them as with the sacred books of other nations. Some say that they are eternal, and that they came directly from the mouth of the deity Brahma. There is nothing in them which requires inspiration, or which professes to be more than the production of ordinary men ; but some of the verses are said to have, when recited, the power of charming birds and beasts. When the primitive natural religion came into the hands of the Brahmans or priests, they alone were permitted to read or interpret the Vedas ; and the priests professed to interpret them as they had always been interpreted—that is, by tradition, or what we would call the consent of Catholic antiquity.

The religion of the oldest portions of the Vedas is the worship of nature. Everywhere natural objects were the first things that inspired reverence in man.

'God, soul, the world,
To primal man were one.'

He did not distinguish them, for the age of reflection had not yet come. His worship was the spontaneous feeling that he was in a beautiful and happy world. The question if such worship was monotheistic or polytheistic is really without meaning. It was neither ; or, rather, it was both. It recognised a living power in nature, but that power was manifested under various phenomena. Natural objects were worshipped as gods, but one deity often had ascribed to him the attributes of another, and sometimes the whole of the power manifest in

nature. Primitive worship was the worship of the one in the
all, but without any distinction between the one and the all.

The first and the last verses in the Rig Veda are addressed
to Agni, the god of fire. Agni might be called the chief
deity in the book, but in other verses other deities take the
chief place. In the first hymn, Agni is called god, priest,
pontiff, and herald of the sacrifice. As the sacrificing god,
he is entreated to be present with the other gods, to come
with that benevolence which a father has for a child, and to
be the friend and benefactor of those who worship him. The
first verse of the last hymn is—

> ' O Agni, generous master !
> Thou minglest thyself with all tha'; is.
> In the dwelling of the sacrifices
> Thou kindlest the fires.
> Bring us riches.'

Agni generally appears as an active deity, and often rather as a
servant of the gods than a god. The Devas are asked to protect him, but with the usual inconsistency of the mythology
of nature, he is sometimes the supreme god, 'surpassing,' as
one verse expresses it, 'all the Devas by his greatness.'

The next important deity in the Rig Veda is Indra, the god
of thunder, who rules the elements and who sends rain upon
the earth, making it fruitful. He also appears as the supreme
god, having all conceivable attributes of power and goodness.
There are hymns addressed jointly to Agni and Indra, in
which both have equal honours. They are called the masters
of all treasures, celestial and terrestrial, and are solicited to
bestow them on their worshippers. In one hymn to Indra,
he is spoken of as a mighty conqueror, whom 'neither earth
nor air can vanquish when armed with thunder.' He is said
to be placed by the gods at the head of the conflict, and his
chariot drawn by beautiful horses. He is again described as
powerful in all regions, as having stretched out the heavens
and the earth, and as the god in whom all worlds repose.

Some Vedic scholars say that there are three chief deities in
the Vedas—Agni, Indra, and Surya, the last being the sun, and
that all the others are the same three under other names and
different aspects. There does not, however, seem to be a sufficient interval between these three and the other gods to

justify this inference. In the Vedas, no deity is before or after another. Any one, at any time, may take the place of the supreme. Altogether equal in dignity and importance with Agni and Indra is Soma, who is the subject of praise and adoration in many hymns. Soma was the juice of the moon-plant used in the sacrifices, and intoxicated with which the gods performed their most famous exploits. Soma is called the support of heaven, the substance of the earth, and the being in whose hands are all beings. In another hymn Soma is addressed as the god who comprises in himself the three-and-thirty gods. It is added: 'Rightly do all wise men assemble round the seat of this pure god. He made the world; he made the heavens.'

Every deity is in the first instance a natural object; it is then invested with all the powers in nature; it has ascribed to it all the qualities of all things cognizable by the senses, and thus it becomes the supreme god, constituting the all of nature.

In one hymn, the supreme deity is addressed as Aditi, the Boundless. He is the sky, the air, the mother, and father, and also the son. He is all the gods, as well as the five classes of men; and lest anything should be omitted necessary to the material infinity of the god, he is addressed as 'whatever has been and whatever shall be born.' In some verses, Purusha Sukta is the god who embraces all things in himself. He is all nature personified as a man. He has a thousand heads, a thousand feet, a thousand eyes. He envelopes the earth on every side, transcending it by his fingers. He is all that is, whatever has been, and whatever shall be. He is diffused among all things, animate and inanimate. The moon was produced from his soul, the sun from his eyes; Indra and Agni from his mouth, and Vayu from his breath. The gods are represented as sacrificing Purusha as a victim, from which some have inferred that this hymn is of late origin, the sacrificial idea being less developed in what are supposed to be the earlier hymns. In the Atharva Veda similar attributes are ascribed to Skambha. This god is a vast corporeal being, co-extensive with the universe, and comprehending in his several members the different parts of the material world. He is also the three-and-thirty gods which sprang from non-being. Being is one of his members, so that he is above being. The other gods are parts of him, as the branches are parts of a tree. They do him homage, and pay him tribute. He and Purusha are both identified with Indra, on the principle, apparently, that they are identical with any of the gods who shall at any time take the place of the supreme. Indra again appears as Visvakarman, and is spoken of in the same manner. He brought forth the earth, and stretched out the majestic vault of heaven. On all sides are his eyes, his heads, his arms, and his feet. God alone has brought forth the heavens and the earth. The one he formed with his arms, the other with his feet. He is our father, who has begotten us. He made the other gods, and he contains all things in himself. It is added : ' The waters have borne in their bosom him who is above heaven and earth, the gods and the Asouras. It is he who gives light to all divine things. It is he who is within you.'

A hymn from the Yajur Veda to a deity, whose name is That, has been thus translated :—

> ' Fire is *That*, the sun is *That* ;
> The air, the moon, so also is that pure Brahma.
>
> .   .   .   .
>
> He, prior to whom nothing was born,
> And who became all beings,
> Produced the sun, moon, and fire.
> To what god should we offer oblations
> But to him who made the fluid sky, and the solid earth,
> Who fixed the solar orb, and formed the drops of rain ?
> To what god should we offer sacrifice,
> But to him whom heaven and earth contemplate mentally?
>
> ' The wise man views that mysterious Being
> In whom the universe perpetually exists,
> Resting upon that sole support ;
> In him is the world absorbed;
> From him it issues ;
> In creatures is he turned, and wove in various forms.
> Let the wise man, versed in Holy Writ,
> Promptly celebrate that immortal being,
> Who is the mysteriously-existing various abode.'

There is variety enough, in the names and characters of the Vedic gods, to furnish any number of mythologic speculations. One eminent writer[*] supposes a monotheism preceeding the polytheism, which he calls the growth of degeneracy and corruption. Another great authority on Vedic deities[†] divides

* Pictet.   † Röthe.

them into the moral and the physical, supposing that the moral were retained by the Iranians, while the Indians had left to them only the physical. Guesses like these are easily made, and any one of them is about as good as another. The only clear inference is, that all these gods are personifications of natural objects, that they have a community of the divine, and that any one of them may at any time take the place of the highest god, embracing all others in himself.

Brahma, the prominent deity of later mythology, is rarely mentioned in the Vedas as the supreme god. The name generally occurs as an attribute, or second name of some other deity. Once, however, in a hymn to Skambha, he appears as the universe. The earth is his measure, the atmosphere his belly, the sky his head, the sun and moon his eyes, and Agni his mouth. To him all the gods are joined as branches to a tree. In another hymn the figure is varied, and the gods are said to be in Brahma, 'as cows in a cow-house.'

BRAHMANISM.

Brahmanas and Upanishads introduce us to later eras in the development of religious thought in India. In the early age, worship was of the simplest kind. The hymns were chanted at morning, noon, and night, under the open vault of heaven. There was no temple and no altar, but such as were made by nature. The father was the priest, the mother the priestess, and the children were the body of the faithful. By the time the Brahmanas were added there was an established priesthood, whose business it was to interpret the ancient scriptures, and to perform the sacrifices. The gods are now more definitely persons. Their names are changed, and their identity with natural objects is not so evident. Brahma and Vishnu, who are only secondary gods in the Vedic hymns, are now the chief deities. This development in the direction of polytheism and sacerdotal religion, was followed by philosophical theology. This is found in the Upanishads, which are also called the Vedanta or Vedic ends. Here we find such passages as this: 'The vulgar look for their gods in the water, men of more extended knowledge in the celestial bodies, the ignorant in wood, bricks, and stones, but learned men in the

universal soul.' This soul is described as ineffable, the unknown god who is all things. 'He is neither great nor small,
large nor long; he is without colour, shadow, smell or taste;
without youth or age, beginning or end, limits or bounds.
Before him there was no one, after him comes no one. He
is unspeakably pure, living in eternal repose and in eternal
joy, stable amid all change, in his grandeur free. He sees
without eyes, and hears without ears; he sees all, hears all,
understands all, but is seen of no one, comprehended by no
one.' This impersonal god or universal soul is called Brahmă,
which is equivalent to absolute being. He is called by all
names to denote, it is said, that the diffusive spirit equally
covers all creatures by means of extension, for in this way his
ominpresence is established; yet he is a being more extensive
than all the extension of space. 'All material extension is
clothed with his existence, for he is not only the efficient but
the material cause of the universe. He proceeds more swiftly
than thought. He seems to advance, leaving behind him intellect, which strives to attain a knowledge of him. He seems
to move everywhere, though in reality he has no motion. He
is distant from those who do not wish to know him, but he
is near those who earnestly seek him. To know God is to
feel that we do not know him, and to suppose that we understand him is to show our ignorance of him. We see his
works, and therefore infer his existence; but who can tell how
or what he is?' He is sometimes distinguished from the universe, yet all the being of the universe is in some way involved
in his being. He is called 'the eternal, the unchangeable,
the ever-present.' He applies vision and hearing to their
respective objects. He is the splendour of splendours. The
sun shines not, with respect to him, nor the moon, nor fire. As
the illusive appearance of water produced by the reflection of
rays in the mirage, so the universe shines in him, the real
and intelligent spirit. The universe had its birth in him; and
as bubbles burst in the waters, so shall it find its destruction in him. He is not only called being, but lest that word
should fail to express his infinitude, he is also said to be non-
being; not in the sense that matter is said not to exist, not
because he is less than being, but because he is greater than
all being. Our thoughts of existence are too mean to be applied

to him. We must declare this insufficiency so as it may be understood that when we, the finite, affirm anything of God, it is imperfect; for no number of finites can ever make up an infinite, no accumulation of being can express him who is the source of all being: therefore Brahma is said to be both being and non-being.

This verbal contradiction pervades the whole of Indian theology. It is an effort to express a being who can only be grasped by infinite thought. It therefore takes refuge in poetry, and struggles to utter by luxuriant similitudes what language cannot accurately express. The deity, as soul, is described as transcending and yet pervading all things. He speaks in the thunder, flashes in the lightning, roars in the cataract; he glances in the sun, smiles in the moon, rolls in the ocean, sparkles in the fountain, reposes on the placid lake; he whispers in the zephyrs, murmurs in the leaves of the forest, and the mighty mountains are the shadows of the ever-present God. He is one, and yet manifold. As the one, no tongue can truly name him, no finite thought can worthily conceive him; as the many, he peoples the heavens the earth, the air, and the sky. Every region is full of gods, for everything that lives and moves is full of the divine. The fields are sacred, for Brahma is there; the rivers are worshipped, for Brahma lives in them. Brahma-putra, as its name implies, is the river of Father Brahma. The Ganges, flowing down from the divine mountains, laden with the richest blessings of the great God of nature, is worshipped as itself divine. The beasts become sacred; and the images of the elephant, the ox, the goat, the hawk, the eagle, and the raven, are found side by side with the idol gods of the Pantheon. Brahma is thus endowed with the attributes of everything, to make up his infinity. The finite is sacrificed to the infinite; but the common understanding of man is conscious of the existence of the finite. It is therefore necessary to deny that this consciousness can be trusted. We imagine the existence of matter. This is the great illusion of life. Matter is called maya, or deception. It seems to exist, but its existence has reality only as the manifestation of Brahma. Creation emanates from him. When he thinks, he becomes object as well as subject—that which is thought of as well as that which thinks. As a man sees himself reflected in a glass, so Brahma beholds himself in creation. That which is to us the manifold world, is to him but the image or reflection of his being. Other representations make creation the divine word or speech. Sometimes Brahma is represented as willing the creation, at other times it is described as flowing from him without his consciousness or will. The substance of created things is his substance. There is nothing out of which he could create them, so he created them out of himself. Creation is thus one with Goda, part of him ; for it is even lawful to speak of the infinite as having parts. As the spider weaves its web from its own bowels, as the tortoise protrudes its legs from the shell, so does Brahma weave or protrude creation. As milk curdles, as water freezes, as vapour condenses, so the universe is formed from the coagulation of the divine substance. These images taken from objects of sense, have an air of materialism ; but though Brahma is thus identified with the material universe, he is essentially spirit. Sometimes creation is the work of inferior gods, who are the agents of the supreme. While the absolute is in repose, the world-makers, who are the word or wisdom of God in activity, are incessantly at work. One legend of creation says, ' In the beginning of all things, the universe, clothed with water, rested on the bosom of Brahmă. The world-creating power swam over the waters upon the leaf of a lotus, and saw, with the eyes of his four heads, nothing but water and darkness. Hence his self contemplation : whence am I ? who am I ? He continued a hundred years of the gods in this self-contemplation, without profit and without enlightening the darkness, which gave him great uneasiness. Then a voice reached his ear : direct thy prayer to the eternal being ! Brahmā (the world-creating power) then raised himself, and placed himself on the lotus in a contemplative position and thought over the eternal being. The Eternal appears as a man with a thousand heads. Brahmā prays. This pleases the eternal, who disperses the darkness and opens Brahmā's understanding. After the darkness had been dispersed, he saw in the exhibition of the Eternal all infinite forms of the earthly world as buried in a deep sleep. Then the Eternal said, ' Brahma, return to contemplation ; and since through penitence and absolution thou hast desired the knowledge of my omnipotence, I will give thee power to bring forth, and to develop the world out of the life concealed in my bosom.'

In this relation of the supreme God to creation, through the mediation of the other gods, we trace the origin of the Hindu trinity, which is simply Brahmă in his manifestations as creator, preserver, and destroyer.   The early gods of the Vedas, representing the powers of nature, disappear, and these three gods, whose images are united into a *Trimurti*, take their place.   They are persons of the impersonal godhead. Each of the three appears as the supreme God, and each of them has traces of some relation to the powers or elements of nature.   To Brahmā the earth is sacred, to Vishnu the water, and to Siva the fire.   In the laws of Menu we have an account of the origin of Brahmā.   The invisible god created the five elements; to water he gave the power of motion.   Through this power arose a golden egg, which shone like a thousand suns, and in this was born Brahmā, the great father of all reasonable beings.   Brahmă, as yet, is scarcely distinguished from Brahmā; for in the same book Brahmă is said to have created the universe.   The following dialogue relates to the creator and creation.   The speaker is Brahmā, who is called the wisdom of God, and Narud, his son, who is also called reason, or the first of men :

Narud.   O father! thou first of God! thou art said to have created the world ; and thy son, Narud, astonished at what he beholds, is desirous to be instructed how all these things were made.

Brahma.   Be not deceived, my son.   Do not imagine that I was the creator of this world, independent of the divine mover, who is the great and original essence and creator of all things.   Look, therefore, upon me only as the instrument of the great will, and a part of his being whom he called forth to execute his eternal designs.

Narud.   What shall we think of God ?

Brahma.   Being immaterial, he is above conception : being invisible, he can have no form ; but from what we behold in his works, we may conclude that he is eternal and omnipotent knowing all things and present everywhere.

Narud.   How did God create the world ?

Brahma. Affection dwelt with God from all eternity. It was of three kinds : the creative, the preserving, and the destructive. The first is represented by Brahma, the second by Vishnu, the third by Siva. You, O Narud! are taught to worship all three in various shapes and likenesses, as the creator, preserver, and destroyer.

Narud. What dost thou mean, O Father ! by intellect ?

Brahma. It is a portion of the great soul of the universe, breathed into all creatures to animate them for a certain time.

Narud. What becomes of it after death ?

Brahma. It animates other bodies, and returns like a drop to that unbounded ocean from which it first arises.

Narud. What is the nature of that absorbed state which the souls of good men enjoy after death ?

Brahma. It is a participation of the divine nature where all passions are utterly unknown, and where consciousness is absorbed in bliss.

Narud. What is time ?

Brahma. Time existed from all eternity with God.

Narud. How long shall the world remain ?

Brahma. Until the four jugs shall have revolved. Then Siva shall roll a comet under the moon, and shall involve all things in fire and reduce them to ashes. God shall then exist alone, for matter shall be totally annihilated."

In the Puranas, or mythological legends, the same doctrines concerning God and creation are repeated in many different forms. The three gods of the Trimurti take the place of the Supreme. They are, so to speak, his manifestations, or the Eternal under forms conceivable by man. Sometimes Brahma is all things, both spiritual and material. In other places Vishnu is all things, all gods and all persons of the godhead. He is at once creator, preserver, and destroyer; he is the sacrifice and the sacrificial rites, the sun, the moon, the whole universe, the formed and the formless, the visible and the invisible. As the wide-spreading tree is compressed in a small seed, so at the time of dissolution the whole universe will be compressed in Vishnu as in its germ; as the bark and the leaves of the plantain-tree may be seen in its stem, so may all things be seen in Vishnu ; as the fig-tree germinates from the seed, and becomes first a shoot and then rises into loftiness, so the created

world proceeds from Vishnu. He is the essence of the gods
and of the Vedas, of everything and of nothing; he is night
and day, he is time made up of moments, hours, and years;
he is mind, intellect, and individuality; he is gods and men,
beasts and reptiles, trees, shrubs, and grasses; he is all bodies,
and all souls that animate bodies.

Brahma and the gods thus address the Supreme: 'We
glorify him who is all things, the Lord supreme over all, the
unperceived, the smallest of the small, the largest of the largest
of the elements, in whom are all things, from whom are all
things, who was before existence, the God who is all beings,
who is the end of ultimate objects, who is beyond finite spirits,
who is one with the supreme soul, who is contemplated as the
cause of final liberation by sages anxious to be free. To him
whose faculty to create the universe abides in but the ten
millioneth part of him, to him who is one with the inexhaus-
tible supreme spirit, I bow; and in the glorious nature of the
supreme Vishnu, which nor gods, nor sages, nor I, nor Sankara
apprehend—that which the Yogis, after incessant effort,
effacing both moral merit and demerit, behold to be contemplated in the mystical monosyllable Om, the supreme glory of
Vishnu and Siva.'

This universality of existence which is ascribed to Brahma
and Vishnu is also ascribed to Siva. In a legend from the
Rudra Upanishad, it is said: 'The gods proceeded to
the celestial abode of Rudra, and inquired, Who art
thou? He replied, I am the fount and sole essence. I am
and shall be, and there is nothing which is distinct from me.
Having thus spoken, he disappeared; and then an unseen
voice was heard saying, I am he who causeth transitoriness,
and yet remaineth for ever. I am Brahma. I am the east
and the west, the north and the south. I am space and
vacuum. I am masculine, feminine, and neuter. I am Savitri,
the Gayatri, and all sacred verses. I am the three fires. I am
the most ancient, the most excellent, the most venerable, and
the mightiest. I am the splendour of the four Vedas and the
mystic syllable. I am imperishable and mysterious. I am all
that is, and all space is comprehended in my essence.'

In the Devi Upanishad, the same attributes are ascribed to
the wife of Siva.

In the Bhagavat Gita, an episode in the great Indian epic, the Mahabharatta, the same things are said of Krishna, who was one of the incarnations of Vishnu. The subject of the poem is the quarrel of two branches of one great family. The hero, Arjuna, looks on his kinsmen, whom he is about to slay, and his courage fails him. Krishna at this moment appears, and exhorts him not to fear. The arguments addressed to Arjuna are derived from the illusive nature of all existences except the divine, which, being eternal, none can injure. Krishna tells Arjuna that kinsmen, friends, men, beasts, and stones are all one; that that which to-day is a man was formerly a vegetable, and may be a vegetable again. The principle of everything is eternal and incapable of destruction. All besides is illusion. If Arjuna will not meet his friends in battle, he is deceived by appearances, mistaking shadows for reality. At last Krishna reveals himself, and tells Arjuna that he appears not only in this form, but in all forms; for he is everything, and is in everything. He is creator, preserver, and destroyer; he is matter, mind, and spirit. There is nothing greater than he is, and everything depends on him as the pearls on the string that holds them. He is the vapour in the water, and the light in the sun and moon; he is the sound in the air, and the perfume in the earth; he is the brightness in the flame, the life in animals, the fervour in zeal, the eternal seed in nature, the beginning, the middle, and the end of all things. Among the gods he is Vishnu, and the sun among the stars. Among the sacred books he is the Canticles. Among rivers he is the Ganges. In the body he is the soul, and in the soul he is the intelligence. Among letters he is Alpha, and in words combined he is the bond of union. He is death, which swallows up all, and he is the germ of those who do not yet exist. To show that he is all things, Krishna thus calls himself by the name of all things.

HINDU PHILOSOPHY.

The history of mind in India corresponds to the same history in Europe. Every system that has appeared in the West, has had its counterpart in Brahmanism. There we have dogmatism, mysticism, materialism, idealism, and scepticism, in all their manifestations, and in all their stages of development. A French writer, M. Martin, even finds 'Positivism' in the Rig-Veda. Sir William Jones compared the six leading philosophies of India, with the principal systems of the Greeks. The two of Nyaya have their counterpart in the Peripatetic and Ionian schools. The two of Mimansa correspond to the Platonic, and the two of Sankya to those of the Italics and Stoics. We noticed in the beginning that if God and the universe are one, if the universe be material, and that which we call matter has any reality in itself, the conclusion is that the deity is matter. ' There is no escape from this alternative but by declaring our ignorance of what matter is, or our conviction that it is not any true being. And this, in the majority of cases, is the declaration of Brahmanism. Yet the Indians, like ourselves, have their systems of materialism. The chief of these is the Sankya of Kapila, who has been reckoned an atheist. This is peculiarly the system of Hindu Rationalism: setting aside the authority of the Vedas, Kapila substitutes for Vedic sacrifices knowledge of the imperceptible one. We are to free ourselves from the present servitude and degradation, not by following the prescriptions of holy books, but by being delivered from our individuality—by ceasing to know ourselves as distinct from other things, and other things as distinct from us. Kapila did not mean to be an atheist, but it has been inferred that he was one from his making some indefinite principle which he called Prakriti, or nature, the first of things. What he meant by this principe may be open to many answers. It was the undefined eternal existence, without parts or forms, which produced all which we see and know. There is an intelligence, indeed, in nature, for nature lives. We see its presence in all thinking and sentient beings : but that intelligence is not the producing cause, it is itself produced. Buddha, or intelligence, is not the first, but the second principle in nature; it depends on the organization of material particles. What is true of this world soul, is also true of the soul of man. It originates with the body, and with the body vanishes. Kapila describes the soul as the result of seventeen anterior principles. He places it in the brain, extending below the skull, like a flame which is elevated above the wick. It is the result of material elements, in the same way as an intoxicating drink is the result of the chemical combination of its ingredients.

The other Sankya bears the name of Patanjali, a disciple of Kapila. He agrees with his master in making knowledge the means of deliverance from this present bondage. Carrying this principle to the extreme of mysticism, he inculcates an entire abstraction from all objects of sense, and a pure contemplation of the deity alone. He exhorts all men to become Yogis, meditators upon God. Patanjali departed entirely from Kapila, in his doctrine of matter and spirit. Regarding bodies as the result of soul, he leaned to idealism, admitting that matter exists as a reflection, an illusion, an appearance. The soul, he says, is placed above sensibility, intelligence above the soul, and being above intelligence. This is that non-being without attributes, which is most truly being, one and all things.

The Nyaya is divided into two schools: the physical and metaphysical. The author of the first is Kanada. Being a doctrine of atoms, it has been compared with the system of Democritus; but the agreement is only in appearance. The atoms of Kanada were abstractions, mathematical or metaphysical points that had neither length, breadth, nor thickness. Though a physical system, it ended in idealism. Kanada judged that material substances had no reality but that derived from their qualities; and these again were derived from the mind perceiving, and were not to be found in the object perceived. The author of the second Nyaya was Gotama. He does not concern himself much with matter, but discourses chiefly of mind. His great question is, 'What is soul?' and he concludes that it is a principle entirely distinct from the body, and does not depend for its existence on any combination of elements. The treatise of Gotama is purely dialectical, and rivals in abstruseness and subtlity, anything that is to be found in the metaphysics of the West.

The third system is the Vedanta, which has two schools: the Parva Mimansa, and the Uttara Mimansa. The first, which is attributed to Jamini, is entirely practical, and seems to have no characteristic beyond the commendation of a virtuous life. The second was taught by Vyasa, and is the one chiefly intended when we speak of the Vedanta. This is, properly, the orthodox philosophy—the generally received exposition of Vedic doctrine. Here Brahma is the axis, the centre, the root, the origin of all phenomena. Mind is not made a product of nature, but nature is declared to be a product, or rather a mere manifestation of mind. The true absorption of man is declared to be not into nature, but into the bosom of eternal Brahma. In the Vedanta Sara, or essence of the Vedanta, Brahma is called the universal soul, of which all human souls are a part. These are likened to a succession of sheaths, which envelop each other like the coats of an onion. The human soul frees itself by knowledge from the sheath. But what is this knowledge? To know that the human intellect and all its faculties are ignorance and delusion. This is to take away the sheath, and to find that God is *all*. Whatever is not Brahma is nothing. So long as man perceives himself to be anything, he is in ignorance. When he discovers that his supposed individuality is no individuality, then he has knowledge. Brahma is the substance, we are his image, and the countenance of Brahma alone remains. Man must strive to rid himself of himself as an object of thought. He must be only a subject, a thought, a joy, an existence. As subject he is Brahma, while the objective world is mere phenomenon, the garment or vesture of God.

The mystical knowledge of God, whereby we become one with him, is said by some to be a later introduction into Brahmanism; but it seems to be as old as the oldest philosophies, and makes an essential part in them all. The ever-repeated doctrine continually meets us: that so far as we exist we are Brahma, and so far as we are not Brahma, our existence is only apparent. To know God is to know ourselves; to be ignorant of him is to live the illusive life. What, then, is our duty and destiny? To be united to Brahma, in other words, to realise that we are one with him. To contemplate merely the world of forms, and the apparent existence, is to contemplate nothingness, to gaze upon delusion, to remain in vanity, yea, to be vanity itself. We must soar above phenomena, above the brute instincts, above the doubts of reason, above intelligence. We must separate ourselves from all which is subject to change, enter into our own being, unite ourselves to pure being, which is Brahma the eternal. He that hath reached this state is free from the bondage of individuality.

He no more unites himself to anything; he has no more passions, consciousness is absorbed in bliss. He has neither fear, nor joy, nor desire, nor activity, nor will, nor thought. For him is neither day nor night, nor I, nor thou, nor known, nor knowing: all is gone. There remains only the universal soul, separated from the world, delivered from the illusions of maya. He is one with the Eternal. He has found the object of his search, and is one with the object of his knowledge. He knows himself in the truth of his being. To reach this elevation is the end and object of all religion, and all philosophy. Every man has a foretaste of this union in dreamless sleep, when the life spirit is simple and free; then speech with all its names, the eye with all its forms, the ear with all its tones, the understanding with all its images returns to Brahma. Then those who at death are not prepared for this union must return to earth, some for one and others for several times, till the soul is sufficiently purified for the final absorption. Yes, the final absorption; for this is the blessed consummation of all things. Their coming forth from the eternal is accounted for in many ways. The general burden of all is, that by creation came imperfection and evil, and therefore we long for deliverance from creation, we long for that existence which was before creation was. That in all things which is real, being eternal, will remain united to him who is eternal; that which is illusory will pass. Brahma will change his form, as a man changes his garment. As the tides return to the ocean, as the bubbles burst in the water, as the snow-flakes mingle in the stream, so will all things be finally lost in the universe of being. Creator and creation are sleep plus a dream. The dream shall vanish, but the sleep shall remain. Individual life will mingle in that shoreless ocean of being, that abyssal infinite which no intellect can comprehend, and even Vedic language fails to describe, the eternal and unchangeable Brahma.

BUDDHISM.

Gotama Buddha, called also Sakya Muni, or the Sakya Sage, lived about six hundred years before Christ. He was, properly, a reformer of Brahmanism; and it is only by remembering his relation to Brahmanism that his life and work can be understood. His religion took its character from his own individuality. It was born of the miseries of human life, and its chief aspect is that of a religion of humanity. Gotama, though a prince, was attended by sorrow from his birth. His mother died when he was seven days old, and he grew up a solitary child. His youth was spent pondering, with a sadness unbecoming his years, over the mysterious problem of being. To induce him to enter on the pleasures of life, his father persuaded him to marry a princess; but he still occupied himself reflecting on the vanity of existence.

The mirth of the palace did not drive from his thoughts the solemn questions, ' What is life ? ' ' What is it worth ? ' ' To what does it tend ? ' Everything was fleeting. Life was a shadow, with no reality, and without satisfaction. Tradition has many stories of Gotama's retirement from the world. It is said that one day, driving in the pleasure gardens of the palace, he saw a withered old man with palsied limbs and faltering speech ; and being informed that he was suffering from old age, the common lot of all men, he exclaimed, ' Alas ! if it be so, what has one to do with pleasure ? ' He then ordered his chariot to be driven back to the palace. Another day he saw a man suffering from a loathsome disease, and on being told that he was a leper, he made similar reflections on the impossibility of taking pleasure while such things were possible to man. A third day he saw a dead body, and learning that death was the end of all, he resolved to withdraw from the world that he might be free from all sorrow, and be able to show to others the way of deliverance. A fourth day he met a hermit, and was told that he was a man who had renounced the world, and who lived on alms that he might give himself wholly to meditation. Gotama then exclaimed that this was the true life, and resolved to follow it, that he might obtain deliverance from age, disease, and death. Accompanied by five Brahmans, he retired into the forest, where he spent six years in meditation and mortification of the body. Not finding deliverance in this way, he began to take more food, on which the Brahmans left him, and returned to Benares. He then retired for forty-nine days of meditation, under a mimosa-tree. Here he was tempted by devils, and had great spiritual conflicts, but at last he was triumphant. He found the way of deliverance. The feeling in which Buddhism originated is not peculiar to India. It is found wherever man is found. There is no one who has not at some moment felt it. We hear it in the sad exclamation of Solomon, 'Vanity of vanities, all is vanity;' in the words of the Greek poet, who said, 'The best of all is not to be born;' and of a modern poet, who, lamenting the condition of the poor, addressed death as 'The poor man's dearest friend.' The soliloquy of Hamlet was the essence of Buddhism, 'Oh that this too, too solid flesh would melt.' The feeling of the vanity of life is universal, but the Buddhist's mode of deliverance is peculiar. The Brahman did call his god Being, and the final absorption was into the eternal and unchangeable essence; but the Buddhist looked and longed for pure nothingness. To most men, non-existence is the most terrible of all things. The loss of being is that from which we naturally recoil, except in moments of the deepest sorrow. But to the Buddhist, annihilation is the consummation of blessedness. Men die, but that is not their end, so long as sins are unatoned for, they must be re-born into existence. Nirvana is the final deliverance when the soul is destined no longer to be. It is that death which is followed by no birth, and after which there is no renewing of the miseries of life. Nirvana is beyond sensation and the world of change. What is in Sansara or the transient world is not Nirvana, and what is in Nirvana is not in Sansara. In Sansara is coming and going, change and motion, fulness and manifoldness, combination and individuality; in Nirvana is rest and stillness, simplicity and unity. In the one is birth, sickness, age and death, virtue and vice, merit and demerit; in the other complete redemption from all conditions of existence. Nirvana is the bank of deliverance nodding to him who is in the stream of Sansara. It is the sure haven to which all souls are directing their course who are seeking deliverance from the ocean of sorrows; it is the free state, which furnishes an asylum to those who have broken the chains of existence and snapped the fetters that bind to the transient life. The soul goes through its transitory existences till the source of its re-birth is exhausted, till it can no longer be re-born, and therefore no longer die. The I is extinguished as plants no longer watered, as trees whose roots have been dug up from the earth, or as the light fades when the oil of the lamp fails.

The Buddhist Nirvana has been understood by some as simply death, the grave, or the land of stillness. Others have taken it as what it plainly seems to be, simple annihilation. But there are others again who have conjectured that it has some analogy to that kingdom of which Jesus spoke, which was not meat and drink but righteousness and joy. Buddha described it by negatives, but in common with the Brahmans, he looked upon what we call being as really non-being, illusion, mere phenomena. Nirvana may thus be the eternal, the unchanging state which is the only true existence. Buddha's mind was not speculative, he always turned to the practical side; he did not profess to describe Nirvana in itself, but only in its relation to the present illusive life. The mode of reaching Nirvana was by faith or intuition, by pure thoughts, pure words, and good deeds. Men were taught to seek after charity, patience, purity, courage, meditation, knowledge, not to kill, not even beasts, not to commit adultery, not to lie or use bad language, and not to take strong drink. That which really is, or that which Nirvana is, Buddha may not have professed to be able to know: what man really knows is the world of phenomena. We plant a seed, from it springs a tree; the tree bears fruit, the fruit bears a seed; from the seed again springs a tree. A bird lays an egg, from it springs another bird; this bird lays another egg, from it again comes a bird: and so it is with the world and with all worlds. They have come from earlier worlds, and these from others that were earlier still. Existence unfolds itself, forms appear and disappear, being alone is unchanged. Life succeeds life, but nothing is lost and nothing is gained. Being is a circle which has neither beginning nor ending. As the moisture is drawn up into the clouds and poured down upon the earth to be drawn up again by the sun's rays, so being undergoes its perpetual and manifold evolutions in the midst of which it remains unchanged. Individuals fall but others rise to take their place; and thus the procession advances apparently in a circle that never ends. But whether or not these worlds are to roll on for ever, the Buddhist does not profess to know. They may have had a beginning and they may have an end. What he really knows, and what it concerns him most to know, is how to work out his own deliverance. He sees an inevitable

connection between existence and actions. Every deed, good
or bad, has an influence through infinite space, and brings with
it a necessary consequence, and will do till Nirvana is reached.
The present state of everyone, his happiness or misery, his joy
or his sorrow, is but the ripe fruit of all the deeds he has done
in his many previous lives. Men will continue to be re-born
into the phenomenal world until they are delivered from the
illusion of personal existence.

It is commonly said that the religion of Buddha was
atheism. The gods of the Vedas and the Vedic mythology he
regarded as no gods. He dispensed with priests and sacrifices,
and substituted a moral life for offerings to the gods, and followed reason rather than antiquity. His religion was more a
life than a creed, and was more concerned with humanity
than with God. The inference that he was an atheist probably rests on the same principles of interpretation as those
which made Nirvana annihilation. He may, like the Brahman,
have regarded God as so entirely unknown that it was
impossible for human thought to grasp him, or for human
language to speak of him, and therefore it was better not to
attempt the impossible. He may have raised a temple to the
unknown, and prescribed silence as the highest worship. God
could not be any of the things of the finite world, and all of
them did not make an infinite. He could not be a person ;
and in the denial of personality, Buddha may have seen a
safeguard against idolatry. We might infer that substantially Buddha agreed with the philosophies of the Brahmans
in recognising the Infinite ; but while they called him by the
name of all things, Buddha called him by no name. By
righteousness we reach Nirvana, and in Nirvana we are one
with the unknown. As Nirvana alone is true existence, so
God alone is true being. Buddha never formulated his
theology ; but this inference that he was not an atheist has
some confirmation from the fact that the Buddhists of Nepaul
and of the North acknowledge a supreme God. Buddha
means intelligence. To come to intelligence was to come to
the light, to receive Buddhahood, or become one with the chief
Buddha. The educated Lamas says that Buddha is the independent being, the principle and end of all things. The earth,
the stars, the moon, all that exists, is a partial and temporary

manifestation of Buddha in the sense that all comes from him as light from the sun.

The account of the Indian religions in the first edition was taken in a great measure from old authors. Creuzer was chiefly followed, though Maurice, Moore, Coleman, Sir William Jones, Rammohun, Roy, Vans Kennedy, Mrs. Spiers, Professor Wilson, Rowland Williams had also been read, with the Oriental Translation Society's publications, so far as they had then appeared. We have now 'The Sacred Books of the East,' edited by Professor Max Müller; the 'Hibbert Lectures,' and other works, by the same author; Dr. John Muir's 'Sanscrit Texts,' and some valuable papers in 'The Journal of the Royal Associate Society for 1865,' by the same writer. 'Dialogues on Hindu Philosophy,' by K. M. Baunerjea; and 'A Rational Refutation of the Hindu Philosophical System,' by Fitz-Edward Hall, were not known to the author when the first edition was published. A recent book is 'Hinduism and its Relations to Christianity,' by the Rev. John Robson (1874). On the special subject of Buddhism, we have Koeppen, in German; Renouf and St. Hilaire, in French; and in English, Spence Hardy's 'Manual.' In the Sacred Books of the East, there are treatises on different forms of Buddhism. The *Contemporary Review*, January, 1877, has an article by Mr. Rhys Davids, who interprets Nirvana as a spiritual reality, corresponding to the Christian idea of the kingdom of God. Mr. Davids also agrees with those who are inclined to regard the Buddhists as Theists. Samuel Johnson, an American writer, also gives a favourable interpretation of Nirvana in a book called 'Oriental Religions.' He says, 'The testimony of the best criticism to the substance of primitive Buddhism establishes the fact that Nirvana, far from meaning annihilation in an absolute sense, was positive exaltation and blessedness expected to follow upon deliverance from special forms and embodiments, through detachment from the elements of individuality, regarded as grounds for successive births, from grief, &c. (Vol. II., p. 211). This writer again says, 'It does not appear that there is any great ground, either in historic fact or rational thought, for attributing absolute atheism to any people.' Koeppen himself, an important authority on the history of Buddhism, gives a long list of authorities, who affirm that it has absolutely no trace of the idea of God; and this is the prevailing opinion of the Christian world. But writers who speak of God will always be found to have given a meaning to the idea of God, which involves, more or less distinctly, the Hebrew and Christian theory of an original creation, proceeding at a given time from a divine pre-existent will. Koeppen has himself quoted passages in which the Buddha is addressed as God of gods, Brahma of Brahmas, Indra of Indras, Father of the world, &c. (Vol. II., p. 194). The French books referred to in the beginning of this chapter are 'Essai sur le Pantheisme,' by M. Maret; and a treatise, 'De l'Humanié,' by Pierre Leroux; also articles by the same author in 'L'Encyclopédie Nouvelle— Christianisme, Ciél, Théologie.'

CHAPTER II.

In the light of the Indian religions we may interpret all the religions of antiquity. They differ, and yet they are alike. We cannot determine if the one sprang from the other, or if each is a natural growth of the religiousness of man ; but they have all a fundamental likeness. Worship of the powers of nature is the origin of them all; and as the mind expands, worship of nature in its infinitude, including, consciously or unconsciously, the whole conceivable assemblage of being as shadowing forth a being infinite and inconceivable, whom we can neither know nor name. Hence, on the one hand, a Polytheism ; and on the other, alongside of it, a Monotheism. While the philosophers contemplated the infinite, the multitude idolized the finite. After the Indian, the religions of the ancient world which are best known to us are those of Persia, Egypt, and Greece.

THE PERSIAN RELIGION.

Of the antiquity of the religion of the Persians we cannot speak with certainty. The sacred books called the Zend Avesta, are the chief sources of information ; but these are only a fragment of the original scriptures — part of the twenty-one divisions into which they were divided. The Zend Avesta was written or collected by Zoroaster, the great prophet of Persia, who may have been contemporary with Buddha, five or six centuries before the Christian era. It is, however, generally admitted that portions of the Zend Avesta writings are of much more ancient date than the time of Zoroaster.

The Parsees, both from their language and mythology, are classed with the Indians as members of the great Aryan family; and as they inhabited the birth-place of the human

race, it is probable that the religion of Persia is the oldest
in the world. When we compare it with Brahmanism, we
find each possessing a sufficiently distinct individuality of
its own. The ingenious mythologer will find many points
of resemblance, but the general student will be more struck
with their difference.

Brahmanism is more metaphysical; Parseeism more ethical.
The spirit of the one is contemplation; that of the other,
activity. The Indian is passive and speculative; the Persian
is not without a speculative tendency, but he is more concerned to oppose the forces of evil which are in the world,
and to subdue which he feels to be the vocation of man.
To the degree that Parseeism is ethically strong, it is removed from what is called Pantheism; but the speculative
side claims our attention, as well for its own sake as for
its subsequent history, and its connection with other systems
of religion and philosophy.

Much has been written, not only in France and Germany
but in England, on the infinite and impersonal God of the
old Persian religion. His name is Zeruane Akerne, time
without bounds, or beginningless time. The idea of his
existence is simultaneous in the mind with the ideas of
infinite time and infinite space. He is the being that must
constitute eternity and infinity. That the Persian had this
idea of an inexpressible being, who is above all the gods as
Brahmă is above the Trimurti, may be considered as settled.
But it appears that the name by which this being is known
to European mythologers is a mere mistranslation of a
sentence in the Zend Avesta. Zeruane Akerne is not a name,
as recent Persian scholars have shown; it simply means infinite time. The passage is : ' Spento-Mainyus (Ormuzd) created,
and he created in infinite time (Zeruane Akerne).' The
infinite being of the Persians was nameless, but sometimes
called by the names of all the gods. He becomes personal.
He is Ormuzd, god of light ; Mithras, the reconciler between
light and darkness ; Honover, the word of him who is
eternal wisdom, and whose speech is an eternal creation.
Hesychius calls Mithras the first god among the Persians.
In his conference with Themistocles, Artabanus describes
Mithras as that god who covers all things. Porphyry,

quoting from Eubulus concerning the origin of the Persian religion, speaks of a cave which Zoroaster consecrated in honour of Mithras, the maker and father of all things. It was adorned by flowers, and watered with fountains, and was intended as an image, or symbol, of the world as created by Mithras.   The same Porphyry records, that Pythagoras exhorted men chiefly to the love of truth, for that alone could make them resemble God.   He had learned, he said, from the Magi that God, whom they called Ormuzd, as to his body resembled light, and as to his soul, truth. Eusebius quotes from an old Persian book as the words of Zoroaster, that 'God is the first being incorruptible and eternal, unmade and indivisible, altogether unlike to all his works, the principle and author of all good. Gifts cannot move him, he is the best of the good, and the wisest of the wise.   From him proceed law and justice.'   The Chaldean oracles, ascribed to Zoroaster, call God 'the one from whom all beings spring.'   On this passage Psellus, the scholiast, says, 'All things, whether perceived by the mind or by the senses, derive their existence from God alone, and return to Him, so that this oracle cannot be condemned, for it is full of our doctrine.'

This original impersonal unity created Ormuzd, who thus becomes the chief of gods.   He is the living personal Deity, first-begotten of all beings, the resplendent image of infinitude, the being in whose existence is imaged the fulness of eternal time and infinite space.   As the manifestation of the impersonal, he is infinite—none can measure him, none can set bounds to his will or his omnipotence.   He is pre-eminently will, altogether perfect, almighty, infinitely pure and holy.   Of all things in heaven, he is supreme; of all things, he is the ground and centre.   The sun is his symbol, yet the sun is but a spark of that unspeakable splendour in which he dwells.   Whatever the original one is, that is Ormuzd—infinite in light, in purity, in wisdom.   But as the first begotten of the eternal, his duration is limited to twelve thousand years. As a personal deity, he is finite. He is a king, and has a kingdom which is not universal, for it is opposed by the kingdom of Ahriman.

It has been commonly believed that the Persians worship-

ped two gods. This is the account given by Mohammedan
and Christian writers, but the Persians themselves have
always denied it. They are not Dualists, but Monotheists
on the one side and Polytheists on the other. Ormuzd
alone is worshipped as the supreme God. His kingdom is
co-extensive with light and goodness ; it embraces all pure
existences in earth and heaven.

Ormuzd's domain has three orders. The first is the Amshaspands, or seven immortal spirits, of which Ormuzd
is himself one. He created the other six, and rules over
them. The second order is the twenty-eight Izeds, and the
third an innumerable number of inferior spirits called the
Fereurs. The Izeds are the spiritual guardians of the earth ;
by them it is blessed and made fruitful. They are also
judges of the world and protectors of the pious. Every
month and every day of the month is under the guardian-
ship of one of the Amshaspands or Izeds ; even every hour of
the day has an Ized for its protector. They are the watchers
of the elements ; the winds and the waters are subject to them.
The Fereurs are without number, because being is without
bounds. They are co-extensive with existence ; sparks as it
were of- the universal being who, through them, makes
himself present always and everywhere. The Fereurs are
the ideals — prototypes or patterns of things visible. They
come from Ormuzd, and take form in the material universe.
By them the one and all of nature lives. They perform
sacred offices in the great temple of the universe. As high
priest, they present the prayers and offerings of Ormuzd.
They watch over the pious in life, receive their departing
spirits at death, and conduct them over the bridge that passes
from earth to heaven. The Fereurs constitute the ideal
world, so that everything has its Fereur, from Ormuzd down
to the meanest existence. The eternal or self-existent
expresses himself in the almighty word, and this expression of universal being is the Fereur of Ormuzd. The law
has its Fereur, which is its spirit. It is that which is
thought by the word as God. In the judgment of Ormuzd,
Zoroaster's Fereur is one of the most beautiful ideals, because
Zoroaster prepared the law.

But there is another kingdom besides that of Ormuzd, king

of light. There is the kingdom of Ahriman, or lord of darkness. He is not worshipped as a god, but he has great power in the world. The effort of the Persian to solve the problem of evil is seen in his idea of the kingdom of darkness. It emerges face to face with the kingdom of light. There is not the hopelessness of human existence which we find in Buddhism; but there is the declaration that evil is inseparable from finite being. The old question had been asked 'What is evil?' How did he who created light also create darkness? If he were good and rejoiced to make the kingdom of goodness, how has he also made the kingdom of evil? The answer is: It did not come from the will of the eternal. The creation of the kingdom of evil and darkness was the inevitable result of the creation of the kingdom of light and goodness. As a shadow accompanies a body, so did the kingdom of Ahriman accompany that of Ormuzd. The two kingdoms, though opposed to each other, have yet a similar organization. The one is the counterpart of the other. At the head of the kingdom of evil is Ahriman. Then seven Erz-dews, and then an innumerable multitude of Dews. These were all created by Ahriman, whose great and only object was opposition to the kingdom of Ormuzd. When light was created, then Ahriman came from the south and mingled with the planets. He penetrated through the fixed stars and created the first Erz-dew, the demon of envy. This Erz-dew declared war against Ormuzd, and then the long strife began. As on earth beast fights with beast, so spirit warred with spirit. Each of the seven Erz-dews has his special antagonist among the Amshaspands. They come from the north and are chained to the planets; but as powers and dignities in the kingdom of Ahriman, they receive the homage of the inferior Dews, and are served by them as the Izeds are served by the Fereurs. The existence of the kingdom of darkness is an accident in creation—a circumstance arising from the infinite manifesting himself as the finite. He permits evil to continue, not because it is too strong for him, but that out of it he may educe a greater good. The limitation will be finally removed. The discord between light and darkness will cease. The reconciler will appear, and then shall begin an eternal kingdom of

light without shadow, and purity without spot. The spirits
of Ahriman shall be annihilated. According to some representations, their chief shall be annihilated with them; but
others think he shall continue to reign without a kingdom.
Now, the Izeds wait for departing souls and preserve them
for the final day ; they shall then be brought forth to be
purified with fire. They shall pass through mountains of
burning lava, and come forth without sin or stain. Ahriman
shall be cast into darkness, and the fire of the burning
metals shall consume him. All nature shall be renewed.
Hades shall flee away. Ahriman is gone. Ormuzd rules.
The kingdom of light is one and all. But who is the reconciler ? Mithras, the human god. He is God, and yet he
is in the form of man. All the attributes of Ormuzd are
gathered up into a human form and make Mithras. He is
fire, light, intelligence, the light of heaven. To the Persian,
the end of all religion is to become light. In all nature he
strives for the victory of the good over the evil. He craves
light for the body and light for the soul, light to guide
his household, light to rule the state. As the symbol of all
that is good in creation, his cry is, Light ! light ! more light !

Mithras is the giver of light. But how is he to be distinguished from Ormuzd, who rules over the kingdom of light ?
This is not so easy to answer. It would perplex the
mythologer to find the place of Mithras in the Persian Pantheon ; yea, to find a place for him at all, without giving
him some of the attributes of Ormuzd, just as Ormuzd had
to get some of the attributes of the ineffable one. But
the perplexity of the mythologer matters nothing. It is
enough for the Persian that Mithras is the mediator—the
human god or the human side of God. It is enough that
he is light, the creator of light, the grand wrestler for
light against darkness, and that he will finally win the victory,
for which the disciple of Zoroaster waits and longs. The
sun must be his image ; he has kindled that globe of fire ;
it is a reflection of his splendour. He is the heavenly light
that came forth from the Eternal, and he is the principle
of material light and material fire. Therefore the Persian
says in his offerings to the sacred flame, 'Let us worship
Mithras.'

When the finite world was created, the darkness placed itself in opposition to Mithras, but this opposition is posited only in time. It is the strife of day and night; the light side of the year striving with the dark side; piety struggling with impiety; virtue with vice. The Eternal only willed the light, but the darkness arose; and as the world emanated from him, he cannot leave it. As Mithras, he mediates and works to hasten the victory. We see the great sun fighting and wrestling; every year, yea, every day, he obtains a fresh victory, and purifies himself from the spots of darkness. Is not this Mithras? What other power is in that sun but the intelligible light which is fighting against darkness? There the mighty principle of right is struggling for victory; there glow sparks of that eternal splendour which is too strong for darkness, and before which all spots must disappear, and all shadows flee away. The kingdom of darkness shall itself be lightened with heaven's light. The Eternal will receive the world back again into himself. The impure shall be purified, and the evil made good through the mediation of Mithras the reconciler of Ormuzd and Ahriman. Mithras is the good, his name is love. In relation to the Eternal he is the source of grace; in relation to man he is the life-giver and mediator. He brings the word as Brahma brings the Vedas, from the mouth of the Eternal. It is he that speaks in the prophets, he that consecrates in priests; he is the life of the sacrifice and the spirit of the books of the law. In heroes he is that which is heroic; in kings that which is kingly; in men he is man. There is a representation of Mithras from old Persian sculpture. It is a young man about to plunge a knife into the equinoctial bull. God condescends to the limits of time and space, becomes incorporated in the world, identifies himself with its perishable nature. Thus by a sort of self-sacrifice originating life year after year, the life of nature falls a victim to the seasons.

Creation is sometimes ascribed to Mithras, and sometimes to Ormuzd. God rises and speaks the word ' Honover.' Through this word all beings are created. The progress of creation advances as Ormuzd continues to pronounce the word, and the more audibly he speaks the more creation

comes into being. From the invisible heaven which he in-
habits he created the surrounding heaven in the space of
forty-five days. In the)middle of the world, under the
dwelling of Ormuzd, the sun is placed. Then the moon
arises, and shines with her own light. A region is assigned
to her, in which she is to produce verdure, and give
warmth, life, and joy. Above this is placed the heaven of
the fixed stars, according to the signs of the zodiac. Then
the mighty high spirits were created—the Amshaspands and
the Izeds. In seventy days the creation of man was completed,
and in three hundred and seventy-five days all which is, was
created by Ormuzd and Ahriman.

Honover, the creative word, 'I am,' or 'Let it be,' is the
bond which makes the all one. It unites earth to heaven,
the visible to the invisible, the ideal to the real. A period
may be assigned for creation, but in truth creation is eternal.
Ormuzd has been always creating. From moment to moment
in eternal ages the word was spoken by the Infinite, by the
Amshaspands, by the Izeds, by the Fereurs, by all spirits
throughout nature. It is the mystery in and by which the ideal
world has its existence. It is the ground of all beings, the
centre of all life, the source of all prosperity. Zoroaster's law
is the embodiment of the law of Ormuzd; hence the Zend
Avesta is itself called the living word.

In this mysterious Honover, the originals and patterns of
visible things existed eternally. Here we catch a glimpse of
the meaning of the symbolic worship of Persia. Regarding all
visible things as copies of the invisible, the ideal was worshipped
through the sensible. Prayers were addressed to fire and light,
to air and water, because the originals of these were in the word
of Ormuzd. But chiefly to fire: temples were erected for its
consecration; liturgies framed for its worship; sacred fire was
carried before the king; it burned religiously in all houses and
on all mountains. Not that adoration was directed to the mere
material element, but to that divine and heavenly existence of
which fire was the copy, the symbol, the visible representation.
What is fire? Manifested spirit; matter in its passage to the
unseen. What is light? Who can describe that splendour which
irradiates the world? Is it not the outbeaming of the majesty
of Ormuzd, the effulgence of the intellect of the infinite, all-em-

bracing one ? This symbolism was seen in all nature, and in all forms of the social and civil life of the Persian. The Iranian monarchy was a copy of the monarchy of the universe. It had its seven orders corresponding to the seven Amshaspands. It had ranks and gradations, which all blended into one. As with the state, so with the family ; it too was fashioned after the pattern of things heavenly. On the same principle all animals were divided between Ormuzd and Ahriman. They were classed as useful and injurious, clean and unclean. As the kingdoms of light and darkness had their chiefs, so had the animal kingdoms their protectors and leaders. The unicorn represented the pure beasts of Ormuzd, while the symbol representative of the animal kingdom of Ahriman was a monster—in part a man, in part a lion, and in part a scorpion. The watching and far-seeing spirits were symbolized by birds : these belonged to the pure creation, and were enemies to Ahriman. Ormuzd was represented by the hawk and the eagle, whose heads were supposed to be images of eternal time. The dragon-serpent is Ahriman ; his spirits are dews, and their symbol the griffin, inhabiting the clefts of the desolate rocks. In this way of difference and intelligible unity, the Persian placed the being as well as the origin of all things in the impersonal One.

The author of the introduction to the English version of the Zend Avesta,* finds, in the Parsee religion, the blending of Aryan with Semetic thought. ' The origin,' he says, ' of many gods and heroes whom the Parsee worships and extols, without knowing who they were or whence they came, were suddenly revealed by the Vedas. The religion of the Magi was the Iranian development of the Indian religion, and makes the second stage of Aryan thought. The supreme, or heaven god, was Varana, a Vedic deity, the all-embracing sky. The spiritual attributes of the heaven god were daily more and more strongly defined, and his material attributes were more and more thrown into the background. Yet many features, though ever dimmer and dimmer, betray his former bodily, or rather his sky nature. He is white, bright, seen afar, and his body is the greatest and fairest of all bodies. He has the sun for his eye, the winds above for his spouses, the fire of lightning for his son. He wears the heavens as a white bespangled garment.'

* James Dermesteter.

The Egyptian Religion.

The gods of a nation take their character from the climate of the country, and from the condition and character of the people. So true is this, that where foreign deities are adopted they become as it were naturalized ; and however great the affinities between the gods of different nations, every country has its own peculiar deities. We notice first the difference ; but when we pass from the mere outward features to the inner reality we find the likeness becoming closer, until we discover the principle in which they have a common origin.

All the great systems of religion that prevailed in the East have their foundation in the doctrine of emanation. On the one side they are the worship of a being infinitely great ; on the other side, the worship of the attributes of that being as these are seen or symbolized in nature. They are different forms of the God-consciousness in man ; and often when the form is most different the substance is most alike. The supreme Deity of the Persians dwelt in light ; but the supreme God of the Egyptians dwells in thick darkness. There is a sphinx at the temple gate : it speaks a riddle ; it proclaims a mystery. Inside the temple are the statues of young men, who intimate, with suppressed speech, that the name of God is secret ; pointing with their fingers, they admonish us to beware that we profane not the divine stillness. The incomprehensible deity must be adored in silence ; we may not speak of him but in words of the most awful reverence. It is permitted us to feel and to know the truth of his presence ; but the amulet of Isis, the voice of nature, is alone the true speech of God.

What then is he ? None can tell. His symbol is a globe or sphere, for he has neither beginning nor end. His duration is eternal, his being infinite. He is present in all things—his centre here ; his circumference nowhere. We may call him Ammon, but this only means that he is hidden or veiled. We can call him by no true name, for no name can express him. ' Call him then by all names,' said Hermes Trismegistus, 'for as much as he is one and all things ; so that, of necessity, all things must be called by his name, or he by the name of all things. We cannot see him, but, says Plutarch, ' he sees all things; himself being unseen.' Material things are the forms of which he is the substance; the garment with which he clothes himself, and by which he is made manifest to men. The workmanship of nature, like the web of Arachne, is wonderful; and by it we can see that there is an intelligence at work, veiled indeed, yet visible in its productions. The work manifests the worker.

The writings that bear the name of Hermes Trismegistus contain a full exposition of Egyptian theology. Our knowledge of Hermes is chiefly through the Neo-Platonists. The books which bear his name are supposed to have been written about the fourth century after Christ, and must only be received as the Neo-Platonic interpretation of Egyptian theology. In them, the identity of God and nature is distinctly taught. Among the infant nations of the world, this identity seems to have been always assumed, not perhaps that they consciously made God and nature one, but that they had not yet learned to separate between nature and the power which works in nature. The ancient Egyptians may not have been philosophers, but Hermes Trismegistus undertook to expound the philosophy which was underlying their religious belief. How far he reads his philosophy into their religion, or how much of it he found already there, we cannot now inquire. For the identity of all things with God he adduced the favourite argument, that they must have existed as ideas in the divine mind. The reality of things, he says, must be eternal, for that cannot be which has not been before. God is not matter, he is the power which quickens matter. The sensuous world is strictly his creation. By his will it exists. It is the receptacle of the forms which he endows with life. All creation is from him and by him, but it is also in him.

The Pantheistic character of these writings may be learned from some words in the eighth book: ' There is nothing in the whole world which God is not. He is being and non-being; he has manifested being, but he has non-being in himself. He is not manifest, and yet he is the most manifest of all. He is whatever may be contemplated by the mind, or is visible to the eye. He is incorporeal and multi-corporeal. There is nothing of any body which he is not, for he is all things. Therefore

has he all names, because he is one father, and, therefore, has
he no name in himself, because he is the father of all things.
Who, therefore, can worthily speak of thee, or to thee? Whither
turning, shall I praise thee? Above, below, within, without?
Neither mode nor place belong to thee, nor anything besides.
All things are in thee, all are from thee. Thou givest all
things and thou receivest nothing, for thou hast all things, and
there is nothing which thou hast not. When, O father! shall I
praise thee? For what shall I praise thee? For those things
which thou hast done, or those which thou hast manifested,
or those which thou hast concealed? But why will I praise
thee? As being of myself, as my own, or as if I were another?
For thou art what I am; thou art what I do; thou art what I
say; thou art all which is produced, and which is not produced.
Thou art an intelligent mind, and efficient father, a God at
work; good, doing all things well. The most attenuated part
of matter is air; that of air, soul; that of soul, mind; that of
mind, God.'

This idea is repeated in all Eastern religions. It is felt that
the highest being must in some way descend through all
spheres and circles and forms of existence. No order is conceivable if God be not conceived as everywhere conditioning
the most conditioned. This presence is not merely passive, but
active. Nor is it merely a presence; it is also a connection.
The Creator is in some way united to his works. The Hindus
used the simple illustration of a spider and its web, or a tortoise
protruding its limbs. The Persian made God the light of creation, and darkness the necessary shadow of the light: so that
light and darkness had been one, and would ultimately be one
again. Sometimes creation was called God's garment, but
Hermes changed the figure, and made God the garment of the
world. 'He embraces it in his bosom; he covers it with his
being; he takes it into himself as the universe includes in its
existence every world of which it is composed.' God is the
supreme world. The constitution of nature is not merely the
work of God, but God is its *compages*—the power which by its
presence and being constitutes nature. And thus God is every
thing, one and yet all things—things which are, for he has manifested them; and things which are not, for their ideals and
patterns are in him. He did not receive things from without,

but sent them forth from his own being. The world is his conception, visible things are his incarnated thoughts. 'Is God invisible?' says Hermes; 'speak worthily of him, for who is more manifest than he? For this very cause did he make all things, that in all things thou might'st see him. As the mind is seen in thinking, so is God seen in working.' Hermes avoids materialism, but he is not afraid of an apparent contradiction. He feels that the truth concerning God must be a contradiction to man. In the spirit of Egypt among sphinxes and beings grotesque and indefinite—after showing how God is the Lord and Maker of all things, yea, and is all things, he concludes, 'that all being parts of God and he the maker of all, he, as it were, makes himself.'

The deities of the Egyptians are arranged into three orders. This was the division made by Herodotus. In the first order there are twelve gods; in the second eight; and according to Bunsen, in the third seven. The only deities that were worshipped throughout Egypt belonged to the third order, these were Osiris and Isis. Ammon, the concealed God, was doubtless worshipped everywhere, for to him all worship was ultimately referred. He was the supreme God. As the Persian One became Ormuzd, or Brahmă became Brahmā, so did the concealed god of Egypt become the revealed. But there were others beside Ammon who stood for the supreme God. The chief of these was the ram-headed god of the Thebaid, the patron deity of Egypt: Ptah, the creator of the world, and the lord of truth, with Neith, the goddess of wisdom, all of the first order, but chiefly Osiris, Isis, and their son Horus, of the third order. Osiris and Isis are the most familiar of the Egyptian gods. They represent singly, or together, the whole of nature, and that being whose power and presence is everywhere manifest in nature. The Egyptians have many legends of Osiris and Isis, of the time when they once reigned in Egypt, of the murder of Osiris by the treachery of Typhon, and of the sorrows and lamentations of Isis. How much of history there may be in these we cannot determine. The interpretation most like the truth is that which regards them as personifications of the operations of nature. Osiris is the deity unveiled, he is sometimes Kneph or Athor, and this Athor is again united to Isis as the hidden principle of the universe, the creative wisdom of the

Deity. She had a temple at Sais, on which was written the famous inscription preserved by Plutarch, 'I am all that hath been, is, and shall be, and no mortal has uncovered my veil.' But Osiris and Isis could only manifest the highest being to the extent that nature reveals him.

'Osiris and Isis,' says Dr. Prichard, 'are the universal being, the soul of nature corresponding to the Pantheistic or masculo-feminine Jupiter of the Orphic verses. Typhon represents physical evil. To him are attributed eclipses, tempests, and irregular seasons. He is the sea which swallows up the good Nile and produces drought and famine. He is the enemy of Osiris, and his wife Nephthys is the enemy of Isis. Nephthys is represented by the desert; and the inundation of the Nile is the deity leaving his garland in her bed. Typhon is the south wind of the desert, and to him all hideous beasts are sacred. Another deity is Horus, the brother of Osiris; he too is the sun, the world, the all of nature. He is supposed to be identical with Harpocrates, who is sometimes called the son of Isis. Harpocrates was the god of silence, the emblem of nature in her silent progress. When the buds opened in spring time, and the tender shoots burst silently from the earth, then was Harpocrates born. Every spring was the festival of his birth. The young god died, but his everlasting mother lived and re-produced him as the seasons changed.' Apuleius, an Egyptian priest of the third century, represents Isis as thus addressing him after he had been initiated into the Egyptian mysteries, 'I am she that is the natural mother of all things, mistress and governor of all the elements, the initial progeny of worlds, chief of divine powers, queen of heaven, the principal of the gods celestial, the light of the goddesses, at my will are disposed the planets of the air, the wholesome winds of the seas; and the silences of the unseen world, my divinity is adored through all the world, in divers manners, with various rites, and by many names. The Phrygians call me the mother of the gods; the Athenians call me Minerva; the Cyprians, Venus; the Candians, Diana; the Sicilians, Proserpina; some call me Ceres, Juno, Bellona, Hecate; the Ethiopians and the Egyptians worship me as Queen Isis.' *

What was said of Isis was said also of Kneph. The Egyp-

* Fable of the Golden Ass.

tians, according to Porphyry, acknowledged one intellectual author and creator of the world under the name of Kneph. They worshipped him in a statue of human form, with a dark blue complexion, holding in his hand a girdle or sceptre, wearing upon his head a royal plume, and thrusting an egg from his mouth. Iamblichus, quoting from the Hermaic books, teaches nearly the same concerning Kneph. This god is placed as the ruler of the celestial gods. He is a self-intelligent mind absorbed in his own contemplations. Before Kneph is a being without parts, the first occult power, and by Hermes called Eikton. He is worshipped only in silence. After these, are the powers that preside over the formation of the visible world. The creative mind which forms the universe is called Ammon Ptah, or Osiris, according to the character it may assume.'

There was another deity to speak the wisdom of God. This was Hermes, the wisdom of Ammon, the teacher of wisdom among men. Osiris was the great body of nature, Hermes the incarnation of the divine intellect. He was called by other names—Anubis 'the golden,' that which shines in the sun, the leader of the stars, the dog star. He was also called Thoth the pillar, because a pillar is the bearer of all the Egyptian wisdom which was preserved by the priests. Hermes is speech and wisdom; he is the discoverer of astronomy, the teacher of science, the inventor of arts. Among the gods he is pre-eminently the good spirit, the giver of gifts intellectual and spiritual. Osiris and Isis are the good king and queen, Hermes the wise priest. As Sirius in the highest part of the firmament overlooks the other planets, and protects the fiery animals of heaven, so does Hermes protect and care for all creatures. The whole of nature is revealed before him, his wise mind rules the world. He is physician, lawyer, judge. He teaches immortality. He guides souls in their wanderings. By imparting wisdom he makes men one with himself—the wise priest becomes Hermes. If all nature be the exteriority of God, the exhibition to the senses of the invisible Ammon, it must then be all divine, and, if divine, why may it not be worshipped? How indeed can we worship the 'veiled God,' but through his works which declare his wisdom and his power? So perhaps the Egyptians reasoned, or rather more probably concluded without reasoning, and consecrated the visible world as an object of worship.

The Persian, with his clear and ever radiant sky, saw God in the light. The Arabian, with his thoughts directed to the starry heavens, saw God in the planets. The Egyptian, too, saw God both in the daylight and in the stars, but much more in that abundant fertility which came he knew not whence, with the overflowing of the Nile, without which Egypt would have been a desert. How sacred then, above all things, the river Nile! How it must have connected itself with the life and thought and religion of every Egyptian! It was the father of the country, on it depended the strength of Pharoah. But the Nile is only an inanimate object. All things may indeed have come from sand and water originally created by the Unknown Darkness. From these has sprung the lotus with which the Nile abounds. But the Nile has higher developments of existence than sand and water, higher forms of life than the vegetable lotus: it has beasts innumerable, the true children of father Nilus, cherished in his bosom, and abundantly provided for. They are very terrible, they are stronger than men and apparently wiser. They are the genii of that bountiful river, the gods of the stream, why may they not be worshipped if only because they are terrible?

But Egypt is peculiarly a land of beasts. It is prolific in animal life: the lion comes from the desert, the ibis gathers its food on the river's banks, the crocodile basks among the rushes. The Egyptian sees all forms of brute life everywhere abundant. They are guided by a wisdom which is above human wisdom; there is a regularity in their movements which is equalled only by the regularity in the works of nature. As the fruitful Nile ebbs and flows, as summer, winter, spring, and autumn come and go, by the same law do the brutes live. They have their part in the same order. In some respects man is superior to these creatures. They build no tents, plough no fields, neither sow, nor reap, nor gather into barns, yet in many respects they are superior to man. Without his cares and disappointments, they lead a joyful life. The law of nature holds its dominion in them, they are determined by a high wisdom. 'The stork in the heavens knows her appointed season.' They live the universal life, and, as the Egyptian would call it, the highest life. They are unconsciously one with the being of the universe. How natural for the Egyptian to worship the brute creation:

to see in the wisdom which guided them a high reflection of that wisdom which is manifest in all nature !

Animal worship is usually the lowest form of idolatry and the mark of a low degree of civilization, but in Egypt it prevailed among a people famed in antiquity for civilization and learning, and it had its roots in a philosophy of being. The following Pantheistic description of Serapis was given by an oracle of the god :—' My divinity shall be described in the words I shall now utter. The canopy of heaven is my head, the sea is my belly, the earth is my feet, my ears are in the ethereal regions, and my eye is the resplendent and far-shining sun.' *

We may distinguish between the worship of animals, and the worship of them as symbols. The latter was that of the Egyptians. It did not obscure the worship of the gods, but was rather a mode of worshipping them. Their deities were mostly represented in the forms of beasts, even Hermes had a dog's head because of his connection with the dog star. Kneph was a good deity, and therefore was represented as a harmless serpent. Osiris had the hawk for his symbol, and his image was usually formed with a hawk's head. This bird was symbolic of the soul. The crocodile was sacred to the highest God. Plutarch assigns as the cause of this, that it is the only animal living in water which has its eyes covered with a transparent membrane falling down over them, by means of which it sees and is not seen, which is a thing that belongs to the supreme God, ' to see all things, himself being unseen.' Plutarch says in another place, ' Neither were the Egyptians without a plausible reason for worshipping God symbolically in the crocodile, it being said to be an imitation of God in this, that it is the only animal without a tongue, for the Divine Logos or Reason does not stand in need of speech, but going on through a silent path of justice in the world without noise, righteously governs and dispenses all human affairs.' Horus Apollo in the hieroglyphics says the Egyptians acknowledged a superior being who was governor of the world, that they represented him symbolically by a serpent, and that they also ' pictured a great house or palace within its circumference, because the world is the royal palace of the deity,' and again he says,

* Macrobius.

' that the serpent, as it were, feeding upon itself, fitly represents
that all things produced in the world by divine providence
are resolved into it again. '   ' The serpent,' says Philo Byblius,
quoting from Sanchoniathon, ' was deified by the Egyptian
Hermes, because it is immortal and is resolved into itself.'
Sometimes the symbol of the deity was a serpent with a hawk's
head, and sometimes the hawk alone.   In the temple of Sais
there was a hieroglyphic which consisted of an old man, a
young man, and a hawk, to make up the meaning, says Plutarch,
' that both the beginning and the end of human life depend
on God.'   We need not suppose that the multitudes of Egypt
who paid their devotions to the sacred beasts had any conscious
conception that in so doing they were worshipping the one
and all of nature.   They saw God in nature, and therefore
they worshipped all the parts of nature as parts of the divine.

> ' God soul, the world, to primal man were one—
> In shapely stone, in picture, and in song.
> They worshipped him who was both one and all ;
> God-like to them was human kind.   God dwelt
> In the piled mountain rock, the veinéd plant,
> And pulsing brute, and where the planets wheel
> Through the blue skies God-head moved in them.' *

THE GREEK RELIGION.

' To understand,' says Mr. Maurice, ' the difference between
the Egyptian and Greek faith, it is not necessary to study
a great many volumes or to visit different lands—our own
British Museum will bring the contrast before us in all its
strength.   If we pass from the hall of Egyptian Antiquities
into the room which contains the Elgin Marbles, we feel
at once that we are in another world.   The oppression of
huge animal forms, the perplexity of grotesque devices, has
passed away ; you are in the midst of human forms, each in-
dividually natural and graceful, linked together in harmonious
groups, expressing perfect animal beauty, yet still more the
dominion of human intelligence over the animal.'†   No truer
contrast could have been made between the gods of Egypt and

---

* Bunsen's Egypt.
† Boyle Lectures, p. 109.

those of Greece.   The former are rarely human, the latter rarely anything but human.   Yet here the contrast ends.   We have passed apparently from the indefinite to the definite, from the infinite to the finite, but it is only apparently, it is only as regards the external form of the mythologies.   In the inner spirit, we are surrounded by the infinite still.   The Greek may be enjoying nature more than the Egyptian, but he still stands in awe of it.   He may feel the dominion of man over nature, and be conscious that the life of human freedom is higher than that of brute instinct, but he is not without thoughts of the Infinite ; he is not without a deep feeling that there is a something or some Being above, and beyond all his thoughts and all his conceptions—a Being but feebly and imperfectly imaged by these human deities which he creates, and which he worships for their wisdom, their power, and their forms of beauty. The Greek, as well as the Egyptian, worshipped nature.   The names of the old deities in the Theogony are a sufficient evidence of this.   Kronos and Chaos, Erebus and Nyx, with Gaea, Ether, and Hermes, testify to their own origin and meaning. An element of history doubtless mingles itself with the legends of the gods.   Mysterious and even foreign deities may have been introduced from other nations, but the evidence is overwhelming that Greek worship was essentially a worship of nature. The heavens, the ocean, the unseen world was each made a kingdom, and had each a divine king or ruler placed over it. All mountains, rivers, lakes, woods, and forests had their presiding deities.   The spirit of poetry could not go further.   An abundant harvest was Ceres rejoicing.   When the wine-press was trodden, it was Bacchus in the revel.   The tempest tossing the ships was Neptune raging in the deep.   Conscience tormenting the evil-doer was the furies seeking revenge.   All virtues and all vices, all endowments, intellectual and moral, became gods.   War was Mars, and Beauty was Venus; Eloquence was Mercury; Prudence was Minerva; and Echo, no more a sound reverberated by the air, but a nymph in tears bemoaning her Narcissus.   They were beautiful human gods, but they owed their existence to Greek imagination, giving life and form to the manifested powers of nature.   They were all created.   Pindar knew them, and spoke of them when he said —‘ There is one kind both of gods and men, and we both breathe from the same mother, and spring from the same original.' Hesiod knew them when he gave their history and origin, and showed how each was produced from each.

Nor are we without traces of a transition period, when the Greek mind was passing from the Egyptian reverence of grotesque forms to the worship of humanised deities. The early Greek gods were monsters. The children of Uranos and Gaea were Titans and Cyclops, and hundred-headed giants. Even the deities that were afterwards the most famous of the Pantheon were originally of monstrous forms. Pausanias mentions a statue of Jupiter which, in addition to its two eyes, had an eye in the forehead. We read also of a four-handed Apollo, and a two-headed Silenus, with a three-handed and three-headed Hermes, reminding us of similar stages in the development of Hindu mythology.

But the Greeks were Monotheists as well as Polytheists. They worshipped one God as well as many. We know this from Greek philosophy, also from St. Paul, who found the Athenians worshipping 'the unknown God,' whom he had come to dèclare to them. That they were inconsistent some of the philosophers felt and thought, and this inconsistency St. Paul made the ground of his argument why they should turn from idols to the living God. St. Augustine adopted the same argument against the philosophical Pagans. In the 'City of God' he asks—'If Jupiter be all, why is Juno added, and the other gods?' And again he says, 'If Jupiter and Janus are both the universe, they should not be two gods, but only one.' That they did worship the one God, who is unlike all the others, is manifest even from their mythology. Homer makes all beings gods, as well as men, come forth from Oceanus, except him who is pre-eminently God, the Father of gods and men. Hesiod, too, gives to all beings a beginning except Zeus. Sophocles says, 'There is in truth but one God, who made heaven and earth,' and Euripides addresses Zeus as the self-existent, as he who upholds all things in his arms, who is resplendent with light, and yet who, because of our weak vision, is veiled in darkness. Pindar distinguished between the created gods and him who is the most powerful of all the gods, the lord of all things, and the maker of the universe. This one god was like the Brahmă of the Indians, the im-

personal and the unknown. In the mythology he is represented
by the greatest of the deities. Zeus bears some of his highest
attributes. Zeus corresponds to Brahmā and Ormuzd. His
name is the name of the highest one. He is nature in its
infinitude. This is the character of Zeus in the Orphic verses.
In later times he became famous as the king of gods and men,
but at first he was a prodigious being, the one and yet all
things, the father, yea the mother of the world, for Zeus was
neither masculine nor feminine, but both genders in one. The
universe is created in him, and by his presence he constitutes
the height of the heavens, the breadth of the earth and the
deep sea. He is the vast ocean, profound Tartarus, the rivers,
fountains and all other things, the immortal gods and goddesses.
Whatsoever shall be, is contained in the womb of Zeus. He is
the first and the last, the head and the middle of all things.
He is the breath of all being, the force of the untamable fire,
the bottom of the sea, the sun, the moon, and the stars, the
king of the universe; the one power and the one god that
rules over all; the great body of Zeus is identical with the
great body of nature. The antiquity of the Orphic verses may
be disputed, but what they say of Zeus agrees with what we
read in other poems. In the hymn of Cleanthes men are called
'the offspring of Zeus.' The universe is there said to emanate
from him, and to obey his sovereign will. He is immanent in
creation, present at all times, filling all places. Heaven, earth,
and ocean present him to our eyes. The verses of Aratus, from
which St. Paul quoted when he addressed the Athenians on
the 'unknown God,' have the same meaning, while they show
us how Zeus stood for him who was omnipotent and omnipresent. 'Let us begin with Zeus. That name should never
be forgotten, for all is full of Zeus: all ways, public places and
all harbours, as well as all seas. He is present always everywhere; all we who breathe do not breathe without Zeus, for
we are all his offspring.'

Nor was Zeus the only universal deity. The Alexandrian
commentators, with some show of reason, brought forward other
deities, to whom were ascribed the high attributes of him who
is infinite. Such were Kronos and Minerva, Necessity and
Fortune, and even Venus and her son Eros, according to the
saying of Zeno, that ' God is called by as many names as there

are different powers and virtues.' In the 'Argonauts' of
Orpheus, Eros is represented as producing Chaos; and Kronos
also, in an Orphic fragment preserved by Proclus, is represented
as coeval with ancient night. In the first satire of Lucilius
one of the gods says, 'There is none of us but is called Best
Father of gods, as Father Neptune, Liber, Saturn, Father
Mars, Janus, Father Quirinus.' One of these chief deities was
Apollo. Under the image of this youthful god, the bearer of
light and joy to the creation, the Greeks adored that majesty
which, as Euripides said, was veiled in light. As the sun re-
joices the earth, giving health to the sick and strength to the
weak, so Apollo, the god of medicine, comes forth with his heal-
ing beams radiant with light. The earth owes the comeliness
of her fields, the music of her groves, and the sparkling of her
streams and fountains, to the glorious king of day. Therefore
Apollo is the god of beauty, the emblem of wisdom, and the
author of harmony. On his temple at Delphi was inscribed the
word *Ei*—'Thou art;' in which Plutarch read the true name
of God. We are but the creatures of a day placed between
birth and death : as soon may we retain the flowing fountain
as our fleeting existence ; being does not belong to us—'*God
alone IS*.' 'This title,' Plutarch says, 'is not only proper but
peculiar to God, because he alone is being; for mortals have
no participation of true being, because that which begins and
ends and is continually changing, is never one nor the same, nor
in the same state.' The deity, in whose temple this word was
inscribed, was called Apollo, which means 'not many,' because
God is one—his nature simple—his essence uncompounded.

'The mysterious physical phenomena were, throughout
ancient mythology, made prolific of moral and mental lessons.
The story of Dionysus was profoundly significant : he was not
only creator of the world, but guardian, liberator, and saviour.
The toys which occupied him when surprised by the Titans—
the top, the wheel, the distaff, the golden Hesperian apples—
were pre-eminently cosmogonic. An emblem of a similar class
was the magic mirror or face of nature, in which, according to
the Platonic notion, but which probably existed long before
Plato, the Creator beholds himself imperfectly reflected, and
the bowl or womb of being, in which matter became pregnant
with life, or wherein the Pantheistic deity became mingled

with the world. Dionysus, god of the many coloured mantle, is the resulting manifestation personified. He is the poly-onymous, the all in the many, the varied year, life passing into innumerable forms. But according to the dogma of antiquity, the thronging forms of life are a series of purifying migrations, through which the divine principle re-ascends to the unity of its source. Inebriated in the bowl of Dionysus, and dazzled in the mirror of existence, the souls, these fragments and sparks of the universal intelligence forgot their nativity, and passed into the terrestrial forms they coveted—Dionysus, the god of this world, the changing side of Deity.'*

The shepherd god Pan occupied, even in the judgment of Socrates, the place of the supreme God, and this because, as his name implies, he was the all-God, the personification of infinite all-embracing nature. Pan was the nature side of the Greek divinities. He ruled over the woods and dwelt in desolate and solitary places. He was nature, as it appeared to herdsmen and shepherds, in its wilder, grander, and more savage aspects, but he is not without gleams of gentleness, and by no means destitute of joy. Every schoolboy knows that he was a merry deity, making music on his pipe of seven reeds, with the glad nymphs dancing to his rustic tunes. His body was rough like the luxuriant earth, but his face beamed with intelligence, which showed the Ammon concealed. As the heavens are radiant with light, so smiled the countenance of Pan. He had horns like the sun and moon, and his garment of leopard's skin was a picture of the varied beauties of the world; but he was not all beautiful. As nature veils some of her secrets, so must we veil the deformities of Pan. In the Orphic verses he is called the All of the universe—heaven and sea, the ruler of the earth, and immortal fire; for all these are but the garments of Pan.

What has been said of the gods of the Greeks may be also said of the deities of Rome. The Romans, too, made God and nature one—finite on the human side, infinite on the divine side. Their mythology, like their literature, was but a feeble echo of the Greek. Their poets and philosophers only repeat what was said before. Their Jupiter is the Greek Zeus; he is primarily the heavens, or that portion of the visible universe which ap-

* Mackay's ' Progress of the Intellect.'

pears to us. This truth is petrified into the Roman language.
Bad weather is ' bad Jupiter ;' to be in the open air is to be
' under Jupiter ;' and to be out in the cold is to be under 'frigid
Jupiter.' 'Behold,' says Ennius, ' the clear sky, which all men
invoke as Jupiter.' And Cato says, ' his seat is heaven, earth,
and ocean. Wheresoever we move, wheresoever we go, whatever we see, that is Jupiter.' Virgil, in imitation of the Greek
poet, says, ' Let us begin with Jupiter ; all things are full of
Jupiter.' In another place he describes ' the prone descending
showers,' as the omnipotent father coming down into the bosom
of his glad spouse. The powers of nature personified ; that is
Greek Polytheism. Nature in its infinitude, embracing the
whole conceivable assemblage of being in which mind is pre-
eminently manifest ; that is Greek Monotheism.

The account of the Persian religion was originally taken from Creuzer's
' Symbolik,' Framjee's ' Parsees,' Hyde's ' Veterum Persarum Religionis
Historia,' and Spiegel's ' Translations of the Zend Avesta.' Some additions
have been made from Dermesteter's Introduction. Bunsen maintains that
Bactria, and not Persia, was the original seat of Zoroaster and his doctrine.
The Fargard, or first book of the Zend Avesta, gives an account of the emigra-
tion of the Aryans to India through Bactria. Now the language of the oldest
portion of the Zend Avesta is High Bactrian, and approaches very near to the
Vedic language, that is, the old East Iranian which is preserved in the Punjab.
Another argument is derived from a comparison of Zoroastrianism with Brahmanism. The old Vedic worship was a worship of nature, but the Zoroastrian
books place a supreme God above nature. 'We may assume,' says Bunsen, 'that
the original Zorathustra founded a new religion before the migration to India
as a mere counterpoise to the earliest Bactrian naturalism, and that the Aryans,
when they migrated, carried with them the primitive Zoroastrian religion on
their great conquering expedition, the last scene of which was the Indian
country. The Agni, or fire worship, of which mention is made in the Vedic
hymns, must be considered as a remnant of the pre-Zoroastrian doctrine.'

On the Egyptian religions, besides the old writers mentioned in the text,
Plutarch, Macrobius, Porphyry, Apuleius, &c., we have Pritchard, Bunsen,
and 'The Egyptian Texts' in ' Records of the Past,' more recently M. Renouf's
' Hibbert Lectures ' and Articles, in the *Contemporary Review*, by Stuart Poole
(Jan., 1879, and May, 1880). In the same *Review*, M. Dermesteter contributed
an article on the whole subject of ' Indo-European Mythology' (Oct., 1879).
Chaeremon (according to Porphyry) explained the Egyptian religion as ignoring
a supreme cause ; Eusebius followed this interpretation, rejoicing to show the
absurdity of Paganism. Depuis extolled it, expecting to prove that the idea of
an intelligent spiritual cause is an invention of modern times, and too absurd
for the wise men of antiquity. Iamblichus refuted Chaeremon. This interpretation of the Egyptian religion is of the same kind with the interpretation
which makes Buddhism atheistic, and thus charges with atheism the most
religious nations of the world. Porphyry gave the rationale of animal worship

from a Pantheistic ground. He says that all living creatures in their degree participate in the divine essence and under the semblance of animals. The Egyptians worship the universal powers which the gods have revealed in the various forms of living creatures (De Abs, IV. 9). M. Renouf quotes hymns to Osiris and other gods, which show the Pantheistic character of Egyptian worship. Osiris has some relation to the Greek Adonis, and is perhaps connected with Thammuz, in the Phœnician mythology.

> 'Thammuz come next behind,
> Whose annual wound in Lebanon allured
> The Syrian damsels to lament his fate,
> In amorous ditties all a summer's day,
> While smooth Adonis from his native rock
> Ran purple to the sea, suffused with blood
> Of Thammuz yearly wounded : the love tale
> Infected Sion's daughters with like heat ;
> Whose wanton passions in the sacred porch
> Ezekiel saw, when, by the vision led,
> His eye surveyed the dark idolatries
> Of alienated Judah.'
>
> *Milton's 'Paradise Lost.'*

When Patricius edited the works of Hermes Trismegistus in the sixteenth century, the Catholic authorities obliged him to add Scholia, explaining that some things, such as the doctrine of creation and the existence of the gods, were not according to the Catholic faith ; but the essence of the theology, such as that God is intellect, that he made the world in imitation of the Word, that perhaps God has no essence—that he brings forth mind as a father generates a son ; that God is masculo-feminine, and that man is made from life and light, were to be understood in an orthodox sense—*sano modo.*

Plutarch, quoting from Hecataeus, says that the Egyptians considered the primitive Deity and the universe as one and identical ; and Eusebius, citing the Genica or old Hermaic books, asks, 'Have you not been informed, by the Genica, that all individual souls are emanations from the one great Soul ?'

Anchises, in the sixth book of the Æneid, explaining to Æneas the law of the transmigration of souls, says, 'The spirit within nourishes heaven and earth and the watery plains, and the enlightened orb of the moon, and the shining stars ; and diffused through the parts, a mind actuates the whole fabric, and mingles itself with the large body : hence the races of men and cattle, and the lives of birds and monsters, which the sea produces under its marble plain.'
'This,' says Bishop Warburton, 'was the doctrine of the old Egyptians, as we learn from Plato, who says, They taught that Jupiter is the spirit which pervades all things.' He adds that the Greek philosophy corrupted this principle into Spinozism, of which we have an instance in the fourth Georgic—
'Some have said that bees have a part of the Divine mind and ethereal draughts, for that God pervades all lands and tracts of the sea and the lofty heavens. Hence flocks, herds, men, all the race of wild beasts, each at birth derive their slender lives.' This might pass for simple Egyptain doctrine, without supposing that it has undergone the *corrupting* (?) influence of Greek philosophy.

The account of the Greek religion is taken from familiar classical authors. 'The gods of Greece,' says Mr. Mackay, in his *Progress of the Intellect,* 'are

D

so fixed and personified in its poetry as almost entirely to conceal their essential generality of character; but in proportion as we approach the Asiatic sources of Greek ideas, or in any way extend our view beyond the limits of the Epic circle, the gods, or the human beings representing them, become more complex, multiform, and independent, until at last all the mysteries and contradictions of genealogies sink into the one mystery of Pantheism.' The notes of Ludovicus Vives, in St. Augustine's *De Civitate Dei*, are full of interpretations of Greek mythology in its aspect of nature worship.

CHAPTER III.

GREEK PHILOSOPHY.

ALL philosophy is a seeking after God—a reiteration of the cry of the patriarch, 'O that I knew where I might find him. And the all but universal answer has been, 'He is not far from any one of us.' This is pre-eminently true of the philosophy of the Greeks in all its stages, and in nearly all its schools.

As to the early Greek philosophers, there are two great difficulties :—first, their own writings are not extant, so that the materials are both scanty and uncertain; secondly, these materials have been used for the most opposite interpretations. Cicero, the Neo-Platonists, and the Christian Fathers held the early Greek philosophers to have been pure Theists. They assumed rightly, unconscious indeed that it was an assumption, that the fact of these old inquirers after truth, being philosophers, was no argument that they were irreligious. Some of them believed in the gods of the mythology, and some of them did not; but they were all seeking after the One who was yet greater than all the gods. Aristotle, to whom we are chiefly indebted for the materials respecting them, refers their speculations to the old 'theologies,' intimating that these are to guide us in the interpretation of their cosmogonies. And this is in the order of things: religion comes before philosophy, men bow in reverence before the unseen, long before it becomes the subject of reason. The view which makes the early Greek philosophers advocates of positive science, without reference to religion, is an anachronism in the history of philosophy. It places them in another age of the world than that in which they lived, and ignores the natural religiousness of man.

THE IONICS.

In the fifth century before the Christian era lived Thales of Miletus, a lover of knowledge, and a seeker after wisdom.

He visited Egypt, at that time the sacred dwelling of
science—sacred, indeed, for out of religion Egyptian wisdom
had arisen. The priests' lips kept knowledge—knowledge
of all kinds. Thales probably learned there of the 'unknown darkness' which produced the 'water and sand' from
which all things were made. He may have compared this
with what we read in Homer and Hesiod about the origin of
all things from Oceanus and Tethys, and hence the thought
arose 'water is the first principle of creation.' Perhaps he
made experiments on matter. A rude chemist he must indeed
have been, yet it was within his reach to know that material
forms are fleeting and unsubstantial. He felt that at the
foundation of nature there was a unity in which all things
were one, a substance of which all partook—a material capable
of being formed into suns and stars, and worlds, trees, animals,
and men, an original element in which all the elements had
their beginning; and what more likely than water to be this
original element? It is the blood of nature, by it all things
live, without it all die. He took a material element for the
original unity, what he meant more we cannot tell. Did he
find that he could go no farther? Did he make no distinction
between the material and the spiritual? We cannot answer.
Aristotle says that Thales believed 'all things were full of
gods.' Laertius, that he called God 'the oldest of all things,
because he was uncreated,' and Cicero, that he held 'water to
be the beginning of things, but that God was the mind which
created things out of the water.'

'But why,' asked Thales' disciple Anaximander, 'should the
preference be given to water over the other elements? That
which you assume to be the ground of all things is finite. By
thus placing it above the others, by making it the one thing of
the universe, you make it infinite. It then ceases to be water.
Why not at once call the one substance 'the infinite,' that
which is unlimited, eternal, unconditioned?' A universe of
opinion has arisen about the meaning of Anaximander's
'infinite.' Was it material? was it incorporeal? We only
know that he believed in an 'infinite' in which all beings have
their being.

Anaximander's successor, Anaximenes, thought it might be
determined what that is which is infinite. It was not water;

that was too gross, too material. Was there no existence conceivable in thought, nor perceptible by sense, that appeared infinite—no essence that is in all things—and yet is not any one of them? There is that which we call breath, life, soul. It pervades all. It permeates all. It penetrates all. Is not that ' the infinite ?' We breathe it. We live in it. It is the universal soul. This may have been what Anaximenes meant; we do not know for certainty. But it is the interpretation of the ' air' by Anaximenes' disciple, Diogenes of Apollonia. He thought the Deity a divine breath, air, or spirit, endowed with the attributes of wisdom and intelligence, and pervading the universe of being. These philosophers begin with inquiries that belong apparently to natural philosophy, but they do not stop there; they cannot—they go beyond the bounds of the finite and the phenomenal.

THE ITALICS.

The Ionics began their search for the truth of the universe from external nature. The Italics began with mathematics. The former declared that all was one—one something, one infinite; they could not explain it further. Pythagoras said it is simply one. What he meant is not easy to determine. In Persia he may have learned of the nameless one, who created Ormuzd and Ahriman. Was not this a monad creating a dyad? Did not one thus become the father of the world, and two its mother? What can be the essence of all things but numbers? Do not all come from the original unity? As the number one is the foundation of the manifold operations of arithmetic and geometry, so the Divine one—the universal soul—is the foundation of the world's manifoldness. The universe is a reflection of the Divine. It is a ' living arithmetic, a realised geometry.' Because of its beauty, and harmony, and everlasting order, it is called the kosmos.

But the monad of Pythagoras; was it a mind, or simply an original something, out of which the all was evolved? If the monad was not the active principle, it is identical with chaos, and the dyad contained in it becomes the active power which causes the harmonious world-development to arise from the chaos. On this supposition the Pythagorean doctrine of the

Deity could have risen no higher than that of an evolution or emanation out of chaos—an original substance from which has proceeded the divine world-soul. But if, as Tenneman thinks, the Pythagorean monad was the active principle, the divine Being, then God is above and before chaos. He is mind, and the producer, not the product of the material; while matter is only God posited on one side, and subject to him. That the latter was the true Pythagorean doctrine is probable from its agreement with the fragments of Philolaus, an old philosopher of the school of Pythagoras. The essence of things is regarded as arising out of two grand elements—the limiting or limit, and the unlimited. Philolaus shows that this takes place through the opposition of the one and the many. The one was unity to many, and the many, as such was the indefinite dyad, through the limitation given by the unity, and through the participation in the unity. But now that the essences of things consist of these two original elements, consequently the principles, or original elements of numbers, must be also the principles of things themselves. The Pythagoreans found the reason of the necessity in this, that only under this condition could things be objects of human knowledge; for neither the one nor the many, in the abstract, can be known by man. The produced alone is cognisable to the human understanding. The union of the limited and unlimited form a kosmos. This kosmos implies a principle of harmony, and this harmony a first cause or author, who is truly and simply God. 'Were there not,' says Professor Böckh, 'above the original one and many, the limited and the unlimited, a highest absolute unity, in which, as in the original ground of all things, these opposites and their harmonious union constitute a kosmos, then in the system of the most religious Pythagoreans would be no trace of the godhead, since neither the limited nor the unlimited appears in this system as God. But now that such a trace exists, and that in the Pythagorean system God is recognised and represented under the idea of the highest absolute outside of, and beyond these opposites, expressly as the first or original cause of harmony, we find established through undisputed testimony of many of the ancients.' According to Aristotle, Philolaus acknowledged one original as the cause of the two principles—as the absolute reality of all, and thus God as the highest unity yet posited above that other unity as different from it. The Pythagoreans regarded this first cause as an intellect; this we may consider as certain. But the limit, the unlimited, and the kosmos were all clearly allied to the first cause. The kosmos consists of decades, each of which has ten bodies. These revolve round a common centre. This centre is the most resplendent part of the universe. It is the seat of the Supreme Deity. From it proceeds that light which gives life and gladness to creation. The stars in the resplendent heavens, outside the centre of light, are dwellings of the gods; if not themselves, divinities. Beneath them in rank are demons or good spirits; then men; and lastly, the brute creation. Through all ranks goes the divine essence of the One. All are in some way allied to God; all are divine.

THE ELEATICS.

The first genuine metaphysicians among the Greeks were the Eleatics. They first doubted the reality of matter, and felt the difficulty of distinguishing between knowing and being, thought and existence. The Ionics evidently assumed the reality of phenomena. The Pythagoreans took the reality of mind or thought, as the substance of matter. The Eleatics annihilated the duality, conceiving the identity of thought and existence.

The transition from Pythagoras to the Eleatics was easy. The reality of phenomena is in some sense admitted, but we are without a certain criterion for a knowledge of its existence. Reason tells us of the One, and this must be absolute and eternal. Xenophanes, the founder of Eleaticism, did not deny, scarcely perhaps doubted the reality of matter. He saw the contradiction between the verdict of reason and the teachings of experience. The one resolved all existence into a unity— an essence eternal, impenetrable, and unchangeable—yet the senses proclaimed the existence of the manifold. The reality of both he admitted, though the mode of their reconciliation could neither be understood nor explained. 'Casting his eyes upwards at the immensity of heaven,' says Aristotle, 'Xeno-phanes declared that the One is God.' But he asked if the One be God, what mean the gods of Homer and Hesiod ? If God is an infinite Being, how base to ascribe to him the foolish actions of men ; how unwise to suppose that he is like themselves, that he has their voice, and shape, and figure. If an ox or a lion were to conceive God, they would conceive him as like themselves. If they had hands and fingers like ours, they would give him an image and a shape like their own. But this is only God finitely conceived ; God so to speak as created by the mind. He that is God must be a being not created by us. He is not anything finite. He is the infinite ; not the infinite as an abstraction, for that, like the finite, may be only a form of our minds. He is an infinite being, independent of all our thoughts and all our conceptions of finity or infinitude. Unlike to men in outward shape ; unlike, too, in mind and thought. He is without parts or organs, but he is all sight, all ear, and all intelligence. He is pre-eminently being, and the only true being. Whatever really exists he is in himself, and all that does exist is eternal and immutable. Nothing can come from nothing. Whatever is must have come from him. The produced is then identical with that which produces. If not, something has arisen which was not in the cause from which it arose. This is absurd, and therefore, said Xenophanes, all that is really being is God. He is one and all things.

Parmenides did not lift his eyes to the immensity of heaven to see the One. He did not believe in the representations of the senses. All that is merely appearance, delusion. Becoming and departing, being and non-being, change of place and vicissitude of circumstance—all which men generally regard as realities, are merely names. Whatever is is, there cannot then be anything produced. It cannot be in part, and in part produced. If it has once been, or is yet to be, then it is not. An existence only to come, or a becoming which implies a previous non-existence takes away all idea of being, so that being must be always or never. There is a reason in man by which he knows that pure being is that which is free from change of time, or of place. The senses reveal the manifold, but that is only deception. Thought acquaints us with pure being, and is itself identical with that being. It is opposed to the manifold, and the changeable which indeed do not exist, and therefore cannot be objects of thought. All things which really exist are one, and this existence is without change. It pervades all space. This one is not the collected manifold as revealed by the senses, but the one substratum which is the foundation and reality of all apparent existence. Parmenides does not call it God. His philosophy is a science of being and knowing. He denies the existence of the many: yet he is compelled to regard it as in some way existing. It exists in the sensuous representation. All men so perceive it to exist. Parmenides must, therefore, make an effort to explain how the world of phenomena has this apparent existence. Being and non-being set themselves as it were over against each other in spite of the philosopher. He denies that the latter is anything, and yet he must treat it as if it were a something. There must be a One prior to the multitude of beings. Every thing which is participated subsists in others which participate it. It has then a progression into being from that which cannot be participated. That which is most profoundly united, or simply being is one or many; but in the order of beings this multitude is occult and characterised by the nature of the One. Since there is then everywhere a monad prior to the multitude, we must suspend all beings from the proper monad. In souls the monad of souls is established in an order more ancient than the multitude of souls, and about this as a centre all souls converge; divine souls in the first rank, their attendants next, and after these the co-attendants, as Socrates says in the Phædrus. Therefore the monad of all•beings is prior to all beings, and so Parmenides calls it the One.

Zeno and Melissus annihilated this lingering duality between the One and the manifold. They did this by showing that no knowledge could be derived from the senses; that from the very conception of being the manifold could not exist, and, therefore, belief in its existence was contradictory and absurd. Zeno maintained the non-existence of the phenomenal. His argument was that in dividing matter, we must in thought reach a stage where divisibility ceases to be possible—where the subject of division becomes a mathematical point, which has no real existence, and as all experience is found to be contradictory, no objective reality can be deduced from it. The only way to certainty of knowledge is to establish the conclusions of the pure reason, and to explain phenomena for a mere illusion of the senses. 'We cannot,' says Melissus, 'determine the quantity of anything without taking for granted its existence. But that which is real cannot be finite, it must be infinite, not in space but in time.' It fills all time, and must always be the same. The multiplicity of changeable things which the senses reveal, can only be deception. The appearance is in us: the reality is nowhere. If the apparent things actually existed, they could not change. A *that* would remain what it is in the reality of its being whatever be the representation to our senses or whatever the subjective condition and circumstances of the representation.

> 'This truth alone it now remains to tell,
> That in this path one Being we shall find,
> As numerous tokens manifestly show ;
> And there its character, without decay ;
> And unbegotten, stable without end—
> Only begotten, whole, nor once it was,
> Nor will hereafter be, since now 'tis all ;
> At once collected, a continued one,
> From whence its source or growth could you explain
> Not from non-being which no mind can see,
> Nor speech reveal ; since as of being void,
> 'Tis not an object of the mental eye,
> But, as from no one it derived its birth,
> Say, why in time posterior, it begun,
> Rather in some prior time to be ?
> Then must it wholly be or wholly not,
> For never will the power of faith permit
> That aught should ever into being rise.'

Parmenides.

HERACLITUS.

The Eleatics tried to end the dualism between the permanent and the changing by denying reality to the latter. But the phenomena remain as that which is given in the experience of the senses. There was still the one and the many. The unity of reason and the sensuous multiplicity. Heraclitus undertook to reconcile them, and to show how both existed in a perfect monism; the one in the many and the many in the one; so that true being was neither the one nor the many, but the union—the flux and reflux—the becoming. Heraclitus's doctrine is generally acknowledged to be obscure.

Cudworth calls him a 'confounded philosopher,' and Socrates, with gentle irony, said of his book concerning nature, that what he understood of it was 'excellent, and he had no doubt that what he did not understand was equally good.   Regarding him as coming after Parmenides and engaged with the same problems as the Eleatics, we may conceive him as asking the question, 'What is the universe?' Is it being or non-being? and he answers, 'It is neither because it is both.' All is and all is not; while it comes into being it is, yet forthwith it ceases to be.   There is no continuance of anything; the only reality is an eternal becoming.   Into the same stream we descend, and yet it is not the same stream.   We are, and at the same we are not.   We cannot possibly descend twice into the same stream, for it is always scattering and collecting itself again, or rather it at the same time flows to us and flows from us.   The reality of being is not an eternal rest, but a ceaseless change.   Heraclitus does not, like the Eleatics, distrust the senses, he holds them for true sources of knowledge, channels whereby we drink in the universal intelligence, and become partakers of the common reason.   We arrive at truth in proportion as we partake of this reason.   Whatever is particular as opposed to it is false; 'Inhaling through the breath the universal ether, which is the divine reason, we become conscious. In sleep we are unconscious, but on waking we again become intelligent, for in sleep, when the organs of the sense are closed, the mind within is shut out from all sympathy with the surrounding ether, the universal reason ; and the only connecting medium is the breath, as it were, a root.   By this separation the mind loses the power of recollection.   Nevertheless, on awakening, the mind repairs its memory through the senses, as it were through inlets, thus coming into contact with the surrounding ether, it resumes its intelligence.   As fuel, when brought near the fire, is altered, and becomes fiery, but on being removed again, becomes extinguished ; so too the portion of the all-embracing, which sojourns in our body, becomes more irrational when separated from it, but on the restoration of this connection through its many pores and inlets, it again becomes similar to the whole.'

This doctrine, as here announced, may be contrasted with Eleaticism, which found certitude only in pure reason, while

Heraclitus finds the senses to be means of communication between the mind and the universal reason; yet after the contrast, the doctrine of the unity of being is the same. With the
one, reality is only in the permanent; with the other, it is in
the becoming. In both cases the One is all. Heraclitus was
originally of the Ionic school, but some call him a disciple of
Xenophanes. Aristotle says that he took fire as the first principle in the same way as Thales took water and Anaximenes
air. 'The universe,' says Heraclitus, 'always was, is, and ever
will be a living fire, unchanged, and at the same time endowed
with the power of thinking and knowing.' The relation between this fire and the becoming we do not know, and can
only conjecture. Had Heraclitus been in Persia? Was he a
worshipper of fire? Had he learned of Ormuzd—the fountain
of light—the all-embracing element whence all things flow?
And did he, like the Persians with an indifferential difference,
call it now the symbol of the first principle of creation, and
again the principle itself? By this fire Heraclitus illustrates
the eternal transformation and transposition of the becoming.
He makes it the substratum of movement, the origin and energy
of existence. In the strife of light and darkness the universe
arose. 'Strife,' he says, 'is the parent of all things. The one,
by separating itself from itself, unites itself again.' In another
place he says, 'Unite the whole and the not-whole, the coalescing and the not-coalescing, the harmonious and the dis-
cordant, and thus we have the one becoming from the all, and
the all from the one.'

EMPEDOCLES.

To what school Empedocles belonged is a question left
undecided by Aristotle. With the Eleatics, he distrusted the
senses. Regarding human and divine reason as one, he
found in reason the source of knowledge. In placing the
origin of the universe in material elements, he seems allied
to the Ionic school; but he separates from them in assuming
four original or root elements instead of one. Of these he
makes fire the most important, and thus seems to approach
Heraclitus. These elements are each original and eternal.

They are mingled again by the working of two powers—strife and friendship. Men call these changes, birth and death, but in reality there is neither birth nor death. Nothing can be produced which has not always existed, and nothing which has once existed can ever cease to be. This indeed is the fundamental doctrine of the philosophy of Empedocles. It is truly Eleatic. But to his doctrine of separating and commingling elements, he seems to have added the becoming of Heraclitus, not, however, purely, for with Empedocles the elements do not change in themselves, but only in their relations. The four elements are eternal, yet not as material elements, but as ideal existences in the divine mind. The world as revealed to the senses is but a copy. The world intellectual is the type. The latter, being the ideal, is the reality of the former, which is only phenomenal. The root elements exist eternally in the One.

The separating and uniting which we see incessantly at work are caused by discord and friendship. As these root-elements are the original thoughts of the Supreme, and as these undergo continual transformations, so the being of the supreme One is interfused throughout the universe. His essence pervades all. All life and intelligence are the manifestations of the divine mind. God is not like anything which can be seen or touched, or imaged by human intellect. He is an infinite mind. Here Empedocles joined with Xenophanes in opposition to the popular deities of the mythology. He was a great enemy to the gods of Homer. Empedocles' theology has been described as an apotheosis of nature and pre-eminently pantheistic, that is, in the sense of merely worshipping external nature. But the verses of Empedocles evidently mean more than this. Polytheism was an apotheosis of nature; but the pantheism of Empedocles was the worship of being. His God is not the phenomenal, but the real, and is allied to the One of Parmenides. Only on this ground could he have opposed the worship of the popular deities. But we have seen in another place that this worship of being had nearly the same origin as the worship of natural powers and objects. The one was the goal of reason, the other was the result of imagination. The one made the theology of the philosopher, the other that of the multitude. Reason protested against polytheism, which Empedocles could not have done had his theology been merely a deification of phenomenal nature. Tradition says that Empedocles proclaimed himself divine, and to prove it, leaped into the crater of Mount Etna. The mountain disproved his divinity by casting up his sandal. This may be true or it may be only the popular interpretation of his identification of the human and the divine reason.

ANAXAGORAS.

To understand fully the development of the theological sentiment among the Greeks, it is necessary to notice Anaxagoras, the great father of all anti-pantheistic theologians. What men are saying to-day against pantheism was said with equal force by Anaxagoras, and the more vulnerable parts of his theology are as ill defended by church doctors as they were by this old Greek. He was no metaphysician, but a man who believed his senses, and had never made sufficient inquiries into the nature of reason to be troubled with the questions that perplexed Zeno or Parmenides. Why should he doubt the reality of the visible world? Was it not there before his eyes? and why should he suppose any hidden relationship between mind and matter? Was not mind the active principle, and matter the passive reality? Why should some material element be the first being, and not that mind which is the ruling power over matter? God is mind, and matter is something arranged by him. What theology can be more simple? No questions of the co-existence of a material finite and an immaterial infinite stood in the way of Anaxagoras. Speculations on the attributes of time and space did not concern him. Why should an infinite being differ from a finite, except in being greater, and why otherwise should an infinite mind not be the same as a finite mind? God made the world as a man makes a machine. He gave it laws and left it to the operation of laws, interfering only when it needs repair. In his far off dwelling-place beyond the boundaries of the universe he beheld his workmanship, and was present to it as a man is present to the objects perceived by his sense of sight.

Compared with the other philosophers of the Ionic school' Aristotle said ' the philosopher of Clazomenæ was like a sober man.' Socrates, however, did not estimate him so highly.

Having one day,' says that philosopher; 'read a book of Anaxagoras, who said the divine mind was the cause of all things, and drew them up in their proper ranks and classes, I was ravished with joy. I perceived there was nothing more certain than this principle that mind was the cause of all things.' Socrates purchased the books of Anaxagoras, and began to read them with avidity, but he had not proceeded far till he found his hopes disappointed. 'The author,' he said, 'makes no further use of this mind, but assigns as the cause of the order and beauty that prevailed in the world, the air, water, whirlwind, and other agencies of nature.'

Aristotle, too, on further study was less pleased with Anaxagoras, and corrected his own views by coming nearer Parmenides. In after times the theology of Anaxagoras developed into the schools of Democritus and Epicurus, who dispensed with the hypothesis of a world maker, or rather left him in his far distant home, reposing in silent dignity, and regarding the world as unworthy of his interference.

SOCRATES AND THE SCEPTICS.

For the same reason that we notice Anaxagoras, a few words are required for Socrates and the Sceptics. The Eleatics had questioned the objective reality of the phenomenal world on the ground of the uncertainty of sense knowledge; but if the objects of sense are denied reality, why, said the Sceptics, should it be granted to the subjects of reason. Knowledge is only relative. Our perceptions are different at different times and in different states. How do we know that truth is not beyond the reach of the human mind? Man, said Protagoras, is the measure of all things: what he perceives is, but its existence is only subjective—it exists only for him. The universal application of this principle ended in universal scepticism. In the light of it, knowledge is a dream, religion is superstition, might is right, and laws, but the conventional regulations of governments and states.

Socrates occupied himself solely with ethics. He tried to find in reason a certain foundation for morals. The Sceptic said 'What I perceive to be true is true only to me; my knowledge is not merely subjective, but it is individual, and therefore empirical.' 'That,' Socrates would have said, 'may be so with you as an individual, but not as a partaker of the universal reason. Human knowledge is not merely relative and empirical, for the measure of all things is not the individual, but the universal man. Morality has a basis in universal reason. It is something eternal, immutable, absolute.'

Consistently with his purely ethical studies, Socrates sought in God a being who answered to the moral necessities of the heart. From his youth he felt himself drawn towards the 'pure and unchangeable mind.' His God was the 'mind' of Anaxagoras; but Socrates did not introduce him as simply making the world. He also preserves it. He is the God of providence as well as of creation. He takes care of all. Nothing is unworthy of his regard—nothing too mean for him to be indifferent to it. He is at once the author and king of the world.

PLATO.

Socrates sought to establish a foundation for moral truth. He found it in absolute reason. In the same reason Plato found a basis for the truth of our knowledge of the reality of being. It comes not from the senses, but from the intercourse of our reason with the Divine. There can be no science derived from the perceptions of sense. They cannot reach that which *is*. They never go beyond phenomena. All their intercourse is with the apparent. But the mind has reminiscences of its former knowledge. Though now imprisoned in the body, it has its home in the bosom of the Eternal. It remembers the truth it once knew when it stood face to face with real existence. Truth belongs to the mind. Thoughts are verities. To limit the reality of existence to the One, Parmenides denied it to the manifold, and Heraclitus denied it to both the One and the many that he might ascribe it to the becoming. But Plato saw in the One the thinker, and in the manifold his thoughts. And who shall separate between the mind and its thoughts? Both are one. Both are realities, and therefore we ascribe real existence both to the One and the manifold. Objects of sense have an existence so far as they participate in the ideal. Thus, man, house, table, exist; but only because the ideas man, house, table, are real existences. Our conceptions become perceptions. The manifold has thus a double existence. One in its ideals, another in phenomena. The latter is the world of sense—what men call the material, and what the vulgar suppose to be reality. But its existence is only borrowed. It is a shadow—a copy of that which is real ; the realities are the ideas, the architypes. The manifold, then, is at once being, and the semblance of being.

But these ideas, are they identical with God, or distinct from God ? Plato answers sometimes that they are identical, and at other times that they are distinct from God. This lies at the root of Plato's theology, and leaves an uncertainty whether God in his system is merely abstract being or a personal creative Deity. In the one case the ideas are the being of God ; in the other, God is a being who creates the universe after the pattern of the ideas. But where is the phenomenal world ? Do the ideas create the phenomenal or is it eternal ? When God made the world, he made it after the ideal pattern, but on what did he impress the idea ? Here Plato ascribes eternity to that which is non-existent, matter. This shadowy semblance of being existed. It was that in which the idea took shape and form, and yet it is nothing. It has the capacity to receive any variety of form, yet it is undetermined, shapeless, and invisible. It receives and preserves being, only as it has in itself the ideal form. The visible universe is the result of ideas with this substratum of non-existence. The universal mind is God. He is the highest of our ideas, and the source of all thinking and knowing. He is 'the Good.' In this supreme idea, all ideas have their ground and centre. Though itself exalted above division, yet in it the perceiver and the perceived, the subject and the object, the ideal and the real, are all one.

In returning to the Socratic faith in the capacity of the mind to know truth, and applying it to the nature of essence, Plato in reality returned to Eleatic ground, and in following out his method, he arrived at the absolute reality in the same way as Xenophanes, Parmenides, and Zeno, had done before him. The God of reason was being absolute. God must be this, and yet Plato recoiled from the immovable Deity of the Eleatics, God is this, but he is something else, even if it be something

E

inconsistent with this. He is movable; he is intelligent; he is mind; the king of the world; the father of the universe; God, who according to reason must be entirely unlike man, must yet again have attributes corresponding to those of men.

ARISTOTLE.

At the point where Plato took up the ground of Socrates, Aristotle differed from Plato. He said that Plato had never proved how ideas have an objective reality, nor had he even rationally explained how objects of sense participate in the ideal. Socrates proclaimed the universal as the essence of the individual—and so far he was right. Plato raised the conception of a universal to the rank of being, independent of the individual, and there, said Aristotle, Plato was wrong. Aristotle's method differed so much from Plato's that these two philosophers have come to be regarded as the respective representatives of the two great classes of minds into which all men may be divided. But their conclusions differ less than their methods.

Aristotle began with observations on the external world, but he found that in this way he could never get beyond the external. Sense acquaints us only with individual existence. We must get beyond this. We do get beyond this, for we have the knowledge of the universals. We have abstract ideas of things. Whence are these? From reason. The universal and the individual are then co-existent. We cannot separate a thing from our conception of it. The universal is immanent in the individual. It is as Plato said, the essence of the individual, but it is not itself independent of the individual, It is like form to the material in which form has its existence, yet only by means of the universal can we know the essence of any one particular thing. Though not independent, it is yet that which is actual, while the individual is only the potential. The absolute actuality is mind, and matter is the same essence in its potential being. There are four first causes, or first principles. Matter, form, moving cause, and end. As in a house there is the matter, the conception, the worker, and the actual house. These four determinations of all being resolve themselves into the fundamental ones of matter and form. The moving cause, form, and end, stand together as opposed to matter. The last is that abiding something which lies at the basis of all becoming, and yet in its own being it is different from anything which has become. Whatever is, has been before potentially. Individual beings are produced by the coalescing of potential being and pure form. Every 'that' is a meeting of potential and actual being. But there is a guiding power superintending these processes of progression. That power is a prime activity, a pure actuality, a first mover. That mover is God. The relation of the divine to the world is left by Aristotle undetermined. In some places he seems to meet Plato, but in others he separates God from all being and becoming, contemplating him as absolutely mind, not dwelling in the universe and moving it as the soul moves the body; but moving it externally, himself unmoved and free from nature. The world has a soul, but it is not God. God is maker of the world soul, which is the movable mover outside of the immovable Mover.

The Stoics.

Plato and most of his predecessors endeavoured to reduce all being to unity by denying reality to matter. As he admitted only reason for a channel of knowledge, he was consistent in regarding matter as non-being. But Aristotle, believing his senses as well as his reason, left the dualism mind and matter unreconciled. With Plato God was one and all things. With Aristotle God was one, and the universe a distinct existence. But as nothing can be which has not been before, as there can be no addition to the totality of existence, Aristotle made two eternals, the one form, the other matter. God and the material from which the universe was made. The Stoics were not satisfied with the duality. They felt, with Plato, that all must be one; that an infinite cannot leave a finite standing over against it. They were willing to trust the testimony of sense, and to admit that logically mind and matter, God and the world, are separate and distinct, yet the Stoics contended that actually they must be one. To show how God and the universe were distinct and yet one, was the problem of

Zeno and his disciples. They did this by a philosophy of
common sense, in which they acknowledged the truth both of
our conceptions and our perceptions. The sensuous impression
of an external object, they looked upon as a revelation to the
mind, of the object itself. Sense furnished the materials of
knowledge. Reason compared them and formed ideas. But
if in this way all ideas came from the senses, how can we have
an idea of pure spirit? The Stoics were consistent, they
denied that we have such an idea, and with that they denied
the existence of anything incorporeal. That every existence
must have a body was the doctrine which moulded the whole
of the theology of the Stoics. They did not define what a
body was, that was impossible, bodies, being of all kinds from
the spiritual to the grossly material. But the very indefiniteness in which they left the idea of the corporeal, showed that
they were far removed from the school of Epicurus. Their
great inquiry was concerning the world—whence it is. Evidently it is not eternal as Aristotle supposed, since it is something produced. What we know of the world producer must
be learned from the world itself. Being is evidently divisible
into the active and the passive. A producing and a produced
are the two obvious principles in the actual world. There must
then be a similar two-foldness in the original of the world, an
active principle and a passive—the one a living power, the
other a passive potentiality—the one that from which everything is, the other that through which everything is. The
passive is the original matter—a lifeless and inert substance.
The active is the efficient cause or producing power. But this
cause must be corporeal, and yet how can we conceive of it
under any known form of body. The Stoics tried to separate
the living power which creates the universe from every idea of
gross matter, and at the same time they felt that to have a
definite conception of that power we must clothe it with some
material form. The active principle was therefore conceived
as having for its substratum the nature of external fire, but to
protect this representation from the misconception of ordinary
minds, they also called it spirit.

The first expression of the working of the active principle is
in forming the primary elements from the original matter; the
second, in forming bodies. The active principle thus working

externally in unorganised nature Chrysippus calls the binding power, and supposes the air to be its substratum or substance. This power acting in its higher operations producing the life of nature, and animating all forms of organism from the humblest plant to the highest spirit-life he calls the ether, but though the one active principle has many powers and functions, it is still but one, as the human mind with all its faculties is an undivided unity. This active principle is again considered as the original source of all right and morality—the principle of law-giving—the world order. The moral order is therefore of the essence of God, or in other words, this moral order is our divinest conception of the nature of God, for in this God appears as the unchangeable and the eternal, the absolute being whose existence implies the highest rectitude, wisdom, and perfection. Tiedemann says of the Stoics—'Among all the philosophers of antiquity, none defended the existence of God with so warm a zeal or so many and so powerful arguments.' The chief of these was the undeniable existence of right in the world. This shows a relationship between man and God, and the existence of a deity as a moral being, as the principle of moral law-giving and world order, that is, of right and morality. In the last analysis there is in reality but one being existing. We may call him God, or we may call him the universe. The one is God active, the other is God passive. The one is the life, the other is the body which is animated by the life. The one is the creative energy, the other is the ground or substratum in which this energy is at work, and to which it is united. God is the soul of the great animal world. He is the universal reason which rules over all, and permeates all. He is that gracious providence which cares for the individual as well as for the all. He is infinitely wise. His nature is the basis of law, forbidding evil and commanding good. By the very order of creation he punishes them that do evil, and rewards them that do well, being in himself perfectly just and righteous. He is not a spirit, for that is nothing; as we have no idea corresponding to such an existence, but he is the subtlest element of matter. He is in the world as those wonder-working powers and ever-creating energies which we see in all nature, but whose essence baffles our reason to penetrate. He is the most mysterious of all things we know, and more

mysterious than all mysteries. He is the divine ether. He is
the breath that passes through all nature. He is the fire that
kindles the universe. From him issues forth that stream of
divine life in which nature lives, and which flowing forth into
all her channels makes her rejoice to live. Seneca, the Roman
representative of the philosophers of the porch, calls God the
maker of the universe, the judge and preserver of the world,
the being upon whom all things depend—the spirit of the
world; and then he adds, 'Every name belongs to him. All
things spring from him. We live by his breath; he is all, in
all his parts; he sustains himself by his own might. His divine
breath is diffused through all things small and great. His
power and his presence extend to all. He is the God of heaven
and of all the gods. The divine powers which we worship
singly are all subject to him.'

That the ground of all things is one reality, and that that
reality is God, is the burden of nearly all the speculations of
the Greeks, and the end of all their inquiries. They deny
reality to created things lest two realities existing together
might imply two everlasting beings, which is contradictory to
the utterances of reason concerning being. The individual
things proceed from God, and so far as they are real they are
of God, but in their individuality they are distinct from God.
What that reality of things is, each school has tried to express,
but all the expressions involve a contradiction as they express
something definite, while God is beyond definition—not only
the undefined but the infinite.

In a summary of Greek philosophy much must depend on conjecture. The
original materials are very scanty, many philosophies being known only from
a few quotations preserved in old writers and often of doubtful meaning.
Laertius says, that at first philosophy concerned itself only with things natural,
then with things moral, and at last with things rational. This division is frequently followed, but more because it is convenient than because it is correct.
It has the apparent sanction of Aristotle, who says, that 'of those who first
philosophised, the majority assumed only material principles or elements.'
But Aristotle also says, that 'Thales believed that all things were filled with
gods,' and he infers that Thales believed that 'soul is mixed with all things.'
'Our ancestors,' he says, 'and men of great antiquity, have left us a tradition
involved in fable that these first essences are gods, and that the Divinity comprehends the whole of nature.' Laertius also says that 'Thales taught that
inanimate things were endued with souls, and proved it from the virtues of
the magnet and water, and that though he made water the first of all things,
yet the world was a living creature full of spirits and demons.'

Anaximander's 'infinite,' seems at first sight to have been merely material. This was the opinion of Aristotle and Plutarch, and is the opinion generally received by historians of philosophy. But there are ample grounds for the contrary opinion. Ritter understands it as an imperishable unity, an ever-producing energy.

The doctrines of Pythagoras are the most uncertain, and as they are usually set forth, the least comprehensible. That Pythagoras was ever in Persia is only conjecture. There is no contemporary evidence that the Greek philosophers learned anything from the East. Aristotle says, the 'Pythagoreans were of opinion that the infinite existence and the one itself are the essence of those things of which they are predicated, and hence they asserted that number is the essence of all things.' Alexander the philosopher, discoursing of the Pythagorean doctrine, says, that 'the one is the formal principle and cause of all things, as in all men is *man*, in all animals the *animal*, and in all beings the *being*. Ueberweg sums up the Pythagorean doctrine, as taught by Philolaeus, in those words, 'The world is eternal and ruled by the one who is akin to it and has supreme might and excellence.'

The Master of Trinity vindicates Xenophanes from the charge of Pantheism. He says, that Xenophanes 'carefully distinguished the Deity from the outward universe on the one hand and from the *Non-ens* on the other. It was Parmenides who first imagined the necessity of identifying plurality with the *Non-ens*, in other words of denying reality to the outward phenomenal world.'

Dr. Thompson also says of Heraclitus, that his 'fire was endowed with spiritual attributes. Aristotle calls it soul and incorporeal. It is the common ground of the phenomena both of mind and matter. It is not only the animating but also the intelligent and regulative principle of the universe. The universal word or reason which behoves all men to follow. This interpretation seems to materialize mind, but it also spiritualizes matter and makes the movable one of Heraclitus, the becoming, as immaterial as the resting one of the Eleatics, which is being.'

Aristotle says, 'Socrates employed himself about ethics, and entirely neglected the speculation respecting the whole of nature, in morals indeed investigating the universals and applying himself to definitions. Plato approving this, his investigation of morals, adopted this much of his doctrine, that these definitions respect other things and are not conversant with anything sensible.'

The connection, in the text, between Socrates and Plato is only inferential, and may be disputed. The 'knowledge,' according to Dr. Thompson, was a knowledge of consequences generalised from experience. On this ground Grote claims Socrates for a 'Utilitarian.'

According to Xenophon, Socrates regarded the soul of man as allied to the Divine mind, not by its essence but by its nature, elevated by reason above the rank of the mere animal creation.

It appears from the *Phaedo* that Socrates had the Buddhist notion of the wretchedness of the present existence. He looks upon the union of a body with the soul as a penalty. By the pre-existence of the soul he seems to mean its identity with the divine being. He calls the soul '*That which is.*' In the *Gorgias* again, he says, 'I should not wonder if Euripides speaks the truth when he says—Who knows whether to live is not death, and to die, life?'

Our interpretation of Plato, like all interpretations of Plato, may be disputed. Dr. Thompson says, 'Plato's one is relation, a thought as against a

thing or perception, a genus as opposed to individuals, &c., he rejects the ab
solute One of Parmenides at least under that name.   Mind is with him the giver
of the "limit" not the limit itself; the efficient rather than the formal cause :
that cause which blends the limit with the unlimited—in short, a creative
energy, if we may not say, conscious Creator.'

Warburton ascribes the notion of the derivation of the souls of men from the
Divine essence, and their final resolution into it to all the philosophers of
antiquity, without exception.   Archer Butler thinks this opinion unsupported
in the case of Platonism, as it came from the hands of Plato ; yet he says,
'Plato may in the last analysis have embraced all things in some mysterious
unity ; an idea which in "some" vague sense it is impossible for human reason
to avoid.'

According to the 'Timaeus' the universe was generated, it was modelled after
an eternal pattern.   It is a blessed god, having its soul fixed in the centre, yet
existing throughout the whole.   The soul was made before the body.   Between
soul and body there is an intermediate, made up of the indivisible and divisible
essence.   The three are mingled into one.   The eternal universe was a living
existence ; so the deity tried to make the sensible universe, as far as he could,
similarly perfect.   Time was generated with the universe.   Eternity is a unity.
The stars are generated gods, living existences endowed with souls.   Fire,
water, &c., should not be called 'this' or 'that,' not being 'things.'   Before the
creation of the universe there were being, place, and generation.   The charge
of producing mortal natures was committed by the Creator to his offspring the
junior gods.

Plato, says Archer Butler, calls matter the unlimited ; intelligence the limit
—one and many—single and multiple—indivisible and divisible—unchangeable
and changeable—absolute and relative—example and copy—the good and the
manifestation of the good—the object of science, eternal being and the objects
of opinions.   Dr. Thompson adds, 'Bare matter he scarcely distinguished from
place.'   He also says, Plato dedicated his mature powers to the task of reconciling the Ephesian doctrine of a flux, and becoming, with the Eleatic principle
of Parmenides.

Mr. Mackay says, Plato, like most philosophers after Anaxagoras, made the
supreme Being to be Intelligence, but in other respects left his nature undefined or rather indefinite though the variety of definition, a conception floating
vaguely between Theism and Pantheism.

The histories of philosophy that have been chiefly followed, are those of
Schwegler, Ueberweg, Brucker, Ritter, and Tennemann ; with the English
histories of Professor Maurice, George Henry Lewes, and especially the lectures
of Professor Archer Butler with Dr. Thompson's notes.

CHAPTER IV.

THE Hebrew Scriptures begin with the creation of the world. The creating God or gods is called Elohim, ' a name,' says Gesenius, ' retained from Polytheism and which means the higher powers or intelligences.' That the sacred writer should use a word borrowed from Polytheism will not surprise those who understand the nature of language, but that the writer himself had passed from Polytheism to the belief of the one God is evident from the whole of the record of creation, and confirmed by the succeeding history. To Abraham, Isaac, and Jacob, the name of God was El Shaddai. To Moses God revealed himself by the new name Jehovah, or I AM. The God of Moses was pure Being. It was the name Jehovah which kept the Jews from idolatry. In proportion as they ceased to think of their deliverer as the unspeakable being, they were in danger of worshipping the gods of the nations. ' This new name,' as Dean Stanley says, ' though itself penetrating into the most abstract metaphysical idea of God, yet in its effect was the very opposite of a mere abstraction.' The old Jews did not speculate about the essence of God, though they had reached the highest conception of that essence. Guarded by the declaration once for all that the nature of God was mysterious and his name ineffable, they were free to make him a person—to ascribe to him attributes, and to represent him as made in the image of man. He has hands and feet. He rules as a king, dwelling with Israel in Canaan, protecting them with his mighty arm, and watching over them with ever open eyes, which are in every place, beholding the evil and the good. All the mighty objects of nature are summoned to express God. The great mountains are the mountains of God ; the tall trees are the trees of God ; and the mighty rivers the rivers of God. He is the rock of safety, whose way is perfect. He maketh Lebanon and Sirion to skip like a young unicorn.

It is his voice that roars in the raging of the waters; his
majesty that speaks in the thunder; and when the storm and
tempest break down the mighty cedars, it is the voice of the
Lord, yea, it is the Lord who breaketh the cedars of Libanus.
This psalm expresses the full extent to which the old Hebrews
went in the identification of God and nature. They never
surpassed this even in poetry; and never forgot that the Lord
sitteth above the water floods, and that the Lord is king for
ever. The personifying tendency natural to a race of men
who had to fight for their own national existence, as well as
for the doctrine of the divine unity, interfered with all speculation concerning the divine essence. It exposed them however to the idolatry against which their national existence was
meant to be a continual witness. The search for symbols led
them to liken God to things in heaven and earth and the
waters under the earth. The world, according to Josephus, is
' the purple temple of God,' and to imitate this temple, the
Jews built the tabernacle, and afterwards the great temple of
God at Jerusalem. The symbols permitted them by Moses
and David and Solomon became objects of worship. The
images borrowed from nature to express God prepared them
for the worship of Baal and Ashteroth, the sun, moon, and
stars, the gods of the Sidonians, of Chaldea, and the nations
round about them.

We may perhaps fairly date the origin of Jewish philosophy
from the time of the captivity. The metaphysical idea involved in the name of Jehovah becomes prominent, and acts its
part as the personifying idea had done before it. The sin of
the Jews is no longer idolatry. They are henceforth without
Teraphim. The unity of God was not unknown either to the
Chaldeans or the Persians. Abraham only conserved a doctrine well-known to his ancestors of Chaldea, but in his day
almost hidden by the prevailing idolatry. When the Jews
went into Babylon and Persia, did they hear again from the
sages the philosophical notion of God, or did the idea implied
in the name, I AM, come naturally to its proper development?
The answer is immaterial. The Jewish Rabbis who prosecuted
the metaphysical idea of God, maintained that their speculations were familiar to learned Jews, and that though the
Scriptures speak of God as a person, which was a necessity of

the popular mind, yet we are to distinguish between the popular aspect of Jewish theology and that theology itself. The latter was the esoteric teaching, the former simply exoteric. To the Rabbis was confided the hidden philosophy which the multitude could not receive. How far Rabbinical philosophy agreed with the Scriptures or differed from them must be left for the present an open question. The Hellenist Jews may have borrowed from the Greeks and Orientals, or the Greeks and Orientals may have borrowed from the Jews. Or, again, it may have been that the philosophies of each were natural developments. Some thoughts belong universally to the soil of the human intellect, and have an independent growth among nations that have no intercourse with each other. But even when a doctrine is borrowed, there must be previously a disposition to receive, for a borrower will only borrow what is congenial to his own mind. Religious teachers, as Schleiermacher says, do not choose their disciples, their disciples choose them. The many points of agreement between Judaism and the philosophies of the Greeks and Orientals, leave it open for us to say either that the heathen got their wisdom from the Jews or that the roots and germs of Christian doctrines are revealed in the universal reason. The speculative Jews have maintained that the philosophy of Judaism as they understand it was the source and beginning of all philosophies. Plato is with them but an Attic Moses, and Pythagoras a Greek philosopher who borrowed the mysteries of Monads and Tetrads from the chosen people.

We have supposed that from the time of the captivity, the Jews had a philosophy of religion; but of this philosophy the traces are few, and the authorities uncertain, until near the beginning of the Christian era. Eusebius has preserved some fragments of Aristobulus supposed to be the Alexandrian Jew mentioned in the Maccabees as King Ptolemy's instructor. In these fragments Aristobulus clearly distinguishes between God himself, as the first God, the ineffable and invisible, and God as manifested in the phenomenal world. And in the letter ascribed to Aristeas, librarian to Ptolemy Philadelphus, we see Judaism and Hellenism forming so near an alliance that each regards the other as but a different form of itself. Aristeas informs Ptolemy that the same God who gave him his kingdom gave the Jews their laws. 'They worship him,' says Aristeas, 'who created all, provides for all, and is prayed to by all, and especially by us, only under another name.' And Eleazar, the high priest of Jerusalem, when asked by Aristeas if it was not unworthy of God to give laws concerning meats, such as those given to the Jews, answered 'that they were indeed insignificant; and though they served to keep the Jews as a distinct people, yet they had beyond this a deep allegorical meaning.' 'The great doctrine of Moses,' said Eleazar, 'is that the power of this one God is through all things;' words in which the students of Alexandrian philosophy have seen an intimation of that Spirit which is through all and in all. It has been thought, too, that in the Greek version of the Scriptures made at Alexandria, there are evident marks of the influence of Greek thought on the minds of the translators, who seem often to have chosen such words as left the ground clear for a Platonic interpretation, and sometimes, even to suggest it. Some of the most remarkable of these are the translation of the name of God. 'I AM THAT I AM,' which the seventy render 'I AM HE THAT IS;' and the second verse of the first chapter of Genesis, where the Hebrew words which simply mean that the earth was confusion, are translated 'The earth was invisible and unformed,' pointing, it has been supposed, to the ideal or typical creation of Plato, which preceded the material. 'The Lord of hosts' is usually translated 'the Lord of the powers,' or, 'the Lord of the powers of heaven,' the Greek name for the inferior gods.

The Books of the Apocrypha, which were mostly written by Hellenist Jews, have also been pressed into this service, but the evidence they furnish is uncertain. Solomon is made to speak of himself as good coming undefiled into a body; which seems to be allied to the Platonic idea of the body being the cause of sin. He is also made to speak of the incorruptible Spirit of God being in all things. But the verses supposed to be most conclusive are those which speak of wisdom as the creative power of God: 'A pure influence flowing from the glory of the Almighty. She is the brightness of the everlasting light—the unspotted mirror of the power of God—the image of his goodness; and being but one she can do all things, and remaining in herself she createth all things new and in all ages;

entering into holy souls she maketh them friends of God and prophets. She preserved the first formed father of the world, who was created, alone, and brought him out of his fall.'

Again, the son of Sirach makes wisdom thus praise herself:

> I came out of the mouth of the most High,
> And covered the earth as a cloud.
> I dwelt in high places,
> And my throne is in a cloudy pillar.
> I alone compassed the circuit of heaven,
> And walked in the bottom of the deep.
> In the waves of the sea, and in all the earth,
> And in every people and nation, I got a possession.
> With all these I sought rest:
> And in whose inheritance shall I abide?
> So the Creator of all things gave me a commandment,
> And He that made me, caused my tabernacle to rest,
> And said, Let thy dwelling be in Jacob,
> And thine inheritance in Israel.
> He created me from the beginning before the world,
> And I shall never fail.
> In the holy tabernacle I served before him:
> And so was I established in Sion.
> Likewise in the beloved city he gave me rest,
> And in Jerusalem was my power.
> And I took root in an honourable people,
> Even in the portion of the Lord's inheritance.
> *   *   *   *   *
> I am the mother of fair love,
> And fear, and knowledge, and holy hope,
> I therefore being eternal, am given to all my children,
> Which are named of Him.

That these verses speak of wisdom as the creative power of God in much the same way as wisdom is spoken of in heathen philosophies, is not to be denied. It is also true that they were composed in Greek, and in a heathen city; but their likeness to the words of wisdom in the book of Proverbs forbids us to say that they were borrowed from heathen philosophy. The writer may indeed have felt the harmony between the thoughts of the Alexandrians and those of the Jews, and may have delighted to show the heathen that his nation was already in possession of a philosophy not inferior to theirs.

Philo Judæus.

If the influence of Greek philosophy is only imperfectly discerned in the Apocrypha, or the fragmentary writings of the Hellenist Jews, all doubt is removed by the works of Philo Judæus—the proper representative of Alexandrian Judaism. We have not indeed any treatise of Philo's on a subject purely speculative, and, consequently, no complete or carefully defined system of speculation; but the ideas scattered through his practical and expository writings, and his unceasing efforts to bring the teaching of the Old Testament into harmony with these ideas wherever it seemed to differ from them, sufficiently evidence his obligations to the Greek philosophers.

But how could the Old Testament be made to teach Greek philosophy? The history of a practical nation like the Jews might be supposed beforehand to have but little relation to the thoughts of philosophers, who spent their lives in the study of causes and essences. Often indeed the connection between thought and action, philosophy and daily life, is closer than we imagine, and the Old Testament writers may have had metaphysical thoughts, though they wrote no books on metaphysics. It is, however, impossible in reading Philo, notwithstanding the advantage he had in using the Greek version of the Seventy, not to feel that his interpretations are more frequently read into the Scriptures than found there. But this need not concern us here; we come to Philo's writings neither to refute his doctrines nor to approve them, but only to trace the character of that philosophy which manifested itself among the Jews of Alexandria.

The Greek translation of 'I AM' as 'HE THAT IS' at once allied the Jewish theology to that of Plato; for 'the Being' was pre-eminently the name of Plato's supreme Deity. From this Philo could at once speak of the God of the Jews as the Eleatics and Platonists had done of the being without attributes, of whom nothing could be truly affirmed; of whom no likeness could be made, for he is unlike anything in heaven or earth. He is infinite, immutable, and incomprehensible; but these predicates do not say what he is; only what he is not. Qualities belong to finite beings, not to God. He is wiser than wisdom; fairer than beauty; stronger than strength. By reason we know that he is; but we have no faculty whereby to know what he is. We aid our feeble thoughts by metaphors and illustrations from things material. We call him the primitive light, from which all light emanates; the life, from which all life proceeds; the infinite intelligence; but of him, as he is in himself, we only know that he is one, simple, and incapable of destruction. He has no name. To Moses he revealed himself as ' I AM THAT I AM,' which, says Philo, is equivalent to saying, 'It is my nature to be; not to be described; but in order that the human race may not be wholly destitute of any appellation which they may give to the most excellent of beings, I allow you to use the word Lord as a name.' He again says, 'So indescribable is the living God, that even those powers which minister to him do not announce to us his proper name.'. After the wrestling with the angel, Jacob said to the invisible Master, 'Tell me thy name;' but he answered, 'Why askest thou my name?' And so he does not tell him his peculiar and proper name. He says, 'It is sufficient for thee to be taught by ordinary explanations; but as for names which are the symbols of created things, do not seek to find them among immortal natures.' Again, 'A name can only designate something that is known; it brings it into connection with something else. Now, absolute being cannot come into relation with something else. It fills itself; it is sufficient for itself. As before the existence of the world, so after it, being is the all. Therefore, God who is absolute being, can have no name.' The name God does not worthily express the highest being. It does not declare him as he is; it only expresses a relation of the highest first principle to the created. In reference to the universe, God is ' the good,' but he is more than that; he is more than God. It is enough for the divine nature to be and not to be known. He must be unchangeable, because he is perfectly simple; and the most perfect of all beings can be united with no other. 'God does not mingle with anything else, for what is mingled with him must be either better than he is, or worse, or equal; but there is nothing better or equal; and nothing worse can be mingled with him, for then he would become worse, or perhaps annihilated, which it is wrong to suppose.' Without attributes, without names, incomprehensible to the intellect of man, God is the One, the Monad, Being; 'and yet,' Philo adds, making a still higher effort to express the ineffable, 'the Therapeutæ reverence God worthily, for they consider him simpler than unity, and more original than the Monad.' He is more than life, for he is the source of life itself.

The necessity of again connecting the divine Being with the created world and things conceivable and sensuous, after entirely separating between him and them, involved a contradiction perhaps more than verbal. God, though a simple essence and unlike things which proceed from each other, is yet the cause of all the created universe. The unchangeable Being thus becomes the cause, and being the ground of all becoming, that is, the phenomenal, he must in some way be related to it. The universe, it is argued, did not owe its origin directly to the first Being. The most beautiful of the sensuous world is unworthy of God, to say nothing of the more unworthy part, which to ascribe directly to God would be blasphemy; and yet without him it could not be. He must therefore be recognised, at least, as the cause of causes. The unknowable thus becomes known, though known only as the unknowable. To be ignorant of him is truly to know him. 'Therefore,' says Philo, 'we, disciples and friends of the prophet Moses, do not leave off the inquiry concerning that which really is; holding fast that to know this is the goal of fortune, is an unbroken life, whilst the law also says, that those who are near God live. Then, indeed, those who are separated from God are dead in soul. An important doctrine, dear to a wise man; but those who have taken their place with God live an immortal life again.' The goal of this life is the knowledge and science of God. He is incomprehensible, and yet comprehensible. Incomprehensible to us men, and yet comprehensible to us so far as we are divine; for man was not made of the dust alone, but also of the divine Spirit. There is in us a germ of the Deity, which may be developed to a divine existence; and though God cannot enter into the circle of the human, we may be raised to equality with him, and then we shall both see and know him. Now we know God imperfectly through his works. He is a God afar off; a being whose

existence is demonstrable by reason; though indeed this knowledge of God is only negative. But we rise to a true knowledge
of him as our being becomes assimilated to his being. We
have visions of God, a pure and perfect knowledge, by
intuition, phantasy, or whatever other name may be given to
that revelation by which God is revealed to the soul. 'It is
such as was given in part to Moses when transcending the
created he received a representation of the uncreated, and
through this comprehended both God and his creation.'

The supreme Being is not the immediate maker of the worlds.
Beginning with the sensuous, which is the first step of the
celestial ladder, we ascend to the spiritual; for the visible
evidently reveals the working of the invisible. But we cannot
here infer only one being. There are, evidently, more than
one, at least two, an original first cause and an intelligent
being, who is the proximate cause. The latter is subject to
the former, and is the mediating power between it and matter.

This mediating power is the Logos, or Word of God, the world
maker. Philo gives the Logos a variety of names. He is the
mediator between mortal and immortal races. He is God's
name, God's interpreter, God's vicar. To man he is God, but
on the divine side, the second God, or the image of God. The
spirit world is the divine thought; the sensuous world, the
divine speech; and the Logos, the capacity of God to think
and speak. As thought, he is the Logos immanent; as speech,
the Logos transient. Philo identifies the Logos with that wisdom which God is said to have created as the first of his
works, and established before the Æons. He calls it the spouse
of God, who is the father and the mother of the all. Sometimes the Logos is plural, not only the word, but the words of
God; and these are identified with the divine powers or attributes. The two cherubim in Genesis are the two highest
powers of God; his goodness and his might. By the one he
has created all, by the other he preserves all. Between these,
as a uniting bond, is the Logos, which embraces both; for by
the Logos God rules, and creates, and shows mercy. The
cherubim were the symbols of these powers, and the flaming
sword that turned either way was the divine Logos. In the
same way the Logos is identified with other attributes, and
distributed into different potencies of the divine Being. As all

F

these potencies are consubstantial, having their substratum in
God, the Logos is identical sometimes with the potencies, and
at other times with the first cause or supreme God. Philo
ends in ascribing to the first cause, through the Logos, those
qualities, works and attributes, which he had otherwise denied
him; considering them unworthy of the first God. The Deity
could not pervade matter, nor come into any relation to it; but
through the Logos he is the maker and preserver of the world.
By the Logos, God is restored to the world, and the oneness of
the created and the uncreated becomes manifest through the
mediating power or powers. These powers are God; they are
also the spiritual world-plan, the perfect world after which this
sensuous world is formed; and even it, so far as it is well
formed, is itself the Logos or word of God. The spirit worlds
are God's first begotten, and the sensuous his younger sons.
Ideas, demons, heroes, angels, the higher powers, have the
same relation to the sensuous creature that God has to the
spiritual. The necessity of personification may cause them to
appear as distinct beings: but they have all in their degrees
a divine existence. Angels and spirits are the divine thought,
and are not separate from him who thinks. According to
Philo, the Chaldeans said either the visible world is itself a god
or God contained in himself is the soul of all things. Philo
intended to differ from the Chaldeans by means of the Logos,
word, words, or invisible powers distinct from God and yet
identical with him; but he differed only in intention, for
Philo's chief God filled all things and went through them all,
and left no place void or empty of himself. The soul of the
universe is God. All the inferior gods, the divine mediating
powers, as well as the world, are parts of the first God. He is
the place of all things—that which embraces all things, but is
himself embraced by none. He extends himself to all visible
things, and fills the all with himself. He is original light,
while matter is the darkness. The circles of being are light
circles about the first being. The Logos is a brilliant far-
shining light, most like to God. The individual powers are
rays which spread wider and wider the light they receive.
The entire creation is an enlightened becoming of matter
through the first light, the one God who is working always
and in all. 'The Lord looked down to see the city and the

tower,' is spoken after the manner of men, since who does not know that he who looks down, necessarily leaves one place and takes another. But all is full of God. Of him alone it can be said that he is everywhere, and yet nowhere. He is nowhere, because he created space and things corporeal; and it is not becoming to say that the Creator is contained in things created. He is everywhere, because he leaves no part of the world void; since by his presence he holds together the earth and water, and the wide heaven, and all things.

The Logos made the world. The ideal of creation, according to Plato, existed in the mind of God. Philo said that the Logos created the world after the pattern set forth in the ideal. But we must take care that the necessity of personifying does not mislead us. We have already seen that the ideal was itself the Logos. God's thought was his image, and as the thought was the likeness cf God, so man was the likeness of the Logos. Creation may thus be regarded either as flowing forth from God, or as being willed by him. It is in reality an emanation; but as we personify God in the Logos, we must consider it as an act of the will. Moses taught that the material or younger creation was formed on the model of the archetypal or elder creation. As a plan exists in the mind of an architect, so did creation exist ideally in the mind of God.' In the beginning, that is, out of time, God created the incorporeal heaven and the incorporeal earth, after the model perceptible by the mind. He created also the form of air and of empty space. He called the air darkness, and the space the deep. He then made the incorporeal substances of the elements, and at last the ideal man. After forming the invisible heaven and earth with their inhabitants, the Creator formed the visible. But he could not be entirely responsible for the creation of mixed natures; so he called in others.—' Let *us* make man.' The creation of Adam was the creation of human reason not yet united to a body. Through its union with the sensuous came the fall. This was a necessity, the natural result of creation; but it was a step in the divine procedure. Man shall rise through the Logos, through the working of the divine reason within him. The mind of man is a fragment of the Deity. His immortal nature is no other than the Spirit of God. It shall yet subdue the body, and rise to the purely divine. To make out for Philo

something like a congruous system, it has been thought desir-
able to pass by his inconsistencies, and especially his allegorical
trifling with the Scriptures. 'It is no easy matter,' says
Dähne, 'to determine the qualities which Philo gives to matter,
since he, like all his philosophical predecessors, in order to
lead over all imperfection to this which he did not know how
to separate in any other way from the most perfect God, placed
matter along side of God as a second principle, which was
naturally bound up with him; but with this the national faith
was at war; and as the faith of the people forbade its entrance,
it was kept in the background; sometimes he seems to forget
it, and sometimes he goes from one school to another. The
same with all the Alexandrians, heathen and Christian, and
the same too with the Gnostic heretics.' Philo calls matter
'the void,' 'that which is empty;' and, like Plato's evil
world-soul, he makes it the cause of evil. He seems to admit
its existence as a something; and though he receives the axiom
that nothing from nothing comes, he speaks, at times, of matter
as if it had been created, having had no previous existence.
Though he has spoken in full, concerning creation and the
first existence of the sensuous world, he yet says that 'It is
the most absurd of all ideas, to fancy that there ever was a
time when the world did not exist, for its nature is without
any beginning and without any end.' God eternally creates.
There was no time before the world. That is constituted by
the movement of the heavens. Eternity has no past or future,
it is *now*. There is no time in God. The days of creation are
merely the order of succession. God speaks, and it is done,
'When God spoke to Moses, all the people saw the voice.
The voice of man is audible, but the voice of God is visible in
truth. What God speaks is not his word, but his works, which
eyes and not ears perceive.'

THE CABBALA.

The Cabbala is the secret tradition of the Jews, which
explains the hidden meaning of the Scriptures, and contains the true esoteric doctrine of Rabbinical Judaism. The
origin of the Cabbala is unknown. The present collection
of books which profess to unfold it are supposed to have ori-

ginated about the first or second century of the Christian era ;
but concerning the age of the doctrines contained in them we
know nothing. The mystical Rabbis ascribe the Cabbala to
the angel Razael, the reputed teacher of Adam, and say that
the angel gave Adam the Cabbala as his lesson book in paradise. From him it descended to generation after generation.
Noah read it in the ark ; Abraham treasured it up in his tent ;
and through Jacob it was bequeathed to the chosen people. It
was the charter of the national wisdom ; their secret masonic
symbol. By its instruction Moses brought the Jews out of
Egypt, and by its cunning wisdom Solomon built the temple
without the sound of a hammer. That the collection of books
which we possess is the original Cabbala may be true, though
its wisdom much resembles that of the schools of Alexandria.
The likeness of the Cabbalistic theology in some points to that
of Zoroaster, has suggested the time of the captivity as the
probable date of the origin of its earlier parts ; but a likeness
of this kind proves nothing. Its nearest kindred is the writings of Philo, and it is of nearly the same intrinsic worth.

The whole conceivable universe of being, spiritual and material, is one. It proceeded from One, and the process of this
procession is the subject of the metaphysics of the Cabbala. It
shows how all spirits and spirit worlds are on the one side
blended with God, and how on the other they flow out into
the visible world, and are connected with it. The first of
beings, the chief being, is En-soph ; eternal and necessary, the
everlasting or the oldest of existences. He is the absolute
unity, the essence of essences, pre-eminently Being. But that
he may not be considered as any one of the things that are
created, he is also called non-being. He is separated from
all that is, because he is the substance of all that is, the principle of all things, both as potential and as actual. Before
creation, he is God concealed, dwelling in the thick darkness ;
but by creation, he is God revealed, with his light filling space
infinite. Unrevealed, he is the unopened fountain of spirit, life,
and light ; with his self-manifestations, these flow forth to all
beings. He opened his eye, according to the Cabbalistic hieroglyphic, and light, spirit, and life streamed forth to all worlds.

This self-manifesting of God concealed, was creation or
emanation. The power of the Infinite flowed forth in its three-

fold form. The first act of unfolding, that which preceded creation, was called the word or speech of God. It is not distinct from God and the world. Priority or antecedence merely expresses the order of sequence. The Cabbalists, like Philo, know nothing of time, but as existing for the human mind. God and his manifestations are eternal. The Word was the first ray, the original, in which the principles of conception and production were united; the father and mother principle of the actual universe; the alpha and omega, the universe of forms; the first-born of God, and the Creator of all things; at once the image of the ineffable God, and the form or pattern of the visible worlds, through which it proceeds as a divine ray in all degrees of light, life, and spirit. At the head of this gradation is the celestial man, Adam Kadmon, the old or first Adam, who is united to the Infinite in and through the first ray, and is identical with that ray or Word of God. He is the macrocosm or great world, the archetype of the microcosm or little world. In the celestial Adam we eternally exist. He is that wisdom, of whom it is said, that of old his delights were with the sons of men.

From En-soph emanate ten sephiroths, or luminous circles. These represent the divine attributes. They manifest the wisdom, perfection, and power of God. They are his vesture : ' He clothes himself with light as with a garment.' By these he reveals himself. They are also called the instruments which the supreme Architect employs in the operation of his ceaseless activity. They are not however instruments like the tools of an artizan, which may be taken up or laid down at pleasure. They are as the flame from the burning coal. They come from the essence of the Infinite. They are united to him. As the flame discovers force which before lay concealed in the coal, so do these resplendent circles of light reveal the glory and the majesty of God. They are from him, and of him, as heat from fire, and as rays from the sun; but they are not distinct from his being. He suffers neither trouble nor sorrow when he gives them existence. They are no deprivation of his being; but as one flame kindles another without loss or violence, so the infinite Light sends forth his emanating sephiroths. When the primordial ray, the first-born of God, willed to create the universe, he found two great difficulties—first, all space was full of this brilliant and subtle light, which streamed forth from the divine essence. The creative Word must therefore form a void in which to place the universe. For this end he pressed the light which surrounded him, and this compressed light withdrew to the sides and left a vacuum in the centre. The second difficulty arose from the nature of the light. It was too abundant, and too subtle for the creation to be formed of it. The creative Word therefore made ten circles, each of which became less luminous in proportion as it was removed from himself. In this way, from En-soph to the meanest existence, we have a connected universe of being. The infinite light is the all God. In his infinitude are placed all ranks and orders of existence. Around him, in what we are compelled by the imperfection of thought and speech to call his immediate presence, are the pure spirits of the highest sphere. Then spiritual substances less perfect. After these are angels or spirits clothed with bodies of light, which serve both as a covering and as chariots to convey them whither they will. Then follow spirits imprisoned in matter, subject to the perpetual changes of birth and death. Last of all gross matter itself, that of which human bodies and the world are composed, the corruption of the pure divine substance deprived of the perfections of spirit, and light, and life—divinity obscured.

The Cabbalists believe in creation, but only in the sense of emanation. They do not find in Scripture that God made the world out of nothing. 'From nothing, nothing comes,' is with them an established doctrine. No one thing, they say, can be drawn from nothing. Non-existence cannot become existence. Either all things are eternal, which, they say is atheism, or they have emanated from the divine essence. If it is objected how matter could emanate from God, they answer, that matter is not an actual existence, and in its logical annihilation they are not less successful than other philosophers. The efficient cause being spirit, must, they say, produce what is like itself. Its effect must be a spiritual substance. True, indeed, there exists something gross, palpable, and material, but its existence is only negative—a privation of existence. As darkness is a privation of light, as evil is a privation of good, so is matter a privation of spirit. As well say that God made darkness, sin, and death, as say that he made the substances

which we call sensible and material. The sum is—all is a
manifestation of God. The divine Word is manifesting itself
always, and in all places. Angels and men, beasts of the
field and fowls of the air, animated insects, grains of sand
on the sea-shore, atoms in the sunshine—all, so far as they do
exist, have their existence in that which is divine.

Ueberweg, speaking of the Septuagint, says, 'We find that as a rule the
notion of the sensible manifestation of God is suppressed; anthropopathic ideas,
such as the idea of God's repenting are toned down in their expressions, the
distance between God, in his essence, and the world is increased, and the
idea of mediating links between the two appears more fully developed than in
the original text. In these peculiarities germs of the later religious philosophy
may undoubtedly be seen, but not as yet this philosophy itself.'

Philo says, 'It would be a sign of great simplicity for a man to suppose that
the world was created in six days; or, indeed, created at all in time; but
naked truth can only be received by very wise men. It must be put in the
form of lies before the multitude can profit by it. The creation of Eve is manifestly a fable. God had put Adam, or human reason into an *ecstacy* (the Greek
word), and the spiritual came in contact with the sensuous.' In Genesis iii. 15,
God says to the serpent, '*It* shall bruise thy head.' Who? Evidently the
woman, says Philo; yet the Greek word is *He*. It cannot refer, grammati-
cally, to the woman, who is feminine; nor to seed, which is neuter; it must
then refer to the mind of man that shall bruise the head of the serpent, which
is the cause of union between the mind and the sense. Eve bare Cain—*possession;*—the worst state of the soul is self-love, the love of individuality. Abel,
or, *vanity*, was next conceived, in which the soul found out the vanity of possession. Cain slew Abel in a field, which is the man in whom the two opposite
principles contended. From Cain sprung a wicked race; the evil consequences
flowing from Cain's victory, when every desire after God was destroyed.
Another interpretation of Cain killing Abel, is, that Cain killed *himself;* showing that the evil-doer naturally reaps the reward of his evil deeds. Abraham
leaving Chaldea was his leaving the sensuous. The Babylonian Talmud complained that the *Seventy* had translated Gen. i. 27, 'Male and Female created
he him.' Philo vindicated this translation, because the ideal man was masculo-
feminine. 'Of every tree of the garden thou mayest freely eat; but of the
tree of the knowledge of good and evil, *thou* shalt not eat of it; and in the day
thou eatest thereof, *thou* shalt surely die.' The Seventy make the pronoun in
the first verse singular; but in the other two, the pronouns are plural, because,
says Philo, the reasonable soul is alone required for the practice of virtue; but
to enjoy the forbidden fruit, there is need not only of the soul but of the body
and of sense, 'Sacrifice and offering thou wouldst not, but a body hast thou
prepared:' the body is given to man for sacrifice. It is to be renounced.
When the high priest entered the Holy of Holies he became God. Where we
read 'There shall be no man in the tabernacle,' Philo interprets, 'When the
high priest shall enter into the Holy of Holies, he shall *be no more a man*, until
he comes forth again.'

There are many books on Philo by German writers, as Dähne, Gfrörer,
Grossman, and Planck. His works were edited in England by Thomas Man-
gey, in 1742. Translations of some of them are in Bohn's library. The
account of the Cabbala is taken from the Cabbala Denudata.

CHAPTER V.

'IT is only Ammonius the porter,' said some Alexandrians to each other. 'He professes to teach the philosophy of Plato;' and they laughed contemptuously, thinking how much better it would suit him to be making his day's wages at the harbour instead of troubling his mind about essences and first principles, entelechies, potentialities, and actualities. But the Alexandrians were earnest truth seekers, and when Ammonius Saccas intimated that he was to lecture on philosophy, an audience was soon collected. Among this audience was a young man with a look of unusual earnestness. He had listened to many philosophers. He had questioned many sages. His search for truth had been deep and earnest, long and ardent; now he is about to abandon it as hopeless. The abyss of scepticism lies before him. He knows no alternative but to go onward to it; and yet his spirit pleads that there must be such a thing as truth within the reach of man. The universe cannot be a lie. On the verge of despair he listens to Ammonius, and ere many words had been spoken, he exclaims, 'This is the man I am seeking.' That pale, eager youth was the great Plotinus, the mystical spirit of Alexandria, who, with Plato in his hand, was destined to influence the religious philosophy of all succeeding ages. With the devotion of a true philosopher, Plotinus sat for eleven years at the feet of the Alexandrian porter. He then visited the East, that he might learn the philosophies of India and Persia. Rich in Asiatic speculation, he returned to Rome, and opened a school of philosophy. Charmed by his eloquence, multitudes of all ranks gathered around him. Men of science, physicians, senators, lawyers, Roman ladies, enrolled themselves as his disciples; nobles dying, left their children to the charge of the philosopher, bequeathing to him their property, to be expended for their children's benefit. Gallienus wished to re-build a city in Campania, and to place him over it, that he might form a new society on the principles of Plato's Republic. Strange and wonderful was the power over men possessed by this mystical philosopher. He discoursed of the invisible; and even the Romans listened. As he himself had been in earnest, so were men in earnest with him. What had he to tell them? What was the secret of his power?

There was a new element in Plotinus which was not found in the old Greek philosophers. He was religious; he wished to be *saved*. Indeed, this word was used by the Neo-Platonists in the same sense in which it was used by Christians; only, the way of salvation for them was through philosophy. They sought to know God, and what revelation of truth God made to the human mind. Aristotle could pass with indifference from theology to mathematics, his sole object being intellectual exercise; but Plotinus regarded philosophical speculation as a true prayer to God. He had, as he explains it, embraced the philosophical life, and it was the life of an angel in a human body. The object of knowledge was the object of love; perfect knowledge was perfect happiness, for, necessarily, from the right use of reason would follow the practice of virtue.

Neo-Platonism has been called Eclectic, and this rightly. It not only borrowed from other systems, but with some of them it sought to be identified; and on many points the identity is not to be disputed. That the senses alone could not be trusted had been abundantly proved, and individual reason only led to scepticism. The one remaining hope was in the universal reason. Individual reason has but a partial participation in the universal, and is therefore defective. Common sense is the judgment of an aggregate of individuals, and is to be trusted to the extent that that aggregate partakes of the universal reason. Beyond this no school of Greek philosophy had as yet advanced. A further step had been indicated by Parmenides and Plato, and is now consistently and logically made by Plotinus. That step was to identify the individual reason with the universal; but this could only be done by the individual losing itself in the universal. There is truth for man just in proportion as he is himself true. Let man rise to God, and God will reveal himself to him. Let man be still before the awful majesty, and a voice will speak. In this divine teaching, inspiration or breath of God passing over us, is the only ground of truth. And the reason is that our home from which we have strayed is in the bosom of the Infinite. He is near us at all times, but we do not feel his presence, because our minds are too much set on things finite. Let us put aside what holds us back from him ; all that weighs us down and prevents us ascending to the heights of divine contemplation. Let us come alone, and in solitude seek communion with the Spirit of the universe, and then shall we know him who is the true and the good. When we become what we were before our departure from him, then shall we be able truly to contemplate him, for in our reason he will then contemplate himself. In this ecstacy, this enthusiasm, this intoxication of the soul, the object contemplated becomes one with the subject contemplating. The individual soul no longer lives. It is exalted above life. It thinks not, for it is above thought. It is not correct to say that Plotinus abandoned reason for faith ; he holds fast to reason, but it is human reason, at one with the divine. To the mind thus true, thus united to universal reason, truth carries with it its own evidence.

Our knowledge begins with the sensuous world. The manifold is, at first, alone accessible to us. We cannot see that which is eternal till purified by long labours, prayers, and this particular illuminating grace of God. At first our weakness is complete. We must penetrate the nature of the world to learn to despise it, or, if it embraces any spark of true good, to seize it and use it to exalt our souls and lead them back to God. As Plato instructed by Heraclitus not to name a river, not even to point to it with his finger, yet fixed his eyes on the fleeting waters before contemplating the eternal essence, so Plotinus stops for a moment among the phenomenal ; seeing in sensation, not the foundation, but the occasion of science. The order of being is not disturbed by the changes in the sensuous world. That order must be the proper object of knowledge, and not those many individuals which are ever changing. There can only be a science of the universal, for that alone is permanent. We quit the phenomenal world for another—the eternal, immutable, and intelligible. There spirits alone penetrate, and there thought directly seizes essences. True knowledge is that which teaches us the nature of things, penetrates directly the nature of objects, and is not limited merely to the perception of images of them. This much had been established by Plato, and some think by Aristotle too; but Plotinus was carried beyond through this rational knowledge to a revelation or vision of the Infinite, granted to the soul that had been purified by mental and spiritual exercises.

The theology of Plotinus was a combination of the theologies of Parmenides, Socrates, Plato, and Aristotle. Parmenides and his followers had carried dialectics to their last consequence, and the result was that God was the immovable One. Socrates rebelled against the Eleatic deity, and, taking up the ' mind ' of Anaxagoras, which created the world, he ascribed to it also the preservation and moral government of the universe. Plato was partly faithful to his master Socrates. He too contended for the movability of God, though had he followed out consistently the dialectical method which he received from the Eleatics, he would have come to the same conclusion as they did; but he recoiled from the theology of Eleaticism, and made God a creator. Aristotle combated the God of Plato as being too much related to the sensuous world, and substituted a mover, who was movable; and above him in another sphere, an immovable mover, who alone is God. Plotinus did not regard these theologies as contradictory. Each contained a truth of its own. He could not reconcile them by reason, but he could receive them and see their harmony by an intuition which was above reason. He admitted Plato's method and Plato's God. He admitted, too, Aristotle's doctrine of the first principle, which must be immovable, and his interpretation of the dialectical method, that it could stop only at simple unity; yet, he said, God must be a cause, hence a threefold God—a God in three hypostases, the unity of Parmenides, the immovable mover of Aristotle, and the Demiurgus of Plato.

The Demiurgus, world maker, or world-soul, is the third hypostasis of the Trinity of Plotinus. It produces things movable, and is itself movable; but it is nevertheless universal, excluding from its bosom all particularity, and all phenomena. It is unlike our souls, which are but 'souls in part.' The Demiurgus is God, but not the whole of God; it is entirely disengaged from matter, being the immediate product and the most perfect image of ' mind.' It does not desire that which is beneath it, but is intimately united to God, and derives from him all its reality, and brings back to him all its activity and all its power. It is one with him, though existing as a distinct hypostasis. It is the all of life in whose essence all things live. Plants and animals—yea, minerals, stones, and pebbles, are all animated by it; for it is the only true element in nature. But, whatever its manifestations, it is still one and the same. We may see it manifested as the divine Socrates; or as a simple brute, leading the mere insect life; as one of the deities of the mythology, as a blade of grass or as a grain of dust. It is at once everywhere, and yet nowhere; for, as spirit, it has not any *where*. It proceeds from 'mind' as the ray from the radiating centre, the heat from fire, or the discursive from the pure reason. This 'mind' from which it proceeds, is the second hypostasis. Plato identified the two. Mind was the Demiurgus, or world-maker, and not different from the archetypal world. Plotinus made the distinction that he might separate God more from the world, and at the same time unite him more closely to it. Mind is the divine Logos, God knowable and conceivable by man; but God is above human knowledge and finite conception; therefore, said Plotinus, repeating Plato, ' O man, that mind which you suppose, is not the first God; he is another, more ancient and divine.' This is the first hypostasis, the simple primordial unity; the being without acts and attributes, immutable, ineffable, without any relation to generation or change. We call him being, but we cannot stop at this; he is more than being; he is above all that which our minds or senses reveal to us of being. In this sense he is above being; he is non-being. The laws of reason cannot be applied to him. We cannot declare the mode of his existence. He is the super-essential unity; the only original and positive reality; the source whence all reality emanates. What more can we say ? In this unity, by means of the Logos or mind, and the Demiurgus, all things exist. It is the universal bond, which folds in its bosom the germs of all existence. It is the enchained Saturn of mythology; the father of gods and men; superior to mind and being, thought and will; the absolute; the unconditioned; the unknown. The three persons of this Trinity are co-eternal and consubstantial—the second proceeding from the first, and the third from the first and second. Duality originates with mind, for mind only exists because it thinks existence ; and existence, being thought, causes mind to stand over against it as existing and thinking. Between the supreme God, or first person of the Trinity, and the Demiurgus, there is the same connection as between him who sows and him who cultivates. The super-essential One, being the seed of all souls, casts the germs into all things, and so all participate in his being. The Demiurgus cultivates, distributes, and transports into each the seeds which come from the supreme God. He creates and comprehends all true existences, so that all being is but the varieties of mind ; and this being is the universal Soul, or third person in the Trinity. Thus all things exist in a triune God. The supreme One is everywhere, by means of mind and soul. Mind is in God, and, in virtue of its relation to the things that proceed from it, is everywhere. Soul is in mind, and in God, and by its relation to the material, it, too, is everywhere. The material is in the soul, and, consequently, in God. All things which possess being, or do not possess being, proceed from God, are of God, and in God.

The material world presented the same difficulty to Plotinus that it had done to other philosophers. It flowed necessarily from God, and being necessary, it could have had no beginning, and can have no end. Yet it was created by the Demiurgus—that is, it existed in the Demiurgus—for creation was out of time, it was in eternity, but not eternal. Eternity meant the plenitude of being. Now the world is divisible and movable ; it is therefore not perfect, and, consequently, not eternal. It has a cause, and that cause is God. Platonists, including Plato, contradict themselves when they speak about creation.

Before the creation, according to Plato, there existed God the Creator, the idea of creation, and the matter from which to create. These three are eternal and co-existent. But the existence of matter is a non-existence ; for, being a thing of change, it is next to nothing, if it is anything ; but more probably it is nothing. The real existences, then, are God and his thoughts, the Creator and the ideas of things. And as these thoughts existed always in the mind of the Deity, creation is eternal ; for the things which we see are but images of those which are not seen. If Plato left any doubt about the nothing-ness of matter, Plotinus expelled it. Like a true chemist, he reduces matter to a viewless state. He deprives it of the quali-ties with which our minds endow it, which we commonly suppose to be its properties, and when deprived of these it evanishes. It is found to be nothing, having neither soul, intelligence, nor life. It is unformed, changeable, indeterminate, and without power. It is therefore non-being, not in the sense in which motion is non-being, but truly non-being. It is the image and phantom of extension. To the senses, it seems to include in itself contraries—the large and the small, the least and the greatest, deficiency and excess ; but this is all illusion, for it lacks all being, and is only a becoming. Often when it appears great, it is small. As a phantom, it is, and then it is not. It becomes nothing, not by change of place, but because it lacks reality. The images in matter are above matter, which is the mirror or image in which objects present divine appearances, according to the position in which they are placed—a mirror which seems full, and appears to be all things, though in reality it possesses nothing, and has no reality except as non-being. God and his thoughts are the only true existences. Material things *are*, only in so far as they exist relatively to true beings. Subtract the true existences, and they are not. God and his thoughts or emanations, in their totality, embrace all existences throughout the universe. God is so far separated from his emanations, that we must not confound him with any one of them ; but they are all in and by him. There are grades of being from that which is everywhere and yet nowhere, to that which must be somewhere ; from God, who is pure spirit, to that which has a finite material form, and occupies a definite space.

Plotinus found the germs, at least, of all his doctrines, in Plato. The supreme good he identified with the absolute unity ; and though in some places Plato calls God a soul, and ascribes to him the creation of the world, yet in the Timaeus he evidently regards mind as the Demiurgus ; and this Demiurgus produces the soul of the world. Plotinus thus sums up Plato's doctrine : 'All is outside of the King of all ; He is the cause of all beauty. That which is of the second order is outside of the second principle ; and that which is of the third order is outside of the third principle. Plato has also said that the cause of all had a father, and that the cause or Demiurgus produced the soul in the vase in which he makes the mingling of the like and the unlike. The cause is mind, and its father the good, that which is above mind and essence. Thus Plato knew that the good engendered mind, and that mind engendered soul.' The human soul was alienated from God by coming into contact with matter; therefore Plotinus despised the material. Our bodies are that from which we should strive to be freed, for they keep us from a complete union with the divine. We ought, then, to mortify the flesh, and live an ascetic life, that we may be delivered from the participation of the body. Plotinus practised what he taught; his mind fixed on the invisible, and foretasting the joys of the divine union, he lived indifferent to sensuous pleasures, wishing to attenuate his body into spirit. Regarding it as a calamity that he had ever been born into this world, he refused to tell his friends his birthday, lest they should celebrate an event so sad. When asked for his portrait, he said it was surely enough for us to bear the image with which nature had veiled us, without committing the folly of leaving to posterity a copy of that image; and when dying, he took leave of his friends with joy, saying that he was about to lead back the divine within him to that God who is all and all.

PORPHYRY.

To follow the other Neo-Platonists is but to follow the copyists of Plotinus. His most ardent and most distinguished disciple was the celebrated Porphyry. Where Porphyry differs from his master, the difference is only in details. His supreme God is the same super-essential unity in three hypostases which, if differently named, are yet the counterpart of the Plotinian Trinity. We have the same discourse of the unity being everywhere, and yet nowhere; all being, and yet no being; called by no name, and yet the eternal source of all beings that have names; outside of whom there is neither thought nor idea, nor existence; before whom the totality of the world is as nothing, but called by pre-eminence, God, because he is pure unity, and superior to all things. With

Porphyry Neo-Platonism made a closer alliance with religion. Philosophy, which had formerly banished the popular deities, now re-called them to its aid. The ancient religion, about to expire, once more glowed with life. At the root of Polytheism there had been a Monotheism, but their harmonious co-existence had hitherto been apparently impossible. Now they coalesce. The philosopher sees his philosophy in the popular worship, and the devout worshipper sees his religion sanctioned by the speculations of philosophy. Plato had conjectured that there was a chain of being from the throne of God to the meanest existence. To make up the links of this chain was the favourite work of the Neo-Platonists of Alexandria, both heathen and Christian. Porphyry undertook it, and for this purpose he required all the gods, heroes, and demons of antiquity, with all the essences, substances, and emanations that had been cogitated by all the schools of all the philosophers. He erected a pyramid of being. First: God, or the One in three hypostases; next the soul of the world. Here Porphyry differed from Plotinus, who made the world-soul the same as the third person of the Trinity. Porphyry admitted it to be a being—the first of creatures but begotten—the great intermediary between God and man. It consists of the world, the fixed stars, the planets, the intelligible gods, all of which are children and servants of the Supreme. Under these were demons, and genii, principalities and powers, archangels, angels, personifications of the forces of nature, and other heavenly messengers; all helping in some way to bridge the distance by constituting grades of being from the Trinity to man.

IAMBLICHUS.

While Porphyry was expounding Plotinianism at Rome, Iamblichus and Hierocles were continuing the succession at Alexandria, but not without some change. The theory of the Triad, as we have seen, was born at Alexandria, through the necessity of reconciling the absolute, immovable God of dialectics with the necessarily movable Demiurgus. Plotinus and Porphyry could not give movement to the absolute God, nor immovability to the creative god; nor could they admit many gods, so they believed in a God, who, without coming out from himself, transforms himself eternally into an inferior order, and thus renders himself by a kind of self-diminution, capable of producing the manifold. To preserve the immovability of the first God, and the movability of the third or manifold, they introduce an intermediary. The doctrine of a Trinity served to preserve the unity, while the hypostases remained distinct. Iamblichus thought to remove the contradiction, by multiplying the intermediaries. In the first rank he put absolute unity, which enveloped in its bosom the first monads. These are the universal monads which do not suffer any division or diminution of their unity and simplicity. The first God is simple, indivisible, immutable. He possesses all the attributes which accord with the plenitude of perfection; the second god possesses the power which engenders the inferior gods, the plenitude of power, the source of the divine life, the principle of all efficacy, the first cause of all good. The third god is the producer of the world. He gives the generative virtue which produces the emanations and makes of them the first vital forces, from which the other forces are derived. All being, that is, God, and the universe, are thus embraced in this Triad of gods. Porphyry had begun to make philosophy religious, but it was reserved for Iamblichus, his disciple, to bring the work to completion. If the gods of the poets and the people are true gods, it must be proper, thought Iamblichus, that temples be dedicated to them, their oracles consulted and sacrifices daily offered. What higher calling then could there be for a philosopher, than to concern himself with that which concerned the gods ? And if the world·soul is so near us that it constitutes the reality of the world, may we not influence it, work upon it, receive communications from it ? Hence divination, theurgy, wonders of magic. The soul of the philosopher drinking deep into the mysteries of spirit, has intercourse with the spirit world. He becomes the high priest of the universe, the prophet filled with deity—no longer a man, but a god having intercourse with, yea, commanding the upper world. His nature is the organ of the inspiring deities. To this sublime vocation Iamblichus was called. He tells us, how communications can be received from the various orders of the spiritual hierarchy. He knows them all, as familiarly as the modern spiritualist knows 'the spheres' of the spirits, with only this difference, that the modern spiritualist evokes the spirits and they come to him ; but the philosopher more properly elevates himself to the spirits. The descent of divinity is only apparent, and is in reality the ascent of humanity. The philosopher by his knowledge of rites, symbols, and potent spells, and by the mysterious virtues of plants and minerals, reaches that sublime elevation, which, according to Plotinus, was reached by prayer and purification, a clean heart and an intellect well exercised by dialectics.

PROCLUS.

In the early part of the fifth century, late one evening, a young man, not yet twenty years of age, arrived at Athens. He had come from Alexandria to complete his studies under the care of some celebrated philosophers. Before entering the town, he sat down to rest by the temple of Socrates, and refreshed himself with water from a fountain which was also consecrated to the Athenian sage. He resumed his journey ; and when he reached Athens, the porter addressing him, said, ' I was going to shut the gate if you had not come.' The words of the porter were in aftertimes interpreted as a prophecy, that if Proclus had not come to Athens, philosophy would then have ceased. He prolonged its existence for another generation. Arrived at Athens he found Syrianus, who was then the master of the school. Syrianus took him to Plutarch, who had been his predecessor, but who had now retired from teaching, having recommended his disciples to Syrianus. Plutarch, struck with the genius and the ardour of young Proclus, wished to be his teacher, and at once they began their studies. Plutarch had written many commentaries on Plato, and to excite the ambition of Proclus he engaged him to correct them, saying, ' Posterity shall know these commentaries under your name.' Syrianus made him read Aristotle that he might be familiar with the inferior departments of science. He then opened to him the holy of holies—the divine Plato. When he had mastered Plato, he was initiated into the mysteries of magic and divination. In time he became famous for his universal learning and his sweet persuasive eloquence, which was made yet more attractive by his solemn and earnest manner, added to great personal beauty.

Proclus combined all former philosophies, religions, and theologies, into one eclectic amalgamation; and brought them to the illustration of Plato, as interpreted by Plotinus, and religionised by Porphyry and Iamblichus. In his hands the harp of every school is vocal with the divine philosophy of Plotinus. We still hear discourses of the one and the many; the sterility of the one without the many; and the lifelessness of the many without the one. We still hear how the all is both one and many; and how existence springs from the multiplication of unity. The universe, says Proclus, is constituted by harmony, and what is harmony but variety in unity. In the mind of the great Architect, ideas exist as one and many. He himself is the One—the highest unity which embraces the three divine unities: essence, identity, variety. This is the first Triad, which Proclus repeats in all forms, and with which repeated he fills all conceivable voids and vacuums in the universe of being. From this first Trinity proceed all others; as simple being is three in one, so are all other beings, each having two extremes and an intermediary. If we realize the Triad; essence, identity, variety, the result is—being, life, mind. Every unity, which is also a trinity, proceeds from the Trinity; and each is of the multiplicity which belongs to the supreme one, the prime unity, who is non-being, because he is above being. But the necessities and limitations of our reason require us to speak of him as being. He is therefore called being absolute, of whose divine substance all things are full. Could we conceive a pyramid of beings, of which each is a trinity in unity, we might have a conception of the favourite aerial image of the brain of Proclus. But as the pyramid of our imagination is finite, we must not think that it truly represents all being, for that is infinite. One moment we may say non-being is at the head of it, for the primal One is above being, and nothing is at the base of it, for beneath it is that which is below all being; but the next moment we must declare that being has no bounds, nor boundary walls, that there is no 'beyond' outside the all of the universe; and therefore it is that God who is beyond being, whom we cannot by reason understand, can yet be known as infinite being. We must then think of a pyramid from the summit of which supreme perfection descends to the lowest degree of being; constituting, preserving, adorning all things, and uniting them to itself. First, we may think of it as descending to beings truly existing, then to divine genii, then to divinities which preside over the human race, then to human spirits, at last to animals, plants, and the lowest forms of matter—that which borders on nothing. In such an image we may have an idea of the eternal procession from him who is super-essential, and therefore most truly essence, to that which is non-essential and no kind of essence. In the primordial one all things have their existence and unity. They derive their multiplicity by a progression which originates in the separating of the one in the same way that rays diverge and proceed from a centre. So that though in nature there be many forms, and in the universe there be many gods, and in waste places many genii, and in heaven many spirits, and in hades many heroes, there is but one essence to all. It is everywhere the same. That essence is in us; God is all; and we and all existence are but the expressions of the One ineffable and supreme.

Proclus was a genuine Platonist. He began and ended with God. He saw all things in God, and God in all things. The world is before us a thing of change, its phenomena are ephemeral. We are spectators of the drama. Is our being only phenomenal? Are we but a part of the world, or is there in us anything of the One, the Eternal? Our feet are in the mire and our heads among the clouds. Our first thoughts reveal to us our greatness and our nothingness; our exile and our native land; God who is our all, and the world through which we must pass and rise to God. This Triad is the foundation of philosophy, the indisputable data from which we must begin. That the most perfect exists, Proclus did not stop to inquire. Our reason proves, clearly and distinctly, that it does. As little does he ask if the world exists, it is before us; we can see it and feel it. Man, by his passions and the wants of his body, is drawn to the earth; by philosophy, inspiration and divination, he is elevated to God.

The contradiction involved in the identity of the One and the many was not less for Proclus than it had been for his predecessors. The One is perfect, the many are imperfect. The One is eternal, the many are temporal. The One existed alone, it is

necessary to his perfection that he be alone, and thus truly the
all before the imperfect was made; but it is also necessary to
his perfection that he be not alone. He must have thought, and
thought must have an object. God must be the absolute unity,
and yet God creating; the one of Parmenides, the 'immovable
mover' of Aristotle and yet the mind or Demiurgus of Plato.
The One is God in himself, the last sanctuary of the divinity.
The other is the God of creation and providence, the Lord and
ruler of the world. Hence a Trinity which did not differ from
that of Plotinus. The super-essential One, mind or the most
perfect form of being, and soul, which is necessary to the existence of mind, and preserves its immovability while it unites it
to the world. 'From the hands of Proclus,' says M. Simon,
'we receive the god of experience, and the god of speculation
separately studied by the ancient schools, reunited by the
Alexandrians in a unity as absolute as the God of the Eleatics,
and mind as free, as full of life and fecundity as the Demiurgus
of Plato.'

The conversion of Constantine checked the career of philosophy. It was restored under Julian, who adhered to the the-
urgical school of Iamblichus. Julian was a lover of divination,
always eager to read the will of the gods in the entrails of the
victims. He worshipped the sun as we may suppose the devout Neo-Platonists were used to do, but it was the intelligible
sun—God veiled in light—the source of essence, perfection, and
harmony. 'When I was a boy,' he says, 'I used to lift up my
eyes to the ethereal splendour, and my mind, struck with
astonishment, seemed to be carried beyond itself. I not only
desired to behold it with fixed eyes, but even by night when I
went outside under a pure sky, forgetting everything besides,
I gazed, so absorbed in the beauties of the starry heavens that
if anything was said to me I did not hear, nor did I know
what I was doing.' The sun which so entranced him in his
youth he afterwards worshipped as God—the parent, as some
philosophers had said, of all animate things. Libanius says,
'He received the rising sun with blood, and again attended him
with blood at his setting. And because he could not go abroad
so often as he wished, he made a temple of his palace and
placed altars in his garden, which was purer than most chapels.'
'By frequent devotions he engaged the gods to be his auxil-

iaries in war, worshipping Mercury, Ceres, Mars, Calliope, Apollo, whom he worshipped in his temple on the hill and in the city.' After Julian, philosophy revived at Athens, where it flourished till 520, A.D., when the schools were shut by the decree of Justinian. The last of the Neo-Platonists was John of Damascus.

The histories of philosophy mentioned at the end of the last chapter, contain accounts of the Neo-Platonic philosophers. This chapter is derived mainly from the work of M. Jules Simon, *Histoire de l'Ecole d'Alexandrie.* Plotinus wrote nothing, but some of his lectures, arranged in nine sections, or *Enneads*, were preserved by Porphyry. Proclus wrote on the theology of Plato, and commentaries on the Timæus ; which were translated into English by Thomas Taylor.

CHAPTER VI.

The Church.

The Neo-Platonist school began with Philo the Jew, and ended with Proclus. This is one account. Another is, that it began in a very different quarter, and is not ended yet. In reality, there were three kinds of Neo-Platonism: one allied itself with the old Gentile religion, another with Judaism, and a third with the new religion of the Crucified. It had formerly been disputed whether Plato or Moses was the founder of Greek philosophy, and now it is disputed if the Neo-Platonic philosophy was borrowed from Christianity, or if the philosophical Alexandrian fathers borrowed their philosophy from the Pagan Neo-Platonists.

The only New Testament authors in whose writings we find definite manifestations of acquaintance with Greek philosophy, are St. John and St. Paul. Indeed John's gospel is so marked by Greek doctrine and philosophical speech, as to have led to the supposition that it could not have been written by the fisherman of Galilee. We must, however, remember that John lived to a great age, and that the latter years of his life were spent in Asia Minor, where he might have come in contact with every form of philosophy then known in the Greek world. It may be true that he did not find the Logos in Plato, but we know from Philo Judæus, and some of his contemporaries, that the Logos in a sense nearly allied to that of St. John's was in common use among the Alexandrian Jews. The Logos was in the beginning. It was at once with God, and it was God. John's Logos had the same relation to God as in Plato's theology 'mind' had to 'being.' Only St. John's went beyond the philosopher. He said that the Logos was incarnate in Jesus of Nazareth, thus making Jesus divine.

St. Paul's writings have more of a Hebrew than a Greek character. His illustrations, his logic, his rhetoric, are all Jewish. But St. Paul, confessedly, was familiar with Greek literature. That he had many thoughts in common with Philo is evident from such passages as that in the Epistle to the Colossians, where he speaks of the Son as 'the image of the invisible God,' and that in the Hebrews, supposing this Epistle to have been written by St. Paul, where it is said that the Father made the worlds by the Son, who is 'the brightness of his glory, and the express image of his person.' That St. Paul did not regard heathen philosophy as purely darkness is manifest from his address to the Athenians, where he quotes and endorses the favourite doctrine of the Greeks, that we are the offspring of God.

JUSTIN MARTYR.

The relation of Christianity to heathen philosophy is more distinctly traceable in the writings of the Christian fathers, especially of those who were educated where philosophy flourished. The first of these is Justin Martyr, who defended Christianity against Jews and Pagans. He had been a philosopher, and to him Christianity was a new philosophy, or rather the consummation of all philosophy. He said that all men were partakers of Christ, because he was the 'very Logos or universal reason.' On this account he said that all who live by reason are in some sort Christians. Such among the Greeks were Socrates, Heraclitus, and the like.* Those who lived in defiance of reason are described as not Christian, and as enemies of the Logos, while all are Christians who make reason the rule of their actions. God, with Justin, was an absolute Being who could not reveal himself except by the mediation of another. He is above every name or title, and only becomes the object of thought or speech in the Logos, who was created before creation, and through whom creation was effected. Justin used the word created, but it is equivalent to begotten, or caused to proceed from himself. The Logos is also called a rational power, and though created as the medium of creation, it seems to be assumed that it was always immanent in God. It became incarnate in Jesus Christ, but in all men there is a germinal or spermatic Logos through participation with Christ.

* Apo. I. 61,

Justin was the first of the fathers who used the term Logos in the sense of its being the divine reason. Hitherto it was simply the creative word. The seed of reason is in all men; but the all of reason is in Jesus Christ. The soul of man has a natural and essential relation to the Logos. But Jesus is the Logos, the primal reason itself; so that Christianity is a divine philosophy.

TATIAN.

Tatian, subsequently a Valentinian heretic, is said by Irenæus to have been a disciple of Justin. He is unlike Justin in his estimate of the philosophers, whom he abuses, but his doctrine of God and the Logos is nearly the same as Justin's. He was by birth an Assyrian, which may account for his contempt of the Greeks. He calls God the hypostasis or being of all beings. Before creation he was alone, but as he was himself the hypostasis or substance of both, the visible and invisible, all things were with him. By the power of reason the Logos which was in him subsists, which seems to mean that the Logos was the divine reason. It emanated or proceeded from God by his will. It is also called the first begotten, and the beginning of the world. It came into being not by division or abscission, but by participation, which is explained to mean that it was not separated from the original substance as light from light. The Logos made the world, having first created the matter out of which it was made.*

ATHENAGORAS.

Athenagoras is confessedly a disciple of Plato, freely using his arguments and adopting his language concerning God and creation. He makes God distinct from matter, but completes the chain of being by a graduating scale of creatures from God to matter. God is eternal, but being from eternity endowed with reason, he had the Logos in himself. The Logos is God's son, and is compared to the sons of the gods, but he is the son as being the divine reason in idea and activity. This is the Platonic notion of God as mind energizing in matter. The

* Address to the Greeks, Ch. V.

Logos was created as the being in whom the ideas that is the archetypes of all things might subsist.*

THEOPHILUS OF ANTIOCH.

Theophilus did not acknowledge the authority of the philosophers. He openly dissented from Plato as to the eternity of matter,† but he spoke of God as ineffable, and of his attributes as transcending all human conceptions. But all things were made by the Logos, and this Logos was the divine reason. To an objection that God in the Scriptures is said to have walked, Theophilus answered that the God and Father of all could not be contained, that there is no place of his rest. It was the Logos in the person or character of the Father who talked to Adam in Paradise. The Logos existed always in the heart of God. Before creation he was God's counsellor, the divine mind and thought. This was the Logos immanent. But when God determined to create, he begot the Logos, uttered the first born of all creation. This was the Logos as manifested. God, however, was not by this act divested of his reason. It seems as if Theophilus meant that the manifestation of this Logos was the beginning of creation.

IRENÆUS.

Irenæus, seeing that these speculations concerning God and the Word were at the root of the Gnostic heresies, maintained the absolute identity of God and the Word. God he said was wholly reason, and that reason was the Son or Logos. There is no Infinite beyond or above the God who is the Word. The supposition of such an infinite led the Gnostics to their Bythos, or the One that could not be known, but God can be known. He is fully manifested in the Word.

HIPPOLYTUS.

Hippolytus is said to have been a disciple of Irenæus. He also wrote against the heretics, and in many things followed

* Petition Ch. 8-10.
† To Autolychus I., Ch. IV.

his master. He ascribed the origin of all heresies to the wisdom of the Greeks. The heretics took nothing from Scripture, but only from mysteries and systems of philosophy. The Greeks are described as being ignorant of the Creator, and as glorifying the parts of creation. Hippolytus, however, in discoursing of the Logos, agrees more with Plato than with Irenæus. God was alone in himself when by an act of will, or as it is otherwise expressed, by an exercise of reflection, he brought forth the Logos. This Logos is further explained as not the word in the sense of a voice, but as the thought of the all in the mind of God. The Father constituted existence, and the Logos proceeding from him was the cause of all creation. The Father ordained the world to come into existence, and the Logos executed the will of God. The world was made from nothing; it is, therefore, not divine. The Logos, on the other hand, is of the substance of God, and therefore is God. Those who are desirous of becoming God are exhorted to obey the Logos who spoke by the prophets. The identity of God and the Logos, as maintained by Irenæus, developed into the Patripassian heresy. If the Son was the same as the Father, then the Father suffered on the cross. To refute this heresy, Hippolytus had recourse to the arguments of Plato for the distinction between God and the reason of God. Dorner says, ' The fundamental idea of his theology is chargeable with approximating in another way to Pantheism through raising a too hasty opposition to Patripassianism.'

TERTULLIAN.

Hippolytus showed how God was once alone and nothing with him, and how he willed to create the world. This was done by thinking, willing, and uttering the idea of the world. But this solitary existence was not real, for God never was without the Word or Wisdom. All was in him and he was himself the all. Hippolytus said, ' The Father is over all, the Son is through all, and the Holy Ghost is in all.' Tertullian, who despised philosophy, had recourse to the same arguments borrowed from the philosopher when he undertook the refutation of the Patripassians. He explained, philosophically, how God was the Logos and yet was not the Logos. God, as the object of his own thought, became the Son of God when he obtained positive reality. He has at first a mere ideal existence in the being of God. He is God's thought, the idea of the world, or the sum of the thoughts of the world. It is involved in this world idea, that when it becomes a reality, it will still have the God who was incorporated with it, that is, the Word. The manifestation of God is thus interwoven with the idea of the world, and all the divine thoughts become realities, so the world is a progressive realization of the thought to which God has given objective existence over against himself. The full realization of the world ideal is completed through the incarnation of Christ. The Logos is thus God immovable and infinite, and yet God associated with the world, God movable and finite.

CLEMENT OF ALEXANDRIA.

The stream of Christian Neo-Platonism can best be traced in the school of Alexandria. The two most famous teachers of this school were Clement and Origen. Clement openly defended the truth of Greek philosophy. He said, 'I give the name philosophy to that which is really excellent in all the doctrines of the Greek philosophers, and above all to that of Socrates, such as Plato describes him to have been. The opinion of Plato upon ideas is the true Christian and orthodox philosophy. These intellectual lights among the Greeks have been communicated by God himself.' Clement repeats what Plato and his disciples had said about the impossibility of man knowing God. Our knowledge of the divine Being, the first cause of all things, is only negative. We know what he is not. We call him by the highest names, and think of him as the best of beings, yet he is without name and without form. He is infinite, and, therefore, not to be defined. He is neither genus, difference, species, individual number, accident, nor anything that can be predicated of another thing. But this unknowable Being may be known in his Son. 'The Logos is the power and the wisdom of the Father, the idea of ideas in the ideal world, the timeless and unbegun beginning.' It issues from the Father like the rays of light from the sun, and is everywhere diffused. It has been in all ages and under all dispensations the light of man. It inspired the Jewish prophets, and it led the Greeks to righteousness. Philosophy prepared the way for the gospel, which was engrafted on it as a new branch on the stem of a wild olive tree.

ORIGEN.

Origen was Clement's disciple, and went beyond his master in the development of Christian Neo-Platonism. The Trinity with Origen, is an eternal process in God. In his time, first arose the question of the eternal sonship of Christ; and no marvel, for it is a doctrine purely Alexandrian. Tertullian made the generation of the Son a divine act, thereby introducing multiplicity into God. Origen made it an act, eternally completed, and yet eternally continued. 'The Son was not generated once for all, but is continually generated by God in the eternal to-day.' The Father is the Monad, absolutely indivisible, and infinitely exalted above all that is divided, or multiplied. He is not truth nor wisdom, nor spirit nor reason, but infinitely higher than all these. He is not being nor substance, but far exalted above all being and all substance. He is the utterly ineffable and incomprehensible One, the Absolute. All truth, goodness and power, are derived from him, but attributes do not adequately describe him. We cannot attribute to him will or wisdom without also ascribing to him imperfection. The super-essential Monad is above all qualities. The Son is being, energy, soul. Origen wishes to make the Son equal to the Father; but his philosophy compels him to make him inferior to the Father as touching his Godhead. The Son is related to the manifold world. He cannot be directly grounded in God the Father, because of the Father's unity and unchangeableness. As Aristotle would say, the Father is immovable, and the Son movable; only the Son is not outside of God, but in God; and in God that he may be the medium by which the world outside of God may be brought into the divine, for we cannot conceive the world existing independently of unity. Necessarily connected with the eternal generation of the Son, is the eternal generation of the world; for the Son is its ideal, its eternal unity. He is the world-principle, that which connects together the universe of individuals in all their divergencies from each other. He is the permeating substance of the world, its heart and reason, present in every man, and in the whole world. The Son is the truth, the life, the resurrection of all creatures; the One who is at the basis of the manifold, having objectively different modes of existence for different beings, without therefore ceasing to be one Logos. The human race consists of those souls that through sin have fallen from the union with the Son. He could not forget them, and to restore them, he became incarnate. His soul and ours thus pre-existed together; and as the Logos came upon the man Jesus and united him to itself, so shall the Logos possess our souls and restore them to itself and God. Origen rivalled Philo Judaeus in his subtle interpretations of the sacred writings. 'The beginning,' in St. John's gospel, he takes for 'the supreme Being.' Thus, the Word was in the beginning will signify, it was in God the Father. 'Christ is also the beginning, being the wisdom of God and the beginning of his ways.' In the first verse of Genesis, the beginning is the Lord Jesus Christ. 'In the beginning, that is, in the Word or reason, God made the heaven and the earth. God is in all respects one, and undivided; but Christ the Logos is many proceeding from the Father as well as from mind.'

The Son participates in all that the Father is, and in this sense there is a community of substance; but the Son is another being, a distinct individuality. He is God, but not the God, a second God and inferior as a copy is to the original.* In the unfolding of the divine unity with plurality the Son is the first term; the Spirit the second, standing next to the created world. The time will come when all spiritual beings will possess the knowledge of God in the same perfect measure in which the Son possesses it, and all shall be sons of God in the same manner in which now the Only-begotten alone is, being themselves deified through participation in the Deity of the Father, so that then God will be all in all.

THE ATHANASIAN TRINITY.

It is a great question among theologians whether the ante-Nicene fathers were Arian or Athanasian. The proper answer would be that they were both. The same writer often maintains

* Ueberweg, Vol. I, p. 317.

both opinions without any apparent consciousness of a contradiction. But the real question is whether they were monarchians like Irenæus and maintained the divine unity, or whether, like the philosophers and philosophical theologians, they introduced multiplicity into the Godhead. Noctus, Beryllus, Sabellius, and Paul of Samosata, were such strict monarchists, that they incurred the charge of heresy. With them the Logos was simply the eternal reason of God, and the reason became incarnate in Jesus Christ. But this involved the denial of the existence of the Logos except as an attribute or mode of the Deity. The Trinity was simply God in three manifestations—God regarded as Father, as Son, and as Holy Ghost. This secured the perfect equality as it secured the complete identity of the Father and the Son.

But this seemed to be a denial of the Trinity, and so the doctrine of these men was condemned by the majority, that is, by those who called themselves the Catholic Church. It was also condemned by Arius, a man who had but little of the philosophy of his age or country. He was an anti-speculative practical common sense theologian, without the remotest element of Pantheism, the truest disciple of Anaxagoras that had yet appeared in the church, one whom Aristotle would have pronounced a sober man. He distinguished broadly and at once between the substance of God and that of creation, as well as between the substance of the Father and that of the Son. He cut away at one stroke all the Alexandrian theories of eternal creation and eternal generation. 'If,' he argued, 'the Son is generated generation is an act, and that implies a beginning of existence.' There *was* when the Son was not, he like other created things is created from nothing, and therefore his substance is different from God's.

The Arian controversy was carried on with so much vehemence, and the history of it is usually written with so much prejudice, that it is hard for the present day student to penetrate to the facts and to see its real meaning. Arius really wished to defend the Trinity. According to Socrates, the historian, Alexander, Bishop of Alexandra, in discoursing to his clergy, insisted so strongly on the unity, that he seemed to be verging on the heresy of Sabellius. Arius bounded to the other extreme, and virtually made the Logos a second and inferior

God. The Trinity thus ended in three Gods. Alexander argued for the divine unity, for the eternity of the Logos, and its identity with the Father. His argument was that God could never have been without his reason. Though the Son is generated, there is yet no interval between him and the Father. This generation surpassed the understanding of the evangelists, and perhaps also that of the angels. Arius said, ' There *was* when the Son was not,' but this, Alexander answered, 'involved the existence of time.' Now, time is created by the Logos. It comes into existence with the world, so that the time supposed to have existed must have existed through him, which is placing the effect before the cause. If time was before the Logos, he could not be the first born of every creature. The Father must always have been Father, and the Son through whom he is Father must have existed always. ' Alexander's aim,' says Dorner, ' was to establish the closest possible connection between the hypostasis of the Son and his eternal divine essence. In carrying out this design he decidedly posits a duality in God, and if we may judge from the images employed by him, he conceives the Logos of the Father to be objectified in the Son. His images in themselves would warrant us in concluding that he conceived the Father to have reason and power, not in himself, but in the Son ; and that consequently the Son was the Father himself under a determinate form, or a determination or attribute constituting part of the full conception of the Father. The council of Alexandria, concurring in the doctrine of Alexander, adopted the Neo-Platonic idea of time to reconcile the Sonship of Christ with his eternity.'

The Alexandrian fathers wished to establish the unity of God, and at the same time preserve the distinct existence of the Son. The tendency of Plato's philosophy was to regard all beings divine and human, spiritual and material, as in some way but one being, that which to human sense is the manifold is in some transcendent way the one. The Christian Platonists regarded the world as an act of creation, and limited the divine emanation to the persons of the Trinity, acknowledging in them that identity and difference that one, and yet more than one, which the philosophers saw in the all of being. The disciples of Arius were always few in number. The numerous body were those called Semi-Arians, who objected to the unscriptural language introduced by the Arians and the philosophical phrases not found in Scripture, which were adopted by the Athanasians. This moderate or middle party reckoned that there was no real difference between Arians and Athanasians. The difference was created by defining that which the Scriptures had not defined. The heretics had led the way in philosophizing. The Manichæans called Christ a 'consubstantial part of God.' The Sabellians, who made the Trinity three modes of God, by necessity made these modes consubstantial. The word was rejected by the Council of Antioch, which condemned Paul of Samosata, but when the Council of Nicæa wished to condemn the Arians, they had to adopt the heretical term and declare the Son to be consubstantial with the Father. If the Logos was to be regarded as distinct from God the Father, subordination, hetereity of substance seemed to follow as a necessary consequence; but the Nicene fathers wished to retain both distinction and consubstantiality. The individuality had been designated by the philosophers hypostasis, but to this there were some objections, as at one time hypostasis was equivalent to being or substance, and in this sense it made for Arianism. It had also the meaning of a character assumed in a play, but this made for Sabellianism. Hypostasis came to be translated person, so that Athanasians avoided both heresies by accepting what is a contradiction, both in word and thought, that Deity is essentially one and yet three; and this is really a confession that neither unity nor plurality adequately expresses God. For as the Alexandrian fathers said, he was above substantiality, and, therefore, above personality. Athanasius combined the unity of the Monarchians with the multiplicity of those who made God a trinity of individuals. His tendency was clearly to unity in the manifold; he made a halt between God and creation, because the creature had fallen into sin, which is a state of deprivation of true being; but the creature was to be delivered. It was through the Word that man was created at first, and by that Word he was to be restored to sonship. To do this the Word must not merely participate in the substance of God as something alien, but must be the very self-communicating divine substance. If not properly the Son of God, he could not make men sons of God. The Son imparts himself to them, dwells in them, and makes them one with him, as he is one with God. A partial Pantheism lies at the root of the Athanasian Trinity; God became man in Christ, that through Christ man might be made divine.

EUSEBIUS OF CÆSAREA.

Eusebius, whose orthodoxy is somewhere between that of Arius and that of Athanasius, is not free from the philosophy of Alexandria: In his inmost essence, says Eusebius, God is one. It is only with an eye to the world and God's relation to it that we can speak of the Trinity. The unity expresses that which is inmost in God. It contains in it no plurality. This one being is the absolute, the primal substance. This Monad or Father cannot communicate his being. He cannot enter into any relation with the world. He could not be a creator. To mediate between him and the world there was need of the Logos. The Son is grounded in God, and is a copy of God. He connects the world with God, and makes it worthy of him. He is the bond that passes through the universe—the world soul. The Son was always with the Father, generated out of time, existing before the Æons, yet his existence was effected by an act of God.

ST. AUGUSTINE.

In Augustine we have the Athanasian theology in its Western form as we are accustomed to hear it in the dogmatic formularies of the church. But Augustine is no mere dogmatist. He has the true spirit of philosophy, and, indeed, openly confesses his obligations to Plato and the Neo-Platonists. He does not positively deny all attributes to the Deity, nor does he, like some of the Greeks, place the Godhead above the Trinity, but he makes all the attributes in God to be the same. His wisdom, his truth, his justice, his being are all one. This either means that we cannot ascribe any attributes to God, or that if he has any they are in him in some way that transcends human conception. In his books on the Trinity, Augustine really makes

God altogether to transcend man's thoughts, and regards the Trinity as an effort to utter what we cannot fully express. ' The Supremacy,' he says, ' of the Godhead surpasses the power of ordinary speech, for God is more truly thought than he is uttered, and exists more truly than he is thought.' God is not properly a person, but each of the three persons is regarded as truly and completely God. The world was created out of nothing, yet God is called the creative substance, everywhere diffused. But for the continual presence of God, creation would cease to exist. Augustine endorses the Platonic distinction between eternity and time. He does not admit unlimited periods of duration before creation. Eternity IS, but time belongs to that which is subject to change. The same with space which is merely the place of created things. All creation is good, everything in its kind and degree perfect. Evil as anything positive does not exist. It is only the privation of good, the want of being, or the product of non-being, which is the true opposite of God. Absolute good is possible, but absolute evil is impossible. The philosophical ideas scattered over Augustine's writings, and chiefly borrowed from the Platonists, might be a good foundation for Pantheistic doctrine, but they are guarded by the acceptance of the dogmatic theology sanctioned by the Church.

SYNESIUS.

But more singular than the Neo-Platonism, even of Origen, was that of Synesius, Bishop of Ptolemais. Synesius, however, scarcely professed to be a Christian in any other sense, but as Christianity seemed to him a form of philosophy, nearly related to what he had learned in the schools. When the bishopric was offered to him, ' he declared candidly,' says Neander, ' that his philosophical conviction did not, on many points, agree with the doctrines of the church, and among these differences, he reckoned many things which were classed along with the Origenistic heresies; as, for example, the doctrine of the pre-existence of souls, his different views of the resurrection, on which point he probably departed far more widely than Origen from the view taken by the church, inasmuch as he interpreted it as being but the symbol of a higher idea.' A few quotations from the hymns of Synesius will show the character of his theology, and its likeness to that of the schools.

Rejoicing in immortal glory,
God sits above the lofty heights of heaven ;
Holy Unity of unities ;
And first Monad of monads.

    *   *   *

A fragment of the divine Parent
Descended into matter ;
A small portion indeed,
But it is everywhere the One in all—
All diffused through all.
It turns the vast circumference of the heavens,
Preserving the universe,
Distributed in diverse forms it is present ;
A part of it is the course of the stars,
A part is the angelic choir ;
A part, with an heavy bond, found an earthly form,
And disjoined from the Parent, drank dark oblivion.
God, beholding human things,
Is nevertheless present in them ;

    *   *   *

Yet a light, a light there is, even in closed eyes,
There is present, even to those who have fallen hither
A certain power calling them back to heaven—
When having emerged from the billows of life,
They joyfully enter on the holy path
Which leads to the palace of the Parent.

    *   *   *

But Thou art the root of things present, past, and future.
Thou art Father and Mother ;
Thou art masculine ;
Thou art feminine :
Hail ! root of the world ;
Hail ! centre of things ;
Unity of divine numbers.

    *   *   *

Father of all fathers,
Father of thyself ;
Fore-father, without father,
Son of thyself ;
Unity before unity ;
Seed of beings ;
Centre of all.
Presubstantial, unsubstantial mind,
Surpassing minds ;
Changing into different parts,
Parent mind of minds ;
Producer of gods.
Maker of spirits,
Nourisher of souls,
Fountain of fountains,
Beginning of beginnings,

Root of roots,
Number of numbers,
Intelligence and intelligent;
Both intelligible and before intelligible,
One and all things,
But the one of all things:
Root and highest branch.

   *   *   *

Thou art what produces,
Thou art what is produced ;
Thou art what enlightens,
Thou art what is enlightened ;
Thou art what appears,
Thou art what is hidden,
By thy own brightness.
One and all things,
One in thyself,
And through all things.
Produced after an ineffable manner
That thou mightest produce a Son
(Who is) illustrious wisdom,
(And) maker of all things.

   *   *   *

Thou art the Governor of the unseen world ;
Thou are the nature of natures ;
Thou nourishest nature—
The origin of the mortal,
The image of the immortal ;
So that the lowest part in the world
Might obtain the other life.

DIONYSIUS THE AREOPAGITE.

The most remarkable resemblance in any Christian writings
to the doctrines of the Platonists of Alexandria, is found in the
once famous works of St. Dionysius.   This saint was the Areopagite who adhered to St. Paul after his discourse at Athens.
It was not known for three or four centuries after the death of
Dionysius that his works were extant, or even that he had
ever written any works.   They appeared suddenly in the controversy between the Church and the Monophysite heretics,
and were quoted in favour of the heretical side.   They have
never been universally received as genuine, but their sublime
speculations and their sweet mystical piety have always pro-
cured them admirers, and even advocates of their genuineness.

The favourite doctrine of three orders in the Church; bishops,
priests, and deacons, as the copy and symbol of the three orders

in the celestial hierarchy, has always made them dear to church-
men. The Abbé Darboy, in a recent introduction to the works
of St. Dionysius, has shown that their author was indeed the
Areopagite converted by St. Paul; that he lived in the days
when St. John was well known as a theologian, apostle, and
evangelist in exile at Patmos; when Timothy and Titus were
bishops of Ephesus and Crete, and when Peter was pope at
Rome. Furthermore, that this Dionysius was certainly present
at the funeral obsequies of the Virgin Mary, that he was made
bishop of Athens; but having left his Greek diocese as a mis-
sionary to France, he became the veritable St. Denys, who
founded the church of the Gauls. ' He did not borrow from
Plotinus,' says the Abbé Darboy, 'but Plotinus borrowed from
him.' Guizot, who is less interested in the advocacy of the
' three orders,' and not concerned for the admission that the
Christian fathers drank of the streams of the Neo-Platonic
philosophy, takes a different view from that of the Abbé Darboy. 'Neo-Platonism,' he says, 'when forsaken and abandoned
by princes, decried and persecuted, had no other alternative
than to lose itself in the bosom of the enemy.' Brucker's
opinion is nearly the same. ' The works of St. Dionysius introduced Alexandrian Platonism into the west, and laid the
foundation of that mystical system of theology, which afterwards so greatly prevailed.' He then describes it as ' a philosophical enthusiasm, born in the east, nourished by Plato,
educated in Alexandria, matured in Asia, and introduced under
the pretence and authority of an apostolic man into the Western
Church.'

Before the Reformation, the genuineness of these writings
was an open question in the Catholic Church, and to some extent it is so still. At the Council of Trent they were appealed
to as genuine. From that time many Catholic theologians have
considered their doctrines in harmony with the teaching of the
Church.

We have already seen how Plato's Alexandrian disciples conceived a universe of being, in which were all grades of existence
from the primal One to that which is nothing. We have seen
how Porphyry and Proclus filled up the intermediate spaces between that which was above and that which was below being,
with hypostases of the Trinity, gods, genii, demons, heroes, men,

animals, vegetables and unformed matter; all of which had, in God, whatever of true existence they possessed. St. Dionysius, as a Christian, had to expel all the gods and demons from this Pagan totality of being; and, as a good churchman, to fill their places with more orthodox existences. Instead of a chain, beginning at God, or a pyramid of which the top was primal unity, St. Dionysius conceived a central and special dwelling of the Eternal, around which were arranged, in consecutive circles, all the orders of being from the highest to the meanest. First, there were cherubim, seraphim and thrones. Behind them dominions, virtues, powers. Then principalities, archangels, and angels. Of the heavenly hierarchy, the ecclesiastical was a copy: bishops, priests, deacons. The 'threes' of Pagan Proclus were beautiful triads with the Christian Dionysius. Were not all things trinities in unity? The supreme one was a trinity. Each grade was a trinity. The ecclesiastical hierarchy a trinity. Outside of the heavenly, that is, immediately behind the angels, is the order of beings gifted with intellect such as men; then those which have feeling but not reason; and lastly, creatures that simply exist. Light and wisdom, grace and knowledge, emanate from the supreme, and spread through all ranks of being. Divinity permeates all. The supreme One has called them in their several degrees and according to their several capacities to be sharers of his existence. His essence is the being of all beings, so far as they exist. Even things inanimate partake of divinity. Those that merely live partake of this naturally vital energy, which is superior to all life, because it embraces all life. Reasonable and intelligent beings partake of the wisdom which surpasses all wisdom; and which is essentially and eternally perfect. Higher beings are united to God by the transcendent contemplation of that divine pattern, and in reaching the source of light they obtain superabundant treasures of grace, and in a manner express the majesty of the infinite nature. All these orders gaze admiringly upwards. Each is drawn to the Supreme, and each draws towards itself the rank next below it; and thus a continual progress of lower being towards that which is higher, and a continual descent of the Divine, elevating all ranks and helping them in their progress towards God. The Divinity surpasses all knowledge. It is above all thought and all substance. As the sensible cannot understand the intelligible; as the multiple cannot understand the simple and immaterial, as the corporeal cannot understand the incorporeal, so the finite cannot understand the Infinite. He remains superior to all being—a unity which escapes all conception and all expression. He is an existence unlike all other existences; the author of all things, and yet not any one thing: for he surpasses all that is. We ought therefore to think and speak of God only as the Holy Scriptures have spoken, and they have declared him unsearchable. Theologians call him infinite and incomprehensible, and yet they vainly try to sound the abyss, as if they could fathom the mysterious and infinite depths of deity. We cannot understand him, yet he gives us a participation of his being. He draws from his exhaustless treasures, and over all things he diffuses the riches of his divine splendours.

St. Dionysius anticipates an objection, that, if God thus exceeds words, thoughts, knowledge, and being, if he eternally embraces and penetrates all things, if he is absolutely incomprehensible, how can we speak of the divine names? He answers, first, that in order to extol the greatness of God and to show that he is not to be identified with any particular being, he must be called by no name. And then, secondly, we must call him by all names, as, I AM, life and truth, God of gods, Lord of lords, wisdom, being, eternal, ancient of days. He dwells in the heart, in the body, in the soul. He is in heaven and upon earth, and yet he never moves. He is in the world, around it and beyond it. He is above the heaven and all being, yet he is in the sun, the moon, the stars, the water, the wind and the fire. He is the dew and the vapours. He is all that is and yet nothing of it all. In the infinite riches and simplicity of his nature, he has eternally seen and embraced all things; so that whatever reality is in anything may be affirmed of him. As, by lines drawn from the centre of a circle to the circumference, so are even the meanest existences united to God. 'The blessed Hierotheos,' says St. Dionysius, 'has taught that the divinity of Jesus Christ is the cause and complement of all things. It keeps all in harmony without being either all or a part; and yet it is all and every part, because it comprehends all, and from all eternity has possessed all, and all parts. August substance! it penetrates all substances, without defiling

its purity, and without descending from its sublime elevation.
It determines and classifies the principles of things, and yet
remains pre-eminently beyond all principle and all classification.
Its plenitude appears in that which creatures have not; and
its superabundance shines in that which they have.' 'As in
universal nature,' says the Areopagite, ' the different principles
of each particular nature are united in a perfect and harmonious
unity—as in the simplicity of the soul the multiplied faculties
which serve the wants of each part of the body are united, so
we may regard all things, all substances, even the most opposite
in themselves, as united in the indivisible unity.' From it they
all proceed. It has an existence which is comprised in God, but
he is not comprised in it. It partakes of him, but he does not
partake of it; for he precedes all being and all duration. From
his life flows all life. Whatever now exists has existed in its
faithful simplicity in him. The Areopagite anticipated an
objection from the existence of evil. He obviated it, as all his
predecessors and successors who felt the same difficulty have
done, by denying its existence. Not that he said there was
no evil in the world, but it was not a real being, and, consequently, could not emanate from being. It is only an accident
of good, having an existence nowhere.

On the impossibility of knowing the Infinite, St. Dionysius
and Plotinus entirely agree. All things speak of God, but
nothing speaks the fulness of his perfections. We know both
by our knowledge and by our ignorance. God is accessible to
reason through all his works; and we discern him by imagination, by feeling, and by thought; yet he is incomprehensible
and ineffable, to be named by no name. He is nothing of that
which is, and nothing of that which enables us to comprehend
him. He is in all things and yet, essentially, he is not one of
them. All things reveal him, but none sufficiently declare
him. We may call him by the names of all realities, for they
have some analogy with him who produced them; but the
perfect knowledge of God emerges from a sublime ignorance of
him which we reach by an incomprehensible union with him.
Then we feel how unsearchable he is; then the soul forgets
itself and is plunged into the eternal ocean of Deity; then does
it receive light among the billows of the divine glory, and is
radiated among the shining abysses of unfathomable wisdom.

Bunsen says in the Hippolytus, vol. i. p. 193, 'Now, before I proceed to this last inquiry, shall I, my dear friend—I believe I must—say something in defence of our author to those who may be inclined to fly off directly, and to despair of his orthodoxy, or to deny the authenticity of our book, on account of certain expressions, in the third and concluding part of his Confession of Faith, which to some people in our time may sound as Pantheistic, if not Atheistic? It seems to me that the orthodoxy of such people respecting the Spirit is as idealess and dead as respecting the Logos and the Son. They have just as much cause for being alarmed by this third article on account of what they call Pantheism, as by the second on account of a supposed incorrect Trinitarianism. If they will read any philosophical father of the first centuries, even Athanasius himself, they will be shocked by expressions respecting the nature and intelligence of man very much like these—expressions certainly abhorrent from the terminology of Paley and Burnet, as much as from the language of the Roman Catechism, but not at all, that I can see, from the words of St. Paul and St. John, nay, of Christ himself. What can they find stronger than St. Paul's saying, " In him we live, and move, and have our being," or than Christ's repeated declarations respecting the identity of the human and divine nature? Before they identify Christianity with a bare Theism, let them look at what it has produced among those who know nothing better—a maimed Judaic Mohammedanism, a system impotent to connect God with his own manifestations, a system which gives us an extra-mundane God, with a godless world and nature, which leaves man, God's image, in a position irreconcilable with Christ's most solemn words and promises, and which degrades Revelation itself to an outward communication, which, as one of their apostles said, might (for aught he could see) have been vouchsafed just as well to a dog, if it had so pleased God.'

In the chapter in Ueberweg on Patristic Philosophy will be found many passages from the Fathers, orthodox and unorthodox, ante-Nicene and post-Nicene, which substantiate all that Bunsen here says.

The book of Dorner's referred to in this text is on the 'Person of Christ.'

At a conference in Constantinople, in the year 533, where the Dionysian writings were first cited, the Orthodox at once refused their authority. In the seventh century a Presbyter, named Theodorus, composed a work in defence of their genuineness ; but long before this their influence was widely spread, or, to speak more correctly, the influence in which they originated. Neander says, ' In the last times of the fifth century, a cloister at Edessa, in Mesopotamia, had for its head an abbot by the name of Bar Sudaili, who had busied himself in various ways with that mystic theology which always formed one of the ground-tendencies of the Oriental Monarchism, and from which had proceeded the writings fabricated in the name of Dionysius the Areopagite ; as in fact he appeals to the writings of a certian Hierotheos, whom the Pseudo-Dionysius calls his teacher. He stood at first on intimate terms with the most eminent Monophysite teachers, and was very highly esteemed by them. But, as his mystic theology came into conflict with the church doctrine, he drew upon himself the most violent attacks. Espousing the peculiar views of Monophysitism, and more particularly as they were apprehended by the party of Xenayas, he maintained that as Father, Son, and Holy Ghost are one divine essence, and as the humanity formed one nature with the godhead in Christ, and his body became of like essence to the divinity (was deified), so through him all fallen beings should also be exalted to unity with God, in this way

would become one with God ; so that God, as Paul expresses it, should be all
in all. If it is true, as it is related, that on the walls of his cell were found
written the words, 'All creatures are of the same essence with God,' we
must suppose that he extended this assertion so as to include not only all rational beings, but all creatures of every kind, and that his theory was—as all
existence proceeded by an original emanation from God, so by redemption all
existence, once more refined and ennobled, would return back to him. But the
question then arises, whether he understood this, after the Pantheistic manner,
as a return to the divine essence with the loss of all self-subsistent, individual
existence (as it has often been observed, that mysticism runs into Pantheism) ;
or whether he supposed that, with the coming into existence of finite beings, sin
also necessarily made its appearance, but that by the redemption this contrariety was removed, and now at length the individual existence of the creature
should continue to subsist as such in union with God. Our information is
too scanty to enable us to decide this question.' In another place, speaking of
the development of doctrine in the Greek Church, Neander says, 'The monk
Maximus, distinguished by his acute and profound intellect, appeared in the
seventh century, as the representative of this dialectic contemplative disposition.
It appears from his works, that the writings of Gregory of Nyssa, and of the
pseudo-Dionysius, had exercised great influence on his theological views. We
may trace the main lineaments of a connected system in his writings. Christianity, as seen in the doctrine of the Trinity, seems to him to form the right
medium between the too contracted view of the idea of God in Judaism, and
the too diffuse notion exhibited in the nature-deifying system of Heathenism.
He considered the highest aim of the whole creation to be the inward union
into which God enters with it through Christ ; whilst, without injury to his
unchangeableness, he brings humanity into personal union with himself in
order to deify man ; whence God becomes man without change of essence ;
and human nature is taken into union with him without losing aught of its
peculiar character. To be able to keep a firm hold of these opinions, it was of
importance to him to possess distinct notions on the union of the two natures,
still retaining their particular properties unaltered. The object of redemption
is not only to purify human nature from sin, but to exalt it to a higher state
than that which it originally enjoyed—to an unchangeable and divine life.
Thus the history of creation becomes divided into two great parts : the one
exhibiting the preparation for the assumption of human nature by God ; the
other, the progressively developed deification of man's nature, commencing with
that act, and carried on in those who are fitted for it by a right will, till the
end is attained in their perfect salvation. Hence he often speaks of a continued
humanizing of the Logos in believers, in so far as the human life is taken into
communion with Christ, and is imbued with his own divine principle of life ;
and he regards the soul of him who is the source of so divine a life a bearer of
God.'

CHAPTER VII.

By heresy we are to understand the doctrines of sects outside of the Church; or doctrines that the Church has openly condemned. Catholic theologians say that Pantheism is the inevitable goal of Protestantism, and therefore they find it among all sects, ancient and modern. But as Catholic theologians are not agreed what Pantheism is, some finding it in books, where others cannot find it, we must for the present leave it an open question to what extent and in what way it is the goal either of Protestantism or of Catholicism.

But if the influence of the Greek philosophers and the Oriental religions was so marked among the Greek fathers, and since even the writings of St. Dionysius have found so many admirers in the Catholic church, it will not surprise us that the same or similar doctrines are found in the writings of heretical teachers. As in the first centuries of the Christian era, Judaism, Neo-Platonism, and Christianity were all struggling for pre-eminence and mutually influencing each other, it was only to be expected that the doctrines common to them all, would be found under manifold forms. To so great an extent was this the case, that some who wished to be considered Christians, were refused that name, and regarded even by the Platonic fathers as corrupters of the Christian faith.

The heresies of the early Church, especially those with which we are concerned here, arose from the predominance of Greek or Oriental speculation over the purely Christian element. Christianity, as taught by Christ and his disciples, was not so much a philosophy as a religion. It led the soul to God by intuition and inspiration, without professing to satisfy the understanding on questions relating to the essence of God, or his relation to the universe. But did it forbid these inquiries? Did it say that they were not proper for man? On this question the fathers were divided; some saying, that we have nothing to do with philosophy, and that the Christian's only business is to learn the doctrines of the Church, others who before their conversion, had been philosophers of the schools, embraced Christianity because it helped them to understand the questions which they had long been studying; and why should they give up the study now?

THE GNOSTICS.

.From the speculative side of the Church sprang the philosophical heretics. The oldest of these were the Gnostics, who are divided into many sects; for Gnostic, which means one that knows, seems to have been applied to all the heretics whose speculations on nature and being did not agree with the speculations approved of by the Church. Perhaps the most marked distinction between the Gnostics and the Alexandrian fathers, is, that the former have more of the Oriental spirit, the latter more of the Greek. The Gnostics had more theosophy; the Alexandrians more philosophy. Plotinus, who had imported into his system more of Orientalism than any Greek before him, wrote against the Gnostics, charging them with perverting the old philosophy of the Greeks.

The general character of Gnosticism does not differ widely from that of contemporaneous philosophies in the Eastern world. It is occupied with the same questions and comes to nearly the same conclusions. The special heresy of the Gnostics, as professed Christians, was the denial of the humanity of Christ; and this arose from the belief which, as philosophers, they entertained, that matter was connected with evil, and that the body was the dwelling-place of sin; and if sin was thus inseparably connected with the material body, they concluded that Christ's humanity must have been illusive. He was man in appearance only. Some of them place so wide an interval between the invisible and the visible, as to separate between the God of heaven and the God of nature. This, indeed, had been done by some of the old philosophers, for they would not admit the creating God to be the same with him who was the immovable essence. The Demiurgus was the 'mind' of God with Plato, and the second hypostasis of the Trinity with Plotinus; but some of the Gnostics went so far as to make the Demiurgus the enemy of

God, like the Ahriman of the Parsees, creating a kingdom opposed to God's; yet this dualism again in some way resolved itself into monism ; the existence of the opposing god and his world of nature being only a necessary result of the emanations of the supreme God.

Gnostic sects are divided into six classes. The first, comprised of the small primitive schools, which having at their head Cerinthus, and Simon, allied to Christianity doctrines borrowed from Judaism, Greek Polytheism, and the East. The second, consisting of the schools of Syria, joined to Christianity some of the fundamental ideas of the East. The third class, which embraced the great schools of Egypt, was hostile in some of its divisions to Judaism, but blended in its teaching the doctrines of Asia, Egypt, and Greece. The fourth, that of the small schools of Egypt, did not much differ from the great schools. The fifth class was that of the Marcionites, which carried its hostility to Judaism very far, but added to Christianity some ideas from the East. Another class was composed of those who professed the principles of the Clementines, which allied Judaism and Orientalism to Christian doctrines.

Of Simon the magician, we know but little beyond the mention of him in the Acts of the Apostles. He was called the ' great power of God;' a designation which is supposed to mean that he was an incarnation of God, or one of the divine powers which surrounded the Eternal, and were, in reality, the divine attributes. When he saw the works of the apostles, he joined himself with them as a disciple of Christianity. For anything we know to the contrary, he may have been a Christian to the end of his life. Tradition makes him an imposter and the head of a Gnostic sect. He supposed that the Holy Ghost could be bought with money; but his answer to Peter, some say, established his good faith and his deference for the apostles— ' Pray God for me that none of these evils of which you have spoken happen to me.'

Cerinthus, as we learn from Theodoret, was a native of Judea. He lived sometime in Egypt, and became familiar with the allegorical system of Philo. He wished to preserve it in Christianity, but was strenuously opposed by the disciples of St. John. He believed the interval between the supreme Being and the material world to be so great, that he was unwilling to attribute creation to the supreme God. The creator of the world was an inferior power, separated from the first principle by a long series of Æons, or inferior powers, who did not know God, or who, at least, as Irenæus expressed it, had less knowledge of him than the Logos had. Jesus of Nazareth, the son of Joseph and Mary, in virtue of his great wisdom and goodness, was united to Christ at his baptism in the Jordan, and the object of this union was the manifestation of the supreme God to men.

Saturninus, who represents the first Syrian school, was more related to the disciples of Zoroaster than any of the other Gnostics; that is to say, he was clearer in his enunciation of the doctrine of the two principles. He identified the 'I AM' of the Jews with the supreme Being of the Zendavesta; calling him not only Father. as Christians had been taught to do, but the 'unknown Father.' He calls him also the source of all that is pure; for the 'powers of being' become weak in proportion as they are distant from the first or primitive source. On the last stage of the pure world are seven angels, which represent what is least perfect in the intelligible world; and these seven angels are the creators of the world which is material and visible. This differs, apparently, from the doctrine of Zoroaster. But it is, probably, only another mode of expressing the same thing, creation frequently being but another word for emanation. The angels made the creature, man; but the breath of the supreme power animated him and elevated him to his position as man. He must be freed from the bondage of matter, and for this work Christ came into the world. He was the first of the heavenly powers; and on earth was without form, without natural birth, and without any material body.

Bardesanes, was the founder of the second school of Syria. He also admitted the two principles; the one the 'Unknown Father,' or the supreme and eternal God, who lives in the bosom of the light, blessed in the perfect purity of his being; the other eternal matter, or that inertness, dark and uninformed, which the East reckoned the source of all evil, the mother and the seat of Satan. The eternal God happy in the plenitude of his life and his perfections, having resolved to spread abroad this life and happiness beyond himself, multiplied himself or manifested himself as many beings, partaking his nature and bearing his name; for the Æons were called El, or God.

The first being, whom the unknown Father produced, was his syzygy, or companion, whom he placed in the celestial paradise ; and who there became, through him, the mother of the Son of the living God, Christ. This is an allegory which means that the Eternal conceived, in the silence of his decrees, the thought of revealing himself by another being, who was his image or Son. After Christ, comes his sister or spouse, the Holy Spirit, whom the Church itself calls the love of the Son for the Father. Bardesanes admitted seven of these syzygies, or seven emanations of mystical couples. With the help of the four Æons, types of the elements, the Son and the Spirit made the heaven and the earth and all that is visible. The soul of man, in the last analysis, was itself an emanation of the supreme Being; one of the Æons. It was the breath of God, the spirit of the Spirit that formed the world.

The third class of Gnostics, that of Egypt or Alexandria, is perhaps the most important of all, and the most marked by Alexandrian doctrine. Basilides the head of this school, like all other Gnostics, placed at the head of all, the unrevealed or ineffable God. From him proceeded emanations, which in their turn were themselves God, for they were in reality but the divine names and attributes personified. With Basilides, the manifoldness of God appears first as an Ogdoad, consisting of seven divine powers, and the primal One. This is the first Octave, the root of all existence. From them are evolved other existences ; each rank being a copy of the preceding one and inferior to it. Every rank or series is composed of seven intelligences, and the total of these three hundred and sixty-five, make the intelligible or celestial world. The soul of man is a ray of the celestial light which has been in a perpetual migration since the beginning of the world. Its end is to be separated from the material, that it may return to the source whence it came ; and not only is this the destiny of the soul of man, but of all life that is now imprisoned in matter. The Word came to accomplish this deliverance, and for this end he was united to Jesus of Nazareth.

The most significant, according to Baur, and that which represents the first chief form of the Gnosis, is undoubtedly the

Valentinian, partly as it is set forth by Valentinus himself, and partly as it is more fully expounded with different modifications by his zealous disciples. Like the system of Basilides, that of Valentinus has a double series of manifestations or of beings, which are all united to a single first cause. Of these, some are the immediate manifestations of the plenitude of the divine life; others are emanations of a secondary kind. The head of both series, who is the immediate head of the first only, is a perfect being the Bythos or abyss, which no intellect can fathom. No eye can behold the invisible and unspeakable glory in which he dwells. We cannot comprehend the duration of his existence. He has always been and he will always be.

The manifestation of this Being gave existence to the intelligible world. To this act we cannot apply the word creation, for it was not a production of that which did not exist. The supreme Being put outside of himself that which was concealed; that which was concentrated in the Pleroma; and the intelligences to which he gave existence, bore the name of manifestations, powers, or Æons. The Cabbalists gave to all superior intelligences, and especially to the Sephiroth, the names, El, Jehovah, Elohim, and Adonai. They wished by this to express that all that which emanates from God, still is God. The Gnostics had the same thought, and gave to the intelligences the name Æon, which means a world; an age; an eternity. The most characteristic attribute for God was eternity; and therefore these emanations of God were called Æons. The Valentinians say, according to Irenæus, that there is in the invisible and unspeakable heights, an Æon of all perfection, who has been before all things. They call him also Bythos.

The Bythos having passed infinite ages in rest and silence, resolved to manifest himself; and for this he made use of thought, which alone belonged to him; which is not a manifestation of his being, but which is the source of all perfection —the mother which receives the germs of his creation. The first manifestation which the thought of the supreme Being produced was mind. In the allegorical language of the Valentinians, thought was impregnated by the Bythos, and thus was produced mind the only begotten Son of the Supreme. Bythos is thus masculine; at other times masculo-feminine, as when regarded as in a state of unity with thought. Bythos and thought have their counterpart in the Ammon and Neith of the Egyptians. Mind is the first manifestation of the powers of God—the first of the Æons, the beginning of all things. By it divinity is revealed; for without the act which gave it existence, all things would remain buried in the Bythos. The Æons are but the more complete revelation of God. They are the forms of the great Being, the names of him, whose perfections no name can express—the names of the nameless One. Of these Æons, some are masculine, and some are feminine. The feminine is the analogue of the masculine; so that the Ogdoad becomes a Tetrad, and can be reduced to these :—Bythos, Mind, Word, Man.

In the Bythos, all things are one. As it unfolds itself there result antitheses, which are formed through all degrees of existence. But these are antitheses of like kinds; syzygies, or unions; copies of Bythos and thought. The one is the complement of the other. The first of the two is the male, the active or forming principle; the second, the feminine, or passive principle. From their union result other Æons, which are the images of these. The union of all Æons forms the Pleroma, or fulness of the divine nature, the plenitude of the attributes and perfections of him whom no man can know, save the only begotten Son.

All the manifestations of God were pure, and reflected the rays of his divine attributes. But the Æons were not equal in perfection. The more their rank separated them from God, the less they knew him and the nearer they were to imperfection; yea, they reached imperfection, and of necessity there was degeneracy, or, as it is otherwise called, a fall. The Æons that were distant from God were animated by a vehement desire to know him; but this was impossible. Eternal silence, which means an impossibility in the nature of things, prevented their attaining this knowledge. The harmony of the Pleroma was troubled; there was need of a restoration, of a deliverance from the fall. This deliverance was wrought by Christ.

This Pleroma, this fall and deliverance, only concerned the celestial or intelligible world; but the inferior or terrestrial world is a copy of the celestial; and though outside of the

Pleroma, what took place in the celestial had its counterpart in the terrestrial. Jesus did for the inferior world what Christ did for the Pleroma, as the Only begotten. He was the first-born of creation, and spread throughout all existence placed outside of the Pleroma the germs of the divine life, which he embraced in his own person.

There was a manifest contradiction in speaking of a Pleroma or fulness, which contained the all of being, and then assuming the existence of matter outside of the Pleroma. But the Valentinians had a ready answer. Though the Father of all things, they said, contains all, and nothing is beyond the Pleroma, yet 'inside of' and 'outside of' are only words adapted to our knowledge or our ignorance, having no reference to space or distance. And when they spoke of matter beyond the Pleroma, they explained matter as the philosophers had done before them ; as not a real existence, but the necessary bounds between being and non-being, a negative something between that which is and that which is not. The existence of a purely divine, and a divine mingled with matter, required Valentinus to acknowledge, in the creative wisdom of God, a two-fold being, a higher and a lower wisdom. The latter is the soul of the world, the immature Æon in its progress to perfection. From the mingling of this Æon with matter spring all living existences, in gradations without number ; higher in proportion as they are free from matter, and lower the more they are in contact with it.

The doctrines of Basilides and Valentinus, under different modifications, were held by all the sects of Egyptian Gnostics, both of the great and the small schools. Neander says, ' There were some among this kind of Gnostics who carried their Pantheism through with more consistency. They held that the same soul is diffused through all living and inanimate nature ; and that, consequently, all, wherever it is dispersed and confined by the bonds of matter within the limits of individual existence, should at length be absorbed by the world-soul or wisdom, the original source whence it flowed. Such Gnostics said, "When we take things for food, we absorb the soul, scattered and dispersed in them, into our own being, and with ourselves carry them upward to the original fountain." Thus, eating and drinking were for them a kind of worship.' In an apocryphal gospel of this sect,* the world-soul or supreme Being says to the initiated, 'Thou art I and I am thou; where thou art I am, and I am diffused through all. Where thou pleasest thou canst gather me, but in gathering me thou gatherest thyself.' Dorner says, 'Epiphanius relates of the Gnostics of Egypt, what proves that they were in part given to a Nature-Pantheism. They called the quickening powers of nature Christ. Those who believed that they had measured the entire circle of nature-life, and had collected and offered all power, said, "I am Christ."'

MANICHÆISM.

After Gnosticism, the other great philosophical heresy was the Church of the Manichees. Manes, the founder of this sect, before he embraced Christianity, had lived long among the Persian Magi, and had acquired a great reputation for all kinds of learning. 'The idea,' *Matter* says, 'which governs all his system, is Pantheism, which, more or less, pervades all the schools of the Gnosis, which he, however, derived from other quarters; doubtless, from its original source in the regions of India and China, which he had visited, in order to satisy his ardour for theological speculation.' According to Manes, the cause of all that which exists is in God; but in the last analysis, God is all. All souls are equal. God is in all. This divine life is not limited to man and animals; it is the same in plants. But the Pantheism of Manes was modified by the dualism of Zoroaster. The kingdoms of light and darkness, spirit and matter, had long contended. Each had its Æons or demons, under the leadership of their chief, as in the kingdoms of Ormuzd and Ahriman. At one time, the kingdom of darkness seemed likely to overcome; but the chief of the kingdom of light, seeing the danger, created a power which he placed in the front of the heavens, to protect the Æons, and to destroy the kingdom of darkness or evil. This power was the mother of life—the soul of the world—the divine principle, which indirectly enters into relation with the material world, to correct its evil nature. As a direct emanation of the supreme, it is too pure to come into contact with matter. It remains on the bounds of the superior region. But the mother of life bore

* The gospel of Eve—The sect, the Ophites.

a son, who is her image ; this son is the first or celestial man. He fights with the powers of darkness, is in danger of being conquered and of falling into the empire of darkness ; but the ruler of the light kingdom sends the living spirit to deliver him. He is delivered ; but part of his armour or light, which, in the Eastern allegory, is called his son, has been devoured by the princes of the kingdom of darkness.

The succession, then, of the first beings of the empire of light is this :—The good God, the mother of life, the first man, the son of man, or Jesus Christ, and the living spirit. The mother of life, who is the general principle of divine life, and the first man are too elevated to be allied with the empire of darkness. The son of man is the germ of the divine life, which, according to the language of the Gnosis, enters the empire, and ends by tempering it or purifying it from its savage nature. The deliverance of the celestial ray which is in the empire of matter, and its return into the bosom of perfection, constitute the end and destiny of all visible existence. This end once reached, the world will cease to be.

The visible Adam was created in the image of the first man. His soul was light and his body matter, and thus he belonged to both kingdoms. Had he obeyed the commandment not to eat of the forbidden fruit, he would have been freed ultimately from the kingdom of darkness, but an angel of light tempted him to disobey. The demons produced Eve, whose personal charms seduced him from the spiritual and plunged him into the sensual. What happened at the creation of the world is repeated by the generation of every human being. The blind forces of matter and darkness are confounded, and enchain the soul, which seeks deliverance. Man is enchained of fate by this act which has given him existence, and which always gives him up weaker to the powers of sense and the charms of the terrestrial world.

JOHN SCOTUS ERIGENA.

It is not with the full permission of the Catholic Church that we place among heretics the name of John Scotus Erigena. Until the year 1583, both the French and English martyrologers celeberated him as a holy martyr, and since the republication of his works in Germany, many Catholic theologians of that country claim him as a sound Catholic. He certainly lived and died in the communion of the Church of Rome—was perhaps an abbot and probably a priest, though evidence is wanting to establish the certainty of this. He first appears in history in a controversy on predestination. Godescalcus, a Saxon monk, had incurred the displeasure of the Archbishop of Rheims, by teaching that God's predestination was two-fold—one of the good to eternal blessedness, and the other of the reprobate to eternal condemnation. Erigena espoused the side of the Archbishop, maintaining that God out of his everlasting love had predestined all men to eternal life. The controversy became so important that an appeal was made to Rome. Nicholas I. approved of the doctrine of Godescalcus, and tried to check the 'poisonous' dogmas of Erigena. 'Nevertheless,' adds his German Catholic biographer, with a feeling of triumph, 'Erigena himself was not condemned.' At the request of Charles the Bald, Erigena translated into Latin the works of St. Dionysius, the Areopagite. This again exposed him to the Papal displeasure. Nicholas blamed him for translating, without the approbation of the Court of Rome, a book so liable to be misinterpreted. His work on the Eucharist, in reply to Radbertus, was condemned and burnt by the Council of Versailles in the eleventh century; but his Catholic advocates in Germany say this book was not written by Erigena, but by Ratramnus. His great work 'on the Division of Nature' seems to have passed without censure till the thirteenth century, when Honorius III., finding it had leavened the sect of the Albigenses, who boasted of their agreement with so great a man as Erigena, ordered all his works to be collected and burnt. In the seventeenth century they were republished at Oxford, and immediately after catalogued at Rome in the index of books forbidden. To what extent Erigena is a heretic the infallible Church has not decided. He believed his speculative theology to be in perfect harmony with the theology of the Church. This has been maintained by some modern Catholic theologians, but denied by others. It is convenient here to place him among heretics, and yet it is improper to separate him from the author of the Dionysian writings.

Of the history of this remarkable man, very little is known.

To his name, John Scotus, was added Erigena, or the *Irish-born*. Tradition brings him from the Irish monasteries, where, it is said, philosophy and the Greek language flourished long after they had fallen into neglect in other parts of Europe; but Scotland and Wales dispute with Ireland the honour of being the country of his birth. He found a liberal patron in Charles the Bald, who made him Director of the University of Paris. His rare acquaintance with the Greek language, his familiarity with the doctrines of Plato and his Alexandrian disciples, seem to have constituted his chief claim to regal patronage and to Papal censure. According to one account, he died in France. According to another, he found a second royal protector in Alfred the Great, who made him teacher of mathematics and dialectics at Oxford, and then Abbot of Malmesbury. He suffered death at the hands of his scholars. A wonderful light shone over the place where his body lay, till it was buried near the altar in the great church of Malmesbury. He was henceforth enrolled in the list of saints and martyrs. Like nearly all great metaphysicians, he was little of stature, and endowed with great subtlety of intellect.

Erigena's great work, we have said, is ' On the Division of Nature.' By ' Nature,' he understands not only all being, but all non-being; things which are, and things which are not. These two are necessary to constitute absolute existence, for being is not the all so long as non-being stands opposed to it. This, however, is but the ground of a further division into four kinds.

1. Nature which creates and is not created.
2. Nature which creates and is created.
3. Nature which is created and does not create.
4. Nature which is not created and does not create.

These four divisions are purely speculative, starting with the idea of existence in which being and non-being, subject and object, God and the world, are all one. The dualism is only apparent, the monism is real. On the human side, that is, in our subjective contemplation, ' Nature' is two-fold and manifold. On the divine side, all is one. The four divisions are justly resolved into two. The first is manifestly God in the Word, as the Original of all things. The second is things in their ideals, which in Plato's sense are the realities. The third is what some would call the reality in the ideals, but, in Platonic language, the phenomenal world. The fourth is God in himself as the source of all things, and as the goal to which all things return. Reduced to two, these four divisions are God from whom all emanates and the things emanating from him. But as the latter have no reality except so far as they derive it from him from whom they emanate, we come back to the Pantheistic formula—God is one and all things.

Erigena dwells much on the incomprehensibility of God. He is so overwhelmed with the thought of the divine infinitude, that he does not imagine God to be known by any created being. Even to expect to know God as he is, is as unwise as the demand of Philip, 'Shew us the Father.' And Christ's answer to Philip is the only answer that will ever be given to our expectations of seeing God. We shall behold him in his theophanies ; in the manifestation of himself in creation, but above all, shall we know him in his Son. We know that God is, and that he is the highest reality ; the essence of all which is, but what that essence is, we know not. It remains above all human thought and all human conception of being. God alone creates, and is alone un-created, he is created by no other because he creates himself. But if thus above us, how can we think of him ? How can we speak of him ? If we cannot know him, is theology possible ? This is a question with which we are still familiar. The different answers to it, and the conclusions from these answers are interesting, when we compare them with the answers and conclusions that were made in the days of Alfred the Great. Erigena did not despair of theology, though he declares God to be the absolutely unknowable and unknown. We can think and speak of him in two ways, negatively and positively. We first deny that God is anything; any of those things which can be spoken of, or understood. Then we predicate of him all things, but affirming that he is not any one of them, and yet that all are by and through him. We can say of God that he is being, but that is not properly being to which non-being stands opposed. He is therefore above being. We can say, he is God. If we take the Greek word for God, as derived from the Greek verb *to see*, then darkness is opposed to vision, and God being more than light, is above God ; if from the verb *to run*, then not running is opposed to running, and he is, in this sense too, more than God. It is written ' His word runneth very swiftly,' which means that he runs through all things which are, in order that they may be. In the same way he is more eternal than eternity, wiser than wisdom, better than goodness, and truer than truth. These attributes are transferred from the creature to the Creator, from the finite to the Infinite. They exist in him, but in a manner so transcendent that we speak most reverently of him when we deny him all attributes, lest we should associate with them anything that is human or finite. Only by predicating all things of God, and at the same time denying him the possibility of these predicates being applied to him, can we speak truly of God. There is more truth in the negation than the affirmation. We know him best by feeling our ignorance of him. This is true divine knowledge to know that we do not know him. The highest name by which he can be called is to call him by no name, and our highest conception of him is not as in reality a being, but as the Absolute Nothing who is above all being.

But Erigena cannot stop here. The dread of limitation accompanying the knowledge of the divine being, is thus the ground of the denial of that knowledge. But another question immediately arises : Does God know himself ? If he does, is not that a limitation, as well as human knowledge of him ? If he knows himself, he must become an object of his own knowledge, and as such he is no longer the infinite and the inconceivable. Erigena comes boldly to the legitimate conclusion of his rigid dialectic. God does not know himself. He knows that he is, but he does not know what he is. If he knows not himself, how are we to know him ? Wherefore need we ask his name since it is so wonderful ? God cannot be known as anything determined, and yet this divine ignorance is in truth the most inexpressible wisdom. And so it is with God's unconsciousness of himself. We say he does not know himself because if he did he would be limited. This attribute like the others must be both affirmed and denied of him ; so as to express that his knowledge of himself is like himself, above all that is being or essence, transcendently divine.

Erigena divided nature, or the all of being and non-being,

into four divisions. These, as we have seen, were reducible to two, and these again to one, in the identity of God and creation. But this identity may be understood in two ways, either that the essence of God goes out entirely into the being of the universe, or that though all things partake of his being, and are manifestations of it, yet he himself transcends all. It is in the latter sense that we are here to understand the identity of God and the universe. He creates all things, and his essence is in all things. It is manifested in every creature, and yet God remains one in himself. He never gives up the simplicity of his being. God moves and extends himself, and therefore the universe, as a visible phenomenon, appears. All is his extension, because all arises from this, that God extends himself; but in this extension he does not give up his being. He still exists, separate from all, just as our spirits exist separate from our thoughts as expressed in words or in writing. His presence in all things does not hinder that he remains one in himself. The universe has no existence independent of God's existence ; it is therefore God, but not the whole of God. He is more than the universe, yet the divine nature is truly and properly in all things. Nothing really is, in which the divine nature is not. God and the creature then do not differ in their essential nature ; they are both divine. The creature subsists in God ; and God after a wonderful manner is created in the creature.

Erigena uses the word creation, and his Catholic advocates plead this as a proof of his orthodoxy ; but we must not be misled by words. Creation, with Erigena, is emanation. His arguments lose their meaning the moment we forget this. Emanation is the chain which unites the created to the uncreated ; the invisible bond which makes Creator and creature one. As the second of the four divisions, we have ' That which creates and is created.' This represents the ideals which constitute the realities of all created things, which the Greeks called prototypes, species or eternal forms according to which, and in which, the visible universe was created. These ideals are God's thoughts—his conception of things before the beginning of time. They are identical with his spirit and will. God cannot exist without creating, for creation is his necessary work. The divine attributes of being, wisdom, good-

ness, and truth require that God create—and these are themselves one with the ideal principles of creation. These ideals
thus become the bridge between the infinite and the finite. As
God's attributes they participate in God, and at the same time
they are the realities of the phenomenal universe. To understand this we must dismiss our ordinary conception of a
thought, as something in the mind distinct from the outward
reality. All God's thoughts, it is maintained, have a real
objective existence in the Logos, which, as Scripture teaches,
existed in the beginning or first principle, the primordial cause
of the heaven and earth. He formed in his Word, which is his
only begotten Son, all the things which he wished to create,
before they came to phenomenal existence. The Word thus is
the unity of the ideals; the original form of all things, which
in an eternal and unchangeable manner are represented in
him, and subsist by him.

Whilst the ideals were regarded as the divine attributes, or
God's necessary thoughts, Erigena found it easy to identify
these with God through the Word. But how is he to bridge
the separation between the ideal and phenomenal universe—
between the second and third divisions of nature—'That
which creates and is created;' and 'That which is created and
does not create?' The ideas are co-eternal with God. This
is settled; but could they be objective realities until they
passed into the phenomenal state? In other words—can
there be a cause until it makes good its existence by an effect?
Is the phenomenal universe co-eternal with the ideal; or did
it take its origin in time? If the latter, then creation was not
eternal, unless there can be a cause without an effect. But
creation is eternal—the ideal universe is eternal, the phenomenal being necessary to its completion, it too must be eternal.
Logically, the effect follows the cause; the creature must come
after the creation; so that here we are compelled to distinguish
between the eternity of God who has his beginning in himself,
and the eternity of things created, which have their beginning
in him. Yet, when he was, they were; the primordial causes
are co-eternal with him, because they always subsisted in him.
What then is matter, time, and space? As realities they disappear. Time is but the continuance and motion of things
mutable. The cognition of it precedes everything known or

belonging to time. Space is a limitation of sensible and intelligible objects. It is not perceivable by sense. It can only be thought in the reason. Time and space are merely subjective existences. Nearly the same is said of matter. It comes to appearance within the bounds of time and space, flowing out from the primordial causes. So far as it has form, it is corporeal, but so far as it is formless it is incorporeal, and can be known only by reason. Aristotle regarded matter as mere potentiality; and form as the actuality which brought the indefinite material to be a something. Erigena's doctrine does not much differ from this. Matter is to him only the participation of form and shape. Whatever wants these is nothing actual. But form and shape are in themselves incorporeal, and can only be known by the reason. It follows then that things formed as well as things formless are originally and essentially incorporeal; the latter, through the want of form, the former, not in themselves, but through the form. But that which is in itself incorporeal becomes corporeal by its participation with another incorporeal; and thus bodies are produced by the coming together of two incorporeals. If so, they can be again resolved into their original states and cease to be bodies. What then is matter? Nothing—or something next to nothing; the mutability of things mutable; the 'without form and void;' the nonentity of a body which remains when deprived of all its qualities—the mere reflection, echo, and shadow of true being.

Man visible has his place at the head of the 'nature which is created and does not create.' As the essence of God is the one substance of all beings, as the Logos is the unity of all the primordial causes, so is man the mediating point of the opposites and differences of the phenomenal world. His being contains all created natures in itself; since in the spirit and reason of man God has created the invisible and intelligible world; and in his body, the visible and sensible. Man is contained in the hidden original cause of nature according to which he was created; and in him is contained the whole creation, so that he has been called, not improperly, 'the workshop of all other creatures.' He understands as an angel; reasons as a man; feels as an animal; lives as a plant; consists of body and soul and is akin to every creature. He was created in God's image, that in him every creature, both intelligible and sensible, might form an undivided unity. Need we marvel then, that if in his suffering, creatures suffer, and that all creation is groaning and travailing together with him, and with him waiting for deliverance ?

The fourth division of nature is, 'That which does not create and is not created.' This, as we have already seen, is God in himself. The difference is, that in the first, God is the Creator, the Word, the being from whom creation emanates. In this he is the being to whom creation returns. This is God in our highest conception of him ; God without attributes ; God in his super-essential essence, neither creative nor created ; God as the original Monad, which, not being any one thing, is yet more than all things, and of whom we speak most reverently and most truly when we call him the absolute non-being.

We have reserved hitherto the application of Erigena's philosophy to the interpretation of Scripture and church dogmas. This arrangement is of our own making. It has no place in the 'Division of Nature.' Scripture, church doctrine and philosophy are brought together to explain each other, the perfect harmony of all these being previously assumed. Erigena was a Christian and a Catholic. Let us see how he understood Christianity.

Neander says:—'The prevailing bent of the theological spirit of that age was to cling, as we have remarked before, to the authorities of the church tradition ; but he was founding a system of truth, which should repose entirely on rational insight, approve itself as true by an inner necessity of reason. Yet even according to his apprehension, the rational and the church-traditional theology, faith and knowledge by reason, philosophy and religion did not stand in contradiction, but in perfect harmony with each other. For, said he, a man can elevate himself to the knowledge of God, which is the end of true philosophy, only by following the mode and manner in which God, who in his essence is incomprehensible and unknowable, letting himself down to the condition and wants of humanity which is to be educated, has revealed himself ; God in his forms of revelation, in his theophanies. After this manner God presents himself in the historical development of religion, through the authority of the church ; but true philosophy, which rises above the theophanies to the absolute itself, which soars beyond all conceptual apprehension, gives insight into the laws according to which God must be known and worshipped. True philosophy and true religion are therefore one. Philosophy veiled in the form of tradition is religion; religion unveiled from the form of tradition by rational knowledge is philosophy. Philosophy is the theoretic side of religion; religion the practical side of philosophy.'

The Catholic faith is, that we worship one God in trinity and trinity in unity. This is a true doctrine. We may object to the contradictory and hard dogmatic form which it takes in the Latin phrases of the creed of St. Athanasius; but in substance it is true. There are not three persons in the Godhead; but substitute the Greek word, which we translate person, explain that the Latin word means no more than is intended by the Greek word, and then the creed of St. Athanasius may be allowed to pass. The Trinity is not so much a God in three persons as God in three operations. He is one cause subsisting by itself, and yet in three self-subsisting causes. The Father is the cause of the Son, not as to nature, for both are of one essence; but according to the relation of him who begets, to him who is begotten, or of the cause that precedes, to that which follows. The Holy Spirit proceeds from the Father, not from but through the Son, for one cause cannot have two causes. Light proceeds from fire by the medium of a ray, but not from both, for the fire is the original cause both of the light and the ray. The ray produces the light, but not as if it were in itself a self-subsisting cause; for it can never be thought of, as separated from the fire from which the ray proceeds, and which is incessantly present in the ray, and suffers the light to go forth from itself. So also the Father is the producing cause of the Son. And he is the essence of all causes which are created in him by the Father; and the Father himself is the cause of the Spirit proceeding from him, but through the Son. The Spirit again is the cause of all division, multiplication, and distribution of all the things, which are made in the Son by the Father, in the general and special workings both in the kingdoms of nature and of grace. Thus the Holy Spirit proceeds from the Father by the medium of the Son; and, again, the Son is begotten of the Father through

the grace of the Holy Spirit.   These forms and modes of representing the Trinity were common among the Greek fathers.
How far they are orthodox is not our present business.   With
Erigena the 'three' that form the Trinity never appear as
persons, but only as powers, names, relations, or operations of
God.   The Father is essence; the Son is wisdom; the Spirit is
life.   The Father is being; the Son is might; the Spirit is
energy.   The Father is mind; the Son self-knowledge; the
Spirit self-love.   As Abraham was not a father in himself, but
in relation to Isaac, nor Isaac a son but in relation to Abraham,
so God is not a Father in himself, nor Christ a Son in himself;
but the one a Father and the other a Son in relation to each
other, the substance of both being the same.   Though the
operations are different, it is one God who works through all.
The Father creates.   Through the Son all is created.   By the
Spirit, as the differential principle, the creation is wrought out
into the manifold.   The Father wills; the Son creates; the
Holy Spirit brings the work to completion.   But for the
Father to will is to do, so that the working of the Son and the
Spirit is but the willing of the Father.   The Father is the
principle of the substance of things—the Son, of their ideal
causes—the Spirit, of their actual manifestation in time and
space.   The operations of the triune three are different, and
yet the worker is One.   This great doctrine of the Church
points to moments in the becoming of nature.   It is a theophany of the truth, nothing more.   God is neither a Trinity
nor a unity.   He is something more than either three in one
or one in three.

The creation of man, too, like the being of God, is altogether
transcendental.   Man existed in the divine mind from all
eternity.   Of old 'the delights of wisdom were with the sons
of men.'   The ideal Adam was completely happy in paradise;
he had a spiritual body like that of the angels.   St. Paul discourses of glorified bodies, and shows by his language that
body and spirit are essentially of one substance.   This primordial Adam was taught to love the spiritual and the invisible;
but he desired the visible and the sensual, and as a punishment he was clothed with this present body of death.   Then,
being subjected to passions and the viler affections, he was
driven from Paradise—that is, he was sent forth from the

spiritual to the material world. He was no more like the angels. Eve was created. Marriage was instituted, and man was doomed to perpetuate his race in the same way as the beasts of the field. This may seem to contradict the narrative in Genesis; but in reality it does not, for the ideal Eve previously existed in the ideal Adam, and represented that principle of sense which seduced him from the spiritual life. In this expulsion from Eden, and this separation of the sexes, the phenomenal world, to speak humanly, has its origin. Man passes from the ideal and spiritual to the phenomenal and material, and as in him are contained all forms and ranks of creatures, these take their beginning as he begins his material existence. In this fall we learn what sin is. It is no real thing, but only a privation of good—an accident of being. It was nothing which happened to man in time, but an original infirmity of his nature. The seed of sin or the possibility of willing evil was always in man. It was suffered by God to be in him. Indeed, the fall was predestined, that out of this seeming evil might be brought a greater good. It is impossible that God could be disappointed, or that any event should arise which he had not pre-ordained. The fall of the ideal Adam, and the creation of this phenomenal world, are but steps in the divine procedure—parts of an eternal working which, in the end, shall contribute to the greater glory of God, and the higher blessedness of all the universe.

And the incarnation of Christ, that too is out of time. It must be, for the thought of it is co-existent with the thought of infirmity in man. As he was predestined to pass the material stage, so was he predestined to return to the spiritual, or rather to pass on to it, for the fall and the incarnation are together processes in the history of the creature's progress towards the Creator. The subject of the incarnation is the eternal Logos; the first principle in and by whom all things were made. In the Logos, man had his being. He fell by the love of the sensual. He participated in the material. It was necessary that the Logos, in order to restore man, should descend in like manner and participate of the material, therefore he took upon him humanity in its fallen state; a body of sense with soul and spirit, and thereby he united in himself the whole sensible and intelligible creation. In taking man's nature he took all

K

the natures below man's, for it includes them all, and thus he
is the Redeemer of the whole creation. The Logos or eternal
cause of all, descended as in his Godhead into the effects of
which he is the cause, that is into the sensuous world, that he
might save according to his humanity the effects of the causes,
which he already had eternally in himself. The incarnation
was no måtter of choice. It was necessary for the cause of all
things, thus to make good the effects by descending into them.
This was done by the Logos, who in this incarnation became
man, and thereby manifested the eternal self-subsisting unity
of the spiritual and the phenomenal; the infinite and the finite
—the eternal immanency of God in the universe. As man is
the content of all effects produced by the ideal cause, so the
Logos is the unity or content of the causes themselves. In
Scripture the incarnation is necessarily represented as taking
place in time, but like the creation, and fall of man, it is in
reality eternal.

The final and complete restitution of man, is the inevitable result of the incarnation of the Logos. The universe has proceeded
from God. It is but the extension of his being; the manifestation
of himself; therefore must it return again to him, not in part,
but as a whole. The predestination of anything to destruction
is but a figure of speech. All men shall be saved. Their return to God is necessary, yea it is not a thing of time, not an
event of which we can speak, as past or future. It is something actual. In the contemplation of God it is eternally
realized, but to man the Logos became incarnate in Jesus of
Nazareth, who by his death, resurrection, and ascension, completed the salvation of men, and angels.

ERIGENA'S DISCIPLES.

Erigena left no school, and if he had any immediate followers
nothing is known of them. 'The century,' says Neander, 'in
which he lived was not prepared for his system; but the
speculative spirit which passed over from the twelfth to the
thirteenth century prepared the way for its acquiring an influence which it was unable to do on its first appearance.'
We are without data for any sufficient history of the heresies
of the thirteenth century; but we have intimations that

they were numerous, and so widely spread as to alarm the authorities of the Church. The chief of these heresies were various forms of what we call Pantheism. In the year 1204, the University of Paris condemned the doctrines of Amalric de Bena, Professor of Theology in the University. As we have none of Amalric's writings, we only know his doctrines from passages preserved by other authors. These agree so entirely with Erigena's doctrines, as to leave no doubt as to the source from which they come. That God alone truly exists,—all else being merely phenomena,—that God and the creature are one and the same, and that all things will finally return to God, are the chief points in the heresy with which he is charged. Then we have in detail the Platonic doctrine of ideas and primordial causes—the forms and patterns which, like the second division of nature, create and are themselves created. They exist in God, and what God is they are. As Abraham is not of one nature and Isaac of another, but both one and the same, so all things are one—all are divine, God being the essence of all creatures. We have the repetition of Erigena's doctrine concerning the fall of man, and the result of that fall in the production of the sensuous body, and the origin of the two sexes. Amalric was removed from his professorship. He appealed to Innocent III., but the sentence of the University was confirmed. Thus condemned by the Roman See, he acknowledged his errors, signed a recantation, and soon after died.

But Amalric's doctrines had taken deeper root than either the Pope or the University of Paris was aware of. His disciple, David of Dinanto, was not less formidable than Amalric had been. To refute David of Dinanto was the work of the theologians of this century, and to extirpate his followers the special vocation of the Church. David wrote a book ' On Divisions,' which, from the portions of it preserved by Albert the Great, seems to have been an imitation of Erigena ' On the Division of Nature.' He is said to have gone beyond his master, in having defined God as ' the material principle of all things,' which was a substitution for Amalric's more idealistic phrase, ' the formal principle.' But the difference appears to be in words more than in meaning. What is ' formal ' in the Platonic philosophy is essential, and perhaps ' material ' is but another name for the same thing. Matter, as such, had no more existence for him than it had for Erigena or Amalric. Whatever he meant, we may safely conclude he did not think that God is material. This distinction between the theology of Amalric and David of Dinanto was first made by Thomas Aquinas, who describes the latter as having taught that God was the first matter; that is, that God is the one substance, essence, or matter which constitutes the universe. He divides the 'all' into 'three indivisibles;' the substratum of the corporeal world; then, that out of which spirit proceeds; and lastly, that of the ideas or eternal substances. The first is called matter, the second spirit, and the third God. But the three are one; they are only different designations of the divine essence according as we consider it in its relation to the corporeal, the spiritual, and the ideal worlds. God alone is true being, the only substance, of which all other beings are but the accidents.

So widely did this speculative theology spread itself both among the clergy and the lay people, that the University of Paris prohibited the reading of all metaphysical books. Aristotle and books ascribed to Aristotle, which had hitherto been read in the University, were publicly condemned. The body of Amalric was ordered to be dug up and burned, or at least cast out of consecrated ground. The work of David of Dinanto was proscribed, with the commentaries of the Arabian Averroes, and the writings of some other Pantheistic heretic, who is called 'the Spanish Maurice;' nor was the opposition of the Church confined to proscriptions of books, and anathemas against their authors. The stake was kindled, and all metaphysical priests and laymen who would not recant their faith in the doctrines of Aristotle and Amalric were consumed. 'But you cannot burn me,' cried Bernard, a brave priest of the Pantheistic sect; 'you cannot burn me, for I am God.' This, however, did not overawe his enemies. They kindled the faggots which they had gathered round him, and soon all that was phenomenal in Bernard disappeared.

Neander says, 'Pantheism, with all the practical consequences that flow from it, was more boldly and abruptly expressed than perhaps the original founders of this school had intended. That distinction of the three ages which had attached itself to the doctrine of the Trinity, and which we noticed in the doctrines of the Abbot Joachim, was employed by this sect also, after their own peculiar manner. As the predominant revelation of God the Father, in the Old Testament, was followed by the revelation of the Son, by which the forms of worship under the legal dispensation were done away; so now the age of the Holy Ghost was at hand—the incarnation of the Holy Ghost in entire humanity, the being of God under the form of the Holy Ghost after an equal measure in all the faithful; that is, the dependence of the religious consciousness upon any one individual as a person in whom God is incarnate would cease, and the consciousness of all alike, that God exists in them, has in them assumed human nature, would come in place of it. The sacraments, under which the Son of God had been worshipped, would then be done away; religion would be made wholly independent of ceremonies; of everything positive. The members of this sect are the ones in whom the incarnation of the Holy Ghost has begun, the fore-runners of the above-described period of the Holy Spirit. Several other opinions are charged upon members of this sect, which certainly accord with their general mode of thinking; as, for example, that God had spoken in Ovid as well as in Augustine; that the only heaven and the only hell are in the present life; that those who possess the true knowledge no longer need faith or hope; they have attained already to the true resurrection, the true paradise, the real heaven; that he who lives in mortal sin has hell in himself. These people opposed the worship of saints as a species of idolatry. They called the ruling Church Babylon; the pope, antichrist.'

A leaven of the heresy of Erigena and Amalric is supposed to have made considerable progress among the order of St. Francis. Abbot Joachim, of St. Floris, a fervent advocate of the speculative and mystical doctrines condemned by the University of Paris, was in great reverence among the Franciscans. Joachim had written a commentary on the Apocalypse. He was a prophet, and an interpreter of prophecy. Among other predictions, he foretold the great success of the order of St. Francis; and among his interpretations of prophecy, he supposed that he had discovered the law of God's progressive revelation of himself in the world. There was first the age of the Father. With the incarnation, was that of the Son; and now the age of the Holy Ghost was about to begin. This age was to be marked by such an increase of light and grace, as to supersede the necessity of a church and priesthood such as then existed. All men were to be equal, free from the cares of the world, and filled with the Spirit of God. This millennium of blessedness was called 'the eternal gospel,' and the order of St. Francis were to be the chief heralds of its approach. The historical question of the eternal gospel we may give in Neander's words: 'As the strict Franciscans entertained a special reverence for the Abbot Joachim, who had foretold their order and the regeneration of the church, of which they were to be the instrument, and occupied themselves a good deal with the explanation of his writings, the interpretation and application of the current ideas in the same, so a great deal was said among them about a new everlasting gospel. The idea of such a gospel belonged really among the characteristic and peculiar notions of Joachim; and we have seen, how by this expression, borrowed from the fourteenth chapter of the Apocalypse, he had understood, following the view of Origen, a new spiritual apprehension of Christianity, as opposed to the sensuous Catholic point of view, and answering to the age of the Holy Spirit. A great sensation was now created by a commentary on the eternal gospel, which, after the middle of the thirteenth century, the Franciscan Gerhard, who, by his zeal for Joachim's doctrines, involved himself in many persecutions, and incurred an eighteen years' imprisonment, published under the title of 'Introductorius in Evangelium aeternum.' Many vague notions were entertained about the eternal gospel of the Franciscans, arising from superficial views, or a superficial understanding of Joachim's writings, and the offspring of mere rumour or the heresy-hunting spirit. Men spoke of the eternal gospel as of a book composed under this title and circulated among the Franciscans. Occasionally, also, this eternal gospel was confounded perhaps with the above-mentioned 'Introductorius.' In reality, there was no book existing under this title of the Eternal Gospel; but all that is said about it relates simply to the writings of Joachim. The opponents of the Franciscan order objected to the preachers of the eternal gospel, that, according to their opinion, Christianity was but a transient thing, and a new, more perfect religion, the absolute form, destined to endure for ever, would succeed it.'

Nearly allied to these zealous Franciscans were the Albigenses who, as we have already mentioned, claimed discipleship from Erigena, and appealed to his works in vindication of their doctrines. Of the tenets of the Albigenses we know nothing, except from their enemies. They are represented as Manichæans and Arians. Many wild doctrines are charged upon them, but with what amount of accuracy we cannot determine.

An affinity of doctrine has also been shown between the ' Division of Nature,' and the book ' On the Nine Rocks,' which, it is said, was the secret oracle of the ' Brothers and Sisters of the Free Spirit.' There are, however, extravagances in this book, which are not to be found in the works of Erigena. The existence of the universe is denied because of its identity with God. It is an emanation from him, and to him it shall return. The soul of man is declared to be uncreated and a part of the divine Being. To abstract ourselves from the finite, is the way to realize our union with the Infinite—to feel that we are God. What the Scripture says of Christ is true of every godly man—he is the son of God, and God. Under the shelter of these doctrines, if history speaks what is true, ' the Brothers and Sisters ' justified practices which are not considered commendable by Catholic Christendom. If, they said, the soul is one with God, then those acts which appear sinful cease to be so, they are essentially acts of God. If God wills that we sin, why should we will not to sin ? And if we have sinned a thousand times, why should we repent ? The sins we commit are parts of the divine plan, which brings good out of evil and makes use of partial ill for the universal well-being of the world. There is often but a narrow line between truth and error, between a man's own doctrines, and the sense in which others understand them, and yet that line is itself a world. St. Jude condemned those who, by apparently legitimate reasoning, turned the grace of God into lasciviousness, and so doubtless, if these things are true, would John Scotus Erigena have rebuked and condemned the ' Brothers and Sisters of the Free Spirit.'

The Tetrad, consists of the Bythos (abyss), Nous (mind), Logos (speech), Anthropos (man). In the Bythos, all is one, its manifestations constitute the degrees of existence ; the four which make the Tetrad, with their syzygies, make the Ogdoad. The syzygy of Bythos is Ennoia (thought), sometimes call Sigé (silence), and Arreton (the unspeakable), the syzygy of Nous is Aletheia (truth). These four make the first Tetrad of the Ogdoad. The syzygy of Logos is Zoé (life), and that of Anthropos, Ekklesia (the Church). These form the second Tetrad. From Bythos proceeds Horos (limitation), the Æon sent to teach the last of the Æons (Sophia), that she could not be united to the Bythos. The desire to know the Bythos, and to return to it, which had seized Sophia, possessed all the Æons which troubled the harmony of the Pleroma. To finish the work begun by Horos, the Nous engendered Christos, and his companion Pneuma (spirit). From Logos and Zoé emanate a decade of Æons ; Bythios (of the nature of Bythos), Ageratos (the ageless), Autophyes (self-produced), Akinetos (the immovable), and Monogenes (the only begotten), with their syzygies, Mixis (alliance), Henosis (union) Hedone (pleasure), Synkrasis (moderation), Makaria (blessedness). From Anthropos and Ekklesia emanate a duodecade ; Parakletos (comforter), and Pistis (faith), Patrikos (paternal), and Elpis (hope), Metrikos (the metrical), and Agape (love), Aeinous (eternal mind), and Synesis (intelligence), Ekklesiasticos (belonging to the church), and Makariotes (the blissful), Theletos (will), and Sophia (wisdom), last of all, the Æon Jesus, who united in himself all the good of all the Æons.

The Marcionites, who in *Matter's* classification are the fifth group of Gnostics, belonged to Asia Minor and Italy. There is nothing in their doctrines to require any particular notice here. The Clementines represented rather the opinions of an individual than a sect. Their fundamental definition of God is that he is a pure being, rest, and out of him is only nothing. As being he is the all. The world, including man, stands over against being as the vacuum which is to be filled by him who IS. God· is good, and especially righteous. This imposes the necessity of thinking God as personal. God, viewed in himself, is eternally united with wisdom as his spirit and his effulgent body. But his manifestation is a movement of *God himself* flowing forth in the double act of expansion and contraction of himself, of which the heart of man is the type, the wisdom, the spirit or word of God, is the eternally outstretched hand which completes the manifestation and forms the world. The world of revelation is God unfolding himself. There are six acts of self-expansion which comprehend the six world epochs, which, in the seventh, find their point of rest in God. God is the eternal Sabbath and the moveless centre. But though the world is a communication of his essence, a momentum of the Monad, God in his inner being remains unchanged. He is personal, but he is also being. Christ, the eternal prophet of truth, is manifested in Adam, Enoch, and Jesus.

The accounts of the Gnostics and Manichæans, and of nearly all ancient and mediæval heretics, have the disadvantage of coming from enemies.· We have chiefly followed the *Histoire Critique*, by M. Matter. In German there are works on Gnosticism by Baur, Neander, Möller. Schmid, and Huber. Hjort and Christlieb have written, on John Scotus Erigena in German ; and in French Taillandier.

CHAPTER VIII.

SCHOLASTICISM.

THE Church doctors of the middle ages were called scholastics, either because they were the learned men of these ages, or because of their connection with the schools that were established by Charlemagne. Philosophy found a home in Paris after its course was run at Athens and Alexandria. Erigena may be considered either as the forerunner of scholasticism, or as the first of the scholastics. M. Rousselot speaks of him as wandering on the mountains of Scotland, or by the banks of the sea which washes the Hebrides, embracing in himself all that the solitary Iona had been able to preserve of philosophical antiquity from the ignorance of barbarians; and, at the same time, concealing in his bosom the fruitful germ of the future. That Erigena was a native of Scotland is only conjecture, but it seems natural to believe that so great a metaphysician belonged to a metaphysical race. The discussions of the scholastics were but a continuation of the discussions of the philosophers, under the restraint of the definitions of the Church. Two centuries had elapsed after the death of Erigena, before the great controversies of the middle ages; but there is evidence that in these two centuries the cultivation of philosophy was not neglected. M. Cousin has shown by a passage in the glosses of Raban Maur, who wrote in the ninth century, that the difference between Nominalists and Realists had already began. Idealism, as the doctrine of Plato, had always been more or less the philosophy of the Church. The wisest, and as we now reckon the most orthodox of the fathers, St. Augustine, was an idealist, believing that ideas are realities—the original types of things and existing before the things themselves. Scholastic realism was but another name for idealism, and as such had been inherited from Plato.

Boethius, in his introduction to Porphyry's Isagoge, had said—'The intention of Porphyry in this work, is to facili-

tate the understanding of the categories by treating of five
things or names—genus, species, difference, property, accident.' In another passage the question was raised whether
universals, such as genera and species, have an external
existence, or if they exist only in our thoughts: again, supposing them to exist externally is that existence material
or immaterial? And further, do they exist apart from the
objects perceived by the senses; or only in and with these
objects. Porphyry had not entered into any special discussion
of these questions, this was reserved for his commentators.
Raban Maur said they were only names, and that Boethius
had shown this in his first commentary on the categories.

ROSCELLIN.

But Nominalism does not appear to have been much in
favour till the eleventh century, when Roscellin carried the
Nominalist principle so far as to come in collision apparently
with the doctrine of the Church. He said that only the individual was the real. He was answered that then the three
persons in the Trinity were only one reality. This he did not
admit, as it implied that God was one being, while Father,
Son, and Holy Ghost were only names. He said rather that
the three persons were three realities, and from this it was
inferred that he taught that there were three gods. We only
know Roscellin's doctrine from those who professed to refute
it. He may be classed with those philosophers who measure
knowledge by sensuous experience, and therefore deny reality
to ideas, that is, he was not a Platonist. As he denied the
objective existence of universals, for the same reason he denied
the existence of parts. He said that to think of a part we
must have the idea of the whole, and the whole again pre-
supposes the idea of the part. This gave Abelard the opportunity of making the famous jest that when Christ, after his
resurrection, ate part of a fish, he could only have eaten a
name. But the jest might have been spared. What Roscellin
denied was the existence of a part as an abstraction, not as
something concrete, separate, or capable of separation.

ANSELM.

Roscellin was condemned by the Council of Soissons, 1093, and was driven from France. He is believed to have came to England, then under the sway of the Normans. About the time of his arrival came also his great opponent, St. Anselm. Roscellin came as a fugitive, quitting his native land to save his life—Anselm to have placed on his head the mitre of the Archbishop of Canterbury. Anselm was by nature the better philosopher; but the bent of his mind was checked by the necessity of his being an orthodox bishop. He was a profound metaphysician, essaying boldly the most exalted questions, but he recoiled before the conclusions to which philosophy led him. He made reason the servant of faith, but when reason asked concerning the ground of faith, Anselm checked the inquiry. Belief should accord with reason, and reason with belief. Only on this assumption is philosophy possible in the church. But Anselm's philosophy was only Erigena's restrained by the dogmas of the church, whenever these dogmas seemed opposed to it. In his 'Dialogue on Truth,' says M. Rousselot, ' he plunges into the metaphysical abyss; into what is true in itself, leading back all to unity. This unity is for him reality. The true is that which is, and all that which *is*, is good. Then the good and the true are identical, and form only one and the same thing, whence it follows, that in the ontological point of view, evil *is* not, it is only a negation. It exists only in the acts of men, and in consequence of human liberty. The true, or that which is truth, is being; then beings or individuals are parts of being, as particular truths are parts of truth.'

The ontological argument for the being of God, which is ascribed to Anselm, can only be understood by its connection with his philosophy. ' It is impossible,' he says, ' to think that God does not exist, for God is, when defined, such a being that we cannot conceive one superior. Now, I can conceive a being whose existence it is impossible to disbelieve; and this being is evidently superior to one whose non-existence I am capable of imagining. Therefore, if we admit the possibility of supposing that God does not exist, there must be a being superior to God—that is to say, a being superior to one than whom we cannot conceive a greater, which is absurd.' There cannot be a question about the conclusiveness of this argument. It is an absolute demonstration of the being of God. But what God ? The God of ontology ; the One of Parmenides—infinite Being. Plato, as we have seen, saved his theology from this purely dialectical God, by adding the 'mind' and the 'Demiurgus.' Anselm, by adhering to the faith of the Catholic Church.

WILLIAM OF CHAMPEAUX.

Roscellin's disciple, William of Champeaux, united with Anselm in opposing the Nominalism of Roscellin, yet he barely escaped the fate of his master. He was not indeed condemned by the church, but if judged as some judge him, he might have been. Bayle describes the Realism of William of Champeaux as ' a Spinozism not yet developed ; ' and even the Abbé Maret says ' that from this opinion to Pantheism there is but one step.' Nominalism denied the Unity because it did not admit the reality of a universal. Realism did not admit the reality of the individual, and therefore involved the denial of the distinction of the three persons. The conclusion was the same— unity of substance—with only this difference, the 'substance' of the Nominalist was matter ; that of the Realist, spirit. The Nominalists were Ionics ; the Realists were Eleatics. The Nominalists were natural philosophers ; the Realists were metaphysicians.

ABELARD.

Peter Abelard appeared as the opponent both of Nominalism and Realism, but in no better harmony with the Church than Roscellin or William of Champeaux. His condemnation by Rome may have been unjust, having been made on the representation of an open adversary ; but though his philosophy was different from the two antagonistic schools, his theology it reckoned equally unsound. Abelard saw in Nominalism the negation of philosophy. It limited knowledge to the senses, excluding even the common sense of reason. In Realism he saw the other extreme, the tendency to exclude the senses, and to find reality only in abstractions of the mind. Speaking of his master, William of Champeaux, he says, 'I then returned to him to study rhetoric, and among other matters of dispute, I set myself to change—yea, to destroy by clear arguments—his old doctrine concerning universals. He was of this opinion concerning the identity of substance, that the same thing, essentially and at the same time, was with the individuals it produces. The difference between the individuals does not then come from their essence, but from variety of phenomena.' Abelard took up intermediate ground, allowing reality both to universals and to individuals. Genus, species, difference, property, accident, what are they? Things, said the Realist. Words, said the Nominalist. Both, said Abelard. Every individual has matter and form, the former from the universal, the latter is its individuality. Humanity, Anselm said, is a reality apart from the individuality, and yet the individuals partake of it, and are themselves each a particular reality besides. Between this theory and orthodox theology, there was no necessary discord, but Abelard was a philosopher. He did not depart from the principle of Anselm, that faith precedes reason, but unlike Anselm, he forgot the boundaries within which the Church wished to confine philosophy. Bishop Hampden, while vindicating the orthodoxy of the Realists, refuses to do the same for Abelard. 'His expressions in his Introduction to theology,' says Bishop Hampden, 'are decidedly Pantheistic, identifying the Holy Spirit with the *Anima Mundi* of the Stoics.'

Abelard, like many of the Church fathers, accepted the doctrines of Plato as almost, if not altogether, those of Christianity. The Platonic Trinity of the One or the good, the mind with the ideas and the world-soul, he understood as the three persons of the Christian Trinity. Bernard of Clairvaux accused him of heresy, in making the world-soul the same as the Holy Ghost. A passage in the 'Dialectic,' where Abelard explains that in Plato the procession of the world-soul from the mind is temporal, while that of the Holy Ghost from the Son is eternal, is believed to have been a recantation in favour of Bernard.

ALBERTUS MAGNUS.

The later Schoolmen were more orthodox. They were not

consistent Realists, though they did not entirely forsake Plato. A leaven of the experimental philosophy of Aristotle guarded them from the legitimate results of pure Realism; yet in their reasonings the Platonic element is predominant. By the *a priori* method of tracing up all existences to the being of God, they virtually admitted that the material was only the phenomenal. All power, wisdom, and goodness in the universe, were emanations of the power, wisdom, and goodness of the divine Being. All earthly relations are copies of archetypes in God. Fatherhood and sonship were of heavenly origin. God is the Father of our Lord Jesus Christ, and from him all fatherhood in heaven and earth is named. The analogies of the physical universe with the divine were positive participations of the divine nature. The purified intellect, that could see God in the manifestation of creation, knows him not in a figure, but in reality. All that was real in nature, was truly God.

Albertus Magnus is the first of the five, in whom, according to Dean Milman, the age of genuine Scholasticism culminates. He undertook to reply to Amalric de Bena, and yet he differs from him only in degree. He affected to reconcile Plato and Aristotle; Philosophy and Christianity, yet he leans more to Plato than to Aristotle. On most of the peculiar doctrines of Christianity he is silent, some of them, such as creation and redemption, he expounds after the manner of Erigena. He holds by the dogmas of the Church, but his philosophy beats against the bars of the cage. Anselm laid down the principle of believing that he might understand, but Albert excluded all the special doctrines of revelation from the category of things knowable of reason. The human soul can only know that of which the principle is in itself. It is a simple essence, and therefore cannot know the Godhead as a Trinity except by divine illumination. The universals he held to be realities, for if not real they could not be known. They do not exist independently of the divine mind, but were eternal emanations from it. The universe has a formal not a material existence. It can give being to a plurality of objects, but its actual existence is in the divine intellect. God is simple truth, not therefore to be identified with the universal substance. Albert was ever repeating the doctrine of the development of the manifold from the unity, and yet ever struggling to establish a real difference between them. 'He accepted,' says Dean Milman, 'a kind of Platonic emanation of all things from the Godhead; yet he repudiates as detestable or blasphemous the absolute unity of the divine intelligence with the intelligence of man. He recoiled from Pantheism with religious horror.' He saved himself by the doctrine of creation out of nothing, and he answered the objection of the philosophers, that from nothing, nothing comes by the observation, that this though true in physics or in secondary causes, is not applicable to God the first cause. He refuted, by order of Pope Alexander IV., the wide spread doctrine of Averroes that there is in reality but one soul, which is the totality of all individual souls. His own philosophy, as founded on Aristotle, interpreted by Averroes, might have led to the identification of the universal in the particulars with the doctrine of one soul in all men, but if philosophy led him one way Church authority led him another.

AQUINAS.

Nor does Thomas Aquinas, 'the angelic doctor,' the greatest of the scholastics, the recognised interpreter of Catholic theology, entirely escape the danger of the 'blasphemy' of Pantheism. As if armed against it, he sets forth with all explicitness the absoluteness of God, and his entire separation from all that is created. No Eastern Anti-Materialist ever guarded the primal Godhead more zealously from any intrusive debasement. But this guarding is no sure protection. If, Aquinas asks, it is the essence of God 'to be,' what is the essence of things created? He answers that it is not being. His world of angels and demons, which corresponds to that of the Dionysian writings, has no being, it is finite. This must be the line which separates it from the Godhead, and yet he admits it has being, and is on one side infinite. The visible world was created according to the ideas existing eternally in the divine mind. These ideas, as Plato and all his true disciples had taught, were the types of the world that appears to our senses. They are parts of God's infinite knowledge; they are the essence of God—they are God. Aquinas' theology was a compromise—an eclectic gathering. His design was to separate God from his creation; but the interests of theology demanded that the separation be in some way abandoned—the chasm bridged over; and this Aquinas did, though contrary to his own design. 'There have been,' he says, 'some, as the Manichees, who said that spiritual and incorporeal things are subject to divine power, but visible and corporeal things are subject to the power of a contrary principle. Against these we may say that God is in all things by his power. There have been others again who, though they believed all things subject to divine power, still did not extend divine providence down to the lower parts, concerning which it is said in Job, "He walketh upon the hinges of heaven, and considereth not our concerns." And against them it is necessary to say, that God is in all things by his presence. There have been again others, who, though they said all things belonged to the providence of God, still laid it down that all things are not immediately created by God, but that he immediately created the first, and these created others. And against them it is necessary to say that he is in all things by his essence.' On the existence of evil, Aquinas made some refined distinctions, the simple meaning of which is, that evil has only a negative and not a positive existence. He did not affirm the eternity of creation; but he said it was impossible to refute it, for a beginning of creation was so opposed to reason that it could only be an object of faith.

BONAVENTURA.

Bonaventura may be ranked with the mystics, who followed a modified form of the doctrines of the Dionysian writings. He was partly influenced by the medieval Aristotle, but he leaned more to Plato, as Plato was then understood. He speaks of God as the beginning, the end, and the archetypal ground of all things. This was following the Patristic and Scholastic interpretation of Plato, that the 'ideas' which were the types of things created were the thoughts of God. 'The seraphic doctor' was the furthest removed from philosophy of all the schoolmen. For Plato and Aristotle, he substituted the life of St. Francis and apocryphal legends of the history of Christ. He exchanged dialectics for contemplation and meditation on the way of man's return to God. Yet that thought of Plato's, that the being of God is the essence of all created things, lay at the basis of his aspirations after the divine. 'His raptures,' says Dean Milman, 'tremble on the borders of Pantheism.'

DUNS SCOTUS.

Nor can ' the subtle doctor,' the great antagonist of Aquinas, be excluded from the category that contains the seraphic and the angelic doctors. The direction, says Ritter, which he gave to philosophy was throughout ecclesiastical. 'He is,' says Dean Milman, 'the most sternly orthodox of theologians.' And yet Duns Scotus is so much a Rationalist as to have denied the necessity of revelation, because of the abundance of knowledge attainable by natural reason. And when he comes to discourse of the relation of God to creation, he falls back on the ultra-Platonic argument of Plotinus, that matter is in its essence but another form of spirit. To call matter immaterial may seem a paradox; but with this definition, how easily does the orthodox Duns Scotus shake hands with the heretical David of Dinanto, and agree to call God the 'material' principle of all things. God is the single Monad above all creation both in earth and heaven. To this dogma of the church, as a churchman, Duns Scotus was pledged, but his philosophy cannot rest here. The primary matter, which is God, must in some way be throughout all things. This is accomplished by its being divided into three kinds: the universal, which is in all things; the secondary, which partakes both of the corruptible and incorruptible; and the tertiary, which is distributed among things subject to change. The schoolmen repudiated the consequences which we draw from their theology. They were the men pre-eminently orthodox—the true sons of the Church—the genuine defenders of the faith; but their history only adds a few more names to the large list of theologians who destroyed what they sought to establish, and established what they sought to destroy. It is satisfying to find the view of scholastic theology here advanced, sanctioned by the great names of Dean Milman and Bishop Hampden. 'In this system,' says Bishop Hampden, 'neither was the Deity identified with the individual acted upon, nor was the individual annihilated in the Deity. The distinctness of the divine Agent and the human recipient was maintained in accordance with the Scripture revelation of God as a sole being; separate in his nature from the works of providence and grace. Still, the notions of him as an energy—as a moving power—entered into all the explanations of the divine influence on the soul. So far, they were strictly Aristotelic; but with this exception, the Platonic notion of a real participation of Deity in the soul of man pervaded their speculations. Aristotle's idea of human improvement and happiness was rather that of a mechanical or material approach to the divine principle—an attainment of the Deity as our being's end and aim. We see a great deal of this in the Scholastic designation of the progress of man in virtue and happiness. Plato's view, on the other hand, was that of assimilation or association with the divinity. This notion more easily fell into the expressions of Scripture, which speak of man as created in the image of God, and which holds out to us an example of divine holiness for our imitation. The Pantheistic notion, then, of a participation of Deity, or the actual deification of our nature is the fundamental idea of the co-operation of grace according to the schoolmen. The Aristotelic idea of motion, of continual progress, of gradual attainment of the complete form of perfection, is the law by which this operation of grace is attempted to be explained. This system, made up of Platonic and Aristotelic views, was regarded as sanctioned by the Apostle, in his application of that text of philosophy, In him we live, and move, and have our being.'

M. Haureau says that Porphyry raised three questions: 1. Is a universal a subsisting reality? 2. If so, is it a body? 3. And does it exist independently of sensible objects—that is, of the individuals which alone appear to sense? The Realists said that genera and species possess being by participation —that which is real is Being. The Nominalists said that the realities of the Realists were only abstractions. M. Haureau also says that Aristotle defined essence as that which is universal to all, but substance as that which constitutes the personality of each. These were confounded by Aristotle's interpretors, which led to Spinozism. Aristotle would have said that there was no being who is the universal substance.

Ueberweg quotes Anselm saying, that only the poverty of languages compels us to express the *trina unitas* by the word *persona*, and that there is in the supreme Being no more a plurality of persons than of substances. This is an advance in the direction of Monarchianism, and departing from the generic Trinity of Basil, Gregory of Nyssa, and other Greek theologians.

Abelard is described by Ueberweg as following Augustine in identifying the

Platonic Trinity with the Christian. The good, the mind with the ideas, and the world-soul are interpreted as corresponding to Father, Son, and Holy Ghost. The earlier Scholastics are described as Platonic, but the later as modifying the doctrine of Aristotle to form ecclesiastical theology. Vol. ii., p. 429.

The English books referred to are Milman's Latin Christianity, and Hampden's Bampton Lectures.

CHAPTER IX.

THE ITALIAN REVIVAL.

WE have already seen how Aristotle agreed with Plato in the transcendentalism of his theology, though he reached that transcendentalism by an entirely different method. M. Rousselot says there were, in fact, two Aristotles in the middle ages, Aristotle the logician, who narrowly escaped being canonized, and without whom, as an Italian Cardinal said, ' the Church would have wanted some of the articles of faith.' The other was Aristotle the metaphysician, proscribed and persecuted, the author of all heresy.

The knowledge of Aristotle came to the schoolmen through a Latin translation, and the commentaries of the Arabian Averroes. That these commentaries did not agree with the text is now generally admitted, but what Averroeism is, is a question as wide as what Aristotelianism is. At one time it is the bulwark of heresy, at another time the refuge of the defenders of the faith. The later schoolmen, particularly Albertus Magnus and Thomas Aquinas, know no greater enemy of the Church than Averroes. The medieval painters gave him a place in inferno with Mahommed and Antichrist. Dante is more tolerant, having placed the philosopher among great men, in a region of peace and melancholy repose. His works had been translated into Latin about the end of the twelfth or the beginning of the thirteenth century, and had found so many advocates in the University of Paris as to provoke a host of opponents, and to bring down the censure of the Church. In a former chapter we classed such heretics as Amalric de Bena, with the Brothers and Sisters of the Free Spirit, as disciples of John Scotus Erigena. Three centuries had intervened, all traces of genealogy were lost, yet the similarity both of words and sentiments made the classification reasonable. There was, however, at work a powerful and living element, and it would be no idle inquiry to examine how far they might be considered children of Averroes. It is certain that most of the heretics of the middle ages sprang from the Franciscans. Almost every great movement for reform, for freedom of speech or thought, had its origin in the bosom of this order. They were the preachers of the ' Eternal Gospel,' the bold spirits that most rebelled against the Court of Rome, the prophets who, not without a mingling of enthusiasm, proclaimed the approach of a spiritual reign. Now the leaders of the Franciscan school favoured the philosophy of Averroes. ' Alexander of Hales,' says M. Renan, ' the founder of the Franciscan school, is the first of the Scholastics who had accepted and propagated the influence of the Arabian philosophy. John of Rochelle, his successor, follows the same tradition, and adopts for his own almost all the psychology of Avicenna. M. Haureau has justly observed that most of the propositions condemned at Paris by Stephen Templier in 1277 belonged to the Franciscan school, and that they had been borrowed by the boldest of Alexander de Hales' disciples, from the long ill-famed glosses of Avicenna and Averroes. The same year the Dominican, Robert of Kilwardby, Archbishop of Canterbury, in the council held at Oxford, the centre of the Franciscan school, condemned propositions almost identical, and in which the influence of Averroes could not be ignored. We may then believe that some of the philosophers against whom William of Auvergne, Albert and St. Thomas express themselves with so much severity, belonged to the order of St. Francis.'

But the history of Averroeism culminates at the University of Padua. It appears there first as a kind of free belief, embraced chiefly by physicians and men devoted to natural studies. From being in disgrace with the Church, it comes into favour. It then provokes opposition both from the side of philosophy and orthodox theology. It mingles its influence with the revival of letters, and then disappears as the morning star before the sun. Plato comes back and Scholasticism vanishes. Aristotle is read in Greek and his Arabian commentator seeks the shade. Cardinal Bembo celebrates in verse the great event. The morning dawns and the shadows flee away.

Nearly all the great men of the Universities both of Padua and Florence in the time of the revival are called Averroeists ; but this only in a very wide sense. They all exhibit in some way the influence of philosophy in its contact with the new direction which had been given to the physical sciences. They are all either metaphysicians or naturalists or both combined.

GIORDANO BRUNO.

Of those who are known as Pantheists, the most celebrated is Bruno, whom we may take as the representative of the Italian school proceeding from Averroes. It has been said above that most of the heretics and Averroeists belonged to the Franciscans, but Bruno was a monk of the order of St. Dominic. His history is well known, having been frequently recorded as that of one of the martyrs of philosophy and freedom of belief. With the zeal of a propagandist he travelled through Europe to disseminate his doctrines. Rome and Geneva expelled him as a dangerous teacher, but England and Protestant Germany permitted him to dispute in their universities. He was favoured by Queen Elizabeth and her court, but as the extravagancies of his doctrine became better known, he was compelled to leave our hospitable shores. At Florence he fell a victim to the Inquisition. After an imprisonment of six years, he expiated his heresies at the stake in presence of the cardinals and the most illustrious theologians of Rome. Bruno was wholly occupied with what Erigena called the higher speculation. At Oxford he declared himself the teacher of a more perfect theology and a purer wisdom than was then taught there. Like Erigena he essayed to harmonise this 'more perfect theology,' with the popular theological teaching. 'I define,' he says, 'the idea of God, otherwise than the vulgar, but it is not for that reason opposed to that of the vulgar. It is only more clear, more developed.' Judged merely by his theology, Bruno's title to be called a Christian is not less than Erigena's, but he is not so reverent. The great Erin-born never forgets that he is a Christian as well as a philosopher, but the Neopolitan is simply a speculator, aiming apparently at little more than the reputation of ingenuity and making a parade of his learning.

The starting point of his philosophy is the infinitude of the universe. A disciple of Copernicus, he denied the immobility of the earth, and with that perished every thought of the universe, having either a centre or a circumference. The saying of Hermes Trismegistus sometimes applied to God and sometimes to the world, is continually on his lips. 'The centre is here the circumference nowhere.' Bruno applies it to God, just because it is applicable to the universe. The infinite is realised in this visible creation in the immensity of celestial space. Nature is but a shadow, a phantom, the mirror in which the Infinite images himself. The basis of all things is mind, not matter. It is mind that pervades all. We ourselves are mind, and what we meet in creation is a corresponding mind. Creation does not present mere traces, or footprints of the Deity, but the Deity himself in his omnipresence.

We are compelled to believe that God is. This is a primal truth so obvious to reason, and so overwhelming in its evidence, that we cannot escape receiving it. The visible universe is an effect, it must have a cause. The worlds are all composed, and they can be dissolved. As they could not give themselves existence, there must be a first principle from whence they come. This principle must be infinite, and yet one. Though reason is impelled to the conclusion that there is a God, it cannot stop there. It must ask what God is ? who he is ? and how he is related to the visible infinite ? There are here two terms logically different, the primitive unity, and manifested nature, or the visible creation. In popular speech these are pure spirit, and matter, but these in their essence, so far as matter has an essence, are only one. The interval between them is filled up by an intermediary. This is the world-soul, which is God, and which yet mingles with matter. As a voice that fills the sphere where it resounds without being lost, so this world-soul becomes the essence of matter without ceasing to be God. It is the source of the general life of the world manifested in different degrees according to the rank of the creatures, the highest form being that of mind or soul. God transcends the world. To behold him in his transcendental character is the object of religion, but to find him in the forms and existences of the universe is the vocation of philosophy. There he is reflected in all his perfection, so that the contemplation of the infinite universe is of necessity the contemplation of God.

To understand this fully we must inquire into the nature of a principle and a cause. A principle is the intrinsical foundation; the eternal reason of a thing—the only source of its

potential existence. Cause is the exterior basis, the source of
the actual and present existence of an object. The principle
remains bound and inherent to the effect, and preserves the
essence of the object. For example, matter and form are united
together in the way of mutually sustaining each other. Cause,
on the contrary, is exterior to the effect and determines the external reality of the object. What an instrument is for a work,
or means for an end, that is a cause for its effect. Causes are
of three kinds, the efficient, the formal, and the final. The
efficient cause of the universe is the Being which acts ever and
everywhere, the universal intelligence, or chief faculty of the
soul of the world. It is this inconceivable power which fills
and enlightens all, which guides nature in the production of
all her works. What the faculty of thinking is in man to the
generation of ideas, that is the world soul to works of nature.
It is what Pythagoras called the mover of the world; Plato,
the architect of the universe; the Magi, the seed of seeds, that
which by its forms impregnates and fructifies matter. Orpheus
called it the eye of the world because it penetrates all things,
and because its harmonies and skilful proportions are found on
all sides. Empedocles called it the discerner because it develops
what is confused and enveloped in the bosom of matter and
death. For Plotinus it was a father, a generator, since it distributes germs and dispenses the forms of which the field of
nature is full and by which it is animated. 'We,' says Bruno,
'call it the interior artist. It is he who from within gives
form to the matter, who sends out from the root and grain, the
trunks and shoots; from the shoots, the branches; from the
branches, the twigs. He disposes and finishes within, the
tender tissue of the leaves, the flowers and the fruit. Again
from within he calls back the juices from the fruits, the flowers,
and the leaves to the branches, from the branches to the trunks,
and from the trunks to the roots. That which the interior
worker performs in the plants, he does also in animals. The
works of nature more manifestly than ours aré the works of
intelligence. We practise upon the surface of nature. We can
produce any work or invention just so far as there is a mind
working within us. Now if for our works we need intelligence,
how much more is an intelligence needed, for the living works
of nature?'

The world-soul is at once interior and exterior, reason, principle, and cause at the same time. A pilot in a ship follows the movements of the ship. He is part of the mass which is in motion ; and yet, as he is able to change the movement, he appears an agent who acts by himself. So it is with the world-soul. It penetrates and vivifies the universe. It constitutes the universal life. It appears but a part ; the interior and formal part of the universe. But as it determines all forms and organisaticns with their changing relations, it assumes the rank of a cause. Every form is the effect of soul. It is the soul's living expression. We cannot conceive anything which has no form. Mind alone is in the state of forming. There is nothing so sensual, nor so vile, that it does not contain mind. The spiritual substance, in order to become a plant or an animal, needs only a proper relation. It does not, however, follow, though soul is the essence of all things, and though life permeates all, that everything is therefore a living creature. The product of our arts, for instance, are not living forms. A table, so far as it is a table, is inanimate ; but since it derives its matter from nature, it is in consequence composed of living parts. All material things have form in them, which is the abiding essence, though they themselves are subject to continual change.

The substance of what Bruno had to say, though spread over many volumes, might be put into a few words. He connected his theology with the system of Copernicus ; but it, in reality, consisted of the idea with which we are now familiar—that the conception of infinity is the conception of God. The infinity of the universe is one and the same infinity as that of God. Its substance is not two-fold, corporeal and spiritual, but in its essence and root simply one, so that God is in all things. Multiplicity and difference are the result of combinations or alterations, the substance being ever the same. Pythagoras is quoted as knowing this, having once said that he did not fear death, for it was only a change. Bruno is generally represented as the forerunner of Spinoza ; but there is nothing in his works to entitle him to this distinction. A more just view is to look upon him as a reviver of old doctrines, which he reproduces with vivacity, and sometimes with eccentricity, but with little originality. He only repeats Aristotle, as he had been interpreted by the Averroeists. He opposed himself to the professed disciples of Aristotle in his time; but these were the disciples of Aristotle 'the logician,' not of Aristotle 'the metaphysician.'

OTHER ITALIAN PHILOSOPHERS.

Any classification of the eminent Italians of this period must be arbitrary. They mostly wished to adhere to the Catholic Church, yet many of them had embraced opinions in entire opposition to Christianity. When Sabinus, a friend of Melancthon's, was at Rome, he visited Cardinal Bembo, who asked him what Melancthon thought of the resurrection of the body and the life everlasting? Sabinus answered that it was evident, from the Reformer's writings, that he held these doctrines. 'Ah,' said the cardinal, 'I should have thought Philip a wise man if he had not believed these things.' When Vanini was in England, his zeal against the Reformation earned him a year's imprisonment. The famous Campanella, too, amid all his troubles, still tried to cling to the church. But the church condemned most of them as atheists, and Protestantism approved the condemnation. 'Modern atheists,' says Archbishop Tillotson, 'came first from Italy. They crossed the Alps into France, and from thence they came into England.'

Bruno's doctrines were received with more or less addition or modification by many eminent Italians, especially in Padua and Florence. It is impossible to classify them as Averroeists, or as opposed to Averroeism; for some taught the Arabian philosophy while they declared themselves opposed to it; and others avowed themselves Averroeists, meaning only that they were students of the commentaries on Aristotle. M. Renan enumerates among those who were Averroeists, in the wide sense of sceptics or enemies of Christianity, Cisalpini, Cardan, Berigard, and Vanini. Of the first, he says 'that his mind was too original to be confounded with a school that wanted originality.' In some points of his doctrine he is related to Averroes; but in his spirit and manner he in no way belongs to Paduan Averroeism. Nicholas Taurel, his adversary, finds his doctrine 'more absurd and more impious than that of Averroes.' Cisalpini says, 'There is but one life, which is the life of God, or the universal soul. God is not the efficient, but the constituent cause of the universe. Divine intelligence is unique, but human intelligence is multiplied according to the number of the individuals, for human intelligence is not actual, but potential.' Cisalpini was physician to the Pope, and was present at the burning of Bruno. He escaped the Inquisition, not because his doctrines were approved, but by the convenient method of professing to renounce philosophy as dangerous. ' I well know,' he said, ' that all these doctrines are full of errors against the faith, and these errors I regret ; but to refute them is not my business. I leave that task to theologians more profound than myself.'

The doctrine of Cardan is not without analogy to that of Cisalpini. All particular souls are regarded as virtually included in a universal soul, as the worm in the plant by which it is nourished. In one of the first treatises which he composed, Cardan admits, without restriction, the Averroeist hypothesis of the unity of intellect. In a later book he retracted his first sentiment, and acknowledged expressly that there could not exist a single intelligence for all animated beings, or for all men. He maintains there that this intelligence is to us purely personal, and that souls are distinct here below, and will be in another life. In a third writing, Cardan undertook to reconcile these two antagonistic opinions. Intelligence, he said, is single, but can be regarded from two points of view—either in its relation to eternal and absolute existence, or in relation to its manifestation in time. Single in its source, it is multiple in its manifestation.

On the individuality of the human soul, Berigard is more orthodox than either Cisalpini or Cardan. His claim to be considered an Averroeist is limited to his being in some measure an unbeliever in Christianity. The want of the spirit of Christianity among the learned Italians of the time of the revival was that which prevented them being among the great reformers of the church. It was seriously proposed to the Pope that the best way of putting down the Reformation in Germany was to circulate the writings of the Neo-Platonists.

To fix Vanini's place is not easy. Like Bruno, he was eccentric, and not over-reverent in his discourse. With a love of paradox, and a talent for disputation, he had enemies everywhere, and was never anxious to make friends. In one of his 'Dialogues' he records an example of his preaching, which shows at once his character and the theology in which he delighted. Preaching on the subject, Why did God create man ? he resolved the question by that famous scale of Averroes, according to which it is necessary that there be a kind of gradation from the lowest of all beings to the most exalted, which is God, or the first matter. At Genoa, Vanini wished to teach according to this doctrine ; but, says his biographer, 'the people there were not prepossessed in favour of Averroes, and he was obliged to depart.' These intimations would justify us in classing Vanini with Bruno. But his published works present some difficulties. He professed to refute the doctrines which it is believed he adopted as his own creed. His 'Amphitheatrum' was a defence of Christianity and the Catholic Church against ancient philosophers, atheists, epicureans, peripatetics, and stoics. As such it was published with the approbation of the divines of the Sorbonne. He expressly refutes the Averroeist theories of the eternity of the world, of intelligence, providence, and the unity of souls ; but the Inquisition thought they discovered that he had not used the best arguments in defence of the Christian doctrines ; and they suspected, too, perhaps not without cause, that what he professed to refute was always the doctrine he wished to inculcate. M. Renan, who is severe on Vanini, thinks that in this interpretation of the 'Amphitheatrum,' the Inquisition were not wanting in discernment. They found him guilty of the charge of atheism, for which, like his brother priest and philosopher, he was burned at the stake. Vanini was surely the most unfortunate of men. No author seems to have had a word of sympathy for him ; and yet science has rarely had a more ardent votary, or theology a more zealous student. When a young man at the University of Florence, though struggling with the hardships of poverty, he was not content with what learning was simply necessary to obtain orders, but devoted himself to physic and the natural sciences. Before he was of age to be admitted to the priesthood, he rejoiced in being 'Doctor of both Laws.' He travelled through Europe, defending the Catholic faith against all 'atheists, infidels, Protestants, and other heretics.' But Vanini himself was at last suspected of something worse than heresy. Though the doctors of the Sorbonne had pronounced his great work 'skilful in argument, and well worthy of type,' the Inquisition condemned it. When the inquisitors examined his property, they found among his possessions a crystal glass containing a live toad. This was proof to demonstration, not only that he denied the existence of God, but that he was in league with some other existence. No protestations of orthodoxy; no confessions of his faith could convince his enemies. They loaded him with insult, calling his confession hypocrisy. The judge asking what he thought concerning the existence of God, Vanini answered:— 'I believe with the church, one God in three persons, and that nature evidently demonstrates the existence of the Deity.' Seeing a straw on the ground, he took it up, and continuing to address the judge, he said—'This straw obliges me to confess that there is a God;' and, after a long and beautiful discourse on Providence, he added—'The grain being cast into the earth, appears at first to be destroyed; but it quickens, then it becomes green and shoots forth, insensibly growing out of the earth. The dew assists it springing up, and the rain gives it yet a greater strength. It is furnished with ears, the points of which keep off the birds. The stalk rises and is covered with leaves. It becomes yellow, and rises higher. Soon after it withers and dies. It is threshed, and the straw being separated from the corn, the latter serves for the nourishment of man, and the former is given to animals created for man's use.'

SERVETUS.

Michael Servetus was a Spaniard, but his doctrines identify him with the philosophers of Padua. He was purely a child of the renaissance, combining the physical studies that were common in his time with the speculations of the Neo-Platonists and the theosophy of such scientific mystics, as Paracelsus. He was burned at Geneva for opposing the ecclesiastical dogma of the Trinity, which he might have interpreted so as to harmonize with the rest of his creed, which would only have been to understand it as it was understood by many of the fathers, the schoolmen, and the medieval mystics. The divine Being, he said, was one and indivisible. The church, as corrupted, has divided this being into three persons, which had been the cause of the unbelief of the Mahommedans, the ridicule of the Jews, and of great perplexity to many Christians. Before Constantine's time the church made no personal difference in God. He was one, but had different modes of manifestation or self disposition, and these were eternal. The Word or Son of God was not a person, but God's idea which was afterwards realized in the creation of the world. He is the archetype or chief of all the ideas or images in the divine mind. The Word acquires personality in time by its miraculous incarnation in human flesh. The Holy Spirit was eternally in the Word, and was the soul of Christ or the Word manifested in time. There were not two natures in Christ, but only one, for his body as well as his soul was divine. It was formed by the divine principle of light. He submitted to a human development, which ended with his resurrection, when he laid aside everything corruptible. 'God,' says Servetus, 'makes himself known in, and through, creation, so that not only is every living but every lifeless thing an aspect of the Deity.' Before creation was, God was, but he was neither light nor spirit, but an ineffable something. Light, word, and spirit are mere dispensations or modes of pre-existing Deity. Again, Servetus says, ' God created the world out of himself, of his substance, and as essence he actuates all things. The Spirit of God is the universal agent; it is in the air we breathe, and is the very breath of life. It moves the heavenly bodies, sends out the winds from their quarters, takes up and stores the water in the clouds, and pours it out as rain to fertilise the earth. God is distinct from the universe of things, and when we speak of the Word, the Son, and the Holy Spirit, we but speak of the presence and power of God projected into creation, animating and actuating all that therein is, man more especially than anything else.'

This chapter is largely indebted to M. Renan's *Averroes et l'Averroisme*, which contains some incredible accounts of the schoolmen's knowledge of Aristotle. A copy of Vanini's *Amphitheatrum* is in the British Museum. Dorner treats of this period in his History of Protestantism. A sketch of Italian Philosophy by Vincenzo Botta is appended to the English edition of Ueberweg.

CHAPTER X.

MYSTICS.

UNDER the head of Mystics, we might class many names that have been already disposed of. All religion is more or less mystical—that is to say, it is an inward intuition, a divine sentiment in the soul. The Brahmans, the Buddhists, the Alexandrians, Jewish, Heathen, and Christian, were all Mystics. In some, this spirit has been so largely developed that they have been called pre-eminently Mystics. Such were Plotinus and St. Dionysius; his successor, Maximus, and his medieval disciples. Every great religious movement has been connected directly or indirectly with some Mystic or some unusual manifestation of the mystical spirit.

The most important of modern Mystics who have been called Pantheists, are those of Germany. Dr. Ullmann traces their origin to the societies of the Beghards, Beguines, and the Brethren of the Free Spirit. If this be correct, and there seems no reason for doubting it, we have all the links of the succession established from Dionysius and the early Mystics, through John Scotus Erigena down to the Reformation. 'The basis of their doctrines (the Beghards),' says Dr. Ullmann, 'was Mystical Pantheism, as that is to be found principally among the Brethren of the Free Spirit.'

Inasmuch, however, as during the whole of the middle ages, the chief object of interest was not nature, but more predominantly man, contemplation was then directed less to the divine Being in the general universe, and almost exclusively to God in mankind; the former being adduced merely as a consequence or supplement of the latter. The great thing was God in the mind, or the consciousness of man. Hence, the Pantheism of these parties was not materialistic but idealistic. The creatures, so they supposed, are in and of themselves a pure nullity. God alone is the true being; the real substance of all things. God, however, is chiefly present where there is mind, and conse-

quently in man.   In the human soul there is an uncreated and
eternal thing, namely, the intellect; that is, the divine principle in man, in virtue of which he resembles, and is one with
God.   Indeed, in so far as he purely exists, he is God himself;
and it may be said, that whatever belongs to the divine nature
belongs likewise, and in a perfect way, to a good and righteous
man.   Such a man works the same works as God.   With God
he created the heavens and the earth, and with God he begat
the eternal Word; and God without him can do nothing.   Such
a man was Christ.   In Christ, as a being both of divine and
human nature, there was nothing peculiar or singular.   On the
contrary, what Scripture affirms of him is likewise perfectly
true of every righteous and good man.   The same divine things
which the Father gave to the Son, he has also given to us; for
the good man is the only begotten Son of God, whom the
Father has begotten from all eternity.   Man becomes like
Christ when he makes his will conformable in all respects to
the will of God, when forsaking all things and renouncing all
human wishes, desires, and endeavours, he so completely merges
himself in, and gives himself up to, the divine being, as to be
wholly changed, and transubstantiated into God, as the bread
in the sacrament is into the body of Christ.   To the man who
is thus united with God, or to speak more properly, who recol-
lects his primeval unity, all the differences and contrarieties of
life are done away.   In whatever he is or does, though to others
it may seem sin and evil, he is good and happy.   For the essential property of the divine nature is, that it excludes all
differences.   God is neither good nor bad.   To call him good,
would just be like calling white black.   His glory is equally
revealed in all things; yea, even in all evil, whether of guilt or
penalty.   Hence, if it be his will that we should sin, whatever
the sin may be, we ought not to wish not to have committed
it, and to be sensible of this is the only true repentance.   But
the will of God is manifested by the disposition which a man
feels towards a particular action.   Hence, though he may have
committed a thousand mortal sins, still supposing him to have
been disposed for them, he ought not to wish not to have committed them.   Neither, to speak strictly, has God enjoined
external acts.   No external act is good or godly; and on such
an act no influence is exerted by God; but all depends upon

the union of the mind with him. That being the case, man ought not to desire or pray for anything, save what God ordains. Whoever prays to God for a particular blessing, prays for a wrong thing, and in a wrong way; for he prays for a thing contrary to God's nature. For this reason a man ought well to consider, whether he should wish to receive any boon from God, because in that case he would be his inferior, like a servant or slave; and God, in giving it, would be something apart from him. But this should not take place in the life eternal; there we should rather reign with him. God is truly glorified, only in those who do not strive after property; honour or profit; piety or holiness; recompense, or the kingdom of heaven; but who have wholly renounced all such things.'

This account of the doctrine of the Beghards, has the disadvantage of coming from enemies; by whom it may have been exaggerated, and perhaps the meaning perverted. The source of it is the bull of Pope John XXII., by whom the Beghards were condemned. Dr. Ullmann has used the terms in which the propositions ascribed to them were set forth, admitting their general accuracy, yet willing to make allowance for the difference between a doctrine in itself and the representation of it by an enemy. But whether the extravagances were in the Beghards' teaching, or only in the Papal representations, need not concern us much. We can see in the general features the reappearance of doctrines which we have already met, clothed in more moderate language, and in a more interesting form. Ruysbroek, who was himself a Mystic, gives a description of the Beghards, which corresponds generally with that of the Papal Bull. He divides them into four classes, ascribing a peculiar form of heresy to each, while he accuses them all of the fundamental error of making man's unity with God to be a unity of nature and not of grace. The godly man, he admitted, is united to God, not however in virtue of his essence, but by a process of re-creation and regeneration. The first class he calls heretics against the Holy Ghost, because they claimed a perfect identity with the Absolute, which reposes in itself and is without act or operation. They said that they themselves were the divine essence, above the persons of the Godhead, and in as absolute a state of repose as if they did not at all exist; inasmuch as the Godhead itself does not act, the Holy Ghost

M

being the sole operative power in it. The second class were heretics against the Father, because they placed themselves simply and directly on an equality with God; contemplated the I as entirely one with the divinity, so that from them all things proceeded, and being themselves by nature God, they had come into existence of their own free will. 'If I had not so willed,' one of them said, 'neither I nor any other creature would ever have existed at all. God knows, wills, and can do nothing without me; heaven and earth hang upon my head. The glory given to God is also paid to me, for I am by nature essentially God. There are no persons in God. But only one God exists, and with him I am the self-same one which he is.' The third class were heretics against Christ, because they said, that in respect of their divinity they were begotten of the Father, and in respect of their humanity begotten in time. What Christ was they were; and when he was elevated in the host, they too were elevated with him. The fourth class were heretics against the church, for they despised not only all its ordinances, but set themselves above knowledge, contemplation, and love. They despised both the finite and the infinite; the present life and the eternal. They soared above themselves, and all created things; above God and the Godhead, maintaining that neither God nor themselves, neither action nor rest, neither good nor evil, blessedness nor perdition has any existence. They considered themselves so lost as to have become the 'absolute Nothing' which they believed God to be. Dr. Ullmann, though far from sympathising with the Beghards, considers even Ruysbroek's delineation as half apochryphal.

MASTER ECKART.

John Eckart, Provincial of the Order of the Dominicans, the most famous of German Mystics, is supposed to have been a Beghard; but there is no evidence beyond the likeness of his doctrines to the propositions condemned by the Bull of John XXII., and the fact that the Beghards, who were numerous in Germany in his time, appealed to his writings as confirming their doctrines. Eckart had been a professor in Paris, where the influence of Abelard, William of Champeaux, and Amalric de Bena could scarcely have been ended. He was familiar with the works of the Areopagite and Scotus Erigena; the Neo-Platonist philosophers; and, above all, of Plato, whom he often quotes, and whom he calls 'the great clerk.' He was not aware that he taught anything different from the doctrines of the Catholic Church, supposing Platonism and Neo-Platonism to be compatible with Christianity. In this belief he clung to the Catholic faith to his last hour, though he had been condemned at Cologne by the archbishop, and though his condemnation was afterwards confirmed by the pope.

Eckart's theology may be learned from some passages in his sermons. 'All that is in the Godhead,' he says, 'is one; thereof we can say nothing. It is above all names and above all nature. The essence of all creatures is eternally a divine life in deity. God works but not the Godhead. Therein are they distinguished in working and not working. The end of all things is the hidden darkness or the eternal Godhead; unknown, and never to be known.' Here we have that hidden darkness which is the same as the Dionysian Abysses of light; and that Godhead, who is above being, and only becomes God as he works, and creates. In the Godhead, Creator and creature are one; but when the creature becomes a creature, God becomes God. 'In himself,' says Eckart in another place, 'he is not God, in the creature only doth he become God. I ask to be rid of God, that is, that God by his grace, would bring me into the essence; that essence which is above God, and above distinction, I would enter into that eternal unity which was mine before all time, and when I was what I would, and would what I was; into that state which is above all addition or diminution, into the immobility whereby all is moved.'

To be rid of God, in order to blessedness, is an expression apparently in contradiction to the system which makes man one with God; but Eckart's meaning is never obscure. He longs for a return to that fountain of the Godhead, when as yet God was not distinct from the Godhead. In another passage, he says, 'In every man who hath utterly abandoned self, God must communicate himself according to all his power, so completely that he retains nothing in his life, in his essence, in his Godhead he must communicate all to the bringing forth of fruit.' Again, 'When the will is so united that it becometh a one in oneness, then doth the heavenly Father produce his only begotten Son

in himself and me, I am one with him. He cannot exclude
me. In this self-same operation doth the Holy Ghost receive
his existence, and proceed from me, as from God. Wherefore ?
I am in God, and if the Holy Ghost deriveth not his being
from me, he deriveth it not from God. I am in no wise
excluded.'

In other places he declares his oneness with Deity, 'God and
I are one in knowing, God's essence is his knowing, and God's
knowing makes me to know him. Therefore is his knowing
my knowing. The eye whereby I see God is the same eye
whereby he seeth me, mine eye and the eye of God are one eye,
one vision, one knowledge, and one love.'

'There is something in the soul which is above the soul,
divine, simple, an absolute nothing; rather unnamed than
named ; unknown than known. So long as thou lookest on thyself as a something, so long thou knowest as little what there is,
as my mouth knows what colour is, or as my eye knows what
taste is. Of this I am wont to speak in my sermons, and sometimes have called it a power, sometimes an uncreated light, sometimes a divine spark. It is absolute and free from all names
and forms, as God is free and absolute in himself. It is higher
than knowledge, higher than love, higher than grace, for in all
these there is still distinction. In this power doth blossom and
flourish God with all his Godhead, and the Spirit flourisheth in
God. In this power doth the Father bring forth his only begotten Son, as essentially as in himself, and in this light ariseth
the Holy Ghost. This spark rejects all creatures, and will
have only God, simply as he is in himself. It rests satisfied
neither with the Father, nor the Son, nor the Holy Ghost, nor
with the three persons, so far as each exists in its respective
attributes. I will say what will sound more marvellous still.
This light is satisfied only with the super-essential essence. It
is bent on entering into the simple ground, the still waste
wherein is no distinction neither Father, Son, nor Holy Ghost;
into the unity where no man dwelleth. Then is it satisfied in
the light, then it is one ; then it is one in itself—as this ground
is a simple stillness, in itself immovable, and yet by this immobility are all things moved.'

'God is a pure good in himself, and therefore will dwell
nowhere, save in a pure soul. There he may pour himself out;

into that he can wholly flow. What is purity? It is that man should have turned himself away from all creatures, and have set his heart so entirely on the pure good, that no creature is to him a comfort; that he has no desire for aught creaturely, save as far as he may apprehend therein, the pure good, which is God. And as little as the bright eye can endure aught foreign in it, any stain between it and God. To it all creatures are pure to enjoy, for it enjoyeth all creatures in God, and God in all creatures. Yea, so pure is that soul, that she seeth through herself. She needeth not to seek God afar off, she finds him in herself when in her natural purity she hath flown out into the supernatural of the pure Godhead. And thus is she in God, and God in her; and what she doeth she doeth in God, and God doeth it in her.'

'I have a power in my soul which enables me to perceive God I am as certain as that I live, that nothing is so near to me as God. He is nearer to me than I am to myself. It is a part of his essence that he should be nigh and present to me. He is also nigh to a stone or a tree, but they do not know it. If a tree could know God and perceive his presence, as the highest of the angels perceive it, the tree would be as blessed as the highest angel. And it is because man is capable of perceiving God, and knowing how nigh God is to him that he is better off than a tree.'

'The words I AM none can truly speak but God alone. He has the substance of all creatures in himself.' 'He is a being that has all being in himself.' 'All things are in God, and all things are God.' 'All creatures in themselves are nothing; all creatures are a speaking of God.' 'Doest thou ask me what was the purpose of the Creator when he made the creature. I answer, repose. Consciously, or unconsciously, all creatures seek their proper state. The stone cannot cease moving till it touch the earth; the fire rises up to heaven; thus a loving soul can never rest but in God, and so we say God has given to all things their proper place. To the fish, the water; to the bird, the air; to the beast, the earth; to the soul, the Godhead. Simple people suppose that we are to see God, as if he stood on that side and we on this. It is not so—God and I are one in the act of my perceiving him.' Concluding a sermon, in a lofty flight of impassioned eloquence, Eckart cries, 'O

noble soul! put on thou wings to thy feet, and rise above all
creatures, and above thine own reason; and above the angelic
choirs; and above the light that has given me strength, and
throw thyself upon the heart of God, there shalt thou be hidden
from all creatures.'

Eckart might well ask his hearers, as it is said he used to do
at the end of his sermon, if they had understood him, telling
those who did not, not to trouble themselves, for only those
who were like the truth could know it.   It was not something
to be thought out by the reason, but something to be received
in the soul's intuition, for 'it came directly out of the heart of
God.'

RUYSBROEK.

When the Beghards had brought down upon themselves the
opposition of the church, their existence as societies was no
longer possible.   At Cologne, their headquarters, many were
cast into the Rhine, and some burned at the stake; while
throughout Germany and the Netherlands the church waged
against them a war of extermination.   From their embers
arose a new fraternity, mystical as they had been, and like
them also celebrated for their pious and benevolent labours.
This was the fraternity of the 'Brethren of the Common Lot.'
But between the Beghards and this new Brotherhood there
was a famous Mystic, whom Dr. Ullmann regards as 'a transition link between them.'   This was John Ruysbroek, who
has been already mentioned.   He was by birth a Belgian, but
in his mind and character a German.   He was destined to
exercise a great influence on the mystical writers who immediately preceded the Reformation.   Ruysbroek's first
appearance was as an opponent of the extravagances of the
Beghards, from whom, as we have already intimated, he differed
materially.   Eckart said that God and man were one 'by
nature.'   Ruysbroek would not admit this, but tried to show
how man might become one with God through contemplation
and purification of the soul; but this union, he continually
repeated, was of such a character that man did not lose his
independent existence, or dissolve into deity.   'God,' he said,
'is the super-essential essence of all being, eternally reposing

in himself; and yet, at the same time, the living and moving principle of all that he has created. In respect of this substance he is everlasting rest, in which there is neither time nor place, neither before nor after, neither desire nor possession, neither light nor darkness. This God is one in his nature and triune in his persons. The Father is the eternal, essential, and personal principle. He begets eternal wisdom—the Son; his uncreated and personal image. From the mutual intuition of the two, there flows an everlasting complacency, a fire of love, which burns for ever between the Father and the Son; this is the Holy Spirit, who continually proceeds from the Father and the Son, and returns into the nature of the Godhead. This triune Godhead is transfused in a threefold way into the human soul, which is its image. The deepest root and the proper essence of our soul, which is this eternal image of God, rests for ever in him. We all possess it, as eternal life, without our own agency; and prior to our creation in God. After our creation, however, three faculties take their rise in the substance of our soul; shapeless vacuity, by which we receive the Father; the highest intellect, by which we receive the Son; and the spark of the soul, by which we receive the Holy Ghost, and become one spirit and one love with God.'

Man having proceeded from God, is destined to return and become one with him again. But this takes place in such a way that God never ceases to be God, nor the creature a creature. This is a sentiment often repeated; but the intenseness with which Ruysbroek expresses this union often leads him, as it were unconsciously, into the language of the Beghards. He has admitted, as we have seen above, that man has the root of his being in God, and speaking of the return of the soul to the divine fountain, he says, 'The spirit becomes the very truth which it apprehends. God is apprehended by God. We become one with the same light with which we see, and which is both the medium and object of our vision.'

Dr. Ullmann, while admitting the doubtful meaning of some passages like this, yet contends earnestly that Ruysbroek was no Pantheist. The ground of his argument is, that Ruysbroek, while recognising the immanence of God in the world, never fails to assert that he also transcends the world. He overflows into the universe; dwells ever originally in all created minds, and unites himself in the closest manner to the pious soul; yet he rests eternally in his own essence, and, independently of the world, possesses and enjoys himself in his Godhead and its persons.

To the practical side of Ruysbroek's Mysticism, Dr. Ullmann traces the establishment of the 'Brotherhood of the Common Lot,' and in the other side, the contemplative, he sees the continuation of the Mysticism which had reached its culminating point in Eckart.

JOHN TAULER.

The mystical succession was continued at Cologne by John Tauler, a monk of the Dominican order. Tauler was a great favourite with the German Reformers. Luther and Melancthon often speak of him. His sermons and religious discourses are devoted chiefly to the points most dear to all mystics—God in his being; our origin in and from him, and our return to him again. His words have the ring of the often condemned speculation, but it is urged for him, as for Ruysbroek, that the union with God of which he speaks is rather religious and moral, than a oneness of essence; that while Eckart was a bold speculator, 'rearing a system which, like the dome of the Cathedral of the city in which he lived, towered aloft like a giant, or rather like a Titan assaulting heaven,' Tauler was more a man of sentiment, expressing the deep feelings of an overflowing soul. There may be truth in this distinction, but it may be urged, on the other side, that the difference is less in the doctrines than in the mental character of the men, which to the same doctrine gives different forms. 'Godly men,' says Tauler, 'are called God-like, for God lives, forms, ordains, and works in them all his works; and doth, so to speak, use himself in them.' Here we have God's immanency in man. Human ife is God's life, for God lives in man. He exists in the human soul, for he uses himself there. This, however, is spoken only of the godly, and must be understood with this limitation. Other passages illustrate the advantages of the annihilation of self that God may become all. 'The created nothing,' says Tauler, 'sinks in the uncreated, incomprehensibly, unspeakably. Herein is true what is said in the Psalter, "Deep calleth unto deep," for the uncreated deep calls the created, and these two deeps become entirely one. There hath the created spirit lost itself in the Spirit of God—yea, is drowned in the bottomless sea of Godhead.' 'God,' he says again, 'is a spirit, and our created spirit must be united to and lost in the uncreated, even as it existed in God before creation. Every moment in which the soul re-enters into God, a complete restoration takes place. If it be done a thousand times in a day, there is each time a true regeneration. As the Psalmist saith, "This day have I begotten thee." This is when the inmost of the spirit is sunk and dissolved in the inmost of the divine nature ; and is thus new-made and transformed. God thus pours himself out into our spirit, as the sun rays forth its material light, and fills the air with sunshine, so that no eye can tell the difference between the sunshine and air. If the union of the sun and air cannot be distinguished, how far less this divine union of the uncreated spirit. Our spirit is received and utterly swallowed up in the abyss which is its source. Then the spirit transcends itself and all its powers, and mounts higher and higher towards the Divine Dark, even as an eagle towards the sun.' 'Let man simply yield himself to God ; ask nothing, desire nothing, love and mean only God—yea, and such an unknown God. Let him lovingly cast all his thoughts and cares, and his sins, too, as it were on that unknown Will. Some will ask what remains after a man hath thus lost himself in God ? I answer nothing but a fathomless annihilation of himself ; an absolute ignoring of all reference to himself personally ; of all aim of his own in will and heart, in way, in purpose, or in use. For in this self-loss man sinks so deep that if he could out of pure love and love-liness sink deeper—yea, and become absolutely nothing—he would do so right gladly. O, dear child ! in the midst of all these enmities and dangers, sink thou into thy ground and nothingness, and let the tower with all its bells fall upon thee —yea, let all the devils in hell storm out upon thee. Let heaven and earth and all their creatures assail thee ; all shall but marvellously serve thee. Sink thou only into thy nothing-ness, and the better part shall be thine.'

Tauler speaks of this ground of the soul as that which is in-separable from the divine essence, and wherein man has by grace what God has by nature. He quotes Proclus as saying 'that while man is busied with images which are beneath us, and clings to such, he cannot possibly return into his ground and essence.' 'If,' he says, 'thou wilt know by experience what such a ground truly is, thou must forsake all the manifold and gaze thereon with intellectual eye alone. But wouldst thou come nearer yet, turn thine intellectual eyes right therefrom, for even the intellect is beneath thee, and become one with the One—that is, unite thyself with the Unity. This Unity Proclus calls "the calm, silent, slumbering, and incomprehensible divine darkness." To think, beloved in the Lord, that a heathen should understand so much and so far, and we be so behind, may well make us blush for shame. To this our Lord Jesus Christ testifies, when he says "the kingdom of God is within you"—that is, this kingdom is born in the inmost ground of all, apart from all that the powers of mind can accomplish. In this ground the eternal, heavenly Father doth bring forth his only begotten Son, a hundred thousand times quicker than in an instant, according to our apprehension, ever anew in the light of eternity, in the glory and immutable brightness of his own self. He who would experience this must turn himself inward, far away from all working of his outward and inward powers and imagination—from all that ever cometh from without, and then sink and dissolve himself in the ground. Then cometh the power of the Father, and calls the man into himself through the only begotten Son, and so the Son is born out of the Father, and returneth unto the Father, and such a man is born, in the Son, of the Father, and floweth back with the Son unto the Father again, and becomes one with them.'

Dr. Ullmann says that Tauler, in respect of doctrine, kept apparently within the limits assigned by the church; and though he raised against him ecclesiastical opposition, it was less for what he taught than for his inward piety and his zeal against the sins of the clergy.

HEINRICH SUSO.

Suso, a disciple of Master Eckart, was another of the celebrated mystics of Cologne. It is said, that though he embraced the principle of union with God by self-annihilation, yet he never entirely occupied the ground of Pantheism on which his master speculated. Suso was a monk of the Dominican order; famous as a preacher and distinguished for his piety and benevolence; an ardent lover of the monastic life, and a great enemy to the corruptions of the church. His definition of God is purely Dionysian—being which is equal to non-being. ' He is not any particular being, or made up of parts. He is not a being that has still to be, or is capable of any possibility of receiving addition; but pure, simple, undivided universal being. This pure and simple being is the supreme cause of actual being, and includes all temporal existences as their beginning and end. It is in all things, and out of all things, so that we may say " God is a circle whose centre is everywhere. his circumference nowhere." ' On the union of man with God he speaks with the same guarded expressions as Ruysbroek, maintaining the unity, yet holding the creature to be still a creature. Man vanishes into God. All things become God, yet in such a way that the created is the created still. ' A meek man,' he says, ' must be deformed from the creature, conformed to Christ, and transformed into the deity; yet the divine thou and the human I continue to exist.' 'The soul,' he says again, ' passes beyond time and space, and with a loving inward intuition is dissolved in God. This entrance of the soul banishes all forms, images, and multiplicity. It is ignorant of itself and all things. Reduced to its essence it hovers on the brink of the Trinity. At this elevation there is no effort, no struggle; the beginning and the end are one. Here the divine nature doth as it were embrace and mildly kiss through and through the soul that they may be one for ever. He who is thus received into the eternal nothing is in the everlasting now, and hath neither before nor after. Rightly hath Dionysius said that God is non-being; that is, above all our notions of being. We have to employ images and similitudes, as I must do in setting forth such truths, but know that all such figures are as much below the reality as a blackamore is below the sun. In this absorption of which I speak, the soul is still a creature; but, at the same time, hath no thought whether it be a creature or no.'

THE THEOLOGIA GERMANICA.

This pious mystical book, the author of which is unknown, belonged to the age of Tauler, and was probably written by some of the mystics of his brotherhood. It begins with an ontological application of St. Paul's words, 'When that which is perfect is come then things which are in part shall be done away.' The Perfect is that being 'who hath comprehended and included all things in himself and his own substance, and without whom and besides whom there is no true substance, and in whom all things have their substance, for he is the substance of all things, and is in himself unchangeable and immovable, yet changeth and moveth all things.' The things which are in part, are explained as those things which may be apprehended, known and expressed; but the Perfect is that which cannot be known, apprehended, or expressed by any creature. For this reason the Perfect is nameless. No creature as a creature can name it or conceive it. Before the Perfect can be known in the creature, all creature qualities such as I and self must be lost and done away. God, or the eternally good, is that which truly exists. Evil has no real being, because it does not really exist. Anything exists just in proportion as it is good. The author of the 'Theologia Germanica' does not hesitate to carry this principle to its utmost extent, even saying that the devil is good, so far as he has being.

Submission to eternal goodness is described as the soul's freedom. He is not free who looks for a reward of his well-doing, or who does what is right through fear of hell punishment. He alone is free who loves goodness for its own sake, and does what is right because in well-doing is blessedness. 'What is Paradise?' the author asks, and he answers, 'all things that are, for all are goodly and pleasant, and therefore may be fitly called a paradise. It is said also that paradise is an outer court of heaven. Even so this world is verily an outer court of the eternal, or of eternity, and specially whatever in time or any temporal things or creatures manifesteth or remindeth us of God or eternity, for the creatures are a guide and a path unto God and eternity. Thus the world is an outer court of eternity; and, therefore, it may well be called a paradise, for it is such in truth; and in this paradise all things are lawful save one tree and the fruit thereof—nothing is contrary to God but self-will; to will otherwise than as the eternal Will would have it.'

This book was a great favourite with the Reformers. Luther edited it and recommended it to the people. Spener says 'that it was the Holy Scriptures, the "Theologia Germanica" and the sermons of Tauler, that made Luther what he was.' From the title of it the German Mystics were called 'German Theologians.' Anticipating the reproach of thus identifying himself with Eckart and Tauler, Luther said, 'We shall be called German Theologians;' and he answers, 'well, German Theologians let us be.'

Of all the German Mystics, Dr. Ullmann considers Eckart alone to be a decided Pantheist. He classes all the others as Theists, except the author of the 'Theologia Germanica.' Of this book, he says that it contains the elements of Pantheism, yet a Pantheism not of speculation, but of the deepest and the purest piety.' He had difficulty, as others before him, in drawing the lines of distinction. This book which, before the Reformation, had great influence among the Catholics of Germany, has since been placed in the index of books forbidden; but among the Lutherans it is still in high esteem.

JACOB BÖHME.

Luther retained much of the spirit of the German Mystics, but neither he nor his immediate followers adopted their theology. The mystical succession was broken in Germany for more than a century. It was then taken up by Jacob Böhme, the philosophical shoemaker of Görlitz. Böhme was a member of the Lutheran church, the authorities of which treated him as the Catholic church did Eckart and Tauler. Böhme's meaning is often obscure. He had not the learning of the pre-Reformation Mystics, but what he wants in learning he amply makes up for in originality.

We can either, he says, begin at man and reason up to God, or we can begin at God and reason down to man; the conclusion either way will be the same. To know ourselves is to know

God, for we are a similitude of the Deity—a living image of the eternal divine nature. That which is in the triune God is manifested in nature, and creation; and of this entire nature and creation, man is the epitome.

Beginning with the consideration of the infinite Being, we can contemplate him as he is in himself; as he is in his Word or eternal nature; and as he is in the visible creation, 'the outspoken or visible word.' In himself, God is an eternal unity; an eternal nothing; an abyss without time or space. He needs no habitation, for he is without and within the world equally alike; deeper than thought; higher than imagination; no numbers can express his greatness, for he is endless and infinite. He manifests himself in his Word, eternal nature—the All of the universe. He fills all things, and is in all things. 'The being of God is like a wheel in which many wheels are made one in another, upwards, downwards, crossways, and yet continually all of them turn together.' The whole of nature; heaven, earth and above the heavens is the body of God. The powers of the stars are the fountain veins in this natural body, which is the world or universe.

The process of the divine going forth from nothing to something is on this wise. In the abyssal nothing there is an eternal will, which is the Father; and an apprehending mind, which is the Son. From the will and mind there is a procession which is the Spirit. The Father eternally generates the Son. The Son is the wisdom in which all things are formed. The Spirit expresses the egress of the will and mind, 'standing continually in the flash wherein life is generated.' This triune Being is yet but one essence, which is the Essence of all essences. It is enough to name him God, but with the very conception of God there is introduced that of eternal nature. Of this nature God is the root and the ground; but he is not before it, for it is co-eternal with him. The external world is the out-birth of this nature. In the one are all the principles that are found in the other. But though eternal nature is divine, for into it God enters as he is in himself an eternal good, yet the external world cannot be so unreservedly called divine, for into it he enters both as wrath and love. God is in all things as the sap in the green and flourishing tree. He lives in the stars and the elements of nature. He is present in the tiniest of insects, and the meanest of herbs. By his wisdom, and of his essence is all creation made. In the stillness of the evening twilight we may feel the presence of the Holy Spirit, in whose kingdom all creatures rejoice to live. If our eyes are purified we may see God everywhere. He is in us, and we are in him, and if our lives are holy we may know ourselves to be God. All lies in man, he is the living book of God and all things.

These doctrines are repeated in Böhme's writings times without number, and with so many modifications and further developments, as to make it difficult to set them forth definitely as constituting an harmonious system. The root idea seems to be a dualism, like what is found among the Gnostics, but with this difference, that Böhme receives no principle as independent of the being of God, but posits a duality of principles in the very essence of God.

In this essence is an opposition of darkness and light, fierceness and tenderness, and from this proceeds all opposition in the life of nature and of spirit, and even the opposition of good and evil. There is a duality of principles of which the first, which is dark, fierce, and astringent, is not God in his highest being; yet it is God, or at least it belongs to the essence of God. 'Since man knows that he is twofold, possessing both good and evil, then is it highly necessary to him that he know himself; how he was created; whence his good and evil impulses; what is good and evil and on what they depend; what is the origin of all good and of all evil; how or when evil came into the devil, or men, and all creatures; if the devil was a holy angel, and man too was created good, why such misery is found in all creatures; and why every one is biting, beating, pushing, and crushing each other, and there is such opposition not only in living things, but in stones, elements, earth, metals, wood, leaves, and grasses: in all is poison and wickedness, and it must be so, otherwise there would be neither life, nor movement, nor colour, nor virtue, nor thickness, nor thinness, nor perception of any kind, but all would be a *nothing*. In such a high consideration we find that all such comes from and out of God, and that it is of his substance, and evil belongs to formation and movement, and good to love, and the severe or counterwilling to joy.' This opposition which Böhme found in all nature, he was compelled to carry up to God; for following the analogy he had laid down, what he saw in the creature he must posit in the Abyssal Deity. Though God, in the first conception, is a simple unity in whom difference is not supposed to exist; yet when we inquire into the origin of love and anger, we find that they come from the same fountain, and that they are the children of one parent. We cannot say that the dark, fiery, astringent principle is *in* God any more than in earth, air, or water, and yet these have all come from God. Sorrow, death, and hell cannot be *in* God, and yet they have their origin in the divine nothing. The inquiry must be into the cause of the evil not only in creatures, but in the divine essence, for in the root or original all is one. All comes from the essence of God considered in his threefold nature. God in the first principle is not properly God, but wrath and terror the origin of bitterness and evil. Though this is not God, it is yet the innermost first fountain which is in God the Father, according to which he calls himself an angry and a jealous God. This fountain is the first principle, and in it the world has its origin. It is the principle of severity and anger, resembling a brimstone-spirit, and constituting 'the abyss of hell in which Prince Lucifer remained after the extinction of his light.' This dark principle is not God, yet it is the essence out of which God's light and heart are eternally produced. In it is the eternal mind which generates the eternal will, and the eternal will generates the eternal heart of God, and the heart generates the light, and the light the power, and the power the spirit, and that is the Almighty God, who is in an unchangeable will. The godhead is thus:—God the Father, and the light which makes the will-longing power, is God the Son, since in the power the light is eternally generated; and in the light out of the power proceeds the Holy Spirit, which again in the dark mind generates the will of the eternal Being. 'See now, dear soul,' says Böhme, 'this is the Godhead, and contains in itself the second or middle principle, therefore God is alone good; he is love, light, and power. Consider now that there would not have been in God such eternal wisdom and knowledge had not the mind stood in the darkness.'

Such is the eternal birth of the divine essence. By this, God himself realizes the eternal idea of his Being. The moments of the eternal birth are differently set forth in

Böhme's writings, according as the divine Being is considered in himself, or in his relation to Satan, the world, or man. Again, in the first relation, there are different points of view under which we may regard the eternal birth of the Deity.

The life process in God constitutes a trinity, which is the eternal and necessary birth of God, who produces himself, and without this life-process could not be thought of as a living God. Böhme says, 'When we speak of the Holy Ternary we must first say there is one God—he who is called the Father and Creator of all things, who is therefore almighty, and all in all. All is his. All has originated in him, and from him, and remains eternally in him. Then we say he is threefold in persons, and has from all eternity generated his Son, who is his heart, light, and love, so that the Father and the Son are not two beings, but only one. Then we say from the Holy Scriptures that there is a Spirit who proceeds from the Father and the Son, and is one essence in the Father, the Son, and the Holy Ghost. 'See then,' says Böhme, 'since the Father is the most original essence of all essences, if the other principle did not appear and go forth in the birth of the Son, then the Father would be a dark valley. You see now that the Son, who is the heart, life, light, beauty, and gentle beneficence of the Father, discloses in his birth another principle, and reconciles the angry, terrible Father, and makes him loving and merciful, and is another person than the Father, since in his centre is nothing but pure joy, love, and delight. You may now see how the Holy Spirit proceeds from the Father and the Son. Böhme had his knowledge of God by visions and revelations, and in expounding it in his books he made use of chemical terms and illustrations which make it impossible for ordinary persons to know what he meant. His disciples say that only those who believe in him can understand him; but all summaries made by his disciples seem more incomprehensible than the original.

In his interpretation of Scripture Böhme is more mystical than all the Mystics. With the revelation within, he made all external revelation to agree. God, he says, made all things out of his own essence, because there was no other essence from which they could be made. The Spirit of God indeed moved upon the water in forming the world, but this is the Spirit's

N

eternal work. In the birth of the Son of God, it moveth upon the water, for it is the power and outpouring of the Father out of the water and light of God. Man is made in the image of the Trinity. Like the Father, he has mind ; like the Son, he has light in that mind : like the Holy Ghost, he has 'a spirit which goes out from all the powers.' His fall was a necessary event, for in Adam were contending principles under the dominion of the more hurtful of which he could not but fall. Like the angels, he was created with a spiritual body, and would have multiplied his kind as they do. But he fell, and then Eve was created, that his posterity might be continued, as they now are. This may not accord with the letter of the Scripture narrative, according to which Eve sinned first and then Adam ; but that is only a mystical representation, of which the sense is, that Adam sinned by desire. He fell into a deep sleep, the death of his soul. When he awoke he found Eve. They both knew that they were naked—the sensual had eclipsed the spiritual, and they were ashamed of their material bodies.

SILESIUS.

The poems of Angelus Silesius, published in the seventeenth century, were the last manifestation of German theosophy. Silesius was long confounded with John Scheffler, who is said to have been a follower of Jacob Böhme, but who was at last a priest of the Catholic Church. It is now considered as proved that they were two different persons. The following verses will be sufficient to show the character of the theology of Silesius :—

> ' God never yet has been, nor will he ever be ;
> But yet before the world, and after it, is he.
> What God is no one knows, nor sprite nor light is he,
> Nor happiness, nor one, nor even divinity,
> Nor mind, love, goodness, will, nor intellect far seeing,
> Nor thing, nor nought, nor soul, nor yet essential being,
> He is what I and thou may vainly strive to learn,
> Until to Gods like him, we worldly creatures turn.

> ' God in my nature is involved, as I in the Divine,
> I help to make his being up, as much as he does mine.
> As much as I to God, owes God to me,
> His blissfulness and self-sufficiency.

I am as rich as God, no grain of dust
That is not mine too, share with me he must.
I am as great as God, and he as small as I ;
He cannot me surpass, or I beneath him lie.

' God cannot without me endure a moment's space ;
Were I to be destroyed he must give up the Ghost,
Naught seemeth high to me, I am the highest thing,
Because even God himself is poor deprived of me.

' While aught thou art, or know'st, or lov'st, or hast,
Nor yet believe me is thy burden gone,
Who is as though he were not, ne'er had been ;
That man, oh joy ! is made God absolute,
Self is surpassed by self-annihilation—
The nearer nothing, so much more divine.
Rise above time and space, and thou canst be,
At any moment in eternity.

' Eternity and time, time and eternity,
Are in themselves alike, the difference is in thee ;
'Tis thou thyself tak'st time, the clock-work is thy sense,
If thou but dropp'st the spring the time will vanish hence ;
You think the world will fade, the world will not decay,
The darkness of the world alone is swept away.'

> ' I bear God's image, would he see himself ;
> He only can in me, or such as I.'

> ' I see in God, both God and man,
>   He man and God in me ;
> I quench his thirst, and he, in turn,
>   Helps my necessity.'

FRENCH MYSTICS.

Fenelon the Archbishop of Cambray, and Madame Guyon
were accused by Bossuet of teaching doctrines that led
to Pantheism. The inference may have been correct, but
Fenelon and Madame Guyon would have recoiled not only
from the bold speculations of Erigena and Eckart, but even
from the more modified doctrines of the other German mystics.
Their mysticism was practical rather than speculative. They
were more anxious to be able to love God than to explain his
essence. But like all great religious souls when they did speak
of God their language overflowed the bounds of the prescribed
theology, and wandered into a kind of religious Pantheism.
' What do I see in all nature,' cried Fenelon, ' God—God is

everything, and God alone.' Fenelon may have paused to explain what he meant; so did Erigena and Eckart; and so did even Spinoza; but the explanation was either at war with the original statement, or it went to establish it. If the former, there was a manifest contradiction, if the latter Pantheism was openly espoused.

From Madame Guyon's writings a few similar sentences might be gleaned, but they are not numerous, and they never express more than that ineffable union of the soul with the Deity, which in some way or other is the hope of every Christian. Her deep piety, and the warmth and earnestness of her spirit may have led to the use of language which reminds us of Brahmanical absorption; but we may plead for her, as Dr. Ullmann did for some of the Germans, that the union of which she spoke was not one of essence, but only moral or religious. In this verse, from one of her hymns, we have an instance of this language, and with it a guide to the meaning—

> ' I love the Lord—but with no love of mine,
>   For I have none to give ;
> I love the Lord—but with a love divine,
>   For by thy love I live.
> I am as nothing, and rejoice to be
> Emptied and lost, and swallowed up in Thee ! '

Again, in describing the mode of the soul's union with God, she says, ' The soul passing out of self, by dying to itself necessarily passes into its divine object. This is the law of its transition. When it passes out of self, which is limited, and therefore is not God, and consequently evil, it necessarily passes into the unlimited and uncreated, which is God, and therefore the true and good.'

WILLIAM LAW.

The mystical spirit has not been fruitful in England. The writings of Jacob Böhme were translated into English in the time of the Puritans by some zealous disciples, but his followers in this country do not appear ever to have been numerous. In the middle of the last century he found an eloquent expounder of his doctrines in William Law, a nonjuring clergyman of the Church of England. Bishop Warburton charged Law with teaching Spinozism, to which his only answer was that ' Spinoza made God matter, and that it surely could not be supposed that he could be capable of any belief so absurd.' Law did not understand Spinoza, but he made no secret of his agreement with Jacob Böhme.

Perhaps the best text for an exposition of Law's theology, is the following passage, ' Everything that is in being, is either God, or nature, or creature; and everything that is not God is only a manifestation of God; for as there is nothing, neither nature nor creature, but what must have its being in and from God, so everything is and must be according to its nature more or less a manifestation of God. Everything, therefore, by its form and condition speaks so much of God, and God in everything speaks and manifests so much of himself. Properly and strictly speaking nothing can begin to be. The beginning of everything is nothing more than its beginning to be in a new state.' Whatever separation may be afterwards made between God and the creature, we see in this passage in what sense they are one. All things live, and move, and have their being in God. This is true of devils, as well as of angels, and of all beings in the ranks between devils and angels. The happiness or misery of every creature is regulated by its state and manner of existence in God. He is all in all. We have nothing separately or at a distance from him, but everything in him. Whatever he gives us is something of himself, and thus we become more and more partakers of the divine nature.

Man was created with an angelic nature. It was intended that he should be the restoring angel who was to bring back all things to their first state as they were before the fall of Lucifer. He was placed in this world which had formerly been the place of the fallen angels. He was in a paradise which covered that earth which is now revealed by sin. He was to keep that paradise, but after his fall he was sentenced to till the ground which now appears, for this world and all that we see in it are but the invisible things of a fallen world made visible in a new and lower state of existence. The first creation which was perfect, spiritual, and angelical, is represented by the sea of glass which St. John saw before the throne of God. That sea is the heavenly materiality out of which were formed the bodies of the angels, and the angelical Adam. In this sea of glass all the properties and powers of nature moved and worked in the unity and purity of the one will of God. Perpetual scenes of light and glory and beauty were rising and changing through all the height and depth of this sea of glass, at the will and pleasure of the angels who once inhabited the region which is now this earth. But these angels rebelled, and by their rebellion this sea of glass was broken to pieces and became a black lake; a horrible chaos of fire and wrath; a depth of the confused, divided, and fighting properties of nature. The revolt of the angels brought forth that disordered chaos, and that matter of which this earth is now composed. Stones and rocks, fire and water, with all the vegetables and animals that arise from the contending and commingling of the elements came into existence through the rebellion of the angels. They exist only in time; they are unknown in eternity. The angelical world or sea of glass had indeed its fruits and flowers, which were more real than those which grow in time, but as different from the grossness of the fruits of this world as the heavenly body of an angel is different from the gross body of an earthly animal. It was the mirror of beautiful figures and ideal forms, which continually manifested the wonders of the divine nature, and ministered to the joy of the angels.

Adam was created with dominion over the fallen world and all the creatures whose existence was mortal, but he himself was immortal and possessed of a heavenly body. He was placed in paradise till he should bring forth a numerous offspring fitted to inhabit the world that had been lost to the angels. The sea of glass was to be restored. The sun, and stars, the earth, and all the elements were to be purified by fire, and when all that was gross and dead was purged away, the sons of Adam were to inhabit the renewed earth and sing hallelujahs to all eternity.

Adam with the body and soul of an angel in an outward body, was thus placed in paradise. He was put on his trial not by the mere will of God, nor by experiment, but by the necessity of his nature. He was free to choose either the angelic life, in which he could have used his outward body as a means of opening up the wonders of the outward world; or to turn his desire to the opening of the bestial life of the outward world in himself, so as to know the good and evil that were in it. He chose the latter. The moment the bestial life was opened within him he died spiritually. His angelic body and spirit were extinguished, but his soul being an immortal fire became a poor slave in prison of bestial flesh and blood.

When Adam had thus fallen it was not good for him to be alone, so God divided the first perfect human nature into two parts. Eve was created, or rather taken out of Adam. She led him further astray by eating of the forbidden fruit, and persuading him also to eat of it. He saw that he was naked; that he was an animal of gross flesh and blood, and he was ashamed of his bestial body. That man was created at first male and female in one person, and that his offspring was to be continued after the manner of his own birth from God, Law endeavours to prove not only from the record in Genesis, but from the words of our Lord to the Sadducees that 'in the resurrection they neither marry nor are given in marriage, but are as the angels in heaven,' or as St. Luke has it, 'they are equal to the angels of God,' which is supposed to mean that the state of angelic being, which Adam had before he sinned, will be again restored to humanity.

That the original substance of humanity was divine is evident from the record of creation, where it is said that God breathed into man 'the breath of lives,' and he became a living soul. That soul did not come from the womb of nothing, but as a breath from the mouth of God. What it is and what it has in itself is from and out of the first and highest of all beings. To this record in Genesis St. Paul appeals where he wishes to show that all things, all worlds, and all living creatures were not created out of nothing. The woman, he says, was created out of the man, but all things are out of God. Again, he says that there is to us but one God, out of whom are all things. Creation out of nothing is a fiction of modern theology, a fiction big with the greatest absurdities. Every creature is a birth from something else. Birth is the only procedure of nature. All nature is itself a birth from God; the first manifestation of the hidden inconceivable God. So far is it from being out of nothing, that it is the manifestation of that in God which before was not manifest, and as nature is the manifestation of God, so are all creatures the manifestation of the powers of nature. Those creatures that are nearest to God are out of the highest powers of nature. The spiritual materiality, or the element of heaven, produces the bodies, or heavenly flesh and blood of the angels, just as the elements of this world produce material flesh and blood. The spiritual materiality of heaven, in the kingdom of the fallen angels, has gone through a variety of births or creations, till some of it came down to the grossness of air and water, and the hardness of rocks and stones.

A spark of the light and spirit of God is still in man. It has a strong and natural tendency towards the eternal light from which it came. This light is Christ in us. He is the woman's seed who from the beginning has been bruising the serpent's head. He did not begin to be a Saviour when he was born of Mary, for he is the eternal Word that has ever been in the hearts of men; the light which lighteth every man that cometh into the world. He is our Emmanuel, the God with us given unto Adam, and through him to all his offspring. To turn to the light and spirit within us is the only true turning to God. The Saviour of the world lies hid in man, for in the depth of the soul the Holy Trinity brought forth its own living image in the first created man, who was a living representation of Father, Son, and Holy Ghost. This was the kingdom of God within him, and this made paradise without him. At the fall, man lost this deity within him, but from the moment that God treasured up in Adam the bruiser of the serpent, all the riches of the divine nature came seminally back to him again, so that our own good spirit is the very Spirit of God.

The Christ within us, is that Christ whom we crucify. Adam and Eve were his first murderers. Eating of the earthly tree was the death of the Christ of God—the divine life in the soul of man. Christ would not have come into the world as the second Adam had he not been the life and perfection of the first Adam. God's delight in any creature is just as his well-beloved Son, the express image of his person, is found in that creature. This is true of angels as well as of men, for the angels need no redemption only because the life of Christ dwells in them.

The work of Christ is not to reconcile or appease an angry God. There is no wrath in God. He is an immutable will to all good. The reconciliation is to turn man from the bestial life, from nature which is without God. The effect of the fall of the angels was to deprive nature of God, that is to say, angels and fallen man turned to nature without God. Nature in itself is a desire, a universal want, which must be filled with God who is the universal All. In this desire is a will to have something which it has not, and which it cannot seize. In the endeavour after what it seeks, it begets resistance. From these two properties arises a third, which is called the ' wheel ' or ' whirling anguish of life.' These three great laws of matter and nature are seen in the attraction, equal resistance, and orbicular motion of the planets. Their existence as pointed out by Jacob Böhme has since been demonstrated by Sir Isaac Newton. These three properties were never to have been seen or known by any creature. Their denseness, and strife, and darkness were brought forth by God, in union with the light, and glory, and majesty of heaven, and only for this end, that God might be manifested in them. Nor could they have been known, nor the nature of any creature as it is in itself without God, had not the rebel angels turned their desire backward to search and find the original ground of life. This turning of their desire into the origin of life was their turning from the light of God. They discovered a new kind of substantiality ; nature fallen from God. To these three properties are added other four ; fire, the form of light and love, sound or understanding, and the state of peace and joy into which these are brought, which state is called the seventh property of nature. The fourth, fifth, and sixth, express the existence of the Deity in the first three properties of nature. Böhme explains the first chapter of Genesis, as a manifestation of the seven properties in the creation of this material temporal system ; the last of which properties is the state of repose, the joyful Sabbath of the Deity. As Adam failed to be the restoring angel it was necessary that God should become man, ' take a birth in fallen nature, be united to it and become the life of it, or the natural man must of all necessity be for ever and ever in the hell of his own hunger, anguish, contrariety, and self-torment; and all for this plain reason, because nature is and can be nothing else but this variety of self-torment, till the Deity is manifested and dwelling in it.'

From this doctrine followed of necessity the perpetual inspiration of the human race. God lives and works in man. It is by his inspiration that we think those things that be good. It is not confined to individuals, nor given only on special occasions. The true Word of God is not the sacred writings, but the in-spoken living Word in the soul. The law was the schoolmaster to bring us to Christ, and the New Testament is but another schoolmaster—a light, like that of prophecy, to which we are to give heed until Christ, the dawning of the day, or the day star, arise in our hearts. The sons of wisdom in the heathen world were enlightened by the Spirit and Word of God. Christ was born in them. They were the Apostles of the Christ within, commissioned to call mankind from the pursuits of flesh and blood to know themselves, the dignity of their nature, and the immortality of their souls.

John Toland.

Toland is not put here because he was a mystic. He had no tendency in that direction. He, however, affected to be a Pantheist, and wrote a book, which was published after his death, called 'Pantheisticon.' He was a man of great reading and great intellect, but deficient in the ordinary wisdom of the world. The publication of this book was simply a freak of his erratic genius. It meant nothing except, perhaps, to confound and horrify the advocates of Christianity, who looked upon Toland as an unbeliever of the worst kind. In the introduction he quoted Thomas Aquinas as saying that, they did not contradict the Mosaic account of creation, who taught that God was the eternal cause of the eternal world, and that all things from all eternity flowed from God without a medium,' and St. Jerome as saying that 'God is interfused and circumfused both within and without the world.' 'The seeds of all things,' Toland says, 'begun from an eternal time, are composed out of the first bodies, or most simple principles, the four commonly received elements being neither simple nor sufficient, for in an infinity all things are infinite, nay, even eternal, as nothing could be made out of nothing. To illustrate this, the seed of a tree is not a tree in mere potentiality as Aristotle would say, but a real tree, in which are all the integrant parts of a tree, though so minute as not to be perceived by the senses without microscopes, and not even then but in a very few things.' The 'Socratic Society,' which indulged in these deep speculations, is represented as singing in alternate parts, after the convivial fashion of a Masonic Lodge, some verses of which the following are a specimen :—

> ' *President.*—Keep off the profane vulgar.
> *Respondents.*—The coast is clear, the door is shut. All safe !
> *P.*—All things in the world are one,
> And one is all in all things.
> *R.*—What is all in all things, is God ;
> Eternal and immense—
> Neither begotten or ever to perish.
> *P.*—In him we live, we move, and have our being.
> *R.*—Everything has sprung from him, and shall be reunited to him,
> He himself being the beginning and end of all things.
> *P.*—Let us sing a hymn
> Upon the nature of the universe.
> *P. & R.*—Whatever this is it animates all things,
> Forms, nourishes, increases, creates,
> Buries, and takes into itself all things,
> And of all things is itself the parent
> From whom all things that receive a being,
> Into the same are anew resolved.'

Sometimes they sing this hymn—

> ' All things within the verge of mortal laws
> Are changed, all climates in revolving years
> Know not themselves, nations change their faces,
> But the world is safe, and preserves its all,
> Neither increased by time, nor worn by age ;
> Its motion is not instantaneous,
> It fatigues not its course, always the same
> It has been and shall be, our fathers saw
> No alteration, neither shall posterity,
> It is God immutable forever.'

Toland professed to refute the blasphemies of Spinoza ! He also translated into English Giordano Bruno's *Spaccio della Bestia trionfante,* but the translation was as destitute of meaning as the original. He wrote a Latin epitaph for himself which has been considered Pantheistic. It reads in English ' The spirit is united with the ethereal father from whom it came. The body yielding to nature is laid in the bosom of its mother earth. It shall rise again in some period of eternity, but it will never again be the same Toland.' A member of the Socratic Society wrote a poem on its founder. After speaking of Master Toland as being now a nonentity, his dust having returned to its native dust and the fluids of his body gone to their mother ocean, and his eloquent breath as being lost in boundless ether, the writer says,

' The purer genial powers, the vital flame
    That moved and quickened this mechanic frame
    Is flown aloft, a spark, a borrowed ray,
    And *re-united* to the Prince of Day.'

John Eckart was accused of being in communication with the ' Brothers of
the Free Spirit.' In 1326 he was deposed from his office of Provincial of the
Dominicans in Saxony. As his doctrine had spread widely among the Dominicans, the whole order was charged with heresy by the Archbishop of Cologne.
Eckart was summoned to appear before the Pope at Avignon, and was condemned on the charge of heresy. His doctrines were so widely spread that in
1430 it was necessary again to condemn them, this time by the University of
Heidelberg.

Professor Pfeiffer, in his work on the German Mystics, has collected one
hundred and ten sermons, eighteen tracts, and seventy single sayings, which
he ascribes to Eckart.

John Tauler was a native of Strasburg. He studied at the University of
Paris, and after his return to Strasburg he became acquainted with Master
Eckart. This part of Germany was then under the sentence of excommuni-
cation, but Tauler preached in spite of the Papal interdict, and great crowds of
people flocked to hear him. While the Black Death was raging in Strasburg,
Tauler and two other priests were the only ministers of religion who adminis-
tered the sacraments to the sick and the dying. He was finally banished from
Strasburg for his bold words against the Pope. He repaired to Cologne, where
he preached for some years in the cloister of St. Gertrude. He afterwards
returned to his native town, where he died in 1361.

Böhme's representations of the Trinity are not always verbally consistent,
and this is one of the things which make him difficult to be understood. The
following passage from the book on the ' Three Principles' seems a definite
expression of his conception of God, though in some points it does not agree
with what is quoted in the text—'The seven spirits are God the Father, the
life of the seven spirits is the light which subsists in the centre of the seven
spirits, and is generated by them. This light is the Son, flash, stock, pith, or
heart of the seven spirits. The splendour, or glance in all the powers which
goes forth from the Father and the Son, and forms or images all in the seventh
nature spirit. This is the Holy Ghost. Thus, O blind Jew, Turk, and
Heathen, thou seest that there are three persons in the Deity, thou canst not
deny it, for thou livest, and art, and hast thy being in the three persons, and
thou hast thy life from them, and in the power of these three persons thou
art to rise from the dead at the last day, and live eternally.

The books referred to are Dr. Ullmann's ' Reformers before the Reformation,'
Vaughan's ' Hours with the Mystics.' ' Tauler's Sermons,' and the ' Theologia
Germanica,' are translated into English by Miss Winkworth ; Schrader's
Angelus Silesium und Seine Mystik. Böhme's Works were translated into
English in the seventeenth century. Law published an edition with preface
and plates. The account of Law's theology is taken from ' The Way a Divine
Knowledge,' ' The Spirit of Love,' and ' The Spirit of Prayer.' The last of
Böhme's English disciples was the late Mr. Walton, jeweller in Ludgate Hill.
He possessed the whole of Freher's MSS. His ' Memorials of William Lato '
is a prodigious book, containing biographies and accounts of many expositions
of Böhme. Mr. Walton spent his last years in bringing Böhme's doctrine to
greater perfection, showing more clearly how God was developed from the
abyssal nothing.

CHAPTER XI.

SUFEYISM.

THE only religion in the world in which we should have concluded, before examination, that the Pantheistic spirit was impossible, is the religion of Mahommed. Islamism is repellant of all speculation about God, and all exercise of reason in matters pertaining to faith. The supreme God of the Arabian prophet was not a being from whom all things emanated, and whom men were to serve by contemplation, but an absolute will whom all creation was to obey. He was separated from everything, above everything, the ruler of all things, the sovereign of the universe. It was the mission of Moses to teach the unity of God in opposition to the idolatry of the nations which, through beholding the worshipful in nature, had put the created in the place of the Creator. For this purpose all images of the divine Being were forbidden to the Hebrews, yet their prophets made use of all the glories of creation to set forth the divine majesty and the splendour of God. His chariots were fire. He walked on the wings of the wind. He clothed himself with light as with a garment. He was in heaven and on earth, and in the uttermost parts of the sea— yea, even in hell. Neither matter, suffering, nor impurity excluded him from any region of the universe. Jesus Christ, even more than the Hebrew prophets, directed his disciples to the natural world that he might show them the Father; nor did he hesitate to point to natural objects as symbols of God and emblems of his glory. St. John tells us of the rapture with which he delighted to repeat the message he heard from Jesus that 'God is Light;' and in setting forth the divinity of the Logos, he pronounced this light to be 'the life of men.' Mahommedanism was at least as clear in its doctrine of the divine Unity as either Judaism or Christianity, and more rigid than either of these in excluding nature from any place in

religion. It recognised no symbols. It learned nothing of God
from creation. The supreme One had spoken by his prophet,
and his word was the essence of religion. Again, Mahommedanism is a religion of dogmas and ceremonies. It rests on
authority. Its doctrines are definite. The Koran is infallible ;
the words are not only inspired, but dictated in Heaven. To
find Pantheism in Mahommedanism is to find it in a system
which of all others is the most alien to its spirit. But in this
as in all other religions, we have the orthodox who abide by
the creeds and the ceremonies, who repose implicitly on the
authority of a person, a book, or a church ; and those of a free
spirit, who demand the exercise of reason, or look for divine
intuitions in individual souls. The one says religion is a creed ;
the other it is a life. The one says God has spoken to some of
old ; the other says he is speaking to us now. The latter class
is represented in Mahommedanism by the Sufis, who are its
philosophers, its poets, its mystics, its enthusiasts. To give a
history of them is not easy, for they are divided into many
sects, nor is it less difficult to find their origin and the genealogy
of their doctrines. Mahommedan authors admit that there
were Sufis in the earliest times of their origin, probably cotem-
porary with the prophet himself. Some trace the origin of the
Sufis to India, and identify them with the mystical sects of
Brahmanism. Others find in Sufeyism unmistakcable remnants
of the old Persian faith. This is the more likely hypothesis.
The spirit of Parseeism, which survived after the victory of the
Mahommedan faith, again awoke, and following a law, which
can be traced in many similar cases, gave birth to the
Puritanism * of Mahommedanism. The Sufis thought that
they believed as Mahommed, and wished to prove that he
also was a Sufi—an effort the accomplishment of which to all
but themselves has appeared impossible. ' Sufeyism,' says an
English writer ' has arisen from the bosom of Mahommedanism
as a vague protest of the human soul, in its intense longing
after a purer creed. On certain tenets of the Koran the Sufis
have erected their own system, professing indeed to reverence
its authority as a divine revelation, but in reality substituting
for it the oral voice of the teacher, or the secret dreams of the
mystic. Dissatisfied with the barren letter of the Koran,

* *Sufi* means pure.

Sufeyism appeals to human consciousness, and from our nature's felt wants seeks to set before us nobler hopes than a gross Mahommedan Paradise can fulfil.'

'The Great Creator,' says Sir John Malcolm, 'is, according to the doctrine of the Sufis, diffused over all creation. He exists everywhere and in everything. They compare the emanation of his divine essence or spirit to the rays of the sun, which they conceive are continually darted forth and re-absorbed. It is for this re-absorption into the divine essence, to which their immortal part belongs, that they continually sigh. They believe that the soul of man, and that the principle of life which exists through all nature, is not only from God, but of God ; and hence these doctrines which their adversaries have held to be most profane, as they are calculated to establish a degree of equality of nature between the created and the Creator.'

This brief description, not only fully declares the character of the Sufi doctrines concerning God, but by the illustration of the sun and its rays points at the same time to their origin. God is light, and that light is all which is. The phenomenal world is mere illusion, a vision which the senses take to be a some-thing, but which is nothing. All things are what they are by an eternal necessity, and all events so predestined that the existence of evil is impossible. On these subjects some of the Sufi sects manifest a wild fanaticism which has caused them to be charged with lawlessness, but their more frequent character is that of extravagant mystics. We are come from God, and we long to return to him again, is their incessant cry. But while acknowledging a separation from God, which they regard as the worst of miseries, they yet deny that the soul of man has ever been divided from God. The words 'separated' and 'divided' may not convey the meaning of the corresponding Persian words, nor make clear to us the distinction which it is intended should be conveyed. Perhaps there is here, logically, a contradiction ; for at one time it is declared that God created all things by his breath, and everything, therefore, is both the Creator and created; and at another time this unity of God and the creature is limited to the enlightened soul. The difficulty is one we have met before, and though admitting the inadequacy of the words, we may yet understand or at least

conjecture the meaning.   To be re-absorbed into the glorious
essence of God is the great object of the Sufi.   To attain this
he has to pass through four stages.   The first is that of obedience
to the laws of the prophet.   The second is that state of spiritual
struggling attained through this obedience when he lives more
in the spirit than in the letter.   In the third he arrives at
knowledge and is inspired.   In the fourth he attains to truth
and is completely re-united with the Deity.   In this state he
loses all will and personality.   He is no more creature but
Creator, and when he worships God it is God worshipping
himself.

The late Professor Palmer says that this system of the Sufis
is an endeavour to reconcile philosophy with revealed religion.
He calls it the esoteric doctrine of Islamism, and finds some
foundation for it in the Koran, though admitting that the Koran
has no tendency to Pantheism.   He describes it as the worship
of the good and the beautiful, the triumph of the soul over the
dominion of sense, and he hoped at some future time to be able
to prove that it was really the development of the primeval
religion of the Aryan race.   The Sufis say that there is no road
from man to God, because the nature of God is illimitable and
infinite.   The Koran says that he comprises everything, and
that there is not an atom from which he is absent.   Another
sect which Mr. Palmer distinguishes from the Sufis, but which
seems to be essentially the same, say that there is no road from
man to God, because there is no existence independent of God.
Nor can there be, because that which really exists is self-
existent, and therefore is God.   When man imagines that he
has an existence other than the existence of God, he falls into a
grievous error and sin, yet this error and sin is the only road
from man to God.   Until this is passed God cannot be reached.
A Sufi poet says :—

> ' Plant one foot on the neck of self,
>   The other in thy friend's domain,
> In everything his presence see,
>   For other vision is in vain.'

While man looks to self he cannot see God, but when he is
not looking to self all that he sees is God.[*]

Dr. Tholuck, in his book on 'Sufismus,' has shown by many

* 'Oriental Mysticism,' by E. H. Palmer.

passages from Mahommedan authors that the Sufi doctrines are identical with those of the Brahmans and Buddhists, the Neo-Platonists, the Beghards, and Beguines. There is the same union of man with God, the same emanation of all things from God, and the same final absorption of all things into the divine Essence—and with these doctrines a Mahommedan predestination which makes all a necessary evolution of the divine Being. The creation of the creature, the fall of those who have departed from God and their final return, are all events preordained by an absolute necessity. The chief school of Arabian philosophy, that of Gazzali, passed over to Sufeyism by the same reasoning which led Plotinus to his mystical theology. After long inquiries for some ground on which to base the certainty of our knowledge, Gazzali was led to reject entirely all belief in the senses. He then found it equally difficult to be certified of the accuracy of the conclusions of reason, for there may be, he thought, some faculty higher than reason which, if we possessed it, would show the uncertainty of reason, as reason now shows the uncertainty of the senses. He was left in scepticism, and saw no escape but in the Sufi union with Deity. There alone can man know what is true by becoming the truth itself. 'I was forced,' he said, 'to return to the admission of intellectual notions as the bases of all certitude. This, however, was not by systematic reasoning and accumulation of proofs, but by a flash of light which God sent into my soul. For whoever imagines that truth can only be rendered evident by proofs, places narrow limits to the wide compassion of the Creator.'

Bustami, a mystic of the ninth century, said he was a sea without a bottom, without beginning, and without end. Being asked what is the throne of God, he answered, I am the throne of God. What is the table on which the divine decrees are written? I am that table. What is the pen of God—the word by which God created all things? I am the pen. What is Abraham, Moses, and Jesus? I am Abraham, Moses, and Jesus. What are the angels Gabriel, Michael, Israfil? I am Gabriel, Michael, Israfil, for whatever comes to true being is absorbed into God, and thus is God. Again, in another place, Bustami cries, Praise to me, I am truth. I am the true God. Praise to me, I must be celebrated by divine praise.

o

Jelaleddin, a Sufi poet, thus sings of himself:

> ' I am the Gospel, the Psalter, the Koran,
> I am *Usa* and *Lat* (Arabic deities), Bell and the Dragon,
> Into two and seventy sects is the world divided,
> Yet only one God, the faithful who believe in him am I,
> Thou knowest what are fire, water, air, and earth,
> Fire, water, air, and earth, all am I,
> Lies and truth, good, bad, hard and soft.
>
> Knowledge, solitude, virtue, faith,
> The deepest ground of hell, the highest torment of the flames,
> The highest paradise,
> The earth and what is therein,
> The angels and the devils, spirit and man, am I ;
> What is the goal of speech, O tell it Schems Tebrisi ?
> The goal of sense ?   This :—THE WORLD SOUL AM I.'

Mr. Vaughan, in his ' Hours with the Mystics,' quotes the following verses from Persian poets :—

> ' All sects but multiply the I and thou ;
> This I and thou belong to partial being.
> When I and thou, and several being vanish,
> Then mosque and church shall find thee nevermore.
> Our individual life is but a phantom ;
> Make clear thine eye, and see reality.'—MAHMUD.
>
> ' On earth thou seest his actions ; but his spirit
> Makes heaven his seat, and all infinity,
> Space, and duration boundless do him service ;
> As Eden's rivers dwell and serve in Eden.'—IBID.
>
> ' Man, what thou art is hidden from thyself ;
> Know'st not that morning, mid-day, and the eve
> Are all within thee ?   The ninth heaven art thou ;
> And from the spheres into the roar of time
> Didst fall ere-while, thou art the brush that painted
> The hues of all the world—the light of life
> That ranged his glory in the nothingness.'
>
> ' Joy ! joy ! I triumph now ; no more I know
> Myself as simply me.   I burn with love.
> The centre is within me, and its wonder
> Lies as a circle everywhere about me.
> Joy ! joy ! no mortal thought can fathom me.
> I am the merchant and the pearl at once.
> Lo ! time and space lie crouching at my feet.
> Joy ! joy ! when I would revel in a rapture.
> I plunge into myself, and all things know.'—FERRIDODDIN.
>
> ' Are we fools ?   We are God's captivity.
> Are we wise ?   We are his promenade.

Are we sleeping ?   We are drunk with God.
Are we waking ?   Then we are his heralds.
Are we weeping ?   Then his clouds of wrath.
Are we laughing ?   Flashes of his love.'—JELALEDDIN.

'Every night God frees the host of spirits ;
Frees them every night from fleshly prison.
Then the soul is neither slave, nor master,
Nothing knows the bondsman of his bondage ;
Nothing knows the lord of all his lordship.
Gone from such a night, is eating sorrow ;
Gone, the thoughts that question good or evil.
Then without distraction, or division,
In this one the spirit sinks and slumbers.'—IBID.

Tholuck quotes this verse from a Dervish Breviary :—

'Yesterday I beat the kettle-drum of dominion,
I pitched my tent on the highest throne,
I drank, crowned by the beloved,
The wine of unity from the cup of the Almighty.'

Some verses from Jami's 'Salaman and Absal' which has
been recently translated into English may conclude this notice
of the Sufis.   The subject of the poem is the joys of divine love
—the pleasures of the religious life as opposed to the delusive
fascinations of the life of sense.   In the prologue the poet thus
addresses the Deity :—

'Time it is
To unfold thy perfect beauty.   I would be
Thy lover, and thine only—I, mine eyes
Sealed in the light of thee to all but thee,
Yea, in the revelation of thyself
Self-lost, and conscience-quit of good and evil.
Thou movest under all the forms of truth,
Under the forms of all created things ;
Look whence I will, still nothing I discern
But thee in all the universe, in which
Thyself thou dost invest, and through the eyes
Of man, the subtle censor scrutinize. ;
To Thy Harim DIVIDUALITY
No entrance finds—no word of this and that ;
Do thou my separate and derived self
Make one with thy Essential !   Leave me room
On that Divan which leaves no room for two ;
Lest, like the simple kurd of whom they tell,
I grow perplext, oh God, 'twixt ' I ' and ' thou.'
If I—this dignity and wisdom whence ?
If thou—then what this abject impotence ? '

The fable of the kurd is then told in verse.   A kurd per-

plexed in the ways of fortune left the desert for the city, where
he saw the multitudes all in commotion, every one hastening
hither and thither on his special business, and being weary with
travel the kurd lay down to sleep, but fearing lest among so
many people he should not know himself when he awoke, he
tied a pumpkin round his foot. A knave who heard him
deliberating about the difficulty of knowing himself again, took
the pumpkin off the kurd's foot and tied it round his own.
When the kurd awoke he was bewildered, not knowing

> ' Whether I be I or no,
> If I—the pumpkin why on you?
> If you—then where am I, and who?'

The prologue continues :—

> ' Oh God ! this poor bewildered kurd am I,
> Than any kurd more helpless !—Oh, do thou,
> Strike down a ray of light into my darkness !
> Turn by thy grace these dregs into pure wine,
> To recreate the spirits of the good ;
> Or if not that, yet, as the little cup
> Whose name I go by, not unworthy found,
> To pass thy salutary vintage round !'

The poet is answered by the Beloved :—

> ' No longer think of rhyme, but think of me ?—
> Of whom ?—Of him whose palace the soul is,
> And treasure-house—who notices and knows
> Its income and out-going and then comes
> To fill it when the stranger is departed.
> Whose shadow being kings—whose attributes
> The type of theirs—their wrath and favour his—
> Lo ! in the celebration of his glory
> The King himself comes on me unaware,
> And suddenly arrests me for his own.
> Wherefore once more I take—best quitted else—
> The field of verse, to chant that double praise,
> And in that memory refresh my soul
> Until I grasp the skirt of living Presence.'

The following fable from Jelaleddin will illustrate the Sufi
idea of identity which, under the image of love, is set forth in
Salaman and Absal : ' One knocked at the Beloved's door ; and
a voice asked from within, ' Who is there ? ' and he answered,
' It is I.' Then the voice said, ' This house will not hold me and
thee.' And the door was not opened. Then went the lover
into the desert, and fasted and prayed in solitude. And after

a year he returned, and knocked again at the door.   And again
the voice asked, 'Who is there?' and he said, 'It is thyself!'
—and the door was opened to him.'

Books which treat specially of Sufeyism, are M. Smoelder's *Essai sur les
Ecoles Philosophes chez les Arabes*; Tholock's *Sufismus*; Professor Palmer's
'Oriental Mysticism'; Sir John Malcolm's 'History of Persia'; and an essay
by Professor Cowell in Oxford Essays, 1855.

CHAPTER XII.

MODERN IDEALISM.

A HISTORY of Pantheism would be, for the most part, a history of idealism. It is not however without reason that we apply the term idealistic philosophy specially to this chapter, for here we find those doctrines concerning God and creation, which have so generally prevailed in the world, relegated entirely to the province of philosophy, supported by vigorous reasoning and an effort made for the absolute demonstration of their truth. And all this is done on the only ground on which it could be done, that of a pure idealism.

Des Cartes.

The founder of modern ideal philosophy was René Des Cartes, a French nobleman. He flourished about the beginning of the seventeenth century, and was distinguished in his life-time as a mathematician, metaphysician, natural philosopher, and soldier. Though an idealist in philosophy he was no visionary, but an experienced open-eyed man of the world, who well knew that

> ' All theory is grey,
> But green is the golden tree of life.'

Despairing of being able to extricate philosophy from the confusion into which it had fallen, he resolved to apply to mental phenomena the same principle which Bacon had applied to physics, that of examination, observation and experience. But before this could be done the authority of two great powers had to be put aside, that of Aristotle, and that of the Church. The influence of the former was already passing away. The new life of the sixteenth century had thrown off the bondage of what was called Aristotelianism. Some theologians there were who still defended the authority of Aristotle, but it had met its death-blow before the appearance of Des Cartes. How he

stood in relation to the Church is not so easily determined.
He openly professed the Catholic faith, and declared his object
to be the discovery of grounds in reason by which he could
defend and uphold the doctrines which he received on the
Church's authority. This complacency towards the Church is
by some regarded as only a polite method of keeping clear of
the ecclesiastical doctors and the Inquisition; but modern
Catholics take Des Cartes seriously, and represent him as a
philosopher whose great object was to refute on Protestant
grounds, that is, on principles of reason, the heresies of the
Reformation.

Aristotle and the Church being thus put aside, the first inquiry was for a ground of certitude. Does anything exist ? It
does not prove that anything is, because some one has said that
it is. Nor are the senses sufficient to testify to the existence
of anything, for they may be deceived. So too with our reasonings ; even those of mathematics are not to be relied on, for
perhaps the human mind cannot receive truth. There is left
nothing but doubt. We must posit everything as uncertain ;
and yet this cannot be ; for the I which thus posits must be a
true existence. He who thus doubts of all things ; he who thus
inquires after truth must himself be. So reasoned Des Cartes,
I doubt, then must there be a subject doubting ; I think, therefore, I exist; or more accurately, I think, and that is equivalent
to saying, I am a 'thinking something.'

The clearness of this idea of self-existence evinces its truth,
and from this Des Cartes drew the principle that whatever the
mind perceives clearly and distinctly is true. Now we have a
clear and distinct idea of a Being infinite, eternal, omnipotent,
and omnipresent. There must then be such a Being—necessary
existence is contained in the idea. If it were possible for that
being not to be, that very possibility would be an imperfection,
and cannot, therefore, belong to what is perfect. None but the
perfect Being could give us this idea of infinite perfection, and
since we live, having this idea in us, the Being who put it in
us must himself be. We are the imperfect. We are the finite.
We are the caused. There must be one who is the complement
of our being, the infinity of our finitude, the perfection of our
imperfection ; a mind which gives us that which we have not
from ourselves. Des Cartes eliminated from the idea of the

divine Being everything which implied imperfection. He was careful to distinguish between God and his creation. He left the finite standing over against the Infinite—the creature absolutely distinct in substance and essence from the Creator. He did not take the step which annihilated the one to make room for the other, and yet he suggested it. Unconsciously, and even in spite of himself, he is carried on towards conclusions from which he shrinks, and to which he refuses to go forward. 'When I come to consider the particular views of Des Cartes,' says M. Saisset, 'upon the perfection of God and the relations of the Creator with the world and with men; when I endeavour to link his thoughts, and to follow out their consequences, I find that they do not form a homogeneous whole, I believe that I can detect the conflict of contrary thoughts and tendencies.' Des Cartes had got on the track of Parmenides, but like Plato and St. Anselm he refused to advance. He preferred a theology not logically consistent to the theology of the Eleatics.

There are but two starting points of knowledge. Either we begin with matter, and assuming the reality of the visible world, we go on to the proof of other existences, but in this way we can never demonstrate the existence of mind by itself; or we begin with mind, and, assuming it as the first certain existence, we go on to the proof of others, but in this way we never legitimately reach the proof of the existence of matter by itself. The existence of mind was, to Des Cartes, an undoubted existence. I think, is a present consciousness, and the existence of an infinite mind was a lawful conclusion from the fact of the existence of a finite mind; but since the senses were distrusted, how was Des Cartes ever to prove the existence of matter? Only by means of the mind. We have no knowledge of the corporeal but through the mental; that we have a body is not a self-evident truth, but that we have a mind is. Yet Des Cartes wanted to have an external world, and as he could not prove its existence he took it on trust as other men do. As he had taken the existence of the mind independently of the body, why should not body exist independently of mind? Even on the principle of clear ideas we have some knowledge of matter, for the thinking substance is different from that which is the immediate subject of extension and the accidents of extension, such as figure, place, and motion.

Des Cartes was satisfied to have proved the existence of God, of mind, and of matter. The first is the uncreated substance, self-existent and eternal; the other two are created substances whose existence is derived from God. Their creation was no necessary act of Deity; their existence in no way flowed necessarily from his existence, but in the exercise of his own free will he created them. Mind is a something which thinks, and matter a something which is extended. God, too, thinks. He is incorporeal, yet we must not deny him the attribute of extension, so far as that attribute can be separated from any idea of imperfection. Extension being pre-eminently an attribute of matter, the transference of it to Deity in any form seems to betray a concealed conjecture in Des Cartes' mind, of some ultimate connection between the spiritual and the material. He had denied it, he had fought against the conclusion to which his method led him, but in spite of his protestation, the tendency is manifest at every step he takes. The attribute of matter has been transferred to God, and now consciously, but with no thought of the result, the attributes of God are transferred to the material world. Des Cartes contemplates the universe, and he is overwhelmed with thoughts of infinity and eternity. Is not the universe infinite ? It is at least indefinite, but this word is used only that the other word may be reserved for Deity. The universe is infinite. There can be no void beyond immensity. Illimitable extension is one of our necessary thoughts. It impinges on our idea of infinity, if it is not one with it. But if the universe is infinite, why not eternal ? If unlimited in space, why limited in time ? Des Cartes having placed the origin of the universe in the free will of God, was compelled to give it a beginning, but the question was urgent; why should it have a beginning ? If it is necessary to constitute infinite space, why is it not also necessary to constitute infinite time ? The necessity for a beginning deprives it of the existence of eternity past; but we may without danger, thought Des Cartes, allow it eternity to come. We have thus an infinite Being, and an infinite universe. At some point or other these two infinites must be only one. Creation is indeed a work, but unlike a human work it cannot exist without the continual presence of the worker. It requires for its existence a continual repetition of the Creator's act.

God is not at a distance from his universe. He is immanent therein; the executor of all laws, the doer of all works, the ever present agency that pervades and upholds the infinite all.

SPINOZA.

Des Cartes died a Roman Catholic, receiving in his last hours the sacraments of the Church. Though in his life-time persecuted for an Atheist, his memory is now revered throughout Christendom. Not so with Des Cartes' disciple, Benedict Spinoza. After two centuries of reproaches, theologians only now begin to do justice to his memory.

Herder and Schleiermacher have wished to claim Spinoza as indeed a Christian, but their claims have been long rejected, not only by the Churches, but by the open enemies of Christianity. Whatever may be said of his doctrines, all agree to represent him as a Christian in heart and life; an example of patient endurance; a man full of faith in the divine goodness, preferring to bring forth the fruits of the Spirit, to bearing the bitter apples of wrath and malice, strife and discord, by which the professed Christians of his day were distinguished. He once wrote, 'I repeat with St. John that it is justice and charity which are the most certain signs, the only signs, of the true Catholic faith ; justice, charity, these are the true fruits of the Holy Spirit. Wherever these are, there is Christ, and where these are not, there Christ cannot be.' It would be no great error to accord to Spinoza the name of Christian. He certainly was no enemy to rational Christianity. Nothing but ignorance could ever have classed him with the French Encyclopedists; and that is only a more culpable ignorance which classes him with any sect of materialists.

Of Spinoza's system, Bayle says that 'but few have studied it, and of those who have studied it but few have understood it, and most are discouraged by the difficulties and impenetrable abstractions which attend it.' Voltaire says 'that the reason why so few people understand Spinoza is because Spinoza did not understand himself.' It is now presumed that Spinoza may be understood, and notwithstanding the great authority of Voltaire, it is more than probable that he understood himself. Spinoza was avowedly a teacher of Cartesianism. His first

writings were expository of Des Cartes' philosophy. To these
he added appendices, explaining wherein he differed from that
philosopher. Spinoza was consistent, and went resolutely to
the conclusion before which Des Cartes stood appalled. His
doctrines were purely Cartesian. Some who would save the
master and sacrifice the disciple will deny this. It has been
maintained that he owed to Des Cartes only the form, and that
his principles were derived from other sources. The Cabbala
has been named as a probable source, and the influence of
Averroes on Maimonides and the Jews of the Middle Ages has
been brought forward as another.* That Spinoza had learned
all the philosophies of the Rabbis before he was excommunicated from the synagogue of the Jews is probable; but
there is no need to seek the origin of Spinozism in any other
system but that in which it had its natural growth—the
philosophy of Des Cartes. Spinoza's doctrines are indigenous
to the soil of Idealism.

Dr. Martineau, in a recent work on Spinoza, has argued that
Spinoza was not a Theist. He takes Kant's definition of God
as a being with 'free and understanding action'—in other
words, ' a living God'—and he infers that as Spinoza denied
God freedom and understanding, he really denied his existence.
But the same argument would have made Atheists of many
great theologians, who have spoken of God as the ineffable;
and therefore without attributes, as man conceives of attributes,
Spinoza would not have admitted the inference, because what he
denied to God after the manner of men, he ascribed to him in
a higher mode. Spinoza's phrases are described as being
ingeniously borrowed from the vocabulary of Theism, but out-
balanced by plainer propositions, which exclude all divine self-
consciousness and personality, and constitute a system of pure
Naturalism. If Spinoza did this knowingly, he did not deserve
the great praise that has been given him for sincerity and love
of truth. If he did it unknowingly, we are bound to give him
credit for saying what he intended, however imperfect or
contradictory his words may sometimes appear to be.

The first and most evident of our ideas, is that of an infinitely
perfect Being, whose existence is necessary. Des Cartes defined
this Being as an infinite substance, but he placed beside him

* Article by Emile Saisset in the ' Revue des deux Mondes,' 1862.

the infinite universe, which was a created infinite substance.
Spinoza could find place for only one infinite, so he denied to
creation the character of substance. It is dependent. It does
not exist in and by itself. It requires for the conception of it
the conception of some other existence as its cause. It is therefore not a substance, but only a mode of that substance which
is infinite. God being the absolutely Infinite, there can be no
substance besides him, for every attribute that expresses the
essence of substance must belong to him. Here Spinoza first
separates from Des Cartes. What one calls created substances,
the other calls modes. 'Substance,' says Spinoza, 'is that which
exists in itself.' 'A mode is that which exists in something
else by which that thing is conceived.' It would seem that the
first object of these two definitions was to mark definitely the
self-existing as substance, the dependent as something so different that it must be called the opposite of substance, that is a
mode. The mode has a substance because it partakes of the
one substance. And thus it is a reality at the same time that
it is only a mode by which the one reality is conceived. By the
Cartesian theory of knowledge we have God, mind or soul, and
matter. Through the medium of mind we arrive at the certitude of the existence of God and matter. Is God of a different
essence from mind ? Is mind of a different essence from matter?
Or is it that in some measure God communicates his essence to
all beings, and that they are, just in proportion as they partake
of his essence ? This last is the Cartesian doctrine which
Spinoza further expounds. 'These axioms,' he says, 'may be
drawn from Des Cartes.' There are different degrees of reality
or entity, for substance has more reality than mode, infinite
substance than finite. So also there is more objective reality
in the idea of substance than of mode, and in the idea of infinite
substance than in the idea of finite. 'God is the infinitely perfect Being, his being is distributed to all orders of the finite
creation in diverse degrees according to the measure of perfection, which belongs to each.' Angels and such invisible beings
as we know of only by revelation do not come within the region
of the philosopher's inquiries, and therefore no account is taken
of them. There is much ground for believing that created
beings of greater perfection than man exist in other worlds;
but man is the most perfect in this. Yet he is only part of

infinite nature, which is but one individual consisting of many bodies, which though they vary infinitely among themselves, yet leave the one individual nature without any change. And as being is constituted by the amount of perfection, that which is without any perfection whatever is without any being, so that what the vulgar say of the devil·as one entirely opposed to God is not true; for being destitute of perfection he must be equally destitute of existence. The philosopher has only to deal with thought and the externality of thought. Now though we may distinguish afterwards finite thinking beings, and finite external objects, yet our first and clearest conceptions both of thought and the externality of thought, are infinite. We first think the infinite, and then the finite. But this perfect Being, whom our mind reveals to us thus directly, is an infinite essence, and in his externality infinitely extended. Here in the very conception of him, the only attributes of which the human mind can have knowledge, are infinite extension and infinite thought. We have not reached the idea of God through external nature, but through the mind. Thought is first, externality follows it and depends on it. But if we call that world, which is exhibited to the senses, created nature, what shall we call that internal thought, whose image and manifestation it is? If the one is 'nature produced,' will it be improper to call the other 'nature producing?' They are so different that the one may be called 'producing' and the other 'produced,' yet they are so like—that is, they have their identity in a deeper aspect—that the word nature may be applied to both. Nature, however, is applied to the second in a supreme sense, and not as ordinarily understood, not the mere workings of the external universe, but the Being whom these workings make manifest.

Spinoza builds his whole system on the ontological argument as revived by St. Anselm and Des Cartes. We have in the mind a clear and distinct idea of an infinitely perfect Being of whose existence reason itself will not allow us to doubt. The two attributes under which we conceive this Being are infinite thought and infinite extension. Spinoza's doctrine seems allied to that ascribed to Plato, that the universe is God's thought realized. God is a being who thinks, and his thoughts under different aspects constitute the ideal, and the phenomenal worlds. As a being who thinks, God is primarily manifested

in the world of thought, that is, in beings who think. Des
Cartes had shown that thought is the essence of soul—the
foundation of spiritual existence, in fact, that the soul is a
thought. Spinoza added that it is a thought of God's; for divine
thought being a form of absolute activity, must develop itself
as an infinite succession of thoughts or ideas, that is, particular
souls. M. Saisset, in an ingenious chapter on this part of
Spinoza's doctrine, has pointed out, in one or two places in
Spinoza's writings, obscure but decided intimations that Spinoza
placed intermediaries between God and the finite modes or
particular souls. Existence had been divided into three kinds:
substance, attributes, modes, yet the last seems to have been
again divided into two kinds. There were modes properly so
called; the finite which are variable and successive, and other
modes of an altogether different nature which are infinite and
eternal. The infinite modes are more directly united to substance than the finite. 'Everything,' Spinoza says, 'which
comes from the absolute nature of an attribute of God must be
eternal and infinite, in other words, must possess by its relation
to that attribute eternity and infinity.'* For an example of
this kind of mode he gives the idea of God, so that between
absolute substance and any particular or finite mode, there are
at least two intermediaries—the attribute of substance and the
immediate mode of that attribute. The idea of God is not absolute thought, but the first of the manifestations or emanations
of absolute thought. It is infinite because it comprehends all
other ideas, and as it is an absolutely simple and necessary
emanation from the divine thought, it must be eternal. It
cannot then be confounded with the changing and finite ideas
which constitute particular souls. From the idea of God emanate
other modifications equally eternal and infinite. We have here
room for such an infinity of intermediaries, that we do not
know where the infinites end, and the finites begin. The chain
is endless. Spinoza did not name any of these infinite and
eternal modifications of the idea of God, but M. Saisset thinks
he is justified in reckoning among them the idea of the extension of God. Thus infinite thought, which has for its object
substance or being absolutely indetermined, is the foundation
of all ideas. 'Now,' M. Saisset asks, 'what does each of

* Proposition XXI., Ethica, Book I.

these ideas of each of these attributes of God contain, say for instance, the idea of extension? It comprehends the ideas of all the modalities of extension. Now what is the idea of a modality of extension? It is a soul—a particular soul joined to a particular body. The idea of extension thus embraces all souls. It is literally the world soul of Plato and the Alexandrians—the universal soul of which all particular souls are the emanations. It is an infinite ocean of souls or ideas. `Every soul is a river of this ocean. Every thought is one of its waves. The idea of extension is the soul of the corporeal world, but the idea of extension is itself a particular emanation of a principle which contains an infinity of ideas, a wave of a still vaster ocean. The idea of extension, and the idea of thought, with an infinity of ideas of the same degree, are included in the idea of God. The idea of God is then no longer merely the soul of the universe known to us. It is the soul of that infinity of worlds, which the incomprehensible fecundity of being is incessantly producing. It is truly the world soul, taking the world in that wide sense in which the infinite universe known to us—the universe of bodies and souls, matter and spirit, is lost as an imperceptible atom.' According to this interpretation of Spinoza's doctrine of intermediaries, we have for 'nature producing' God and his infinite attributes, thought, and extension, with all the infinity of attributes beyond the reach of the reason of man; and for 'nature produced,' we have the idea of God with an infinity of emanations, or modes both infinite and finite.

The world of bodies corresponds in its development to the world of souls, that is of ideas or thought. Spinoza defines a body as 'a mode which expresses after a certain determinate fashion the essence of God considered as something extended.' Des Cartes said that every body is a mode of extension. Spinoza added, a mode of the extension of God; for infinite extension, like infinite thought, is one of the attributes of God. But extension is nothing more than space, and the secondary qualities of bodies are but impressions of sensibility, from which it follows that bodies themselves are only ideas or expressions of thought taking definite forms in space. The only thing which bodies have in common is extension, and this is one of the two attributes by which God is known to the human mind.

The participation of bodies in this attribute is that which makes them alike. It is, so to speak, their substance while the modifications constitute the differences. But bodies and souls are distinct existences. The body does not depend on the soul, nor the soul on the body. The one exists as God's thought, the other as God's extension. They have their identity only in that substance, of which thought and extention are the attributes, that is in God.

The passage from the eternal to the temporal, from the infinite to the finite, is left by Spinoza in some obscurity. When did bodies begin to be? This question seems to have been answered when it is said that the only attribute which they have in common is one of the attributes of God. But extension is nothing more than infinite length and breadth, infinite height and depth; when and how do bodies become actual objects? Leibnitz answers for Spinoza, that he made his actual bodies from abstraction; with ciphers he made unities and numbers. In this he approached some of the old philosophers, who made corporeals by the meeting of incorporeals. And this was not some process which had a beginning, but one that was necessary and eternal. Spinoza accounts for the transformations of bodies by the mathematical laws of movement. In nature there is neither birth nor death. What we call birth is but the composition of simple modes of extension. Their decomposition we call death. For a time they are maintained in a finite relation, that is life. The inert elements of the corporeal universe are simple modes uncomposed. The most simple combinations of these modes form inorganic bodies. If we add to these combinations a higher degree of complexity, the individual becomes capable of a greater number of actions and passions. It is organized. It lives. With the increasing complexity of parts the organization becomes perfect. By degrees we arrive at the human body: that wonderful machine, the richest, the most diversified, the most complete of all, yea, that masterpiece of nature which contains all the forms of combination and organization which nature can produce; that little world in which is reflected the entire universe. The whole of nature is one individual. Its parts vary infinitely, but the individual in its totality undergoes no change.

P

The division of the all of existence into 'nature producing' and 'nature produced,' carries with it Spinoza's doctrine of creation. He clings tenaciously to the word creation, though he denies with all explicitness the doctrine of creation from nothing. This doctrine he calls a fiction and deceit of the mind, by which nothing is made a reality. God is not a great Being who works outside of his own essence. He is being itself—the Being who is all being. Creation depends immediately upon God without the intervention of anything with which or upon which he works. God is essentially a cause—the cause of himself and all things. Creation resembles the work of preservation, which, as Des Cartes has shown, is but a continual repetition of the work or act of creation. Yet that which is created is not substance, for no substance can be created by another. The essence of everything is eternal, for it is the essence of God. From the bosom of his unchanging eternity he unceasingly creates. He fills infinite duration with the exhaustless variety of his works; the effects of which he is the cause. But these works are not themselves infinite or eternal. The finite never becomes the Infinite. 'Nature produced' can never become 'nature producing.' Both are called God, but the one is only God in his finite modes, the other is God in his eternal activity. As we thus distinguish between infinite and finite, so must we distinguish between eternity and time. The first IS, the second is constituted by duration. Created things are necessary to its existence. 'Before creation,' says Spinoza, 'we cannot conceive either time or duration, for these began with created things. Time is the measure of duration, or rather it is nothing but a mode of thinking. Not only does it pre-suppose something created, but chiefly thinking beings. Duration ends when created things cease to be, and begins when they begin to be.' Eternity, which belongs to God alone, is distinct from all duration. Make it as vast as we may, the idea of duration still admits that there may be something vaster still. No accumulation of numbers can express eternity. It is the negation of all number. It follows then that nothing could have been created from eternity. The favourite argument of those who maintained an eternal creation is founded on the necessity of an effect following wherever there is a cause. And if God is the cause of creation, it must, they said, be eternal like him. Referring to these, Spinoza says, 'There are some who assert that the thing produced must be contemporaneous with the cause, and that seeing God was from eternity, his effects also must be from eternity. And this they further confirm by the example of the Son of God, who was from eternity begotten of the Father. But it is evident from what we have said above that they confound eternity with duration, and attribute to God only duration from eternity, which is evident from the very example they bring forward, for they suppose that the same eternity which they attribute to the Son of God is possible for creatures. They imagine time and duration before the foundation of the world, and they wish to establish a duration separate from things created; as others wish to make an eternity distinct from God. Either of which is very far from the truth. It is altogether false that God can communicate his eternity to creatures: the Son of God is not a creature but eternal as the Father. When we say that the Father has an eternally begotten Son, we only mean that the Father has always communicated his eternity to the Son.' Spinoza's idea of creation differs on the one side from the ordinary idea that God works on something external to himself, and on the other side it differs from the pre-eminently Pantheistic notion of an eternal emanation, from and out of the essence of the divine Being. Created things are indeed emanations but not eternal, for God is still God, and the creature is still a creature. M. Saisset compares Spinoza's doctrine of creation with that of the Church fathers, quoting St. Augustine who says in the 'City of God,' 'Before all creatures God has always been, and yet he has never existed without the creatures, because he does not precede them by an interval of time, but by a fixed eternity.' This seems to be the very doctrine of Spinoza, but how it differs from that of an eternal emanation, depends on the meaning given to the word eternal, which, with some of the old philosophers, meant unending duration, but with S. Augustine and Spinoza it is the negation of all duration.

Since created things are the modes of the Deity it follows that their existence is necessary. Des Cartes said that creation was due to the will of God uninfluenced by any motive. From this, Spinoza concluded that God must then act from the necessity of his own nature. God is free to create, that is, there is no motive from without, no subjection to fate, no compulsion to call forth creation, but this freedom is regulated by the nature of God, so that he acts by a free necessity. 'I am far from submitting God in any way to fate; only I conceive that all things result from the nature of God, in the same way that everyone conceives that it results from the nature of God that God has knowledge of himself. There is certainly no one who disputes that this really results from the existence of God, and yet no one understands by this, submitting God to fate. Everyone believes that God comprehends himself with a perfect liberty, and yet necessarily.'* We cannot ascribe will to God. In fact, will apart from volitions is a chimera; a scholastic entity or nonentity, as humanity abstracted from men, or stoneity abstracted from stones. Will is only a series of volitions, and a series of volitions is merely a series of modes of activity. But God is the absolute activity, even as he is the absolute existence, and the source of all existence. He acts because he is. For him to exist is to act. He is absolute liberty just as he is absolute activity, and absolute existence. In the words 'free necessity' Spinoza introduces a verbal contradiction, which he tries to explain. He controverts the popular belief in the freedom of the will. We act and we know that we act, but we do not know the motives which determine our actions. Liberty does not consist in the will being undetermined, but in its not being determined by anything but itself. Hence the definition:—'A thing is free when it exists by the sole necessity of its nature, and is determined to action by itself alone; a thing is necessary, or rather constrained when it is determined by another thing to exist, and to act according to a certain determined law.' God is free because he acts from the necessity of his own nature. 'All things result from the nature of God in the same way as it results from the nature of God that he has consciousness of himself; God comprehends himself with a perfect liberty, and yet by necessity.' Things which follow from the nature of God must necessarily exist. To imagine that God could order it otherwise is to suppose that the effect of a cause is not something necessary, or that in a triangle God could prevent that its three angles be equal to two right angles.

* 'Letter to Oldenburg.'

Spinoza's doctrine of the necessity of creation will help us to understand what he says about final causes. He does not deny that God thinks, for thought is one of his infinite attributes, nor does he deny that God is a living, conscious being who creates freely, though his freedom is regulated by his own nature, but he does deny that God works for an end. 'Men commonly suppose,' says Spinoza, 'that all the beings of nature act like themselves for an end. They hold it for certain that God conducts all things towards a certain definite end. God, they say, has made everything for man, and he has made man to be worshipped by him.' Spinoza introduces some confusion into his argument by identifying the doctrine of final causes with the belief that all things were made specially for the use of man. God may work for an end, though that end may not be to make all creation the servant of man. Yet this is the belief which Spinoza has chiefly before him when he speaks of final causes. 'Men,' he says, in the next page, 'meeting outside of themselves a great number of means, which are of great service to procure useful things, for instance : eyes to see, teeth to masticate, vegetables and animals to nourish them, the sun to give them light, the sea to nourish fishes, &c.; they consider all beings of nature as means for their use, and well knowing besides that they have met these means, and have not made them, they think that there is reason for believing that there exists another being who has disposed them in their favour.' It does not appear that Spinoza meant that men should not conclude from the works of nature that there is a manifest intelligence at work in creation. What he chiefly objects to, is that men judging of all things by their utility to man, suppose that for this end they were made, so that the master or masters of nature being themselves like men, have taken care of mankind, and made all things for their use. Spinoza denies God design just as he denied him will, because design is human ; a mode of finite working which cannot be supposed to exist in God. Infinite wisdom must differ from finite. God is intelligent ; yea he is intelligence infinite. He thinks though he has not understanding, just as he acts though he has not will, for understanding like will is a mere abstraction ; a succession of modes of thought, as will is of volitions. But God's thought cannot be a succession of ideas. It is infinite, and therefore we cannot

call it understanding without ascribing to the all-perfect the
conditions of imperfection. Understanding implies a process of
reasoning. It consists in passing from one idea to another;
going from the known to the unknown, till that becomes the
known; but all thinking and all knowing is included in the
ideas of infinite thinking and infinite knowing, so that understanding in the sense in which it belongs to man cannot be
predicated of God.

In this way Spinoza eliminates all imperfection from human
attributes before he ascribes them to God, lest he should carry
over into the divine nature the limitations of the human. This
principle which he had learned from Des Cartes he pushed to
its last consequence, even denying that God has the same attributes as man, or if he has, it is in a way so different that the
theological distinction between attributes, communicable and
incommunicable, disappears. Understanding and will have
been denied to God, and on the same principle he is incorporeal.
Extension is one of the two known attributes of God. It is
also an attribute of bodies; that which constitutes bodies, or
rather that in which bodies have their constitution. That God
is corporeal seems the necessary conclusion from extension being
one of his attributes; and so it would be if Spinoza were in any
sense a materialist. But though Divinity be exhibited to all
our senses by modes, it does not follow that these modes are in
themselves God. If they were anything real they would be
God. If they were God they would not be modes. But their
very name declares that they are not the essence, though the
eseence is manifested in them. God, therefore, is not corporeal,
for though the subject of extension, he is not the subject of
motion or division. He cannot be divided into parts; that
would clearly imply imperfection, to affirm which of God would
be absurd. 'Substance absolutely infinite is indivisible.' The
division which we see in the world is in the modes, not in the
substance. It is not extension which constitutes a body, but
division, so that God is not necessarily corporeal because he is
the subject of extension. It does not follow that whatever
substance is extended, is finite, for to be finite is contrary to
the nature of substance. We can conceive corporeal substance
only as infinite. In the same matter parts are not distinguished,
except as we conceive the matter as affected in different ways;

so that the distinction is not as to the essence, but only the modes. Water, for instance, we may conceive to be divided and separated into parts, so far as it is water, but not as it is corporeal substance; for as such it can be neither separated nor divided. The one substance, whose attributes are infinite thought and extension, is incorporeal; for extension is not body but being infinite it excludes the idea of anything corporeal. Although it is granted that God is incorporeal, yet this is not to be received as if all the perfections of extension were removed from him, but only so far as the nature and properties of extension involve any imperfection. This distinction between extension and corporeity, though not admitted in ordinary thinking, explains how God is incorporeal and yet infinitely extended.

Can we ascribe duration to God? Sir Isaac Newton defined God as that Being who endures always, and thereby constitutes duration. Spinoza says, we call God eternal that we may exclude from him the idea of duration. He does not endure, he IS. Duration is an affection of existence, but not of essence, and cannot be attributed to God, whose existence is one with his essence. No one can say of the essence of a circle or a triangle so far as it is eternal truth, that it has existed longer to-day than it had existed in the days of Adam. To ascribe duration to God would be to suppose him capable of division, and this would be contrary to his infinite nature. God does not, like created things, possess existence. He is himself existence, as he is himself essence. Has God life? As with duration and existence in the sense in which the created thing has it; God has it not. 'By life we understand the force by which things continue in their own being. And because that force is different from the things themselves, we say properly that the things have life. But the force by which God continues in his being, is nothing but his own essence, so that they speak right who call God life. There are theologians who think that because God is life, and not distinguished from life, is the reason why the Jews did not swear by the life of Jehovah as Joseph swears by the life of Pharaoh, but by the living God.' Again, God does not love, or hate. He is not angry with any man; he is without passions. The Scriptures indeed ascribe love and hatred to him, but they are altogether different from the human

emotions that go by these names. St. Paul understood this well,
when he said God loved Jacob and hated Esau before they were
born, or had done good or evil.

The effort to keep the perfection of God free from every
human element, led Spinoza to make the difference between the
human and the divine attributes, not merely one of degree but
of kind. He even denied that there was anything in common
between the divine understanding and the human, saying that
when we ascribe understanding to God, that attribute in the
divine Being has no more resemblance to human understanding than the dog—'the celestial sign,' has to the dog which
barks. Spinoza seems here for a moment to have lost himself
in the abyssal sea of the infinite. Every rational theology,
that is, every theology which has been reasoned out, can only
depend for its conclusions on the belief that the human mind
is a copy of the divine : that the one resembles the other, and
that the human mind is capable of knowing God, and to some
extent of understanding his ways. If there is no analogy between the mind of God and the mind of man, theology and
rational religion are impossible. The infinite, indeed, can never
be brought under the limitations of the finite, but if the difference is in kind, why did Spinoza attempt to tell us what God
is, or how he is related to creation ? The ground of his denying this analogy was that the divine thought was the cause of
human thought. One of his friends reminded him that he had
said, ' If two things have nothing in common they cannot be
the cause of each other, from which it follows that if there was
nothing in common between the divine and the human understanding, the divine could not be the cause of the human.' To
this, Spinoza answered that all beings differ from their causes
both as to essence and existence, excepting where like produced
like ; and referred to a scholium and corollary, where he had
shown in what sense God was the efficient cause of the essence
of created things. What he meant may be conjectured, but
the objection was never really answered.

Spinoza had used a strong and unfortunate comparison,
which expressed more than he intended. To another friend he
wrote, ' As to what you maintain that God has nothing formally
in common with created things, I have established the contrary
in my definition, for I have said, God is a being constituted by

an infinity of infinite attributes, that is to say perfect, each in
its kind.' The attributes which correspond to human attributes, he considered as existing in God after an infinite manner
indeed, yet not as differing in kind from the finite. That
Spinoza believed in the humanity of God is evident from what
he says in another place: 'The will of God, by which he wills
to love himself, follows necessarily from his infinite understanding, by which he knows himself. But how these are distinguished from each other, namely, his essence, the understanding
by which he knows himself, and the will by which he wills
to love himself we place among the things which we desire to
know. Nor do we forget the word personality, which theologians
sometimes use to explain this matter. But though we are not
ignorant of the word, we nevertheless confess our ignorance of
its meaning, nor can we form any clear and distinct conception
of it, although we constantly believe in the most blessed vision
which is promised to the faithful that God will reveal even
this to his own. That will and power are not distinguished
from the understanding of God we have shown from this, that
he not only decreed things to exist, but to exist with such a
nature, that is, that their essence and their existence depended
on the will and power of God; from which we plainly and
distinctly perceive that the understanding of God, his power
and his will, by which he has created and has known created
things, preserves them and loves them, are in nowise to be
distinguished but only in respect of our thoughts.'

Spinoza ascribed to God a kind of freedom: a free necessity.
But to created existences even this kind of fredom is denied.
'There is nothing contingent in the nature of beings; all things
on the contrary are determined by the necessity of the divine
nature, to exist and to act, after a certain fashion.' 'Nature
produced' is determined by 'nature producing.' It does not
act; it is acted upon. The soul of man is a spiritual automaton.
It is not an empire within an empire. It does not belong to
itself; it belongs to nature. It does not make its destiny; it
submits to a destiny made for it. Every individual acts according to its being, and that being is grounded in the being of
God. There can be nothing arbitrary in the necessary developments of the divine essence. There can be no disorder in that
perpetual movement which incessantly creates, destroys, and

renews all things. The harmony of the all is so perfect in itself, and all its unfoldings, that no possibility is left for free
will in the creature. Every being is determined to existence
and to action by another being, and so on for ever. Movements
produce movements, and ideas generate ideas according to a
law founded upon the very nature of thought and extension,
and in a perfect correspondence which again has for its foundation the identity of thought and extension in God. We imagine
ourselves to be free, but it is only imagination. It is a delusion
arising from our ignorance of the motives which determine us
to action. When we think that in virtue of any self-determin-
ing power in the soul, we can speak or be silent as we choose,
we dream with our eyes open. Were a man placed like the
schoolmen's ass between two bundles of hay, each of which
had equal attractions for him, he could decide for neither. If
hay were his food he would die of hunger rather than make a
choice. And if equally placed between two pails of water he
would die of thirst. Of course he would be an ass if he did,
says a supposed objector, to which Spinoza has no other answer,
but that he would not know what to think of such a man.
The old and stubborn objection to this doctrine will arise in
every mind. Is God then the author of sin? Spinoza answers
that sin is nothing positive. It exists for us but not for God.
The same things which appear hateful in men are regarded with
admiration in animals; such, for instance, as the wars of bees
and the jealousies of wood pigeons. It follows then that sin,
which only expresses an imperfection, cannot consist in anything which expresses a reality. We speak improperly, applying human language to what is above human language, when
we say that we sin against God, or that men offend God. Nothing can exist, and no event can happen, contrary to the will
of God. 'The command given to Adam consisted simply in
this, that God revealed to him that eating the forbidden fruit
would cause death. In the same way he reveals to us, by the
natural light of our minds, that poison is mortal. If you ask
for what end was this revelation given? I answer: to render
him so much more perfect in the order of knowledge. To ask
then of God why he did not give to Adam a more perfect will
is as absurd as to ask why he has not given to the circle the
properties of the square.' The consequence, which seems to us

naturally to follow from this doctrine, is that there is no difference between virtue and vice, good and bad. But this Spinoza
does not admit. There is a difference between perfection and
imperfection. The wicked, after their own manner, express
the will of God. They are instruments in his hand. He uses
them as his instruments, but destroys them in the use. It is
true they are wicked by necessity, but they are not on that
account less hurtful or less to be feared. We are in the hands
of God as the clay in the hands of the potter, who, of the same
lump, makes one vessel to honour and another to dishonour.

In a system where all is necessary, and where sin is only a
privation of reality, the distinction between good and evil cannot be more than relative. Our knowledge of things is imperfect. When we imagine, we think that we know. If nature
and the chain of causes were not hidden from our weak sight,
every existence would appear to us, as it is, finished and perfect.
Our ideas of good and evil, perfection and imperfection, like
those of beauty and ugliness, are not children of reason but of
imagination. They express nothing absolute—nothing which
belongs to being. They but mark the weakness of the human
mind. That which is easily imagined we call beautiful and
well-formed, but that which we have difficulty in imagining
appears to us without beauty or order. What we call a fault
in nature, such as a man born blind, is only a negation in nature.
We compare such a man with one who sees, but nature is no
more at fault than denying sight to stones. For man, however,
there exists good and evil relatively if not absolutely. But
these are resolved into the useful and the injurious. A thing
at the same time may be good, bad, or indifferent. Music for
instance is good for a melancholy man, but for a deaf man it is
neither good nor bad. Goodness is but the abstraction we make
from things which gives us pleasure. We do not desire them
because they are good, but our desire invests them with a supposed goodness. To the pursuit of what is agreeable, and the
hatred of the contrary, man is compelled by his nature, for
'every one desires or rejects by necessity, according to the laws
of his nature, that which he judges good or bad.' To follow
this impulse is not only a necessity but it is the right and the
duty of every man, and everyone should be reckoned an enemy
who wishes to hinder another in the gratification of the impulses

of his nature. The measure of everyone's right is his power. The best right is that of the strongest, and as the wise man has an absolute right to do all which reason dictates, or the right of living according to the laws of reason, so also the ignorant and foolish man has a right to live according to the laws of appetite.

The introduction of predestination, or necessity, into Spinoza's system gives it an aspect of terror. The heart of man recoils from that stern fatalism which makes men good or bad, and leads them on to reward or punishment, not according to what they are by choice, but according to what necessity has made them. But like all predestinarians, Spinoza was happily inconsistent. The fact that we are predestined must not influence us in our efforts. We must act as if no such predestination existed. The end Spinoza had in all his speculations, was to find a supreme good, such as would satisfy an immortal spirit. He exercised his reason with all earnestness, that he might know himself and God, and find that which would give him joy when temporal pursuits and pleasures failed him. The existence of good and evil, perfection and imperfection, taken in the moral sense given to them in the human consciousness, he denied. But he denied their existence only to re-affirm it in a higher, and as he reckoned, the only true sense. He had started with the perfection of God. We have an idea of such a perfection: an adequate idea of One who is the perfect. The infinite number of modes which emanate from the divine attributes are less perfect, and yet each in its rank of being expresses the absolute perfection of being in itself. There is then an absolute perfection and a relative perfection; the latter including a necessary mixture of imperfection. Everything is perfect according to the measure of reality which it possesses, and imperfect just as it lacks reality. What is good for man is that which is useful—that which brings him joy and takes away sorrow. Joy is the passage of the soul to a greater perfection, and sorrow to a less perfection; in other words, joy is the desire satisfied, and sorrow the desire opposed. The ruling desire in man is to continue in being: to be more that which he is. Our duty is to know what is the supreme good—the good of the soul. We need not interrupt Spinoza with any questions about duty when he has denied us free will. He will answer, that is alto-

gether a different question, and one that should not interfere
with our striving after perfection. It is a man's right, as well
as the law of his nature, to strive to continue in being. But
there are two ways by which this may be done: one is blind
brutal appetite, the other is the desire which is guided by reason. Now reason avails more than appetite. Reason is master
of the passions, appetite is their slave. Reason thinks of the
future, appetite only of the present. It belongs to reason to
think of things under the form of eternity; it affects the soul
as powerfully with the desire of good things to come, as with
those that now are. Its joys are not delusive and fleeting, but
solid and enduring. It nourishes the soul with a blessedness
which no time can change. Reason leads us to God and to the
love of God. The life of reason is then the highest life, the
happiest, the most perfect, the richest, that is to say, the life in
which the being of man is most possessed and increased. By
reason, man is free. He then regulates his life by a clear and
adequate idea of the true value both of the temporal and the
eternal. The cause of this we can see in the very nature of the
soul. It is an idea, a thought. Its activity is in the exercise
of thought. The more it thinks, the more it is, that is, the
more it has of perfection and blessedness. True thought is in
adequate ideas. All others lead to error and sorrow, and make
men slaves to their appetites and passions. The life of reason
is the most perfect life, because it is the life in God. 'The
supreme life of the soul is the knowledge of God.'

Spinoza's object was the same as that proposed by Des Cartes
—to prove that religion is the highest reason; that the doctrines
of religion are in accordance with reason, that is to say, rational.
Starting with the existence of God, which he held for a primary
truth, he went on to demonstrate the immortality of the soul.
This was involved in the definition of soul. It is an idea, a
thought of God's. As such it is an eternal mode of the eternal
understanding of God. It does not belong to time. Its existence is as immutable as that of its divine object. It does not
perceive things under the form of duration, that is, successively
and imperfectly, but under the form of eternity, that is, in their
immanent relation to substance. The human soul is thus a
pure intelligence entirely formed of adequate ideas, entirely active and altogether happy; in a word, altogether in God. But

the absolute necessity of the divine nature requires every soul
in its turn to have its career in time, and partake the vicissitudes of the body, which is appointed for it. From eternal life
it falls into the darkness of the terrestrial state. Detached in
some way from the bosom of God, it is exiled into nature.
Henceforth, subjected to the laws of time and change, it perceives things only in their temporal and changing aspect, and
with difficulty seizes the eternal bond which binds the entire
universe and itself to God. It does, however, seize it, and by a
lofty effort, surpassing the weight of the corporeal chain, it
finds again the infinite good which it had lost. The human
soul is thus immortal. The senses, memory, and imagination
being passive, faculties appropriated to a successive and changing existence, perish with the body. Then, too, the soul loses
all its inadequate ideas, which were the cause of the passions,
prejudices, and errors which enslaved it and led it astray while
it was in the body. Reason, which enables us to perceive things
under the form of eternity, alone subsists. 'The human soul
cannot entirely perish with the body. There remains something of it which is eternal.'

We have come from God. Once we existed in the bosom of
God, and loved him with an eternal love. Our souls fell from
eternity into time. They came into material bodies. We have
reminiscences of our former blessedness in that reason which
tells us that God is the highest good : the only true joy of the
soul. When the body is dissolved, and that order of things
which is constituted by the union of our souls with bodies is
ended, then we shall find the good which we lost, or rather
which was for a time hidden from our eyes. This is life eternal;
this is true blessedness, to find, in the contemplation of the
perfect Being, the satisfaction of the desire of our souls. Those
who now live rationally have a foretaste of this blessedness,
which they shall enjoy in its full fruition when all dies but
reason, and God shall love us in himself, and we shall perfectly
love God in us.

Spinoza pursues, throughout, the object which Des Cartes
had proposed—to show the reasonableness of religion; yea, to
demonstrate that religion is reason itself, and that reason is
religion. The highest life is the most rational, and that must
be religious. For what is reason ? That which gives us such

clear and adequate ideas of God, of ourselves, and of the eternal
relations of the universe, that we cannot do otherwise than love
God, and all mankind. And to be thus guided by reason is to
preserve and increase our being. It is to nourish the eternal
life within us. Our being is in thought, and the very essence
of thought is the idea of God. To know God is then our
highest knowledge. To love him is our highest joy. And
this participation in blessedness, leads us to desire that other
men may enjoy it too. It then becomes the foundation of
morality; the only true source of all good in men. The divine
law is thus a natural law—the foundation of religious instruction, the eternal original of which all the various religions are
but changing and perishable copies. This law, according to
Spinoza, has four chief characters. First, it is alone truly universal, being founded on the very nature of man, so far as he is
guided by reason. In the second place, it reveals and establishes itself, having no need of being supported by histories and
traditions. Thirdly, it does not require ceremonies, but works.
Actions which we merely call good because they are commanded
by some institutions, are but symbols of what is really good.
They are incapable of perfecting our understanding. We do
not put them among works that are truly excellent—among
such as are the offspring of reason, and the natural fruits of a
sound mind. The fourth character of the divine law is that it
carries with it the reward of its observance, for the happiness
of man is to know and to love God with a soul perfectly free,
with a pure and enduring love; while the chastisement of those
who break it is a privation of these blessings, slavery to the
flesh, and a soul always restless and troubled.

Spinoza starting with reason, and the reasonableness of
religion, of necessity came into collision with those parts of
Christianity which are at present above our reason. While he
could aim a deadly blow at superstition, and recommend the
general precepts and doctrines of Christianity, he was yet compelled to put aside, or relegate to the category of impossibles,
other doctrines or events which did not seem according to
reason. There was no revelation for him in the ordinary conventional sense of that word. Revelation was in the human
soul; in the light that God himself is kindling in men's
hearts. What we call revelation is but the gathering up of

the greatest and most important truths which God has revealed
to the human race. But they were revealed through the
human mind in the natural order of things, and while our
reason endorses them as rational, we are not compelled to
believe that the wisest of those through whom they were made
were free from the errors and prejudices of the age in which
they lived.

Revelation or prophecy Spinoza defines as 'a certain knowledge of anything revealed to men by God.' He immediately
adds that from this definition, it follows that natural knowledge may also be called prophecy, for the things which we
know by the natural light depend entirely on the knowledge
of God and his eternal decrees. The difference between
natural knowledge and divine is one of degree. The divine
passes the bounds which terminate natural knowledge. It
cannot have its cause in human nature, considered in itself,
but there is a light which lightens every man who comes into
the world, and we know by this that we dwell in God, and God
in us, because he hath made us to participate of his Holy
Spirit. The prophets, by whom the Scripture revelations were
made, had imaginations which reached after higher truths.
They saw visions that were not given to other men; visions of
which they themselves did not always understand the meaning.
But to Jesus was given an open mission. He saw and comprehended truth as it is in God. He was not a mere medium of
the divine revelation; he was the revelation, the truth itself.
'Though it is easy,' says Spinoza, 'to comprehend that God
can communicate himself immediately to men, since without
any corporeal intermediary he communicates his essence to
our souls, it is nevertheless true that a man, to comprehend by the sole force of his soul truths which are not contained in the first principles of human knowledge, and cannot
be deduced from them, ought to possess a soul very superior to
ours, and much more excellent. Nor do I believe that any one
ever attained this eminent degree of perfection except Jesus
Christ, to whom were immediately revealed, without words
and without visions, these decrees of God which lead men to
salvation. God manifested himself to the apostles by the soul
of Jesus Christ, as he had done to Moses by a voice in the air,
and therefore we can say that the voice of Christ, like that

which Moses heard, is the voice of God. We can also say in the same sense that the wisdom of God—I mean a wisdom more than human—was clothed with our nature in the person of Christ, and that Jesus Christ was the way of salvation.' Spinoza's relation to Christianity is a vexed question among his critics. In this passage he evidently presents Jesus Christ as the very incarnation of truth, which is the wisdom of God, and which, with the Greek fathers, was God himself or God the Son. He openly admitted that he did not hold the ordinary beliefs concerning God, the Trinity, and the doctrine of the incarnation. In a letter to a friend he wrote: 'To show you openly my opinion, I say that it is not absolutely necessary for salvation to know Christ after the flesh; but it is altogether otherwise if we speak of the Son of God, that is, of the eternal wisdom of God, which is manifested in all things, and chiefly in the human soul, and most of all in Jesus Christ. Without this wisdom, no one can come to the state of happiness, for it is this alone which teaches what is true and what is false, good and evil. As to what certain churches add, that God took human nature, I expressly declare that I do not know what they say, and to speak frankly, I confess that they seem to me to speak a language as absurd as if one were to say that a circle has taken the nature of a triangle.' He calls this the doctrine of certain modern Christians, intimating that there was no such doctrine in the early Church. God dwelt in the tabernacle and in the cloud, but he did not take the nature either of the cloud or the tabernacle. He dwelt in Jesus Christ as he dwelt in the temple, but with greater fulness, for in Christ Jesus was the highest manifestation, and this St. John wished to declare with all possible explicitness when he said that the Word was made flesh. Spinoza's doctrine will be best understood by comparing it with what the Alexandrian fathers have written on the Trinity and the incarnation of the Word or wisdom of God.

The fall of man was explained by Spinoza as we have more than once seen it explained by others. Man lost his liberty by eating of the fruit of the tree of knowledge of good and evil. Adam having found Eve, discovered that there was nothing in nature more useful to him than she was. But as he found that the beasts were like himself, he began to imitate their passions and to lose his liberty. He came under the dominion

Q

of his passions, which is the real bondage of the soul. To be
freed from this dominion is liberty. Redemption, or the
restoration of this liberty, began immediately after the fall.
The patriarchs were guided by the spirit of Christ, that is
to say, the idea of God. And this restoration, begun in the
patriarchs, will be carried on till man completely regains the
freedom which he lost in Adam. As the record of the fall of
man represented the loss of human liberty, so the resurrection
of Christ represented the rising from the death of sin. Christ's
resurrection was altogether spiritual, and revealed only to the
faithful, according as they could understand it. ' I mean,' says
Spinoza, ' that Jesus Christ was called from life to eternity,
and that after his passion he was raised from the bosom of the
dead (taking this word in the same sense as where Jesus
Christ said : " Let the dead bury their dead "), as he was raised
by his life, and by his death, in giving the example of an un-
equalled holiness.' Spinoza gave this instance simply as a
mode that might be adopted to interpret those parts of the
Scriptures which speak of things beyond or out of the course
of nature as known to us. But this was only an indifferent
and secondary matter. He was in reality opposed to explaining the mysteries of religion by subtle speculation, declaring
that those who did this found nothing in the Scriptures but
' the fictions of Aristotle and Plato.' He saw in the Scriptures
a practical religion : instructions how men may live righteous
lives, and the histories of men who have lived such lives. The
sum of all religion, both as taught by the Scriptures and by
the light within, is that there is one God ; that he loves justice
and charity ; that all men ought to obey him, and that the
obedience with which he is most pleased is the practice of
justice and charity towards our neighbour—in the words of
him who was pre-eminently the Teacher of religion to men, to
love the Lord our God with all our hearts and minds and
strength, and our neighbour as ourselves.

MALEBRANCHE.

To Malebranche the difference between himself and Spinoza
seemed infinite. And externally it was great. Spinoza was a
Jew, excommunicated from the synagogue ; Malebranche a

Christian priest. The one had been educated in the Cabbala, the other clung to the writings of St. Augustine. But great as were the external differences, impartial judges justly reckon them teachers of kindred theologies. Des Cartes, as we have seen, admitted two kinds of substance—the created and the uncreated—but in reality the latter was the only real substance. Spinoza saw this inconsistency, and made the created substances accidents or modes of the uncreated. But these created substances are evidently of two kinds—the spiritual and the material. Can these be reduced to one, or are they in their essence entirely distinct? Des Cartes was of the latter opinion. Spinoza held the former. From this resulted his belief in the original unity of the thinking and the extended substance; of God as thought and extension. Malebranche wished to keep the Cartesian ground, that they were distinct substances, and at the same time to remove the Cartesian dualism. He did this by supposing them distinct in themselves, yet finding their unity in God. As all things exist spiritually and ideally in the divine mind, God is, as it were, the higher mean between the I and the external world—'We see all things in God.' Malebranche, as a Cartesian, started with thought. We are a something which thinks; we have ideas. Whence have we these ideas? Some are immediate, but others are the ideas of things material. The latter we may have either from the objects themselves, from the soul having the power of producing them, or from God's producing them in us, which he may have done, either at creation, or may do every time we think of any object; or we may conceive the soul as having in itself all the perfections which we discover in external objects, or, lastly, as united with an all-perfect Being, who comprehends in himself all the perfections of created beings. Malebranche examines each of these five ways of knowing external objects, to find out the one that is most probable. He finds objections to them all except the last. His arguments for this are founded on the old Neo-Platonic doctrine of ideas. 'It is absolutely necessary,' he says, 'for God to have in himself the ideas of all the beings he has created, since otherwise he could not have produced them, and he sees them all by considering those of his perfections to which they are related.' God and the human soul are supposed to be so united that God may be called the 'place' of souls, as extension is the place of bodies. Spinoza could not have expressed this so well, nor could he have wished it expressed better. The chief attribute of the corporeal is extension. In it bodies have their being and essence. And as bodies are constituted in extension, so are souls constituted in God. 'It is the divine Word alone which enlightens us by those ideas which are in him, for there are not two or more wisdoms, two or more universal reasons. Truth is immutable, necessary, eternal; the same in time and in eternity; the same in heaven and in hell. The eternal Word speaks in the same language to all nations.' This speaking in us of the universal reason is a true revelation from Gôd. It is the only means of our possessing any true knowledge of things external. 'To see the intelligible world, it is enough to consult the reason which contains these ideas, or these intelligible, eternal, and necessary essences which make all minds reasonable and united to the reason. But in order to see the material world, or rather to determine that this world exists—for this world is invisible of itself—it is necessary that God should reveal it to us, because we cannot perceive those arrangements which arise from his choice in that reason which is necessary.'

The ideas of material things we see in God, but spiritual things we see in God immediately without the medium of ideas. In the spiritual, internal, or ideal world we are face to face with truth and reason. There we see, not ideas, but realities. There we know the Infinite, not through the idea of him, but immediately, and it is through him that we have our knowledge of all things finite. In him the material exists spiritually. Before the world was created God alone existed. To produce the world he must have had ideas of the world and all that is in it. And these ideas must have been identical with himself, so that in creating the world, he communicated himself to external objects. God eternally beholds his ideas. This is his converse with the eternal Word. This is God as Being, giving himself to God as Thought—the Father giving all things to the Son. This divine Word shines in our souls. By it we see in God some of the ideas unfolded in the infinite essence. God sees all things in himself, but a created spirit does not see all things in itself, because it does not contain all things in itself. It sees them in God, in whom they exist. When, for instance, we see a square, we do not see merely the mental idea within us, but the square itself, which is external to us. God himself is the immediate cause of this divine vision. He instructs us in that knowledge which ungrateful men call natural. He hath shown it unto us. He is the light of the world, and the father of light and knowledge. St. Augustine says that 'we see God in this life by the knowledge we have of eternal truths. Truth is uncreated, immutable, eternal, above all things. It is true by itself. It makes creatures more perfect; and all spirits naturally endeavour to know it. Nothing but God can have the perfections of truth; therefore, truth is God. When we see some eternal and immutable truths we see God.' After quoting from St. Augustine, Malebranche adds, 'These are St. Augustine's reasons; ours differ a little from them. We see God when we see eternal truths, not that these are God, but because the ideas on which these truths depend are in God— perhaps Augustine had the same meaning.' In starting from thought, Malebranche, like Des Cartes and Spinoza, had found the idea of the infinite to be the first and clearest of our ideas. 'This,' he said, 'is the most beautiful, the most exalted, the soundest and best proof of the existence of God.' It is the idea of universal Being, which includes in itself all beings. The human mind can know the infinite, though it cannot compre- hend it. We conceive first the infinite, and then we retrench the idea to make it finite, not, however, that the idea represents the infinite Being, for so far as it is an idea it represents some- thing determinate, but though our vision be dark and finite, we yet see and know God as the infinite. He is then identical with universal Being. We call him a Spirit, but this is not to declare what he is, but what he is not. He is not matter. He is as much above spirit, as spirit is above matter. The highest attribute which we know of that can belong to being is thought or mind, and therefore we call God a Spirit, but he is the infinitely perfect Being. As we deny him a human shape, so should we deny him human thoughts. His mind is not like ours. We only compare it to our own because mind is the most perfect attribute of which we know anything. As he includes in himself the perfections of matter, though he is im- material, so does he include in himself the perfections of spirit without being a spirit, as we conceive spirits. His name is HE

THAT IS. He is being without limitation; all being; being
infinite and universal. And as we have this distinct idea of
God as being, so have we another idea also necessary, eternal,
and immutable—that is, the idea of extension. It is impossible
to efface this idea from our minds, for infinite extension belongs
to being, or, at least, to our idea of being. Malebranche does
not make extension one of the attributes of God, but he ought
to have done, after what he has said of being and extension.
He maintains that the idea of extension is eternal and immutable; common to all minds, to angels—yea, to God himself
—that it is a true being, and identical with matter. We need
not draw any inferences from Malebranche's doctrines. It is
enough at present to show the parallelism between his views
on God, being, spirit, and matter, with those of Spinoza. As
our souls are united to God, and see all things in God, so our
bodies have their essence in extension. Between the substances, matter and spirit, there is no necessary relation. The
modalities of our body cannot by their own force change those
of the mind, and yet the modalities of the brain are uniformly
in connection with the sentiments of our souls, because the
Author of our being has so determined it.

And this immediate action of God is not limited to the mind
of man. It is the same through all nature. God has not given
up his creation to secondary causes; what we call such are but
the occasions whereby God, who is the universal cause, executes
his decrees as he wills they should be executed. It is true that
Scripture in some places ascribes events to secondary causes, as
in the book of Genesis, when it is said, 'Let the earth bring
forth;' but this is said improperly. In most parts of the
Scriptures God is spoken of as the immediate actor. He commands the children of Israel to honour him as the only true
cause, both of good and evil, reward and punishment. 'Is
there any evil in the city,' said the prophet Amos, 'and the
Lord hath not done it?' The works of nature are God's immediate works. He forms all things. He giveth to all life and
health, and all things. He causeth grass to grow for the cattle,
and herb for the service of man, that he may bring forth food
out of the earth. God never leaves his world. He is present
in it now as much as in the first moment of creation—in fact,
creation never ceases. The same will, the same power, and the

same presence that were required to create the world, are required every moment to preserve it. What we call the laws of nature are but the expressions of the will of God. He works by laws, but the working is not, therefore, less immediate or less dependent on his will and power.

Malebranche reminds us of Spinoza when he discourses of the passions. The human mind has two relations essentially different—one to God, and the other to the body. This is no meaningless comparison, as we may at once conclude from what has been said of our seeing all things in God. The union of the soul with God is not less than that of the soul with the body. By the union with the divine Word, wisdom, or truth, we have the faculty of thought. By our union with the material we have the perceptions of sense. When the body is the cause of our thoughts we only imagine; but when the soul acts by itself, in other words, when God acts by it, then we understand. Passions in themselves are not evil. They are the impressions of the Author of nature which incline us to love the body and whatever is useful for its preservation. Whether our union with the body is a punishment for sin, or a gift of nature, we cannot determine. But we are certain of this, that before his sin man was not a slave to his passions. He had a perfect mastery over them. But now nature is corrupted. The body, instead of humbly representing its wants to the soul, acts upon it with violence, becomes its tyrant, and turns it aside from the love and service of God. Redemption can be nothing else but the restoration of man to the dominion of the soul over the body, for this is to have God reigning within him.

But this question of the passions involves a further inquiry —what is sin? If God works whatever is real in the emotions of the mind, and what is real in the sensations of the passions, is he not the author of sin? Malebranche gives the old answer that sin is nothing real. God continually impels man to good, but he stops, he rests; this is his sin. He does not follow the leading of God, he does nothing, and thus sin is nothing. So far we have followed Malebranche simply as a philosopher, but how could he as a priest of the Roman Catholic Church, reconcile his speculations with the Scriptures, and the decrees of the councils? He did not attempt to reconcile them, or if he did the reconciliation was but partial. Where the Church has not spoken reason is free, but where the Church has spoken, whatever be our conclusions from reason, we must submit to the decisions of the Church. We have no evidence of the existence of an external world, but we receive it on the Church's authority. Our reason cannot be trusted with the mysteries of the faith. They are beyond the limits of our faculties. The incarnation, the Trinity, the changing of the bread and wine in the eucharist into the real body and blood of Christ, who can understand? It is well to exercise our reason on subtle questions that its presumption may be tamed, for is not reason the author of all the heresies that have rent the Church? Yet Malebranche used his reason, for after all a man cannot help using his reason, even if he be a priest in the Roman Catholic Church. Malebranche had a grand theory—worthy of Jacob Böhme—that all things were made for the redeemed Church. This world is finite and imperfect, but in Jesus Christ it becomes perfect, and of infinite value. Jesus Christ is the beginning of the ways of God—the first-born among many brethren. God loves the world only because of Jesus Christ. Even had God willed that sin should never have come into the world, yet Christ, the eternal Word, would have united himself to the universe, and made it worthy of God. Christ had an interest in man, independent both of sin and redemption. God foresaw the existence of sin. He decreed to give Jesus Christ a body to be the victim which he was to offer, for it is necessary that every priest have something to offer. God thought on the body of his Son when he formed that of Adam, and he has given every one of us a body which we are to sacrifice, as Christ sacrificed his body.

BERKELEY.

Bishop Berkeley's idealism ended in a kind of Pantheism. The first stage of his philosophy was the denial of matter in itself apart from the percipient mind. Locke had denied the secondary qualities of matter, but he believed in a substance which was the reality of the phenomenal world. For Berkeley, the phenomenal has reality only as the activity of the eternal Mind. Creation was not the coming into existence of things that did not exist before, but only their being perceived by other intelligences besides the divine. 'I do not,' he says, 'deny the existence of sensible things which Moses says were created by God. They existed from all eternity in the divine intellect and then became perceptible in the same manner and order as is described in Genesis. For I take creation to belong only to things as they respect finite spirits, there being nothing new to God.'* Things as revealed to sense are merely phenomenal. They have no substance in themselves, but depend on God for their permanence and substantiality. It has been shown † that the common accounts of Berkeley's philosophy are generally taken from his earlier books when his object was to prove the phenomenal character of the things of sense. In his later books he is more engaged in showing that the things of sense are a revelation of spirit. Berkeley's works are nearly all written in defence of religion. He flourished when the Deist controversy had reached its crisis. The Deists he often treats as atheists, and applies his philosophy in defence of Theism. His great argument is that the manifestations of mind throughout the universe show a living Agent as clearly as the works of a man show a human mind. It is the mind of which we are cognisant. Creation cannot be separated from mind. It does not exist, but as it is connected with mind, God speaks to man by sensible signs as plainly as men speak to each other, and the same evidence which we have of the existence of other men we have of the existence of God.

The development of Berkeley's philosophy into a kind of Pantheism took an eccentric form. He wrote a treatise on the virtues of tar-water, in which he imagined he had found a remedy for all the ills to which human flesh is heir. The acid spirit, or vegetable soul, which was extracted from tar by the help of water he believed to be something divine. The invisible firelight or ether with which it is charged, he called the vital spirit of the universe. When Berkeley wrote this treatise he had studied the ancient philosophers and the philosophy of the ancient religions, which in their Pantheistic form he defended as not atheistic, inasmuch as they recognised a mind or spirit presiding and governing the whole frame of things. The invisible fire or ether extracted from tar was in some way con-

* 'Letter to Lady Percival.'
† By Professor Fraser.

nected with the universal reason which pervaded all things.
It was the soul of the world, as set forth by Pythagoreans
and Platonists, but especially by the Neo-Platonists with whose
mystical speculations Berkeley, in this treatise, manifests increasing sympathy. As the phenomenal world is the sphere of
the divine activity, God is recognised as always present, behind
all phenomena, so that what we call the laws of nature are the
immediate working of the divine Agent, who is his own true
cause, and the cause of all the so-called effects in the physical
world.

LEIBNITZ.

Lessing once said to Jacobi that Leibnitz was as much a
Pantheist as Spinoza. Jacobi would not admit this, and on
further acquaintance with the writings of Leibnitz, Lessing
gave a different judgment. Indeed Leibnitz was so thoroughly
opposed to most of Spinoza's doctrines that our only reason for
introducing him here is to complete the history of Cartesianism.
Leibnitz wished to return to Des Cartes, and so to re-construct
Cartesianism as to refute on Cartesian ground the errors of
Spinoza and Malebranche. But he was only in a very limited
sense a disciple of Des Cartes. Locke said that there is nothing
in the mind which does not come through the senses. Leibnitz
added, ' except the mind itself.' So far as he agreed with Locke
he was a materialist, but so far as he differed from Locke he
was an idealist. Des Cartes had cast doubts on the existence
of matter, and from the idea of the infinite given in consciousness, he had proceeded to construct a universe. This universe
was in reality nothing more than space or extension—something
destitute of energy; an abstraction; a nothing. Now, said
Leibnitz, if Des Cartes' universe is not something real, then
God produces no ' reality ' external to himself, and if God produces nothing real—that is, if he is not a creative God—he is
only an abstraction. Into the conclusiveness of this argument
we need not make any inquiry. Des Cartes and Spinoza would
both have exclaimed that they were misunderstood. This
matters nothing here. The argument gives Leibnitz's point of
departure from Des Cartes.

Substance with Leibnitz was not an idea as it was with the

idealists, nor was it a substratum of matter as it was with the materialists, but a force; a dynamical power. The simple originals of beings he calls monads, which are metaphysical points to be thought of as we think of souls. God is the chief monad; the others are of different ranks and degrees from the humblest forms of matter to the highest spiritual substance. These monads are the true atoms of nature, so to speak, the elements of things. They are imperishable, simple, and original—they have no windows by which anything can enter into them or come out of them. And yet they have qualities, for without qualities they could not be distinguished from each other. Every monad must differ from every other, for there never were in nature two beings perfectly like each other. Being created, as they all are except the chief monad, they must be subject to change, but the principle of change must be from within, for no external cause can influence them. They are also called entelechies, because as simple substances they have a certain perfection. These have a sufficiency of themselves which makes them the source of their own internal actions. They are, so to speak, incorporeal automatons. Every body has a monad belonging to it. This monad is its entelechy or soul. The body with the monad constitutes a living creature, or an animal. Every body is organized. It is a divine mechanism, every part of which is again a mechanism, and so on infinitely for every portion of matter is infinitely divisible, so that there is a world of creation endowed with souls in the least part of matter. With Des Cartes and Spinoza, Leibnitz admits the infinity, and, after a fashion, even the eternity of the universe. But he defines infinity and eternity, when applied to the universe, as different from the same terms when applied to God. There is everywhere a relative infinity—in every particle of the universe an infinity of creatures, each of which again embraces another infinity, and so on for ever. This infinity extends to duration, and constitutes the eternity of the universe. Creation and annihilation do not take place in time but in eternity. To speak properly, nothing perishes and nothing begins to be. All things, even the most inanimate, are naturally immortal. But the immortality of a self-conscious monad is necessarily different from that of one which wants self-consciousness. It is not only

a mirror of the universe of creatures, but also an image of the
Deity. The human mind has not only a perception of the
works of God; it is even capable of imitating them. The soul
of man can discover and understand the laws by which God
made and governs the universe, and in its own little world it
can do the same things as God does in his great world. And
thus it is that men are capable of religion. They can know
the infinite. In virtue of their reason and their knowledge of
eternal truths, they enter into a kind of society with God.
They are members of the city of God.

Leibnitz as an idealist necessarily held to the ontological
argument for the existence of God. He even put it into the
form of a demonstration :—the being whose essence implies existence, exists, if it is possible ; that is to say, if it has an
essence. This is an axiom of identity which requires no demonstration.

Now God is a being whose essence implies existence.
(Through definition.)

Therefore, if God is possible he exists. (By the very necessity of the concept of him.)

The conception of perfect being is more than possible, it is
necessary. It is an absolute necessity of reason. Leibnitz
tried to strengthen this position by arguments drawn from experience, especially that which is found upon the non-necessity
of creation, or the contingent existence of the world. If necessary being is possible it must also be real, for if it be impossible
all contingent beings would also be impossible : if it did not
exist, there would be no existence at all ; which is what we
cannot suppose.

While Leibnitz remained on the ground of ontology he had
much in common with Des Cartes and Spinoza, but he wished
to escape their errors. To do this he gives prominence to the
other two great arguments which were either ignored or denied
by Des Cartes and Spinoza ; these were the cosmological, and
the argument from final causes. The world is manifestly a
work, and God is the worker. All phenomena must have a
producing cause—a sufficient reason. Nothing can happen
without a cause or antecedent. In the whole range of contingent, that is, created beings, there is not one which does not
take its origin in another. ' Every particular being includes

other anterior contingent beings.' Carry up the analysis as
far as we will, let us mount unceasingly from ring to ring, we
must stop at a first cause or reason placed outside of this long
chain; at the necessary Being in whom the series of events
and agents exist as rivers in their fountain heads. This Being
is the *ultima radix*; the last root of things. The cosmological
argument with Leibnitz runs into the teleological, and this it
ought to do, for the proper doctrine of final causes is not that
all things were made for the use of man, but that all things
manifest the wisdom of the great Author of nature. The end
may be the general good of the whole universe; it may be the
glory of God, or both of them together. Leibnitz often speaks
of the Divinity as the true end of all the movements in the
world. He identifies the life eternal, or the final goal of the
career of man with the very essence of the Divinity, and regards the moral activity of intelligent beings as an element
necessary to the felicity of God. God is free, and yet the divine
freedom with Leibnitz does not differ from the free necessity
of Spinoza. 'That pretended fate,' says Leibnitz, 'which
necessitates even the Divinity, is nothing but the proper nature
of God—his understanding, which furnishes laws for his wisdom and his goodness. It is a happy necessity, without which
he would be neither wise nor good.'

But though Leibnitz in some parts of his theology approaches
the Cartesians, his escape from everything Pantheistic is
supremely manifest in his denying the immanency of God in
the world. Des Cartes thought that an infinite, omniscient,
and omnipresent Being must be ever in his universe, and that
what is done in it must be done immediately by God. Leibnitz
thought this unworthy of God. If man can make a machine that
will work by itself, how much more can God? Why may not
he, like the human mechanist, retire from his work? 'He
would be,' says Leibnitz, 'a bad workman whose engines could
not work unless he were himself standing by and giving them
a helping hand; a workman who having constructed a time-
piece would still be obliged himself to turn the hands to make
it mark the hours.' God has made a perfect machine. It is
governed by immutable laws. We cannot even suppose, as
Locke and Newton did, that God sometimes interferes to restore it, or to keep it in repair. The very perfection of his

workmanship must exclude every such thought. He is a perfect worker, and therefore his work must be perfect too. But is it perfect? Leibnitz says this is the best of all possible worlds. Voltaire says it is the worst. Leibnitz says that out of an infinity of possible worlds infinite wisdom must have formed the best. It is not indeed a world without evils, but

> ' Discord is harmony not understood,
>   All partial evil, universal good,'
> ' Then say not man's imperfect, heaven at fault,
>   Say rather, man's as perfect as he ought,'
> ' Respecting man, whatever wrong we call,
>   May, must be right as relative to all.'

The divine mind has so arranged that all things shall work together for good. In making a contingent world, God foresaw what would happen through the action of moral agents and natural causes, and provided for these accidents, that they might be over-ruled for the general welfare of the universe. There was a pre-established harmony by which all things were necessary, and yet man was left free ; God

> ' Binding nature fast in fate
>   Let free the human will.'

This universal order we see everywhere rising above apparent disorder, and triumphing over it. How numerous are the marks of wisdom, visible in creation ! How beautiful the proportions ! How benevolent the intentions ! How wisely are the relations calculated, and how solidly organized ! The harmony in which they are maintained is permanent and universal. That harmony has an author. It is he who has arranged that this infinite diversity of beings shall maintain their places in the order of creation ; that there be a continuous gradation and a mutual dependence among all kingdoms, species, families, and individuals. Leibnitz explained all things by his pre-established harmony. By it the monads come together to form composite beings. By it all monads and composite beings maintain a perfect order in their existence. By it God operates upon mind and matter. He wound them up like two clocks, so that when we see a thing it is not because mind acts upon matter, or matter upon mind, but because it was pre-arranged from eternity that the object and the fact of our seeing it should occur at the same instant.

The rational explication which Leibnitz gave of the world, and his vindications of the perfections of God through maintaining that after all it is a perfect world, necessarily brought him in collision with the commonly received doctrine of original sin. If the world was once better, and may be better again, how is it now the best of all possible worlds ? Leibnitz's answer has been partly anticipated in his doctrine of relative perfection, and the educing of good from seeming evil. But to meet the objection fully, he divides evil into three kinds : metaphysical evil or imperfection, physical evil or suffering, and moral evil or sin. The two first he ascribes directly to God. The evil of imperfection is inevitable : it belongs to the creature. Everything created must be limited. In a relative and dependent world weakness must be mingled with strength, and light with darkness. The uncreated alone can be free from fault, infinite, and truly perfect. As to physical evils, we cannot say that God has absolutely willed them. He may have willed them conditionally, that is to say, as suffering, justly inflicted, for our faults, or as the means of leading us to good : the true end of man and only source of happiness. As to moral evil, Leibnitz falls back on the metaphysical doctrines of the fathers and the schoolmen. God gives us liberty. He respects that liberty in us. He sets before us good and evil, and leaves us to choose. We cannot charge human perversity upon God. He gives all things—that is true. He is the first cause of all things ; the first original of the power which we have to do evil ; the material element of sin, as St. Augustine expressed it. But this power, indispensable to every action, good or bad, is itself a boon, and in giving it God bears witness of his goodness. That, then, in sin which is real and positive comes from God ; that which is unreal and accidental belongs to us.

On the great question of the conformity of faith and reason, Leibnitz, like Spinoza, was purely Cartesian. The spirit of wisdom is the spirit of liberty. The wise man alone is free, said the ancient Stoics. Where the Spirit of God is, there is liberty, said St. Paul. And what is wisdom but the Spirit of God ? That which constitutes a created monad is its power of thinking. Much more must God, who gives us this power, possess it supremely in himself. God is thought, yea, the very essence of all intelligence, of all reason, and all knowledge.

The first original of things is a supreme mind. The doctrines of religion, if they come from God, must be rational. This was a great question in Leibnitz's day, and always will be a great question with men who think earnestly, and who are sincere and honest with themselves. For those who are too idle to think, or who are attached to some favourite dogma, it is convenient to decry reason and philosophy. The most enlightened theologians of the Roman Catholic Church—Pascal, Malebranche, Bossuet, and Fenelon—received what they called Catholic doctrines as mysterious dogmas, to which no principles of reason could be applied. Some even said that the more the mysteries shocked the reason and the conscience the more devoutly they were to be believed. Baronius called reason that Hagar who was to be cast out with her profane Ishmael. Nor was this spirit confined to the Catholic Church. Luther is full of it. The more, enlightened Protestants tried to harmonize the teachings of the Bible with those of reason and conscience, the more those who had to defend the dogmatic forms of the churches cried out against reason. Bayle, with his encyclopædic learning, had set forth all the received doctrines of Christianity, and in a spirit of the deepest scepticism had tried to show how incompatible they all are with reason. From this armoury in later times Voltaire drew the darts, which, winged with sarcasm, he aimed at the theologians who defied reason. Leibnitz had Bayle before him when he discoursed of the conformity of faith with reason. He maintains that what God reveals to man must agree with what man knows to be right. God's goodness and God's justice cannot differ from ours, except in being more perfect. They may be revealed doctrines above our reason, but not contrary to it. Even the mysteries may be explained so far as it is necessary for us to believe them. The Lutherans defended the doctrine of consubstantiation as rational. The Trinity is no contradiction in reason. When we say the Father is God, the Son is God, and the Holy Ghost is God, and yet these are not three but one God, the word God has not the same meaning at the beginning of the sentence which it has at the end. In the one case it signifies a person of the Trinity, and in the other the divine substance. The old fathers refuted the heathen religions by arguments drawn from reason, and defended the Christian doctrines as in the highest sense rational.

It is beside our purpose to follow Leibnitz further. Though sprung from the school of Des Cartes, he is henceforth the representative Theist of Germany.

In the former book, Mr. Maurice and Mr. Froude, the one in his 'Modern Philosophy' and the other in the 'Westminster Review,' July, 1855, were mentioned as all we had on Spinoza in English worth reading. We have now elaborate works by Dr. Willis, Dr. Martineau, and Mr. Pollock, with many articles in Reviews. Dr. Martineau has come to the strange conclusion that Spinoza was not a Theist. Mr. Maurice, who dreaded all philosophies of the Godhead, yet wrote, in his 'Modern Philosophy,' these words concerning Spinoza:—' He did not merely receive the witness of a one God from his mother's lips. The voice which spoke to Moses out of the bush was uttering itself in his generation. It was no cunningly devised fable, no story of another day. There was a witness for it in the very nature and being of man ; it might be brought forth in hard forms of geometry. In those forms it necessarily became contracted. Its life, its personality, were always threatening to disappear. The I am seems in the act of passing into the Being. (Mr. Maurice means Plato's ontological Deity, whom we have identified with the One of Parmenides.) But the change is never fully accomplished. The living God spoke still to the modern sage. He could not shake off the belief that His voice was in some way to be heard in the Bible. With all his physical science, all his reverence for the light of nature, he bows before the God of his fathers. There is awe and trembling in the worshipper. Though so clear in his perceptions, though so calm in his utterances, he often shrinks and becomes confused in that presence. He does not feel that he is alone in it : all men are dwelling in it : were it withdrawn all would perish.'

An account of the attempts to refute and criticise Spinoza would make a curious chapter. The first great effort was that of Bayle, who is generally said to have refuted the whole of Spinozism. Bayle's argument was very profound and very conclusive. It consisted in disregarding Spinoza's definition of substance, and then going on to prove that everything had a substance of its own. Voltaire suspects that Bayle did not quite understand Spinoza's substance, and suggests how Spinoza might really be refuted. This is the process : Spinoza builds his theory on the mistake of Des Cartes, that 'Nature is a Plenum.' As every motion requires empty space, what becomes of Spinoza's one and only substance ? How can the substance of a star, between which and me there is a void so immense, be precisely the substance of this earth, or the substance of myself, or the substance of a fly eaten by a spider ? Voltaire's argument is as ingenious as Bayle's is profound and conclusive. Even Emile Saisset, who is by far the best expositor of Spinoza, is not always to be trusted. Both in his introduction to Spinoza's works, and in his 'Essay on Religious Philosophy,' he makes a rhetorical picture of Spinoza finishing the first book of his 'Ethica,' pronouncing, with perfect serenity, 'I have explained the nature of God.' These words are certainly in the 'Ethica,' but there is a comma after God, and the sentence goes on 'as that which necessarily exists,' &c. The Latin is, *His Dei naturam ejusque proprietates explicui, ut quod necessario existat, quod sit unicus, &c.* M. Saisset translates it apparently to make way for his own rhetoric, *J'ai explicui dans ce qu'on vient de lire la nature de Dieu et ses proprietés; J'ai montré que Dieu existe nécessairement, qu'il est unique, &c.* Mr. Froude, misled apparently by Saisset, has repeated this criticism. Voltaire complained of the difficulty of understanding Spinoza, but surely Spinoza has cause to complain of the want of understanding in his critics. An English clergyman has prefixed an introduction to a tract of Leibnitz's recently discovered, which has been published as a refutation of Spinoza. The tract does not profess to deal with more than one point of Spinoza's philosophy, and that a subordinate one, but the editor lauds it as a complete refutation. 'Unnecessary, indeed,' he goes on to say, 'for we all know that Dr. Adam (!) Clark refuted Spinoza a hundred years ago.'

Voltaire's article on Spinoza is in the 'Philosophical Dictionary.'

CHAPTER XIII.

TRANSCENDENTALISM.

FROM French Idealism to German Transcendentalism we pass over nearly a century. That century was the remarkable eighteenth, generally despised as superficial, and lamented as Godless. The philosophy of Locke, which did not concern itself with ' being' and ' essence,' represented the disposition of the English mind in its relation to all doctrines that savoured of Pantheism or mysticism. Carried into France, that philosophy, developed on its materialistic side, bore its legitimate fruit; an atheism such as the world had never seen. It was reserved for Germany to revive idealism; to re-assert that there is in the human soul an overwhelming conviction of the existence of God, and with this to restore the rejected Pantheisms and neglected mysticisms of past ages.

KANT.

Transcendental philosophy, which is merely another name for German idealism, takes its beginning from Kant. He, however, only laid the foundation : his successors reared the superstructure. Kant, like Locke, was a reformer in philosophy, concerning himself not so much with being as with our modes of knowing being. So far as he was instrumental in the restoration of a philosophy of being and essence, he was only an unwilling contributor. Idealism in the hands of Hume had met the same fate that materialism had met in the hands of the idealists. Hume returned to absolute doubt. We have ideas, but we know nothing more. We have no right to identify thought with reality.

Cartesianism, as interpreted by Leibnitz, and systematized by Christian Wolf, was the orthodox philosophy of Germany. It had grown into an extravagant dogmatism, no longer tenable in the presence of the scepticism of France and

England. Kant applied himself to the criticism of philosophy
that he might save it both from this dogmatism and this scepticism. He tested the powers of the intellect, and essayed to fix
the limits of reason. He tried to hold the balance between the
materialist and the idealist, maintaining with the one the
necessity of experience to give validity to our intellectual
cognitions; with the other, that the intellect is the basis of our
knowledge, and that it contains *a priori* the conditions on
which we know anything by experience. A criticism of reason
naturally led to a criticism of the conclusions of reason, or
rather it included them. Prominent among these were the
proofs of the being of God, in the Cartesian and Leibnitzian
philosophies, the 'ontological,' and 'cosmological,' and peculiarly in the original philosophy of Locke, the 'physico-
theological.' To the first, Kant objected that though we have
the idea of an all-perfect Being, the existence of that Being is
not formed by our having the idea, any more than the existence of a triangle is formed by the definition of a triangle.
In the second he objected that from the contingent or conditioned which we know, to the necessary or unconditioned which
is beyond experience, we can make no valid inference. The last
he showed to be imperfect, as from design we cannot argue the
existence of any being greater than a designer. The argument
proves a world maker, but not a Creator; a framer, but not a
maker of matter.

The idea of God, which Des Cartes recognised as in-born in
the human mind, had been elaborated by a process of dialectics
into a demonstration of the existence of God. Kant objected
to the conclusion, and yet admitted the fact of the existence of
the idea, and while admitting it, endeavoured to determine how
far, and in what manner, our reasonings concerning it are justified. In objecting to the idealistic arguments as theoretical
demonstrations, he opposed the idealists. In again establishing
their practical validity, he opposed the sceptics. His guide,
however, was not eclecticism, but criticism. His object was
not idealistic, nor realistic, but to find exactly what was true
in idealism and in realism.

The idea of God is in the mind, but his existence is not
verified by experience, for it transcends experience. So on the
other hand, the idea of the external world is derived through

the senses. We have experience, or empirical knowledge of its existence. Practically it exists; but as we have no cognition of anything external, by, and in itself, without the mind accompanying the cognition, so in pure reason its existence cannot be demonstrated. In the external world we have phenomena. Beyond this we can demonstrate nothing. True to his principle of a critical investigator, Kant wished to stop here, as having reached the furthest boundary of the possibility of human knowledge. Further than this, he was not an idealist, and only thus far is he the founder of Transcendentalism. In the first edition of his 'Critique of the pure Reason,' he threw out a conjecture that perhaps the reality of phenomena was only the I that contemplates it; that the thinking mind and the thing thought are perhaps one and the same substance.

On this conjecture Fichte started the doctrine of the I-hood. Kant disowned Fichte's doctrine, and protested that he was not responsible for the development of his ardent disciple. He omitted this passage in all subsequent editions of the 'Critique.'

The primitive duality, then, of subject and object was left untouched by Kant. The one he maintained to be the complement of the other, and both were reckoned necessary to make knowledge possible—subject as the form or the principle of our representations, and object as the principle of the matter of these representations. The one being thus necessary to the other, it could not be proved that either of them was a real being. Something real in their internal nature there must be, but what this substratum of phenomena is, what this being is which unites subject and object, was not only left by Kant undefined, but even declared to be beyond our knowledge.

FICHTE.

It might have been supposed that the critical philosophy of Kant was omnipotent to check all further speculation concerning the nature of that which IS. Had he not fixed the limits of the human mind, and shown the impossibility of any science of the absolutely unconditioned? Had he not shown that it was impossible to demonstrate the truth, either of idealism or materialism; that, in the one case, we had no means of verifying by experience the ideas in the mind, and, in the other, no means of knowing the existence of objects independent of the mind always present in the cognition of them. Philosophy seemed to have spoken its last word. Materialism and idealism had been fairly weighed, and the truth in each impartially acknowledged. 'But,' said Fichte on the side of idealism, 'is not our knowledge of the subject greatly more than that of the object, and, moreover, prior to it? We know that we have an internal world, and only through the medium of it do we know that there is an external world. The existence of my I, my consciousness, is a primary fact. The existence of anything external is only seen in the mirror of this I. Its existence, therefore, is dependent, and may be only apparent. The subject is the manifest reality; the primitive ground of knowledge; the true foundation of philosophy.

On this consciousness Fichte based his philosophy, and from the given existence of the I it received its first form. We think it our most certain knowledge. What it is which thinks need not concern us. Of its essence we know as little as we do of the substance of the world. Indeed we may not be justified in concluding that such an essence exists. We need not suppose its existence; it is enough to take by itself the simple fact of consciousness. This is only cognised by us as an activity. It is the act of forming and representing internal images. We must, however, distinguish between the act and the image—the one is the acting process, the other the process by which it acts. In this way the I creates itself. By thus acting it becomes actually what it is potentially. It renders itself self-conscious. And in this act of the I we have a duality, itself and the object it evokes. The I, in positing its own existence, posits also that of the non-I. These two principles stand in the consciousness opposed to each other—the one limiting and determining the other, for what the I is the non-I is not, and what the non-I is the I is not. But the I, in determining itself to a representation, does so with the consciousness that the representation is only a modification of itself; so that the I and the non-I are again united in one and the same consciousness. The formula is thesis, antithesis, synthesis.

Jacobi called this philosophy 'an inverted Spinozism.' In place of the absolute substance Fichte substituted the I. He thought by this to avoid Spinoza's theology, but the endeavour was vain. He had ultimately to go beyond the I, for in no other way could he reach the Infinite. The finite consciousness disappeared in the infinite consciousness. The I found nothing but its own reflex. It sought a God, but it only found itself—the I answering to the I. Freed from the limits which it produces for itself, our I is the infinite I of the universe; that in which all finite I's lose their existence, and in which are embraced as its representation all the varied phenomena of the external world. There is originally and essentially but one consciousness—that of the absolute infinite I. Every effort to represent this I as conceivable by the human intellect was rejected by Fichte as anthropomorphism. The supposition of a personal God was a mere transference of human limits and imperfections to the Divine Being; for when we ascribe to him such attributes as consciousness, or extra-mundane existence, we only make him finite, for these qualities necessarily include the idea of substance extended in time and space.

God is not substance. The attributes ascribed to him by Spinoza are liable to the same objections as were made to the common anthropomorphism. If they do not make God man, they yet limit him. They make him corporeal, and substitute a substratum of the universe for the divine activity. Nor do we escape this result by calling God a spirit. What is spirit? A mere negation of body, a term which as a positive definition of God is wholly useless, unless by a deception of the mind we ascribe to spirit some of the qualities which constitute a body. For the same reason that we deny to God consciousness, personality, and substantiality, we also deny him reality; all reality being to us only finite. God cannot be adequately conceived, defined, or represented; for conceptions, definitions, and representations are only applicable to things limited and determined. 'If,' says Fichte, 'we call God a consciousness, it follows that we apply to him the limits of the human consciousness. If we get rid of this limit of thought, then there remains to us a knowledge which is quite incomprehensible, and this might well be ascribed to God, who, so to speak, is in this sense pure consciousness, intelligence, spiritual life, and activity, save only that we could form no notion of such attributes, and on that account would rather abstain from the approximate definition, and that, too, out of strict regard to

philosophical accuracy, for every conception of the Deity would
be an idol.'

God is the infinite I, clearly incomprehensible. The finite
I is known only as an activity, and so likewise only as an
activity do we know God. We are constituted in a moral
order. As finite I's we have duties and destinies. By fulfilling
these we realise our place in the moral order of the universe.
And this order is the highest idea of God to which we can
attain. We need no other God, we can comprehend no other.
Only by this moral order living and working in us do we perceive anything divine. God is not a being or an existence, but
a pure activity—the life and soul of a transcendent world
order, just as every personal I or finite intelligence is no being,
but a pure activity in conformity with duty, as a member of
that transcendent world order.

This form—the form of morality—is the second phase of the
development of Fichte's philosophy. It incurred, as we might
have expected, the charge of atheism. Jacobi said it was the
'worship of mere universality,' and even Schelling said 'that
it swallowed up all religion.' Fichte defended himself, and in
his later works so explained his meaning as to leave no doubt
of his firm faith in God. Jäsche says, ' The idealist's religious
faith in a moral order of the world is now raised to a higher
standpoint ; to the realistic religious faith in a living and
independent intelligent principle of the world order ; and for
the proud self-feeling of absolute freedom, we now have
humility and submission to an absolute will.' These later
writings were addressed to popular audiences. A mystical
faith had taken the place of metaphysical reasonings. Man
reaches the knowledge of God in pure thought, which is the
eye of the soul. By this he perceives God, for what is pure
thought but the divine existence ? Of the mode of God's being
we know nothing, nor do we need to know. ' We cannot
pierce the inaccessible light in which he dwells, but through
the shadows which veil his presence there flows an endless
stream of life, and love, and beauty. He is the fountain of our
life, the home of our spirits, the one Being, the I AM, for whom
reason has no idea, and language has no name.' In conscious
union with the Infinite, addressing him as a ' sublime and
living will,' Fichte exclaims, ' I may well raise my soul to thee,

for thou and I are not divided. Thy voice sounds within me, mine sounds in thee, and all my thoughts, if they are but good and true, are in thee also. In thee the incomprehensible, I myself and the world in which I live, become comprehensible to me. All the secrets of my existence are laid open, and perfect harmony arises in my soul. I hide my face before thee, and lay my hand upon my mouth. How thou art and seemest to thine own being I can never know, any more than I can assume thy nature. After thousands upon thousands of spirit lives I shall comprehend thee as little as I now do in this house of clay. Thou knowest, and willest, and workest, omnipresent to finite reason, but as I now and always must conceive of being, thou art not.'

God knows, wills, and works. He is something more than a principle, just as he is something more than a person. Yet our highest conception of him is as a principle, as the world order; and our most convincing proof of his existence is in the realization of our place in this order. Then we become conscious of our oneness with him. We cannot become God, but when we annihilate ourselves to the very root, God alone remains, and is all in all. We speak of our existence as something distinct from God's, but ours is only the negation of existence. Apart from the being of God our being is a mere semblance, which has assumed the form and appearance of being. That, alone, is reality, which is good and true. Our highest conception of being is identical with our highest conception of good—a principle of right. What then is blessedness, but to seek this true life ? The eternal is in us and around us on every side. Would we realize this presence ; would we feel that this eternal being is our being, then must we forsake the transitory and apparent, and cling with an unfailing love to the unchangeably true, and everlastingly good. God is goodness unceasingly active, in what the holy man does, lives, and loves, God appears in his own immediate and efficient life. Nor in man only does God appear, but in all nature the soul purified from the love of the transitory and unreal may see him immediately present. ' Through that,' says Fichte, ' which seems to me a dead mass, my eye beholds this eternal life and movement in every vein of sensible and spiritual nature, and sees this life rising in ever-increasing growth, and ever purifying itself to a more spiritual

expression. The universe is to me no longer that eternally repeated play; that monster swallowing up itself only to bring
itself forth again as it was before. It has become transformed
before me, and bears the one stamp of spiritual life; a constant
progress towards higher perfection in a line that runs out into
the infinite. The sun rises and sets. The stars sink and re-
appear, and all the spheres hold their circle-dance, but they
never return again as they disappeared. And even in this light-
fountain of life itself, there is life and progress. Every hour
which they lead on; every morning and every evening sinks
with new increase upon the world. New life and love descend
from the spheres, and encircle nature as the cool evening encircles the earth.'

Wherefore, it is asked, should man doubt of life and immortality? Are they not clearly revealed to the soul that loves
the true life? Being passes through its phases, but it does not
cease to be. A dark soul not recognizing its root in the Godhead may be troubled at the changes in nature, and made sad
by the passing away of that which to it alone seems real. But
is not all death in nature birth? In death itself visibly appears
the exaltation of life. There is no destructive principle in
nature, for nature throughout is free and unclouded life. It is
not death which kills, but the new life concealed behind death
begins to develop itself. Death and birth are but the struggle
of life with itself to assume a more glorious and congenial form.
'And my death,' said Fichte, speaking as one who participated,
in this blessed and unchanging life, 'how can it be aught else
but birth, since I am not a mere sham and semblance of life,
but bear within me the life which is one, true, original, and
essential. It is impossible to conceive that nature should annihilate a life which does not proceed from her: nature exists for
me, I do not exist for her.'

Fichte did not profess to derive his doctrines from Christianity, yet he did maintain, that between them and Christianity
the identity was complete. He lived in that life in which
Christ lived, and drew his inspiration from the same fountain
of truth. All true men have found their strength there, and
Christ above all others because he was supremely true. Christianity then is no external revelation, but God speaking and
working in humanity. By Christianity, however, Fichte only

meant what he called the Johannean gospel. He rejected St. Paul and his party as unsound teachers of Christian doctrine. They were but half Christians, and left untouched the fundamental error of Judaism and Heathenism. St. John was the disciple who had respect for reason: He alone appealed to that evidence which has weight with the philosopher—the internal. 'If any man will do the will of him that sent me he shall know of the doctrine whether it be of God.' The preface to St. John's gospel is not to be regarded as a merely speculative prelude to an historical narrative, but is to be taken as the essence and standpoint of all the discourses of Jesus. In the sight of John this preface is not his own doctrine, but that of Jesus, and indeed is the spirit, the innermost root of the whole doctrine of Jesus. And what is the doctrine of that preface? Its subject is creation. Precisely that on which Judaism and Heathenism had erred. Compelled to recognize the absolute unity and unchangeableness of the divine nature in itself, and being unwilling to give up the independence and real existence of finite things, they made the latter proceed from the former by an act of absolute and arbitrary power. The Jewish books begin:—'In the beginning God created.' No, said St. John, in express contradiction to this. In the beginning; in the same beginning which is there spoken of; that is, originally and before all time, God did not create, for no creation was needed, but was there already. 'In the beginning was the Word; and all things were made by it.' In the beginning was the Word; in the original text the Logos, which might be translated reason, or as nearly the same idea is expressed in the book called the 'Wisdom of Solomon,' wisdom. John says that the Word was in the beginning, that the Word was with God, that God himself was the Word, that the Word was in the beginning with God.

Fichte asks—'Was it possible for John to have more clearly expressed the doctrine which we have already taught in such words as the following:—Besides God's inward and hidden being in himself, which we are able to conceive of in thought, he has another existence which we can only practically apprehend, but yet this existence necessarily arises through his inward and absolute being itself; and his existence, which is only by us distinguished from his being, is in itself and in him not distinguished from his being, but this existence is originally before all time, and independently of all time, with his being, inseparable from his being, and itself his being—the Word in the beginning, the Word with God, the Word in the beginning with God, God himself the Word, and the Word itself God. Was it possible for him to set forth more distinctly and forcibly the ground of this proposition, that in God and from God there is nothing that arises or becomes, but in him there is only an IS; an eternal present, and whatever has existence must be originally with him, and must be himself? "Away with the perplexing phantasm," might the Evangelist have added had he wished to multiply words. "Away with that perplexing phantom of a creation from God, of a something that is not himself, and has not been eternally and necessarily in himself; an emanation in which he is not himself present, but forsakes his work—an expulsion and separation from him that casts us out into desolate nothingness, and makes him an arbitrary and hostile Lord."'

The immediate existence of God is necessarily consciousness —reason. In it the world and all things exist, or as John expresses it, they are in the Word. They are God's spontaneous expression of himself. That Word or consciousness is the only Creator of the world, and by means of the principle of separation contained in its very nature, the Creator of the manifold and infinite variety of things in the world. This Word manifested itself in a personal, sensible, and human existence; namely, in that of Jesus of Nazareth, of whom the Evangelist truly said, he was 'the eternal Word made flesh.' In and through him, others were to be partakers of the divine nature. His disciples were to be one with him as he was one with the Father. This is the characteristic dogma of Christianity as a phenomenon of time; as a temporary form of the religious culture of man. But the deep truth which it reveals is the absolute unity of the human existence with the divine. Christ does not constitute that union, but reveals to us the knowledge that it exists. Before him it was unknown, and all who have since known it, may ascribe that knowledge to him. The philosopher may indeed discover it, but it is already revealed to him in Christianity. All Christ's discourses as recorded by John are full of it. We must eat his flesh and drink his blood—that is, we must be transformed into him. We must live his life, not in imitation merely, but in a faithful repetition. We must be like him, the eternal Word made flesh and blood. For those who repeat the character of Christ he prays that they all may be one, as 'Thou Father art in me and I in thee that they also may be one in us.' One in us—all distinctions are laid aside. The whole community, the first-born of all, with his more immediate followers, and with all those who are born in later days, fall back together into the one common source of all life, the Godhead. Thus Christianity, its purpose being obtained, falls again into harmony with the absolute truth, and maintains that every man may and ought to come into unity with God, and in his own personality become the divine existence in the eternal Word. 'No man had ever a higher perception of the identity of Godhead and humanity than the founder of Christianity. He never supposed the existence of finite things; they had no existence for him. Only in union with God was there reality. How the nonentity assumed the semblance of being, the difficulty from which profane speculation proceeds, he never cared to inquire. He knew truth in himself, he knew it solely in his own existence. He knew that all being is founded in God alone, and consequently that his own being proceeds directly from him. When he showed his disciples the way to blessedness, he told them to be like himself, for he knew of no blessedness but in his own existence. They were to come to him for life, and they were to find it by being in him as he was in the Father, and being one with him as he was one with the Father.'

SCHELLING.

With Fichte the reality of the object had disappeared. The non-I was only the production of the I. Here he departed from Kant, who left subject and object as correlates, the one giving validity to the other. At the same point Schelling departed from Fichte. The arguments which rendered the existence of the object uncertain prevail equally against the existence of the subject. But why should we not believe in the existence of the external world, or why should we doubt our own existence? After all our reasonings, the fact still

remains that we do exist, and with our existence emerges face
to face an existence which is not ours. The I and the
non-I continue to assert their being—the subject as validly
as the object, and the object as validly as the subject.
Is either of them real, and which ? Fichte said the subject.
Schelling said both are real, but they have their reality
in the identity of the two. The thinking process reveals
to us not merely a subject or an object, but both as one—
the mind thinking and the thing thought. We cannot
separate them, because we cannot have the one without the
other. The I is then evidently a subject-object. It is a mind
possessing in itself the potentiality of all that is out of itself,
and its own spontaneous evolution evolving the potential into
the actual. Thinking is thus identical with being, for there
can be no thinking without a thing thought, and this thing
thought cannot be separated from the mind thinking. There
can be no knowledge without a thing known. A true knowledge, therefore, can be only a knowledge of self as subject and
object—in other words, a self-consciousness. What is thus
true of the human I is equally true of the I of the universe—
the absolute or fundamental I. It, too, is a mind knowing,
identical with the things known, an absolute reason in which
all things exist as potentialities, and come forth as actual.
That I, to use Fichte's expression, is an absolute activity whose
movements are represented to us in time and space. The
activity of the finite I is the result of its being acted upon by
the I of the universe. The world spirit is knowing itself as
subject and object in every individual, so that in his internal
essence every man is real and actual; but as to his form and
personality, he is imaginary and unsubstantial.

We have just said that Schelling at the point of the reality
of the external world departed from Fichte, yet only to give
reality to the external world from its necessary connection
with the ideal. It may be maintained, and justly, that as yet
he is on Fichte's standpoint, for nature is wholly deduced
from the essence of the I. Schelling's earliest writings do not
show a sudden departure from Fichte, but a gradual development, imperceptible, it would seem, to himself, from the doctrine
of the I to a philosophy of nature. In the later writings, the
standpoint is frequently changed. Schelling felt that among

real philosophers the harmony was greater than the difference. In every new form which the expression of his own philosophy took, he identified it with that of some other philosopher who had gone before him. Having died without giving to the world the long-expected exposition which would show the agreement of all the forms his doctrine assumed, we have no alternative but to follow them in their historical development. This is divided by Schwegler into five periods. In the first, Schelling agrees with Fichte. In the second, he has advanced to the recognition of a science of nature as distinct from the science of mind. In the third, he agrees with Spinoza. In the fourth, with Plotinus; and, last of all, with Jacob Böhme, of whom he boasts that he is not ashamed.

I. Schelling agrees with Fichte. He discourses of the I, and from it deduces nature. He sees in this nature processes corresponding to those of mind. As feeling, perception, and knowledge are the result of the antagonism of the two potencies—the unlimited and the limited—which constitute mind, so is matter the production of attraction and repulsion. These forces being its original, matter is not something gross and inert, as we might suppose, but of the nature of those forces which, though called material, are yet more like something immaterial. Force is that which we may compare to mind. The conflict which constitutes mind being precisely that conflict of opposite forces which constitutes matter, we must look to a higher identity for the union of the two. The same absolute is manifested in the external world as in mind. Nature is visible mind, and mind is invisible nature. The standpoint being the I, the internal world comes first. It is then followed by the external world as its copy. The mind produces this copy in its way to self-consciousness. In the copy the successive mental stages are visibly marked. Organic life being the highest, in it especially does mind behold the production of itself. In everything organic there is something symbolical. Every plant bears some feature of mind. Each organism is an interpenetration of form and matter. Like mind, nature, too, strives towards a purpose, and presses from within outwards. All nature proceeds from a centre progressing onward and outward to higher stages. The prevailing mode of its activity, the element, so to speak, of its existence, is the conflict of opposing forces. These are one in a higher unity, and, taken together, they lead to the idea of an organizing principle which makes of the universe a system ; in other words, to the idea of a world soul. Though nature and mind are but two sides of the same Absolute, yet the science of each is a distinct science by itself. Here Schelling progresses to the second form of his philosophy, where he distinguishes between a philosophy of nature and a philosophy of mind.

II. The distinction, however, is only provisional, and for the purposes of philosophy. The development of the fundamental unity is ever kept in view. We may begin with nature, and trace backwards the progress from mind, or we may begin with mind and study the procession from it of the external world. The one gives us natural philosophy, which aims at an explanation of the ideal by the real ; the other, transcendental philosophy, which seeks to explain the real by the ideal.

Nature, which to other men seems dead, and moved only by a power external to itself, is to the true philosopher a living self-unfolding energy. It is the absolute Unity manifesting itself on the phenomenal side. It is the movement between the producing activity and the product. Taken absolutely, it is infinite activity or productivity, but, this being hindered in expressing itself, gives finite products. These individual finite products are only phenomenal, beyond each one of which nature herself advances. The individual is contrary to nature ; she desires the Absolute, and to express it is her constant effort. All different as these finite products are, nature yet leaves on all the impress of her unity. We may divide and subdivide, but only to return again to the original identity. The powers in nature are distributed in different measures to various classes of beings, yet the organization of all things organic is one. The life of a plant is but the smallest degree of the life which is enjoyed by man. In the inorganic world we seem to lose the trace of this unity. Yet here we find gradations and processes, corresponding to the gradations and energies of organic existence. There must be a third principle or medium by which organic and inorganic are again united—some ultimate cause in which they are one, and through which, as through a common soul of nature, both organic and inorganic have at once their origin and identity.

On the transcendental side philosophy concerns the I, the beholding subject. Starting from mind, we must establish the validity and explain the character of mental cognitions. The common understanding gives a world existing outside of ourselves. The first problem of transcendental philosophy is to explain this pre-judgment of the common understanding. This constitutes theoretical philosophy, which, beginning with the I, develops the history of self-consciousness through its different stages of sensations, intuitive abstraction, and will. It explains the origin of the external world in the productive intuition, and the existence of time and space in the outer and inner intuition.

With the act of the will arises the second problem: How we can produce an effect upon the objective world according to representations which arise freely in us. The solution of this is practical philosophy. Here the I is no longer unconsciously beholding, but consciously producing. The Absolute is revealing himself in the self-determinations of the human spirit. In the effort to solve these problems, transcendental philosophy finds itself engaged in the solution of a problem yet higher, that is, the reconciliation of the subjective and the objective. This can only be done on the ground that the activity through which the objective world is produced is originally identical with that which utters itself in the will. This identity of the conscious and unconscious in nature is shown by the philosophy of art. The peculiarity of nature is that it exhibits itself as nothing but a blind mechanism, and yet it displays design. It represents an identity of the conscious subjective, and the consciousless objective activity. In nature the I beholds its most peculiar essence, which consists alone in this identity. That contradiction between the conscious and the consciousless, which is unconsciously reconciled in nature, finds its perfect reconciliation in a work of art. There the intelligence finds a perfect intuition of itself. The unknown, which perfectly harmonizes the objective and the conscious activity, is nothing other than that absolute and unchangeable identity to which every existence must be referred.

III. In the third period Schelling has advanced from the idealism of Fichte, to the idealistic realism of Spinoza. The second period is the history of that progress. Now the stage is reached and Schelling adopts Spinoza's definition of matter, as that which expresses in itself an infinite and eternal Being. He repeats, too, with increased conviction of its truth, another of Spinoza's sentiments, ' that the more we know individual things, the more we know God ; ' and to those who seek the science of the eternal I-hood, he says, ' Come to physical nature and see it there.' It may, he said, satisfy such pretenders to philosophy as Epicurus and his disciples, to regard matter as simply atoms ; but it was partly guessed, and partly known by all the wise men of antiquity, that matter had another side than the apparent one, and that a duality lay at its root. And since the question has been raised again in modern times, it has been concluded that the duality was due to a third principle, and therefore matter represents a triplicity enclosed in itself, and identical with itself. The first glance of nature teaches us what the last teaches us. Matter expresses no other nor closer bond than that which is in the reason, the eternal unity of the infinite with the finite. In visible things we recognise the pure essence which cannot be further explained, yet we never see the essence by itself, but always and everywhere in a wonderful union with that which cannot of itself be, and is explained only by the being of the essence. This which cannot be an essence by itself is called the finite or the form. It is not first a something by the infinite coming to it, nor by its going to the infinite, but in the identity with the infinite. These always appear united. The necessity which makes them one, is the bond or copula, which must be itself the only real and true Infinite.

Schelling repeats this idea in a multitude of forms. The Absolute is the copula of the finite and infinite, the being of the ideal and real, the identity of subject and object, the unity of mind and matter. The one side is the real, or nature, the other side is the ideal. The symbol of the Absolute is the magnet where one principle constantly manifests itself as two poles, and still rests in the midst as their identity. Divide the magnet, every part will be a complete system in itself : two poles and a point of divergence. Just as every part of the magnet is the entire magnet in miniature, so also every individual development in nature is a miniature universe ; since, however, the preponderance of the real is the characteristic of nature, the ideal, though present, is held as it were in the bondage of matter, spell-bound in the embrace of reality. But in an ever-rising gradation the ideal effects its disenchantment, the members of that gradation again embodying the type—real, ideal, identity, where it is to be remembered that in each of these three, both principles are present, so that the powers or potencies in nature represent only their particular quantitative differences.

We need not follow Schelling into the details of his nature philosophy. It is enough to mark the principle on which it is grounded; the identity of the object with the subject. The ideal is represented as shadowing itself over into the real. Ideas are produced, and these again are necessarily productive. They are related to each other as they are related to the original unity. The entire result of continued subject-objectiving, which according to one of the first laws of the form of the absolute, goes into the infinite is this—that the entire absolute universe with all ranks of being is reduced to the absolute Unity. In it nothing is truly individual, and nothing as yet is, which is not absolutely ideal, entire soul—pure 'nature producing.'

The ancients said of God, that he was that being whose centre is here, his circumference nowhere. 'Were we on the other hand,' says Schelling, ' to define space, we might say that it is that which is everywhere merely circumference, and nowhere centre, space as such is the mere form of things without the bond.' Its unreality then is evident, for it shows nothing but its want of power, its destitution of being. We cannot define space, because there is nothing in it to define, nor can we say how it was created, for how can we speak of the creation of that which is non-being? The bond as the one in the multiplicity negatives the multiplicity as self-subsisting, and this at the same time negatives space in the form of this self-subsisting multiplicity. Whilst the bond thus negatives space as the form of the self-subsisting multiplicity, it also posits time—the other form of finitude. Time is the expression of the one in opposition to the many. Its centre is everywhere, its circumference nowhere. Temporal things have, as it were, bubbled over from the eternal, and been posited in time. In the being-less-ness of time, the real is the eternal copula without which time would not flow over. Every moment is an undivided eternity. If we did not see eternity in the moment, we could see nothing anywhere, and the moment itself would be unfulfilled. The universe is beyond all time and space. It is only the imagination which changes the actual infinity of the all into the empirical of time and space. In the true infinity of the all the greatest does not differ from the least and endless duration does not differ from a moment. It has neither beginning nor end, but both at once, because the all is neither in time nor in space. Duration is short, but eternity is shorter still. Eternity is all in a moment, as substance is also the all in a point and infinite. Infinite duration, were it conceivable, could not create eternity, neither can the smallest duration annihilate it.

IV. In the fourth period, Schelling's philosophy is allied to Neo-platonism. He had passed from the I-hood of Fichte, to the ideo-Naturalism of Spinoza; and now he has come to recognise with Plotinus a ground of absolute knowledge in the mind itself. We say he has passed from Fichte, and Spinoza, but the transition was no violent effort. There was no barrier to be crossed. The in-itself of the I freed from all limits and opposition was itself the Absolute. Spinoza, as well as Schelling, recognised the intuition of the intellect as the ultimate ground and certainty of knowledge. Reason has not only an idea of God, but it is itself that idea. In the identity of subject and object, the knowing and the known is an immediate revelation of God. 'I know,' says Schelling, 'something higher than science. And if science has only these two ways open before it to knowledge—*viz*, analysis or abstraction, and that of synthetic derivation, then we deny all science of the Absolute Speculation is everything—that is, a beholding of that which is in God. Science itself has worth only so far as it is speculative—that is, only so far as it is a contemplation of God as he is. But the time shall come when the sciences shall more and more cease, and immediate knowledge take their place. The mortal eye closes only in the highest science when it is no longer the man who sees, but the eternal beholding which has now become seeing in him.' But Schelling's agreement with the Neo-platonists did not merely consist in adopting their starting-point of intellectual intuition. He had hitherto made natural philosophy the science of the divine, and had shown the identity of the ideal and the real. But the external world still presented a difficulty which he could not ignore. That would stand forth as something distinct from the Absolute and as opposite to the Absolute. True, indeed, finite things have no reality in themselves; but whence is their unreal existence? Whence had this science world its origin? Not, certainly, in any reality imparted to it from the Absolute, but in a complete falling away and separation from the Absolute. To restore it is the work of time. History is the record of the progress of reconciliation, God is manifesting himself there, and when that manifestation is complete, so also will be the world's restoration.

V. The mystical element, which appeared so decidedly in the fourth period of Schelling's philosophy, was yet more fully developed in the fifth and last. He expressly abandons Spinoza for the company of Jacob Böhme. The philosopher of Görlitz, while maintaining the fundamental union between God and nature, had yet definitely distinguished between them. Schelling had done the same in the earlier forms of his philosophy, but the method of Böhme seemed to lead to a more definite theism, and to be free from the objections to which Spinozism was exposed.

This method was to recognise an abyssal Nothing, in which God and nature had their beginning eternally. Schelling called it the 'original ground,' or rather the 'un-ground.' It is not merely an idea, but a something real and actual. It is not God himself considered in his actuality, but only the ground of his existence. It is nature in God; an essence inseparable from him, and yet different. The relation is explained analogically through the power of gravity and light in nature. The power of gravity goes before the light in its eternal dark ground of being, which is not itself actual, and which disappears in night whilst the light goes forth. This 'original ground,' or 'un-ground' is the absolute indifference. Now indifference is not a product of opposites, nor are they implicitly contained in it, but it is an essence different from all opposites, and in which all opposites are broken. It is nothing but their annihilation, and therefore it has no predicate but that of predicatelessness. The 'un-ground' goes before all existence. But the precedence is not one of time. There is here no first nor last. The one is not without the other, so that God is both that which exists; and again the prius of the ground—since the ground as such could not be, if God did not exist.

This ground of the existence of God is nature in God. It is also described as the non-intelligent principle in God, not only as a mere non-intelligent, but because it is the potentiality—the ground and beginning of the existing God—that is of God as intelligence. It is a medium which works indeed with wisdom, yet, as a blind, in-born intuition, and not a conscious wisdom. 'I posit God,' says Schelling, 'as the first and the last, as Alpha and Omega; but he is not as Alpha what he is as Omega.' In the one he is God involved; in the other he is God evolved. For the evolution of Deity it is necessary that God have before him an object, and this object must be himself. To reach self-consciousness, the Absolute comes from his unconscious envelopment, which is his first state. He comes out of it by a necessary evolution, which is the revelation of himself—creation. As yet he is but half-conscious, his wisdom is but a blind instinct. This is the condition of nature—this is the God of pure naturalism. He then becomes the pure and holy divinity whom we worship—a personal God. He is thus the first and the last. As Alpha, he is God involved, as Omega, he is God evolved. True religion reconciles the worship of both in the worship of the higher identity, who is at once Alpha and Omega.

This nature in God is the bond which unites Naturalism and Theism. This is Schelling's passage from Spinozism to the recognition of a conscious, personal God. Without this bond there would be on the one side God without nature; on the other, nature without God. It may be asked concerning the perfect, the actual, why is it not so from the beginning? The answer is that God is not merely a being, but a life, and all life has a destiny, and is subjected to suffering and becoming. Every life, without distinction, goes forth from the condition of evolution, whence, as regards its next condition, it is dead and dark. Even so is it with the life of God. Personality rests on the union of one independent with one dependent on it, so that these two entirely penetrate each other and are one. Thus God, through the union in him of the ideal principle with the independent ground, is the highest personality.   And since the living unity of both is spirit, then is God, as the absolute bond, spirit in an eminent and absolute sense.

We have followed Schwegler's five divisions of Schelling's philosophy, but in reality the five may be reduced to two—that in which Schelling agrees with Spinoza, and that in which he follows Böhme.   He repudiated the epithet 'Pantheistic,' and strongly expressed his belief in the personality of God.   But whether Spinoza or Böhme was the more Pantheistic, or which of them most believed in the divine personality, is 'among the things which we desire to know.'

'The God of pure idealism,' said Schelling, 'as well as the God of pure realism is necessarily impersonal.   That is the God of Fichte and of Spinoza, but to me God is the living unity of all forces—the union of the ideal principle with itself in the bosom of its own dependence.   This is spirit in the only true sense.'

On the immortality of the soul, Schelling differs in nothing from Spinoza.   'The I,' he says, 'with its essence undergoes neither conditions nor restrictions.   Its primitive form is that of being, pure and eternal.   We cannot say of it, it was or it will be, we can only say, it is.   It exists absolutely.   It is then outside of time and beyond it.   The form of its intellectual intuition is eternity.   Now since it is eternal it has no duration, for duration only relates to objects, so that eternity properly consists in having nothing to do with time.'   This is the eternity which belongs to God, and, therefore, belongs to the human soul, which finds its true life in God—whose essence is the essence of God, and as it returns to the source of its life, it loses its individuality, and knows itself as one with the Absolute and the Eternal.

When Schelling gave to the world his philosophy of revelation, he declared that all his former philosophy was only a poem, a 'mere poem.'   The public, it is said, never took it for anything else, even including the 'last development.'

HEGEL.

There is nothing new in Hegel.   After mastering his fearful verbology we have gained no new ideas ; but he inherited the

riches of all previous philosophers. The whole world of speculation lay open before him. He made a system, grand, compact,
logical. He summed up the entire wisdom of the world and
spoke the last word of philosophy. With him philosophy
stands or falls. A disciple and fellow student of Schelling he
had much in common with his master, but he came out from
Schelling, as Schelling came out from Fichte, and Fichte from
Kant. For 'the poetical rhapsodies, the dithyrambic inspira-
tions, the capricious contemplations, and the brilliant disorders'
of Schelling, he substituted an inflexible method by which he
submitted to the yoke of philosophy all the triumphs of science.
But how shall we explain Hegel? When M. Cousin asked
Hegel for a succinct statement of his system, the German
smiled ironically and said, 'it was impossible, especially in
French.' What cannot be explained in French is surely incapable of explanation. Mr. Stirling traces the immediate
origin of Hegel's philosophy to Kant. Perhaps he is right.
We might trace it to Hume, which is nearly the same thing.
The idealists, Bishop Berkeley for instance, had denied the existence of matter, that is abstract matter. Phenomena, the
things apparent to sense—these are the all of the material. By
the same reasoning which led Berkeley to his conclusions, Hume
showed that mind had no existence as abstracted from our
thoughts. Impressions, ideas—these are the all of the mental.
Hegel's position is precisely Hume's; we know nothing of
matter but as phenomena, we know nothing of mind but
as a thought, an idea. This then is the reality, both of
mind and matter. Thought is existence. The rational is the
actual, and therefore the supreme reality is absolute thought,
mind, or idea. The unfolding of this thought is its development into the manifold; for the order of the actual or phenomenal world has a perfect correspondence with the order of
the ideal or intellectual. Kant had said that 'there are two
stocks or stems of human knowledge, which arise perhaps from
a single common root, as yet unknown to us, namely, sense and
understanding; through the former of which, objects are
given, and through the latter, thought.' This common root
was Fichte's synthesis which united the I and the non-I. It
was Schelling's identity, in which the ideal and the real were
one. It corresponded, too, with Spinoza's substance, of which

the two attributes were thought and extension. Hegel made
it thought itself, the absolute idea. Sensation and understanding are virtually one—the former bring externally what the
latter is internally.

Hegel objected to the term substance as applied to God. It
has a sound of materialism. Doubtless there may be a spiritual
substance, but the word is borrowed from sense-objects.
Spinoza applies it to that absolute Being in whom mind and
matter have their identity, with the obvious conviction that
his nature is not definable beyond a describing of some of his
known attributes. Hegel, on the other hand, defines God as
the absolute mind; he accepts and endorses the Christian
definition that God is a Spirit; not as Malebranche, Augustine,
and others had explained this passage as declaring what God
is not; but as affirming, and possibly defining, what he is. God
is not merely being and substance, he is not merely intelligent
and living, but he is Spirit. 'The spiritual nature,' says Hegel,
'is alone the true and worthy starting-point for the thought of
the Absolute.'

Beasts have no religion; they do not know God, 'because
they do not transcend the sensuous. It is only for thought
that there is being or substance. Only for thought does the
world manifest almighty power and exhibit marks of design.
The so-called proofs of the being of God are only descriptions
and analyses of the coming of the spirit, which is a thinker,
and which thinks the sensuous. The elevation of thought
over the sensuous; its going out beyond the finite to the infinite, the leap which is made by the breaking off from the
sensuous into the super-sensuous; all this is thought itself.
This transition is only thought. If this passage were not
thought it would not be made.

Starting with absolute thought, Hegel constructs a universal
philosophy. There is nothing new in this conception. Schelling had discoursed of the absolute science to which all sciences
were subordinate. Others had done the same before him, but
Hegel's system has an interest for its completeness, its order,
and the universality of its applications. The study of all
things is the study of mind, and mind is God. We have
then :—

I. Logic, or the science of the idea in-and-for-itself.

II. Nature philosophy; or the science of the idea in its otherness.

III. The philosophy of spirit; or of the idea which, from its otherness, returns to itself.

I. Logic, with Hegel, is not mere reasoning, but the whole science of reasoning. It is that which treats of the Logos; the thought of the universe in itself, and all its manifestations. Thought is known to us in its three forms:—subjective, objective, and the union of these two; or thesis, antithesis, and synthesis. Corresponding triads form the 'rhythmus of the universe.' All things are trinities in unities, from the supreme idea to the humblest phenomenal existence. The first division of logic is into

1. The doctrine of being.
2. The doctrine of essence.
3. The doctrine of the notion or idea.

The first definition of the Absolute is being. It is that in which thought is the most primitive, abstract, and necessary. Being, simply, is the indefinite immediate. It is pure indefiniteness and necessary. At this stage, and under this aspect, it is not to be distinguished from nothing. Pure being and pure nothing are the same. They are united in a becoming. Nothing has passed over into being, and being into nothing, so that, though they are the same, they are yet absolutely distinguished. Their truth is the immediate disappearance of the one into the other. This movement we call a 'becoming.' The abstract Being of Parmenides was really identical with the Nothing of the Buddhists, though Parmenides did not see it. He said, 'Only being is, and nothing is altogether not.' 'The deepthinking Heraclitus,' said Hegel, 'brought forward against that simple and one-sided abstraction the higher total notion of becoming, and said—Being is as little as nothing is, for all flows—that is, all is a becoming. We never pass through the same street; we never bathe in the same stream. Neither being nor nothing is, what is is only their union, and that is becoming, for becoming is nothing passing into being, or being passing into nothing; and this truth is the foundation of all the Oriental wisdom; that everything has the germ of its death even in its birth, while death is but the entrance into new life.' 'It does not require much wit,' says Hegel, 'to turn this principle into jest, and to ask if it matters not whether my house, property, the air, this town, the sun, right, spirit, yea God, be or be not? The end of philosophy indeed is to free men from the multitude of finite objects, and to make it a matter of no importance whether they are or are not. But those who ask this question do not understand the subject. Our inquiry is not concerning concrete existences, whether their content is the same as nothing. Our discourse is entirely of being and nothing in the abstract. If it be said that this identity of being and nothing is inconceivable, it is illustrated by the idea of becoming. When we analyse the conception, it is found to contain not only the determination of being, but also another, that of nothing. These two determinations are in this conception one, so that becoming is the unity of being and nothing.' The old argument against a beginning of any-thing was grounded, according to Hegel, on the philosophical opinion that being is only being, and nothing is only nothing. On this supposition it was correct to say 'from nothing, nothing comes.' But the later Christian metaphysic rejected this axiom, for it involved the denial of creation from nothing. This was the error of Parmenides and Spinoza, and the result was 'Pantheism.'

The outcome of the becoming is there-being—in plain Eng-lish, individual things. There-being is to be discussed (1) as such; (2) in its other or finitude; and (3) as qualitative infini-tude. There-being in general is the simple oneness of being and nothing; but as yet it exists only for us in our reflexion. As it is something definite, a concrete, it has qualities, and is determined to a something which evokes its other. This is considered in itself, in its qualification, and its finitude: Through the removal of this limit it passes into the infinite. It is then considered as the infinite in general; the infinite as the negative of the finite; and, lastly, as the affirmative infinite. Being-foritself is the ultimate of the passing over of there-being, or finitude, into the infinite. It is considered (1) as such; (2) as the one and the many; and (3) as repulsion and attraction. Being, which refers only to itself, is the one; but, by its repelling others, it posits many ones. These are not, however, to be distinguished as to essence. The one is what the other is. The many are therefore one, and the one is the many.

Essence is being, as phenomena. The same developments which logic treats of in the doctrine of being, it now treats of in the doctrine of essence, but in their reflected, not their immediate form. Instead of being and nothing, we have now the forms of positive and negative; and instead of individual existence, we now have existence. Phenomenon is the appearance which the essence fills, and which is hence no longer essenceless. There is no phenomenon without essence, and no essence which may not enter into phenomenon. It is one and the same content, which at one time is taken as essence, and at another as phenomenon. When the phenomenon is a complete and adequate manifestation of the essence, then we have an actual something as distinct from the essence of which it forms a part. The individuality of every individual thing is thus reconciled with the unity of absolute essence. This union of being and essence takes place through the notion, which, being rational, is the true actual.

The notion appears first as subjective, then in its objectivity. The union of these is the idea, which is the highest definition of the Absolute. The absolute idea in its reflecting, discharging, or overflowing itself into space, constitutes nature. This gives rise to

II. The philosophy of nature, or the idea in its otherness. This evolution is marked by three epochs—the mechanical, the physical, the organic. Nature, as mechanic, constitutes time and space, matter and movement. As physical, it consists of individualities, general, particular, total. As organic, it is at one time geologic, at another vegetable, another animal. Nature is mind estranged from itself—Bacchus unbridled and unrestrained. Its products do not correspond to our conceptions. They represent no ideal succession, but everywhere obliterate all limits, and defy every classification. The province of philosophy is to trace the return of nature to mind. This stage it reaches in the self-conscious individuality, man. At this stage begins

III. The philosophy of spirit, or the doctrine of the idea in its return from nature or its otherness. In this process the I separates itself from nature and rises above it. The spirit is first subjective in its transition from general consciousness to self-consciousness. As subjective it creates anthropology, phenomenology, psychology. Objectively it appears in right, morality, politics. As spirit absolute it gives birth to religion, esthetics, philosophy. This last, which is the knowledge of knowledge—the knowledge of the absolute Being—is the crown and termination of all the evolutions of the idea.

We need not go further into the details of Hegel's philosophy. The whole secret of it seems to be that it realises thought, Logos, or Logic ; concatenates or classifies all sciences as the expressions of the Logos ; divides each into a ternary, and subdivides each member of the ternary into another. Everything has a beginning, an existence, an end. There is a birth, a life, a death. We have sowing, growing, seed time ; all is a three in one, and a one in three.

Hegel appeared first as the disciple and advocate of Schelling. At this stage he did not seem to differ from Schelling, except that he applied a more rigorous method, and tried to systematize Schelling's rhapsodies. This stage is marked by the 'Phenomenology of Spirit.' Hegel's object in this work is to show how the spirit, both in an individual and in a nation, rises above the vulgar consciousness, or what we call common sense, to the height of absolute science. In its progress it passes through four phases—self-consciousness, reason, morality, religion. These phases Hegel calls spiritual phenomena, and he endeavours to prove that they are the result of the mediate labour of thought, and not as Schelling said, the fruit of an immediate intuition. This is the ladder which intelligence passes over after it has overcome the feeling of individual existence, and before it arrives at the full possession of universal knowledge—that is, of that knowledge which shows to the individual intelligence that it is identical with the universal and absolute spirit—with the world soul. Man only knows just as he has knowledge of this identity. So long as he has not reached this, he has a soul, but he has not a spirit. So long as he is divided by the opposition of being and thought, he distinguishes between his I and his knowing. He does not yet know that he is one with pure knowledge. He does not know that 'the spirit which, in developing itself, teaches to know that it is spirit, is knowledge itself. Knowledge is its life ; it is the reality which it creates, which it draws from its own substance.' Absolute or speculative knowledge does not

begin till after this evolution of spirit. It constitutes the
sphere in which the pure idea reigns—that is, the whole of the
laws which govern all that which can exist and can be conceived, the whole of the categories, the conditions which reason
fulfils in accomplishing the end which it has before it—which
is, to reach the state of perfect reason. The phenomenology
thus ends where the 'Logic' and the 'Encyclopædia' begin.

Hegel has now fairly parted with Schelling. Starting, where
Spinoza stopped, with the abstract conception of pure being,
the Hegelian Logic arrives at a concrete idea whose manifestation is the universe. This idea, whose developments are traced
in the 'Logic' and the 'Encyclopædia,' is God himself—God,
anterior to the creation of the world, viewed in his abstract
universality and eternity. It belongs to his nature to be unfolded in the opposites—general and particular, infinite and
finite, internal and external, ideal and real.

Hegel's last writings were devoted to developing particular
parts of his doctrine, such as the philosophy of right, the
philosophy of history, and the philosophy of philosophy. This
evolution of spirit is Hegel's Theodicea—the knowledge that
spirit can only free itself in the element of spirit, and that what
is past and what is daily passing, not only comes from God, but
is the work of God himself. History is but the successive
revelations of spirit. Each of these revelations is an epoch in
which there appears a new manifestation of spirit. Every
people, representative of an epoch, expresses a given form—a
factor, so to speak, of the unceasing development of spirit.
These manifestations constitute a part of the grand drama of
the universe. They are united to the revolutions of nature, to
the destinies of the terrestrial globe and the vicissitudes of
time and space. History has presented four great ages, each of
them representing a distinct principle, and yet all the principles are closely allied to each other. The first is that of the
East—the theatre of the idea of the infinite, which is there
still absolute and undetermined, immovable, and as it were,
self-involved. There the individual has no part to perform ;
the theocratic power has united the political and the religious
in a unity as indissoluble and compact as it is overpowering
and oppressive. Among the Greeks we see the idea of the
finite everywhere triumphant. The free and varied activity

of the most complete of finite beings, man, has signally disengaged itself from Oriental confusion. It has shaken off Asiatic apathy, and is producing marvels of sentiment and independence ; at the same time maintaining its relation to the infinite, considering this relation as one of dependence, which it expresses under the power of symbol and myth. At Rome, the idea of the finite reigns alone. The worship of the infinite is banished as the worship of a mere abstraction. In the German world the fourth age of the manifestation of spirit in history, on the ruins of the Egoistic empire of Rome, the divine unity better understood, and human nature entirely free are met and reconciled in the bosom of a harmonious identity. From this alliance there has sprung forth, and will yet spring forth more and more, truth, liberty, morality—the peculiar perfection of the modern spirit.

The philosophy of religion shows similar manifestations, or developments of spirit. In every religion there is a divine presence, a divine revelation, but it does not follow that because it is a religion it is therefore good. On the contrary some religions are bad. If the spirit of a people is sensual, so will be its gods. Of these gods it may be said 'they that made them are like unto them.' But all religions seek the reconciliation of the finite and the infinite—man and God—and all point to an absolute religion, in which God will be revealed in his entireness, and in which this reconciliation will be realised. In the great religions of the Eastern world man is overpowered by nature. In the first and lowest forms of them he worships the objects around him. His God is a fetisch. To nature in her more sensuous forms he addresses his prayer. By adorations and conjurations he struggles to be free from that brute force, which he worships in a spirit of superstition and fear. In Hinduism we have a higher form. Nature is still powerful, but God is viewed as present, diffusing himself over all things. Between Creator and creature there is no determined and marked line. The greatest of truths is here divinely shadowed forth—not reached by thought, but by imagination. It is a poetical Pantheism, in which God, man, and nature are undistinguished, and hence the most sublime verities are mingled with the vilest superstitions. In the Persian religion, God or the principle of good, is more precisely determined as spirit, but this only in opposition to the principle of evil, which is matter. In the religion of ancient Egypt the personality of God emerges yet more distinctly. It now appears as it is, and has no need of a principle of opposition for its manifestation. But though God appears as distinct from nature, he remains, as to form, entirely undetermined. Hence the Egyptians worshipped him, now as a man, and again as an animal. Fetischism was still blended with the worship of him who is a spirit. The religion of Egypt was the highest form of the religions of nature.

These were followed by the religions of spiritual individuality. In them, spirit is independent of the external world. The first is Judaism. Here the spiritual speaks itself absolutely free form the sensuous, and nature is reduced to something merely external and undivine. This is the true and proper estimate of nature at this stage; for only at a more advanced phase can the idea attain a reconciliation in this its alien form. The Greek religion also decidedly consecrated the personality of God. Hence mind freed itself from the dominion of nature. The gods are creations of the intellect—arbitrary expressions of the good and the beautiful. In the Roman religion the nature-side of spirit dies. The world has reached that stage of life where it feels nature unsatisfying. It is melancholy, hopeless, despairing, unhappy. From this feeling arises the super-sensuous, the free spirit of Christianity. The Christian religion is the highest determination of the spirit in the religious sphere. Here the spirituality of God is clearly defined. The finite and the infinite are seen both in their separation and in their unity. God and the world are reconciled. The divine and the human meet in the person of Christ. The intellectual content of revealed religion in Christianity is thus the same as that of speculative philosophy.

The Roman world, in its desperate and abandoned condition, came to an open rupture with reality, and made prominent the general desire for a satisfaction, such as could only be attained in the new man—the soul. Rome was the fate that crushed down the gods and all genial life, in its hard service, while it was the power which purified the human heart from all speciality. Its pains were the travail throes of another and higher spirit; that which manifested itself in the Christian religion.

This higher spirit involves the reconciliation and emancipation of spirit, while man obtains the consciousness of spirit in its universality and infinity. The absolute object, truth, is spirit; and as man himself is spirit he is mirrored to himself in that object, and thus in his absolute object has found essential being and his own essential being. But in order that the objectivity of essential being may be done away with, and spirit be no longer alien to itself, the naturalness of spirit, that in virtue of which man is a special empirical existence must be removed, so that the alien element may be destroyed, and the reconciliation of the spirit accomplished. With the Greeks the law for the spirit was 'man know thyself.' The Greek spirit was a consciousness of spirit, but under a limited form, having the element of nature as an essential ingredient. Spirit may have had the upper-hand, but the unity of the superior and subordinate was itself still natural.

The element of subjectivity which was wanting to the Greeks we find among the Romans, but it was merely formal and indefinite. Only among the Jewish people do we find the conscious wretchedness of the isolated self, and a longing to transcend that condition of individual nothingness. From this state of mind arose that higher phase, in which spirit came to absolute consciousness. From that unrest of infinite sorrow is developed the unity of God with reality, that is, with subjectivity, which had been separated from him. The recognition of the identity of subject and object was introduced into the world when the fulness of time was come, the consciousness of this identity is the recognition of God in his true essence. The material of truth is spirit itself, inherent vital movement. The nature of God as pure spirit is manifested to man in the Christian religion.

Hegel's great object, like that of his predecessors, was to show the rationalness of Christianity. He was, or at least he meant to be, thoroughly orthodox. The mysteries, as Malebranche and the Catholic theologians called them, were no mysteries to Hegel. 'That Hagar and her profane Ishmael' were not to be banished, for they were satisfied that Christianity, in all its fulness, as taught in the Holy Scriptures, and interpreted by the Lutheran church, was in perfect agreement with reason. The Hegelian philosophy is the scientific exposition of historical

Christianity. The religion of Christ was the point in the world's history when the spirit awoke to a clear consciousness of its absolute essence, and made a decided beginning to return to itself out of nature, or its otherness. Hegel's Christology proves how earnestly he strove to embrace in his philosophy the whole content of the Christian faith. Not only is the historical account of the incarnation received in all its fulness, but it is shown that God became man; that he appeared in the flesh as manifesting and accomplishing the unity of God and man. Jesus Christ conquered death. He was the death of death. He annihilated the finite as something evil and foreign, and so he reconciled the world with God.

The idea being reason or spirit, it cannot be said that we do not know God, for this is the starting-point of our knowledge. The Trinity is in no wise a mystery. It is the first Triad of being. God, as the absolute Spirit, eternally distinguishes himself, and in this distinction he is eternally one with himself. The true forms of the divine manifestations are (1) The kingdom of God the Father—that is, the idea, in and for itself. God, in his eternity, before and out of the world, in the element of thought. (2) The kingdom of the Son in which God is in the moment of separation—the element of representation. In this second standpoint is contained all that, which in the first was the other of God. Here nature is the other—the world and the spirit which is manifested there—the nature spirit. (3) The kingdom of the Spirit which contains the consciousness that man is reconciled with God. The difference and determination of these three forms is not directly explained through the idea of the Trinity. Each form contains all the three forms—the one, the other, and the removing of the other. There is thus, in all the three forms, a unity as well as a difference, but in a different way. The Father is the abstract God—the universal—the eternal unrestrained total particularity. The other is the Son, the infinite particularity—the manifestation. The third is the Spirit—the individuality as such. The difference, then, is only between the Father and the Son, and, as the Father and the Son are one, the third is also the first.

Hegel as a Christian often speaks with a firm conviction of the reality of the future life. As a philosopher he explains his belief. The explanation differs from that of Spinoza, Fichte, and Schelling only by the form it takes in connection with the idea. Death, which can only happen to a living organism, stands between it and the moment of its other life, which is the life of the spirit. The reason of the dissolution of a living being is to be found in its idea. Organism is the culminating point, and, as it were, the unity of nature; but, it is only an external unity, and does not reach the simple and internal unity of thought and spirit. Death is but the necessary act—the mediating idea—by which the reality of the individual is raised from nature to spirit. It is but the natural progress of the idea which, to produce temperature and colour, goes from heat and light to their negatives, and so to posit spirit it goes to the negative of life—which is death. What we call death marks a higher degree of existence. Beings which do not die are those which are furthest removed from spirit; such as mechanic and inorganic nature. 'At death, the external other of nature falls from us, we are born wholly into spirit, spirit concrete, for it has taken up unto itself nature and its natural life. Nature is to Hegel much as it is to Kant. It is but the phenomenon of the noumenon—it is but the action of what is, and passes, while the latter is and remains. Time and space, and all questions that concern them, reach only to the phenomenon; they have no place in the noumenon. There is but one life, and we live it with, as the Germans say, That life we live now, though in the veil of the phenomenon. There is but an eternal now, there are properly no two places, and no two times in the life of spirit, whose we are, and which we are, in that it is all. So it is that Hegel is wholly sincere and without affectation, when he talks of its being in effect indifferent to him, how and whether he is in the finite life. He is anchored safe in thought, in the notion, and cares not for what vicissitude of the phenomenal may open to him.'* In everything Hegel wishes to be orthodox. He defends the validity of the three great arguments for the being of God—the ontological, the cosmological, and the teleological. He dreads nothing so much as 'Pantheism.' But which of all the systems we have examined is the most Pantheistic, or what Pantheism is, we do not yet know. Hegel concludes his 'Encyclopædia' with some verses from a Persian poet, which express,

* 'Secret of Hegel.'

as well as poetry can express, the great idea of his philosophy. As they are no less applicable to the doctrines of all our preceding chapters, we shall quote them as a fitting conclusion for this. They are, perhaps, the most accurate expression of what is called Pantheism which we have yet met.

> I looked above and in all spaces saw but one ;
> I looked below and in all billows saw but one ;
>
> I looked into its heart, it was a sea of worlds ;
> A space of dreams all full, and in the dreams but one.
>
> Earth, air, and fire and water in thy fear dissolve ;
> Ere they ascend to thee, they trembling blend in one.
>
> All life in heaven and earth, all pulsing hearts should throb
> In prayer, lest they impede the one.
>
> Nought but a sparkle of thy glory is the sun ;
> And yet thy light and mine both centre in the one.
>
> Though at thy feet the circling heaven is only dust,
> Yet is it one, and one my being is with thine.
>
> The heavens shall dust become, and dust be heaven again,
> Yet shall the one remain and one my life with thine.

The books on Kant are too numerous to be mentioned. In English we have an elaborate exposition by Edward Caird, and in the 'Blackwood Series' a succinct treatise by William Wallace. Mr. Wallace sets forth Kant's position in a few words. He says : 'Locke had made psychology the starting-point, affirming that there were just two orders of facts to be examined, the material and the mental ; but this supposes these two as distinct, and as constituting all. It overlooked another fact, that there was a subject by which material and psychological facts were perceived. The philosophy of Kant was called transcendental, because it inquired into the conditions on which the subject is cognisant of the material and the psychological.' He adds, ' A transcendental inquiry is not an inquiry into things in general, or into any particular sort of things, but into the conditions in the mental constitution, which makes us know or estimate things in the way we do,' p. 160. In the same series Robert Adamson has written on Fichte, and Edward Caird on Hegel.

In a short poem, in which Schelling sets forth his nature-philosophy, he contemplates man looking at nature and saying, 'I am the God whom it cherishes in its bosom, the mind that moves in all things. From the first struggling of unseen forces to the outpouring of the first juices of vegetation, when force grows into force, and matter into matter, and the first buds and blossoms swell—and to the first ray of new born light, which breaks through night like a second creation, and from the thousand eyes of the world by day and by night illuminates the heavens, there is one force, one changing play, and one interweaving of forces, one bent, one impulse towards ever higher life.' Schelling's philosophy, though a ' mere poem,' like all true poetry was pregnant with truth. Among his disciples in nature philosophy—those who looked upon all the forms of nature as a picture of the divine life—were Oken Klein and Blasche. Among his mystical disciples—those who considered the spirit as produced by nature, and yet capable of rising above it—were Schubert, Steffens, and Baader. The famous Romantic School also claimed discipleship from Schelling—Novalis, Solger, Frederic Schlegel, and Schleiermacher.

'The Secret of Hegel' referred to in the text, is by Dr. J. H. Stirling. There was no question of Hegel's orthodoxy till some of his professed disciples went into atheism. But what right they had to call themselves his disciples is not easily made out. His first and true disciples were orthodox theologians of the Protestant Church. The attempt of Strauss to connect his doctrine with Hegel's, was as unwarrantable as the claim of the Antinomians to be followers of St. Paul. The whole spirit and character of Strauss's 'Life of Jesus' is contrary to Hegelianism. Hegel was constructive. He acknowledged the good which the 'Illumination' had done, but its day was past. He wished to build up again by philosophy to the full extent of what the Church believed. Some later German philosophies, which profess to be developments, read like burlesques of Hegel.

CHAPTER XIV.

To see all nature blooming of God, is one of the most beautiful of our sentiments. To behold the green and variegated mantle, which in the glowing spring-time is flung over mountain and valley, as the living garment of God, is the sublimest poetry. There cannot be a diviner feeling than that which hears all birds singing of God, and sees all the powers of nature whether in terrific grandeur or in placid repose, as the working of the ever-present Deity. To the pious soul, nature is God's speech ; every little flower peeping from the ground is a silent memorial ; the daisies and the cowslips, the blue bells and the hyacinths, are all speaking of God. This is the marriage of religion and poetry where both as one are penetrated with the presence of the true and the divine. Where the poetical spirit is absent, nature appears but a dead mass, destitute of divinity, and deserted of God. Where the religious spirit is absent or deficient, God is lost in nature, and the nature spirit alone remains. If this beholding of God in nature be so common to poetry and religion, it will not be surprising that we find Pantheism in our poets, even in those of them whose religious sentiments are the most unlike.

The first passages we have selected are from Goethe. What was Goethe's creed we scarcly know. He is generally considered a mere Pagan, though he professed to be a Christian. Goethe lived when Spinoza was being revived in Germany. He does not conceal his obligations to the Portuguese Jew. In his autobiography he speaks of the delight with which in early life he read Spinoza's 'Ethica.' The dry abstractions of the geometrical and metaphysical universe-expounder appeared fresh and beautiful to Goethe. He was fascinated with Spinoza's gentle and humble, yet sublime spirit. And then that lofty doctrine of unselfishness was so charming that even Goethe was disposed to say that God should be loved for his own sake, and without

reference to reward.　But before Goethe met Spinoza's ' Ethica '
he had embraced a similar theology, as we may see from this
passage : ' To discuss God, apart from nature, is both difficult
and dangerous.　It is as if we separated the soul from the body.
We know the soul only through the medium of the body, and
God only through nature.　Hence the absurdity, as it appears
to me, of accusing those of absurdity who philosophically have
united God with the world.　For everything which exists
necessarily pertains to the essence of God, because God is the
one Being whose existence includes all things.　Nor does the
holy Scripture contradict this, although we differently interpret
its dogmas, each according to his own views.　All antiquity
thought in this way—an unanimity which, to my mind, is of
great significance.　To me the judgment of so many men speaks
highly for the rationality of the doctrine of emanation.'

In the prologue of Faust the second person of the Trinity pronounces a benediction.　Instead of the Semitic form, ' May the
holy Spirit '—the corresponding philosophical speech is used,
' May the Becoming, which works and lives through all time,
embrace you within the holy bonds of love.'　This use of the
becoming might be related to the Hegelian philosophy, but it is
said that Goethe never understood Hegel, nor had any interest
in Hegel's development.　In another place Mephistopheles tells
Faust that he is ' a part of the part which in the beginning was
the all '—a blasphemous utterance, and as destitute of the
spirit of philosophy as of the spirit of reverence.　But the
speaker is Mephistopheles.

The earth spirit says :—

> In the floods of life, in the storm of deeds,
> I move up and down,
> I go to and fro,
> Birth and the grave,
> An eternal sea,
> A changing strife,
> A glowing life.
> Thus I create at the roaring loom of time,
> And weave the living garment of the Deity.

Faust says to Margaret, when she doubts if he believes in
God—

> Who dares to name him ?
> And who dares to acknowledge :

I believe him?
Who can feel,
And presume
To say, I believe not in him?
The One who embraces all,
The preserver of all.
Does he not keep and preserve
Thee, me, himself?
Does not the sky arch itself above?
Does not the earth lie firm below?
And do not friendly looking stars ascend?
Do I not behold eye in eye in thee,
And does not everything throng
Towards head and heart in thee,
And hovers in eternal mystery
Invisibly, visible near thee?
Fill with it thy heart, large as it is,
And when thou art quite blissful in that feeling,
Name it then, as thou likest,
Call it happiness, heart, love, God!
I have no name for it!
Feeling is all,
Name is sound and smoke,
Surrounding with mist the glow of heaven.

In Faust's interpretation of the first verses of St. John's gospel we have the doctrine of creation.

It is written—'In the beginning was the Word.'
Here I am at a stand already, who will help me on?
I cannot possibly value the word so highly,
I must translate it differently,
If I am really inspired by the Spirit.
It is written—in the beginning was the sense.
Consider well the first line,
That your pen does not out-run you.
Is it the sense that influences and produces everything?
It should stand : in the beginning was the power.
Yet even as I am writing this
Something warns me not to keep to it.
The spirit comes to my aid.   At once I see my way
And write confidently.   In the beginning was the deed.

In some verses entitled ' God, soul, world,' Goethe says,

What were a God who only wrought externally,
And turned the all in a circle on his finger?
It becomes him to move the world in its interior,
To cherish nature in himself and himself in nature ;
So that whatsoever lives and weaves and is in him
Never lacks his presence and his Spirit.

There is less theology in Schiller's poetry than in Goethe's. The following extract from one of his letters is Platonic, but not extravagant :—' The universe is a thought of God's. After this ideal image in his mind burst into reality and the new-born world filled up the sketch of its Creator—allow me this human representation—it became the vocation of all thinking beings to re-discover in the existent whole the original outline. To seek in the machine its regulator; in the phenomena the law of its production ; in composition its several unities ; and thus to trace back the building to its plan or scheme, is the highest office of contemplation. Nature has for me but one phenomenon—the thinking principle. The great composition which we call the world is to me only remarkable because it is able to indicate to me symbolically the various properties of the thinking Being. Everything within me and without me is the hieroglyphic of a force, and analogous to my own. The laws of nature are the ciphers which the thinking being adopts to make himself intelligible to other thinking beings. They are but the alphabet by means of which all spirits converse with the perfect Spirit, and with each other. Harmony, order, beauty, give me pleasure, but they put me in the active state of a possessor, because they reveal to me the presence of a reasoning and a feeling Being, and reveal to me my own relation to that Being. A new experiment in this kingdom of truth ; gravitation, the detected circulation of the blood, the classifications of Linnæus, are to me originally just the same as an antique dug up at Herculaneum ; both are reflections of a mind—new acquaintance with a Being like myself. I converse with infinitude through the organ of nature, through the history of the world, and I read the soul of the Artist in his Apollo.'

Novalis has been mentioned as a disciple of Schelling, and a leader of the Romantic school. Like Schelling, he had do defined system. His doctrines were poetical, mystical, ecstatical. The desire for the Absolute is, he said, universal. The human spirit is tormented with the desire of returning to its native land, of being with itself. It seeks this country everywhere. What are all the yearnings of man after a being beyond himself—what are all the philosophies of the world but the utterance of this desire for the Infinite ? ' In philosophy,' says Novalis, 'I hold converse with my true I, with that ideal and better I, which is the sole centre of my being. God converses with my soul, and thereby nourishes and strengthens it, making it like himself. Nature, too, converses with me. It is an immense and eternal converse, where thousands on thousands of voices relate the history of God. God speaks to nature and by nature, lives in it and reveals himself by it, just as he lives and reveals himself in man. Our I enters into a living and spiritual relation with an unknown Being. This Being inspires us to become spiritual as he is. By his inspiration we come to know that our I is but the reflex of the true I. This knowledge is produced in us just in the degree that the false individuality evanishes. Then the marriage of spirit and nature is completed for us in the unity of the Being of beings. God is truly known, when to our restless inquiring I there is an answer from the world-soul; the great I of the universe.' Novalis objected to Fichte's evolving all from the individual I. We must begin rather with putting our I to death, and this suicide is that which will meet true life. Then shall be opened to it the life of the universe, the life of God, and it shall live again in the universal and perfect I. 'No mortal hath yet uncovered my veil,' said the inscription on the temple of the goddess at Sais. 'If no mortal,' cried one of her disciples, 'has been able to lift the veil of the goddess, then we must become immortal, for he who does not lift this veil is not a true disciple.'

> One succeeded—he lifted the veil of the goddess at Sais,
> But what did he see ?—he saw, wonder of wonders, himself.

The following lines are from Wieland's ' Hymn to God :'—

Great and lofty art thou ! An unsearchable darkness
Covers thee from man (that is made) of dust. Thou art ! We are like the
    dreams
Which with the breath of the morning move over the head of him that
    slumbers.
Thy presence holds the worlds in their obedience
Beckons to the comet from the vanishing distances. Thou sendest, O Creator
A ray of the light, in which thou dwellest, into the deep,
And it curdles to a sun, which pours out life and blooming beauty
Over young worlds crowding towards it.

In solitary eternity stood in spiritual beauty
All ideas before him, manifest only to his sight,

Charming rivals for life, and to whichever he beckoned ;
Lo, they were.   The unmeasurable, as he looked wide around
Rustled from the rising spheres ; the becoming cherub
Stammered, half-created, towards him, his hymn,
But his stammering was more than the ardent quivering
Of a human soul when, shadowed by thy being,
It receives thee, O God ! with all its wings outspread,
And with all (its) thoughts sinks into thy mystery.

Truth, O God ! is thy body, the light of the air thy shadow
Cast forth through creation.   I borrowed the wings of a seraph
(And) flew to the borders of heaven to find the throne of the King,
But the spheres said—we have never seen him,
And the deep—(said)—he dwells not in me.   Then whispered a breath,
Of an ethereal voice, in my listening soul,
Soft as the first longing of love, like a tender sigh
It whispered to my thought : He whom thy soul
Seeketh is everywhere !   His arm embraces the universe ;
His look all the thoughts of spirits.   What is manifest streams out
Something divine.   Whatever moves speaks of him,
From the songs of heaven to the song of the songster in the meadow,
Or to the whisper of the zephyr, which pastures among the lilies.
To think him is to be continually the highest striving of the deep thought
Of every inhabitant of heaven ; they will strive for ever.

These are from Rückert's ' Wisdom of the Brahmans : '—

Thought, indeed, produces the whole world,
That, O fool ! which God has thought, not what thou thinkest.

Thou thinkest it, but not on this account does the world arise ;
And, without your thinking it away, does it pass away.

Out of Spirit the world arose, and into Spirit it goes again.
God is the ground out of which the world comes, and into which, having
    made its cycle, it returns.

The spirit is a suckling, nature is its nurse ;
She nourishes it till it feels that it does not spring from her.

The dark mother wishes to hold her child in slumber.
From above breaks in a ray through the cleaving of her house.

Thou feelest in thyself (that thou art) infinite, yet finite
Externally, and thou art incomprehensible to thyself.

Understand ; infinite and finite, what appears to thee
So irreconcilable, is yet reconciled through One.

Thou art a becoming, not yet an I become,
And all becoming is a contradiction in itself.

Whence I come, whither I go, I know not.
Only this is my trust—from God to God.

M. Claudius, in a beautiful summer poem, makes Frau Rebecca thus speak to her children :—

> This violet, this tree covered with blossoms
> Which stretches out its branches,
> Are, O children ! the hem of his garment
> Which covers him from our sight.

The poetical works of Lamartine are full of the Pantheistic sentiment. This is from *La Prière* in *Méditations Poétiques.*

> Salvation, principle and end of thyself and of the world !
> Thou who with a glance renderest immensity fruitful,
> Soul of the universe, God, Father, Creator,
> Under all these different names I believe in thee, Lord,
> And without having need to hear thy word,
> I read in the face of the heavens my glorious symbol.
> Extension reveals to my eye thy greatness,
> The earth thy goodness, the stars thy splendour.
> Thou thyself art produced in thy shining work !
> All the entire universe reflects thy image,
> And my soul in its turn reflects the universe.
> My thought embracing thy diverse attributes,
> Everywhere around thee discovers thee and adores thee ;
> Contemplates itself, and yet discovers thee there :
> Thus the day star shines in the heavens,
> Is reflected in the wave, and is painted on my eye.
>
> It is little to believe in thee, goodness, supreme beauty ;
> I seek thee everywhere, I aspire to thee, I love thee !
> My soul is a ray of light and of love,
> Which, detached from the divine centre for a day,
> Consumed with devouring desires far from thee,
> Burns to re-ascend to its burning source.
> I breathe, I feel, I think, I love in thee !
> That world which conceals thee is transparent for me.
> It is thou whom I discover at the foundation of nature,
> It is thou whom I bless in every creature.
> To approach thee, I have fled into the deserts ;
> There, when the day-break, waving its veil in the air,
> Half-opens the horizon which colours a rising day,
> And sows upon the mountains the pearls of the dawn,
> For me it is thy glance which from the divine dwelling
> Opens upon the world and sheds over it the day.

These lines are from the poem 'Dieu,' addressed to the Abbé Lamennais :—

> As a drop of water in the full ocean,
> The Infinite in his bosom absorbs my thought ;
> There, queen of space and of eternity,
> It dares to measure time and immensity,

To approach the nothing, to run over existence,
And to conceive the inconceivable essence of God.
But so soon as I wish to picture what I feel,
Every word expires in powerless efforts ;
My soul believes that it speaks ; my embarrassed tongue
Strikes the air with vain sounds ; shadow of my thought.

He is, all is in him : immensity, times
Are the pure elements of his infinite being ;
Space is his dwelling—eternity his age ;
The whole universe subsists by the shadow of his hand,
Being in eternal billows flowing from his bosom
Like a river fed by this immense source
Escapes from him, and returns to finish where all begins.

Like himself without bounds, his perfect works
Bless as they are produced, the hand which has made them ;
He peoples the infinite each time that he breathes ;
For him to will is to do, to exist is to produce !
Drawing everything from himself, relating all to himself.
His supreme will is his supreme law,
But this will without shadow and without weakness,
Is at once power, order, equity, wisdom.

He is the end of all things, and he alone suffices himself.
Behold ! behold the God whom every spirit adores ;
Whom Abraham served, of whom Pythagoras dreamed,
Whom Socrates announced, with whom Plato conversed ;
That God whom the universe reveals to reason,
Whom justice waits for, whom the unfortunate hopes for,
And whom at length Christ came to show to the world ;
This is not that deity fabricated by man,
That God ill explained by imposture,
That God, disfigured by the hands of false priests,
Whom our credulous ancestors trembling worshipped ;
He alone is, he is one, he is just, he is good ;
The earth sees his work, and the heaven knows his name.

Among English poets, the representative Pantheist is Shelley. He denies explicitly the existence of a personal or creative God.

> Infinity within,
> Infinity without belie creation,
> The interminable spirit it contains
> Is nature's only God.

His God is the soul, life, or activity, of nature.

> Throughout the varied and eternal world,
> Soul is the only element, the block
> That for immortal ages has remained
> The moveless pillar of a mountain's weight,
> Is active living spirit.

Spirit of nature! here!
Is this interminable wilderness
Of worlds, at whose immensity
Even soaring fancy staggers.
Here is thy fitting temple,
Yet not the lightest leaf
That quivers to the passing breeze
Is less instinct with thee.
Yet not the meanest worm
That lurks in graves and battens on the dead
Less shares thy eternal breath.
Spirit of nature! thou!
Imperishable as this scene,
Here is thy fitting temple.

Throughout these infinite orbs of mingling light,
Of which yon earth is one, is wide diffused
A spirit of activity and life,
That knows no term, cessation, or decay;
But, active, stedfast, and eternal, still
Guides the fierce whirlwind, in the tempest roars,
Cheers in the day, breathes in the balmy groves,
Strengthens in health, and poisons in disease;
And in the storm of change, that ceaselessly
Rolls round the eternal universe, and shakes
Its undecaying battlement, presides,
Apportioning with irresistible law
The place each spring of its machine shall find.

In the following lines this 'spirit of nature' seems to be identified with 'necessity:'—

Soul of the universe! eternal spring
Of life and death, of happiness and woe,
Of all that chequers the phantasmal scene
That floats before our eyes in wavering light,
Which gleams but on the darkness of our prison,
Whose chains and massy walls
We feel, but cannot see.
Spirit of nature! all-sufficing power,
Necessity! thou mother of the world!
Unlike the God of human error, thou
Requirest no prayers or praises.

Shelley denies that he 'deifies the principle of the universe.' He calls the Divinity a pervading Spirit, co-eternal with the universe; and yet unconsciously as it were, he acknowledges a personal and creative God, possessing will, and to whose wisdom the world owes its happiness and its harmonies:—

Spirit of nature! thou
Life of interminable multitudes;
Soul of those mighty spheres

Whose changeless path thro' heaven's deep silence lies ;
  Soul of that smallest being,
    The dwelling of whose life
  Is one faint April sun-gleam—
    Man, like these passive things,
Thy will unconsciously fulfilleth :
  Like theirs, his age of endless peace,
    Which time is fast maturing,
    Will swiftly, surely come ;
And the unbounded frame, which thou pervadest,
    Will be without a flaw
  Marring its perfect symmetry.

     Nature's soul
That formed the earth so beautiful, and spread
Earth's lap with plenty, and life's smallest chord
Strung to unchanging unison, that gave
The happy birds their dwelling in the grove ;
That yielded to the wanderers of the deep
The lonely silence of the unfathomed main,
And filled the meanest worm that crawls the earth
With spirit, thought, and love.

Pope's 'Essay on Man' is said to have been written to advocate the doctrines of Leibnitz, as they were made known to Pope by Bolingbroke and Shaftesbury. In what Pope says of natural laws and the perfection of the universe as a divinely constituted machine, there is much of Leibnitz, but Leibnitz would not have sanctioned :

All are but parts of one stupendous whole,
Whose body nature is, and God the soul ;
That, changed through all, and yet in all the same ;
Great in the earth, as in the ethereal frame ;
Warms in the sun, refreshes in the breeze,
Glows in the stars, and blossoms in the trees,
Lives through all life, extends through all extent,
Spreads undivided, operates unspent ;
Breathes in our soul, informs our mortal part,
As full, as perfect, in a hair as heart ;
As full, as perfect, in vile man that mourns,
As the rapt seraph that adores and burns :
To him no high, no low, no great, no small ;
He fills, he bounds, connects, and equals all.

nor this,

One all-extending, all-preserving soul
Connects each being, greatest with the least ;
Made beast in aid of man, and man of beast ;
All served, all serving ; nothing stands alone ;
The chain holds on, and where it ends, unknown.

An immanent, ever-present, all-extending soul in nature was just what Leibnitz emphatically refused to admit.

Thomson, in his 'Hymn on the Seasons,' has beautifully blended the impersonality and the personality of God:

> These, as they change, Almighty Father! these
> Are but the varied God.   The rolling year
> Is full of thee.   Forth in the pleasing spring
> Thy beauty walks, thy tenderness and love.
> Wide flush the fields; the softening air is balm;
> Echo the mountains round; the forest smiles;
> And every sense and every heart is joy.
> Then comes thy glory in the summer months,
> With light and heat refulgent.   Then thy sun
> Shoots full perfection thro' the swelling year;
> And oft thy voice in dreadful thunder speaks;
> And oft at dawn, deep noon, or falling eve,
> By brooks and groves, in hollow-whispering gales,
> Thy bounty shines in autumn unconfin'd,
> And spreads a common feast for all that lives.
> In winter awful thou! with clouds and storms
> Around thee thrown! tempest o'er tempest roll,
> Majestic darkness!   On the whirlwind's wings,
> Riding sublime, thou bid'st the world adore,
> And humblest nature with thy northern blast.

In the conclusion of this hymn, the poet rises to a sublime expression of 'all for the best.'

> Should fate command me to the farthest verge
> Of the green earth, to distant barbarous climes,
> Rivers unknown to song, where first the sun
> Gilds Indian mountains, or his setting beam
> Flames on th' Atlantic isles, 'tis nought to me;
> Since God is ever present, ever felt,
> In the void waste as in the city full!
> And where he vital breathes there must be joy.
> When e'en at last the solemn hour shall come,
> And wing my mystic flight to future worlds,
> I cheerful will obey; there with new powers
> Will rising wonders sing.   I cannot go
> Where universal love not smiles around,
> Sustaining all yon orbs, and all their suns,
> From seeming evil still educing good,
> And better thence again, and better still,
> In infinite progression.   But I lose
> Myself in him, in light ineffable:
> Come then, expressive silence! muse his praise.

Cowper did not mean to be a Pantheist when he wrote

> There lives and works
> A soul in all things, and that soul is God.

U

John Sterling was once in a company where the conversation turned on poets and which of them were Christian. One gentleman was claiming Wordsworth as a Christian poet. ' No !' said John Sterling, emphatically, ' Wordsworth is not a Christian. He is nothing but a Church of England Pantheist.' That Wordsworth should have been Pantheistic is the more remarkable in that he avowedly belonged to that party in the Church whose tendency is to localise the Deity ; to consecrate temples and cathedrals for his special dwelling place. Wordsworth's Pantheism is found in some passages in the ' Excursion,' but especially in the lines on Tintern Abbey.

> I have felt
> A presence that disturbs me with the joy
> Of elevated thoughts, a sense sublime
> Of something far more deeply interfused,
> Whose dwelling is the light of setting suns,
> And the round ocean and the living air,
> And the blue sky and in the mind of man,
> A motion and a spirit which impels
> All thinking things, all objects of all thought,
> And rolls through all things.

His Platonism, or belief in the pre-existence of souls, is found in the well-known lines,

> Our birth is but a sleep and a forgetting ;
> The soul that rises with us, our life's star,
> Hath had elsewhere its setting,
> And cometh from afar ;
> Not in entire forgetfulness,
> And not in utter nakedness,
> But trailing clouds of glory do we come
> From God, who is our home.

Coleridge has these lines :

> Father of earth and heaven,
> All-conscious Presence of the universe,
> Nature's vast, ever-acting energy,
> In will, in deed, impulse of All-in-All.

And again—

> And what if all of animated nature
> Be but organic harps divinely framed,
> That tremble into thought, as o'er them sweeps,
> Plastic and vast, one intellectual breeze,
> At once the Soul of each, and God of all?

This sonnet is by Henry Kirke White :

> What art thou, mighty One, and where thy seat ?
> Thou broodest on the calm that cheers the lands,

And thou dost bear within thine awful hands
The rolling thunders and the lightnings fleet.
Stern on thy dark wrought car of cloud and wind
  Thou guid'st the northern storm at night's dead noon ;
  Or on the red wing of the fierce monsoon
Disturb'st the sleeping giant of the Ind.
In the drear silence of the Polar span
Dost thou repose ? or in the solitude
Of sultry tracts, where the lone caravan
Hears nightly howl the tiger's hungry brood ?
  Vain thought, the confines of his throne to trace,
  Who glows through all the fields of boundless space.

Mr. Matthew Arnold's sonnet, ' The Divinity,' might be interpreted as bearing on our subject.

THE DIVINITY.

' YES, write it in the rock,' Saint Bernard said,
' Grave it on brass with adamantine pen !
  'Tis God himself becomes apparent, when
  God's wisdom and God's goodness are display'd,

' For God of these his attributes is made.'
  Well spake the impetuous saint, and bore of men
  The suffrage captive ; now, not one in ten
Recalls the obscure opposer he outweigh'd.*

God's wisdom and God's goodness !—ay, but fools
Mis-define these till God knows them no more.
Wisdom and goodness, they are God !—what schools

Have yet so much as heard this simpler lore?
This no Saint preaches, and this no Church rules ;
'Tis in the desert, now and heretofore.

Mr. Arnold puts these words in the mouth of Empedocles :

EMPEDOCLES ON ETNA.

ALL things the world which fill
  Of but one stuff are spun,
That we who rail are still,
  With what we rail at, one ;
One with the o'er-laboured Power
  That through the breadth and length

Of earth, and air, and sea,
  In men, and plants, and stones,
Hath toil perpetually,
  And travails, pants, and moans ;
Fain would do all things well, but
  Sometimes fails in strength.

* Gilbert de la Porrée, at the Council of Rheims, 1148

Mr. Tennyson has a poem called 'The Higher Pantheism.'

THE HIGHER PANTHEISM.

THE sun, the moon, the stars, the seas, the hills and the plains—
Are not these, O Soul, the Vision of him who reigns?

Is not the Vision he? tho' he be not that which he seems?
Dreams are true while they last, and do we not live in dreams?

Earth, these solid stars, this weight of body and limb,
Are they not sign and symbol of thy division from him?

Dark is the world to thee: thyself art the reason why;
For is he not all but thou, that hast power to feel 'I am I?'

Glory about thee, without thee; and thou fulfillest thy doom,
Making him broken gleams, and a stifled splendour and gloom.

Speak to him thou for he hears, and Spirit with Spirit can meet—
Closer is he than breathing, and nearer than hands and feet.

God is law, say the wise; O Soul, and let us rejoice,
For if he thunder by law the thunder is yet His voice.

Law is God, say some: no God at all, says the fool;
For all we have power to see is a straight staff bent in a pool;

And the ear of man cannot hear, and the eye of man cannot see;
But if we could see and hear, this Vision—were it not He?

Bailey's 'Festus' has some Pantheistic lines.

> The visible world
> Is as the Christ of nature.   God the maker
> In matter made self-manifest;
> All things are formed of all things, all of God.
>   A world
> Is but perhaps a sense of God's, by which
> He may explain his nature and receive
> Fit pleasure.

Our religious poetry—that is, our hymn literature—is peculiarly destitute of the Pantheistic sentiment. This verse in Wesley's hymns approaches the raptures of the mystic.

> Ah! give me this to know,
> With all thy saints below;
> Swells my soul to compass thee;
> Gasps in thee to live and move;
> Fill'd with all the Deity,
> All immersed and lost in love!

The following is more to our purpose :—

> In thee we move : all things of thee
> Are full, thou source and life of all ;
> Thou vast unfathomable sea !
> (Fall prostrate, lost in wonder, fall,
> Ye sons of men, for God is man !)
> All may we lose, so thee we gain.

This hymn seems to be a translation of Tersteegen's hymn on the ' Presence of God.'   The literal translation is—

> Air, which filleth all,
> Wherein we always move ;
> Ground and life of all things !
> Sea without bottom or shore,
> Wonder of all wonders,
> I sink myself in thee,¶
>   I in thee,
>   Thou in me.
> Let me entirely vanish
> To see and find only thee.

It was impossible for Wesley to translate this literally to be sung by English congregations.   For ' air which filleth all,' he wrote, 'In thee we move.'   This had the sanction of St. Paul ; but, the next words, ' All things of thee are full,' is the most familiar sentiment of the Greek and Roman poets.   If the third line is to be interpreted by the original, ' the God is man ' is not more true and marvellous than the converse, ' man is God,' ' I in thee,' and ' thou in me.'

Bryant, the American poet, is as little Pantheistic as Cowper, yet he writes—

> Thou art in the soft winds
> That run along the summit of these trees
> In music, thou art in the cooler breath
> That in the inmost darkness of this place
> Comes scarcely felt—the barky trunks, the ground,
> The moist fresh ground, are all instinct with thee.
>   That forest flower,
> With scented breath and look so like a smile,
> Seems, as it issues from the shapeless mould,
> An emanation of the indwelling life,
> A visible token of the upholding love,
> That are the soul of this wide universe.

He describes creation as—

> The boundless visible smile of him,
> To the veil of whose brow our lamps grow dim.

The following lines are in Emerson's 'Wood Notes.' The pine
tree sings—

> Hearken ! once more ;
> I will tell thee mundane lore ;
> Older am I than thy numbers wot,
> Changes I may but I pass not.
> Hitherto all things fast abide,
> Safe anchored, in the tempest ride.
> Trendrant time returns to hurry
> All to yean and all to bury.
> All the forms are fugitive,
> But the substances survive,
> Ever fresh, the broad creation,
> A divine improvisation,
> From the heart of God proceeds
> A single will, a million deeds.
> Once slept the world, an egg of stone,
> And pulse and sound and light were none,
> And God said 'throb,' and there was motion,
> And the vast mass became vast ocean.
> Outward and onward the eternal Pan,
> Who layeth the world's incessant plan,
> Halteth never in one shape,
> But forever doth escape,
> Like wave or flame into new forms.
> Of gem and air and plants and worms,
> I that to-day am a pine
> Yesterday was a bundle of grass.
> He is free and libertine
> Pouring of his power the wine.
> To every age and every race,
> Unto every race and age,
> He emptieth the beverage
> Unto each and all,
> Maker and original
> The world is the ring of his spells
> And the play of his miracles.
> 　　*　　　*　　　*　　　*
> Thou seekest in globe and galaxy,
> He hides in pure transparency,
> Thou askest in fountains and in fires.
> He is the essence that inquires ;
> He is the axis of the star ;
> He is the sparkle of the spar ;
> He is the heart of every creature ;
> He is the meaning of each feature ;
> And his mind is the sky ;
> Than all it holds more deep, more high.

CHAPTER XV.

MODERN THEOLOGIES.

IT is a common complaint that Pantheism, or something which goes by that name, pervades our literature. Heterodox writers are often described as on the confines of Pantheism, and how easily the line may be crossed by the orthodox we have already seen. It has never been possible to exorcise the theology of Plato and Parmenides from the Christian Church. What the satirist said of nature may be said of Pantheism, that though thrust out with a pitch-fork it will ever return. Of modern writers who are said to be Pantheistic the first to be noticed is

SCHLEIERMACHER.

Neander did not over-estimate Schleiermacher when he announced his death in these words,—'We have now lost a man from whom will be dated henceforth a new era in the history of theology.' Schleiermacher gave the death-blow to the old rationalism of Germany, and he sowed the seeds of the new. He regenerated theology, and what is more he revived religion. His Moravian piety was combined with the speculations of Schelling; and the glowing 'Discourses,' by which he recalled the educated classes of Germany to a sense of religion, took for their standpoint the philosophy of Spinoza. 'Piety' he says, ' was the maternal bosom in the sacred shade of which my youth was passed, and which prepared me for the yet unknown scenes of the world. In piety my spirit breathed before I found my peculiar station in science and the affairs of life. It aided me when I began to examine into the faith of my fathers, and to purify my thoughts and feelings against all alloy. It remained with me when the God and immortality of my childhood disappeared from my doubting sight. It guided me in active life. It enabled me to keep my character duly balanced between my faults and my virtues. Through its means I have experienced friendship and love.' The ' God and immortality ' of his childhood disappeared. The personal God whom the Moravians worshipped was exchanged for the superpersonal Divinity of philosophy. Nor did this theology seem impious. No, it was the very essence of true religion. The pious soul has an immediate knowledge of the Infinite in the finite—of the Eternal in the temporal. True piety is to seek this infinite; to find it in all that lives and moves, in all which is born and changes, in all acting and suffering. It is a life in the all. It is to possess all in God and God in all. Nature becomes a continuous action of the Deity in the world, and in the sons of men. Religion, as the highest science, tries to comprehend the unity of the divine works—the unchangeable harmony which vivifies the world. In one of the ' Discourses on Religion,' Schleiermacher exclaims, with enthusiastic adoration,—' Offer up reverently with me a lock of hair to the manes of the holy, repudiated Spinoza! The high world-spirit penetrated him; the Infinite was his beginning and his end; the universe his only and eternal love. In holy innocence and lowliness he mirrored himself in the eternal world, and saw himself as its most loveworthy image. He was full of religion and of the holy Spirit; and therefore, he stands alone and unreachable, master in his art above the profane multitude, without disciples and without citizenship.' ' When philosophers,' he says again, ' shall be religious, and shall seek God like Spinoza, when poets shall be pious and love Christ like Novalis, then will the great resurrection be celebrated in the two worlds.'

The old Rationalists placed religion in reason; the orthodox in authority. Schleiermacher, following Jacobi, placed it in devout feeling, or an immediate self-consciousness. Out of this he drew his entire theology, and on this ground he harmonised theology with philosophy. To describe the forms of this religious feeling; the conditions of the pious consciousness, is the work of theology. Now the first and most obvious of these is a consciousness of ourselves as completely dependent, which is the same thing as a consciousness of ourselves in our relation to God. This feeling is the divine element in our constitution. By it we are capable of fellowship with God. It proclaims the presence of God in us, and shows how we may be one with the Infinite.

Jesus Christ differed from other men in this, that in him there was a perfect consciousness of God. He was actually what all men are potentially. He was the realization of our humanity; a perfect indwelling of the Supreme constituted his inner-self. The divine activity, which is in humanity, was chiefly manifested in him. The divine Word was not an eternal 'person.' It only became a person in Jesus of Nazareth. As the Divinity is potentially a person in every man, we may at once conclude that the Trinity in the orthodox, or western view of it, was rejected by Schleiermacher. There are not three persons, but three activities—the Father in creation; the Son in redemption; the Holy Spirit in sanctifying the Church. It is only in an improper sense that we apply the word person to Deity at all. He is the infinite Being, the universal substance. We may think of God as a person if we can separate from his personality everything incompatible with his infinity. Indeed it is a necessity of our minds that we do form a personal conception of God, yet God is more than a person. The question, he says, ' between us and the material Pantheist is not whether there is a personal, but whether there is a living, God.' The attribute 'living,' Schleiermacher regarded as not placing the same limitations to the divine Being as that of personal. It might be objected that the humblest beings, even unorganized matter, possess life, and that Schleiermacher, instead of raising our views of the attributes of God, as he intended to do, in reality lowers them. But this would be an irrelevant objection, for Schleiermacher is showing the materialist that God is a living being, and not a blind necessity. What kind of a being he is, and in what respect he is personal, is to be discussed, not with the materialist, but with the believer in God.

Schleiermacher's doctrine of creation was the same as Spinoza's. There is a creation, but it is eternal. God as the absolute causality could never have been without a something caused. He dwells immanently in his universe, and creates unceasingly. The fall was a necessary step in human progress. It was inevitable from the existence of the sense element in man. Redemption is, therefore, a necessary result, or a con-

tinuation of creation. Its object is to raise men to a perfect
communion with God, such as was possessed by Jesus Christ.
Revelation is the revealing of God in us. Inspiration is the
growth of the Christ within. In the life of Christians, the resurrection of Jesus is completed and his earthly life perpetuated.
We are progressing God-wards. In Christ humanity becomes
divine, and this by an eternal predestination, not of some men
only, but of all men, to eternal life.

Schleiermacher said that the immortality as well as the God
of his childhood disappeared. ' The last enemy to be destroyed
is not death, but the hope of immortality,' said Strauss; but
Schleiermacher had said before that—' Life to come, as actually
conceived, is the last enemy which speculative criticism has
yet to encounter, and, if possible, to overcome.' He means
individual immortality—an immortality apart from God; a
continuance of our present unreal existence. The true eternal
life is that of which the religious soul has a foretaste in communion with God. Thus to lose ourselves—thus to abandon
ourselves to the universe, to our eternal interest; to know that
we are a part of the all, and one with the Eternal is not to be
lost without a return, not to be annihilated without reward.
On the contrary, it is to create the true personality, to know
that we are not a mere transient mode of the Infinite, but its
enduring expression, its chosen and wished for instrument.
These doctrines were called Pantheistic. Schleiermacher maintained that they were not. His critics say that these were
merely the doctrines of his youth, and they trace in his writings
modifications, gradual changes, approximations to a belief in
the personality of God. Schleiermacher, in his old age, declared that he retracted nothing. He added explanatory notes
to his ' Discourses on Religion;' but these were only to confirm what he had taught, and to show the harmony of his
earlier and his later teaching. His critics found in this but
' the weakness common to great men, of believing that he had
never erred.'

Schleiermacher's strength lay in the religious life within
him; his weakness was his faith in criticism. It was necessary
that the spirit of inquiry should be permitted free course, but
the grounds on which he rejected some portions of the Scriptures were arbitrary without measure. His classification of the

dialogues of Plato from internal evidence has not been sanctioned by any eminent Platonist. That kind of criticism which gave but a faint probability as to Plato, ought surely never to have been applied to the writings of the New Testament. It must be very questionable criticism which rejects from internal evidence the first two chapters of St. Luke's gospel, and retains the rest as genuine.

FREDERICK ROBERTSON.

The next writer is Frederick Robertson. Shall we call him a disciple of Schleiermacher? His favourite doctrine of the heart preceding the intellect in all matters of eternal truth reminds us of Schleiermacher's devout feeling, and immediate consciousness of God. In Robertson's sermons there is the same mystical piety combined with a healthy freedom of inquiry, the same faith in the inherent power of truth, and the same placing of the personal or internal possession of 'eternal life,' above all external authority. And, more than this, Robertson's view of the relation of God to the world is as near to Schleiermacher's as it can well be. 'The world,' he says, 'is but manifested Deity—God shown to eye and ear and sense; this strange phenomenon of a world, what is it? All we know of it; all we know of matter is that it is an assemblage of powers which produce in us certain sensations, but what these powers are in themselves, we know not. The sensations of colour, weight, form we have, but what it is which gives us these sensations—in the language of the schools, what is the substance which supports the accidents and qualities of being, we cannot tell. Speculative philosophy replies, it is but ourselves becoming conscious of ourselves. Positive philosophy replies, what the being of the world is we cannot tell, we only know what it seems to us. Phenomena, appearances, beyond these we cannot reach. Being itself is, and ever must be, unknowable. Religion replies that something is God, the world is but manifested Deity. That which is beneath the surface of all appearances, the cause of all manifestations is God. The sounds and sights of this lovely world are but the drapery of the robe in which the invisible has clothed himself.'

'Go out at this spring season. See the mighty preparations

for life that nature is making; feel the swelling sense of grate-
fulness, and the persuasive, expanding consciousness of love
for all being, and then say whether this whole form which we
call nature is not the great sacrament of God—the revelation
of his existence, and the channel of his communication with the
spirit?' 'What is this world itself but the form of Deity,
whereby the manifoldness of his mind and beauty manifests
itself, and wherein and whereby it clothes itself? It is idle
to say that spirit can exist apart from form. We do not know
that it can.' He then quotes the words of Dr. Channing in his
Essay on Milton. 'Perhaps even the Eternal himself is more
closely bound to his works than our philosophical systems
have conceived. Perhaps matter is but a mode of thought.' *

'The Spirit of God lies touching, as it were, the soul of man
—ever around and near. On the outside of earth man stands
with the boundless heaven above him—nothing between him and
space, space around him and above him—the confines of the sky
touching him. So is the spirit of man to the spirit of the Ever-
Near. They mingle—in every man this is true. God has placed
men here to feel after him, if haply they might find him, albeit
he is not far from any one of them. Our souls float in the im-
measurable ocean of spirit. God lies around us; at any
moment we might be conscious of the contact.'

THEODORE PARKER.

The influence of Schleiermacher may be distinctly traced in
the writings of Theodore Parker. His chief work, 'A Discourse
of Matters pertaining to Religion,' was obviously suggested by
Schleiermacher's 'Discourses.' It proceeds on the same doctrine
of religious consciousness—a sense of dependence; or, as it is
otherwise called, the religious element in man. This sense of
dependence does not disclose the character, still less the nature
and essence of the object on which it depends. It is but the
capacity of perception—the eye which sees or the ear which
hears. But it implies the Absolute. The reason spontaneously
gives us by intuition an idea of that on which we depend.
This is natural religion or revelation, for all actual religion is
revealed in us. There is but one religion, and it is always the

* Sermon on the death of Queen Adelaide.

same. Theologies are men's thoughts about religion, and these
have never-ending differences, no two men having precisely
the same theology.   There have been, then, forms of religion of
all kinds, from the worship of the fetisch to the worship of him
who is a Spirit.   God has spoken most clearly in Jesus of
Nazareth ; but he is speaking in all men—speaking most
audibly in those who listen most attentively, who honestly use
the faculties which God has given them, and are in earnest to
know and do his will.   Jesus of Nazareth taught the absolute
religion, but the churches have never realized what he taught.
The Christianity of the churches is, therefore, transient, and,
like all other passing forms, will have its day, and give place
to something higher and better.   Parker discourses of the
workings of the religious sentiment, and after the fashion of
the Germans, traces its development from the lowest to the
highest forms.   Of the ' One-and-All ' doctrine, he says, ' Pantheism has, perhaps, never been altogether a stranger to the
world.   It makes all things God, and God all things.   This
view seems at first congenial to a poetic and religious mind.
If the world be regarded as a collection of powers—the awful
force of the storm, of the thunder, the earthquake ; the huge
magnificence of the ocean, in its slumber or its wrath ; the
sublimity of the ever-during hills ; the rocks, which resist all
but the unseen hand of time ; these might lead to the thought
that matter is God.   If men looked at the order, fitness, beauty,
love, everywhere apparent in nature, the impression is confirmed.   The all of things appears so beautiful to the comprehensive eye, that we almost think it is its own cause and
creator.   The animals find their support and their pleasure ;
the painted leopard and the snowy swan, each living by its
own law ; the bird of passage that pursues, from zone to zone, its
unmarked path ; the summer warbler which sings out its melo-
dious existence in the woodbine ; the flowers that come unasked,
charming the youthful year ; the golden fruit, maturing in its
wilderness of green ; the dew and the rainbow ; the frost-flake
and the mountain snow ; the glories that wait upon the morning, or sing the sun to his ambrosial rest ; the pomp of the sun
at noon, amid the clouds of a June day ; the awful majesty of
night, when all the stars with a serene step come out and tread
their round, and seem to watch in blest tranquillity about the

slumbering world; the moon waning and waxing, walking in beauty through the night; daily the water is rough with the winds—they come or abide at no man's bidding, and roll the yellow corn, or wake religious music at nightfall in the pines,— these things are all so fair, so wondrous, so wrapt in mystery; it is no marvel that men say, this is divine; yes, the all is God; he is the light of the morning, the beauty of the noon, and the strength of the sun. The little grass grows by his presence. He preserveth the cedars. The stars are serene because he is in them. The lilies are redolent of God. He is the One; the All. God is the mind of man; the soul of all; more moving than motion; more stable than rest; fairer than beauty and stronger than strength. The power of nature is God; the universe, broad, and deep, and high, a handful of dust, which God enchants. He is the mysterious magic that possesses the world. Yes, he is the all; the reality of all phenomena.'

Material Pantheism, as thus described, is supposed to have been the doctrine of Strabo, of Lampsacus, of Democritus, and perhaps of Hippocrates; but the description, though beginning with matter, or the external aspect of nature, rises into the higher Pantheism which sees God in all nature.

The writer then goes on to describe what he calls spiritual Pantheism. This denies the existence of matter, and resolves all into spirit, which is God. The material is but phenomenal, and the reality of it is God. This, Parker describes as the Pantheism of Spinoza, of the Medieval Mystics, of St. John, and of St. Dionysius the Areopagite. We may add that it is the Pantheism of Theodore Parker, at least it is difficult to distinguish it from what he says soon after about the relation of nature to God:—' If infinite, he must be present everywhere in general, and not limited to any particular spot, as an old writer so beautifully says: " Even heaven and the heaven of heavens cannot contain him." Heathen writers are full of such expressions. God, then, is universally present in the world of matter. He is the substantiality of matter. The circle of his being in space has an infinite radius. We cannot say, Lo here, or Lo there, for he is everywhere. He fills all nature with his overflowing currents; without him it were not. His presence gives it existence; his will its law and force; his wisdom its order; his goodness its beauty.'

Parker argues—'It follows unavoidably, from the idea of God, that he is present everywhere in space ; not transiently present now and then, but immanently present, always ; his centre here ; his circumference nowhere ; just as present in the eye of an emmet as in the Jewish holy of holies, or the sun itself. We may call common what God has cleansed with his presence ; but there is no corner of space so small, no atom of matter so despised and little, but God, the infinite, is there.

'Now, to push the inquiry nearer the point. The nature or substance of God, as represented by our idea of him, is divisible or not divisible. If infinite, he must be indivisible ; a part of God cannot be in this point of space, and another in that ; his power in the sun, his wisdom in the moon, and his justice in the earth. He must be wholly, vitally, essentially present, as much in one point as in another point, or all points ; as essentially present in each point at any one moment of time as at any other or all moments of time. He is there not idly present, but actively, as much now as at creation. Divine omnipotence can neither slumber nor sleep. Was God but transiently active in matter at creation, his action now passed away ? From the idea of him it follows that he is immanent in the world, however much he also transcends the world. "Our Father worketh hitherto," and for this reason nature works, and so has done since its creation. There is no spot the foot of hoary time has trod on, but it is instinct with God's activity. He is the ground of nature ; what is permanent in the passing ; what is real in the apparent. All nature, then, is but an exhibition of God to the senses ; the veil of smoke on which his shadow falls ; the dew-drop in which the heaven of his magnificence is poorly imaged. The sun is but a sparkle of his splendour. Endless and without beginning flows forth the stream of divine influence that encircles and possesses the all of things. From God it comes ; to God it goes. The material world is perpetual growth ; a continual transfiguration, renewal that never ceases. Is this without God ? Is it not because God, who is ever the same, flows into it without end ? It is the fulness of God that flows into the crystal of the rock, the juices of the plant, the life of the emmet and the elephant. He penetrates and pervades the world. All things are full of him, who surrounds the sun, the stars, the universe itself ;

goes through all lands, the expanse of oceans, and the profound heaven.'

After seeing God in all nature, the writer goes on: 'Since these things are so, nature is not only strong and beautiful, but has likewise a religious aspect. This fact was noticed in the very earliest times ; appears in the rudest worship, which is an adoration of God in nature. It will move man's heart to the latest day, and exert an influence on souls that are deepest and most holy. Who that looks on the ocean, in its anger or its play ; who that walks at twilight under a mountain's brow, listens to the sighing of the pines, touched by the indolent wind of summer, and hears the light tinkle of the brook, murmuring its quiet tune—who is there but feels the deep religion of the scene ? In the heart of a city we are called away from God. The dust of man's foot and the sooty print of his fingers are on all we see. The very earth is unnatural, and the heaven scarce seen. In a crowd of busy men which set through its streets, or flow together of a holiday ; in the dust and jar, the bustle and strife of business, there is little to remind us of God. Men must build a cathedral for that. But everywhere in nature we are carried straightway back to him. The fern, green and growing amid the frost, each little grass and lichen, is a silent memento. The first bird of spring, and the last rose of summer ; the grandeur or the dulness of evening or morning ; the rain, the dew, the sunshine ; the stars that come out to watch over the farmer's rising corn ; the birds that nestle contentedly, brooding over their young, quietly tending the little strugglers with their beak—all these have a religious significance to a thinking soul. Every violet blooms of God, each lily is fragrant with the presence of Deity. The awful scenes of storms, and lightning and thunder, seem but the sterner sounds of the great concert, wherewith God speaks to man. Is this an accident ? Ay, earth is full of such " accidents." When the seer rests from religious thought, or when the world's temptations make his soul tremble, and though the spirit be willing, the flesh is weak ; when the perishable body weighs down the mind, musing on many things ; when he wishes to draw dear to God, he goes, not to the city—there conscious men obstruct him with their works — but to the meadow, spangled all over with flowers, and sung to by every

bird; to the mountain; "visited all night by troops of stars;"
to the ocean, the undying type of shifting phenomena and unchanging law; to the forest, stretching out motherly arms, with
its mighty growth and awful shade, and there, in the obedience
these things pay, in their order, strength, beauty, he is encoun-
tered front to front with the awful presence of almighty power.
A voice cries to him from the thicket, "God will provide." The
bushes burn with Deity. Angels minister to him. There is no
mortal pang, but it is allayed by God's fair voice as it whispers,
in nature, still and small, it may be, but moving on the face of
the deep, and bringing light out of darkness.'*

From the immanency of God in the universe, Parker argues
for the in-dwelling of God in man—the natural, perpetual, and
universal inspiration of the human race. He supposes that the
spiritual Pantheists, especially the German philosophers, did
not allow God any existence beyond the sum total of finite
spirit; and thus, God, with them, was variable and progressive,
growing in wisdom as the ages roll. From this view of the
Deity, he differed widely, as God must infinitely transcend both
the worlds of matter and of spirit. The progress is not in
God, the manifestor, but in nature, which is the manifestation
of him.

EMERSON.

We have already quoted from Emerson's poetry. His prose
writings abound with sentiments similar to those in his verses.
Emerson is usually classed with Theodore Parker as representatives of a far gone school of Unitarianism, but this, like all
such classifications, is open to many exceptions. A similarity
of sentiments is indeed found, but the differences are manifest.
For some to whom Parker is reverent, Emerson seems to border
on blasphemy.

The Egyptian Hermes said, 'Let us call God by all names,
or rather let us call him by no name, for no name can express
him.' The latter is more reverent, and Parker has followed it.
Emerson delights to give God names, which according to the
wise rule of Des Cartes should be rejected as expressing imperfection in the divine nature. But Emerson does not forget

* 'The Relation of God to Nature' in the 'Discourse of Religion.'

the wisdom of Hermes. If he calls God by any name, it is with the distinct remembrance that no name can express him. He says that Empedocles spoke a great truth of thought when he declared that he was God, but it was a lie before it reached the ear, for every expression of the Infinite must be blasphemous to the finite. To determine is to deny. Yet Emerson calls God the 'Oversoul,' within which every man's particular being is contained, and by which it has its unity with all other beings. God is the impersonal—the common nature—which appears in each of us, and which is yet higher than ourselves. We, as individuals, live in succession, in division, in parts, in particles; but within, in the universal-soul, the wise silence, the universal beauty, to which every part or particle is equally related—the eternal One. And the deep power in which we all exist—this beatitude, which is all accessible to us, is not only perfect and self-sufficient, but it is at once the act of seeing, and the thing seen, the subject and the object in one. Time, space, and nature vanish before the revelation of the soul. The simplest person, who in integrity worships God receives God, yet for ever and ever the influx of this better and universal self is new, and unsearchable. Man, the imperfect, adores his own perfect. He is receptive of the great Soul, whereby he overlooks the sun and the stars, and feels them to be accidents and effects, which to-day are, and to-morrow change and pass. Man is nothing. As a transparent eyeball he sees all the currents of universal being circulate through him. He is a part or particle of God. Humanity is a façade of Deity. Let man but live according to the laws of his being, and he becomes divine. So far as man is just and pure and good—he is God. The immortality of God, the safety of God, the majesty of God have entered into his soul. There is but one mind everywhere —in each wavelet of the pool, in each ray of the star, in each heart. Whatever opposes that mind is baffled. When man becomes unjust or impure, he comes into collision with his own nature. Of his own will he subjects himself to the opposition of that mind, which, with rapid energy, is righting all wrongs.

'Jesus Christ,' says Emerson, 'belonged to the true race of prophets. He saw with open eye the majesty of the soul. Drawn by its severe harmony, ravished with its beauty, he lived in it, and had his being there. Alone in all history he estimated the greatness of man. One man was true to humanity. He saw that God incarnates himself in man, and goes forth evermore anew to take possession of the world. He felt respect for Moses and the prophets, but no unfit tenderness at postponing their initial revelation to the hour, and man that now is—to the eternal revelation in the human heart. Thus was he a true man.'

M. RÉNAN.

A theology, corresponding to Theodore Parker's, is at the foundation of the celebrated 'Life of Jesus,' by M. Rénan. Describing the theology of Jesus and its relation to other religions, the author says, 'Deism and Pantheism have become the two poles of theology. The paltry discussions of scholasticism, the dryness of spirit of Des Cartes, the deep-rooted irreligion of the eighteenth century, by lessening God, and by limiting him in a manner, by the exclusion of everything which is not his very self, have stifled in the breast of modern rationalism all fertile ideas of the Divinity. If God, in fact, is a personal being outside of us, he who believes himself to have peculiar relations with God is a "visionary," and as the physical and physiological sciences have shown us that all supernatural visions are illusions, the logical Deist finds it impossible to understand the great beliefs of the past. Pantheism, on the other hand, in suppressing the divine personality, is as far as it can be from the living God of the ancient religions. Were the men who have best comprehended God—Sakya-Muni, Plato, St. Paul, St. Francis d'Assissi, and St. Augustine (at some periods of his fluctuating life)—Deists or Pantheists? Such a question has no meaning. The physical and metaphysical proofs of the existence of God were quite indifferent to them. They felt the divine within themselves. We must place Jesus in the first rank of this great family of the true sons of God. Jesus had no visions; God did not speak to him as to one outside of himself; God was in him; he felt himself with God, and he drew from his heart all he said of his Father. He lived in the bosom of God by constant communication with him; he saw him not, but he understood him, without need of the thunder and the burning bush of Moses, of the revealing

tempest of Job, of the oracle of the old Greek sages, of the
familiar genius of Socrates, or of the angel Gabriel of Mahommed.
The imagination and the hallucination of a St. Theresa, for
example, are useless here. The intoxication of the Sufi pro-
claiming himself identical with God is also quite another thing.
Jesus never once gave utterance to the sacrilegious idea that
he was God. He believed himself to be in direct communion
with God; he believed himself to be the Son of God. The
highest consciousness of God which has existed in the bosom
of humanity was that of Jesus.' *

What M. Rénan means by ' Pantheism,' is evidently materialism or the denial of a living God. It is not that of the ancient
religions nor of the old philosophers. But the doctrine which
he attributes to Jesus, and Jesus' view of his relation to God,
are not widely different from what was taught by Spinoza and
Schleiermacher. In another chapter Rénan says, ' The idea
which Jesus had of man was not that low idea which a cold
Deism has introduced. In his poetic conception of nature, one
breath alone penetrates the universe; the breath of man is that
of God; God dwells in man, and lives by man, the same as man
dwells in God, and lives by God. The transcendent idealism
of Jesus never permitted him to have very clear notions of his
own personality. He is his Father, his Father is he; he lives
in his disciples; he is everywhere with them; his disciples are
one, as he and his Father are one. The idea to him is everything; the body which makes the distinction of persons is
nothing.' † In another place Rénan seems to adopt Schleiermacher's view of immortality, which indeed is only a part of the
same theology. ' The phrase, " Kingdom of God," ' he says ' expresses also very happily the want which the soul experiences
of a supplementary destiny, of a compensation for the present
life. Those who do not accept the definition of man as a compound of two substances and who regard the deistical dogma
of the immortality of the soul as in contradiction with physio-
logy, love to fall back upon the hope of a final reparation, which
under an unknown form shall satisfy the wants of the heart of
man. Who knows if the highest term of progress after millions
of ages may not evoke the absolute consciousness of the universe, and in this consciousness the awakening of all that have

* ' Vie de Jesus,' chap. v.   † Ibid., chap. xv.

lived ? A sleep of a million of years is not longer than the sleep of an hour. St. Paul, on this hypothesis, was right in saying, *In ictu oculi !* It is certain that moral and virtuous humanity will have its reward, that one day the ideas of the poor but honest man will judge the world, and that on that day the ideal figure of Jesus will be the confusion of the frivolous who have not believed in virtue, and of the selfish who have not been able to attain to it. The favourite phrase of Jesus continues, therefore, full of an eternal beauty. A kind of exalted divination seems to have maintained it in a vague sublimity, embracing at the same time various orders of truths.' *

THOMAS CARLYLE.

It is doubtful if we are justified in ascribing any theology to Carlyle. No believer in God, if we except Sakya Muni, ever said so little about him. Carlyle assured his mother that in religion there was little difference between them. Yet his would be the first name that would occur to the multitude of Englishmen as a representative Pantheist. His God was the abysses, the immensities, the infinities, and the eternities ; the unknowable rather than the known. Mr. Froude says, that Carlyle rejected Christianity, and held it as certain as mathematics that no such thing as the Bible miracles could ever have happened. The argument of Teufelsdroeck that miracles might be in accordance with laws unknown to us agreed better with the confession of the unknowable, with the belief that the universe itself was a miracle, and that all its phenomena were in themselves equally incomprehensible. We do not know how far Teufelsdroeck is to be taken as representing Carlyle himself, but we seem to have no nearer expression of his opinions. Nature is spoken of as the living garment of God, who is said to live and to love in man. His glory as that of an ever present God beams in every star, through every grass blade, and through every living soul. Nature reveals God to the wise and hides him from the foolish. To Carlyle, as to Spinoza and others who have been called Pantheists, the existence of

* Ibid., chap. xvii.

God was the most certain of all things. He reasoned that as
we have intellect and conscience, we cannot suppose it possible
that the Being who gave us these could himself be without
them. But the name of God was regarded as too sacred for
common ʼuse. The truest worship was silence in the divine
presence ; according to the saying of Goethe that the Highest
cannot be spoken of in words. Mr. Froude, in a brief chapter
on Carlyle's religion, says, ' He looked on the whole system of
visible and spiritual phenomena as a manifestation of the will
of God in constant forces—forces not mechanical, but dynamical,
interpenetrating and controlling all existing things from the
utmost bounds of space to the minutest granule on the earth's
surface, from the making of the worlds to the lightest action of
a man. God's law was everywhere, and man' welfare depended
on the faithful reading of it.' As all nature was God working
by miracle, so all history was a Bible.

MATTHEW ARNOLD.

Mr. Arnold has said a great deal about God and a great deal
about what other people have said of God. He dreads the
anthropomorphic in the same degree that Mr. Maurice dreaded
the Absolute. He finds the God of the Bible very different from
the God of the theologians, more, as he supposes, a God and
less a man. That there is a great personal first cause, the moral
and intelligent governor of the universe, Mr. Arnold calls an
assumption, with which all the churches and sects set out, but
which can never be verified. What we know of God is, that
he is ' not ourselves,' and that ' he makes for righteousness.'
Mr. Maurice objected to translating Jehovah by self-existent.
He preferred I AM, evidently because that had more in it of
human personality. Mr. Arnold proposes to translate Jehovah
by Eternal, evidently to avoid the idea of human personality.
In the words of Isaiah, God is the high and holy One that in-
habiteth eternity. He is not moral, not intelligent, not a
governor, not a person ; that is to say, he is none of these things
as man conceives them. He may be all of them in a way transcending man's understanding, and as they are applicable to a
Being who is infinite. Scientific theology loses all the magni-

ficence of Deity which was known to Isaiah, who had but poetry
and eloquence and no system. It is to system, or 'the licence
of particularity,' that we owe all the difficulties which torment
theologians. God's justice and God's mercy would never seem
at variance if we did not look too much on God as if made in
the image of man. To avoid the anthropomorphic conception
of God, Mr. Arnold prefers to speak of God as 'an influence,'
'a stream of tendency,' 'a not ourselves,' or in such words as
declare rather what he is not, than what he is. In replying to
the criticisms of the first book, he said, 'We do not profess to
have discovered the nature of God to be impersonal, nor do we
deny God conscious intelligence. We do not assert God to be
a *thing*. All we say is, that we do not know enough about the
Eternal that makes for righteousness to warrant their pronouncing this either a person or a thing. We say that no one
has discovered the nature of God to be personal, or is entitled to
assert that God has conscious intelligence. Theologians assert
it and make it the basis of religion. It is they who profess to
assert and know, not we. We object to their professing to
know more than can be known, and their insisting we shall
receive it, to their resting religion upon it. We want to rest
religion on what can be verified.' Mr. Arnold adds, 'We have
really no experience whatever, not the very slightest, of persons who think and love except in man and the lower animals.'
The idea of miracles corresponds with the idea of God as 'a
magnified and non-natural man at the head of mankind and
the world's affairs.'* But miracles cannot be verified. There is
no complete induction either for or against them. The Christian miracles are admitted to be possible, but the history of all
miracles is against their probability. We cannot, therefore,
build on miracles. It is denied that we have an idea of the
Infinite, so that at the hands of Mr. Arnold, metaphysicians do
not fare better than theologians.

PRINCIPAL CAIRD.

We might be content to describe Dr. Caird's theology as
orthodox, but Hegelian It is a philosophy of religion, or

* 'God and the Bible,' p. 36.

rather it is orthodox theology shown to be rational philosophy.
He argues that finite spirit or mind, considered in itself, and
not as the co-relate of infinite spirit, is a mere abstraction.   On
the other hand, the infinite, apart from its relation to the
finite, is also a mere abstraction.   Both, therefore, must yield
to a higher idea—that is, to an organic whole—which is the
unity of both the infinite and the finite.   This is the infinite
of religion, which cannot be a mere self-identical Being, but
one which contains organic relations to the finite.   The world
of finite intelligence, though distinct from God, is still in its
ideal nature one with him.   The conclusion may be given in a
few brief passages, such as, 'That which God creates, and by
which he reveals the hidden treasures of his wisdom and love,
is still not foreign to his own infinite life, but one with it.   In
the knowledge of the minds that know him, in the self-surrender
of the hearts that love him, it is no paradox to affirm that he
knows and loves himself.'   Again, 'Nor is the mere numerical
principle of distinction less fallacious when applied to those
religions which are usually classed as monotheistic.   The God
of Christianity is not any numerical unit.   In whatever way
we may conceive of the doctrine of the Trinity, it forces us to
ascribe distinction to the divine nature, to include plurality as
well as unity in our conceptions of the Godhead, and even in
the strictest monotheism of the Jewish religion the idea of God
is not a bare unity, for Jehovah is a spiritual Being who manifests himself in a diversity of attributes or names, and therefore his nature can only be apprehended as that which involves
diversity as well as unity.   In another place it is said that the
divine and the human, the infinite and the finite, must be
apprehended as only moments of an organic whole in which
both exist at once in their distinction and their unity.'   The
following passage is not likely to escape being called Pantheistic : 'Thought of any kind, positive or negative, doubting
or assenting, postulates not the thought of the individual
thinker, but a thought of self-consciousness that is prior to all
individual thinking, and is the absolute element or atmosphere
in which it lives and breathes.'   Further on, 'As a thinking
being, it is possible for me to suppress or quell my consciousness, every movement of self-assertion, every notion and opinion
that is merely mine, every desire that belongs to me as the

particular self, and to become the pure medium of thought or intelligence that is universal; in a word, to live no longer my own life, but let my consciousness become possessed and sufficed by the infinite and eternal life of Spirit.*

* Introduction to 'The Philosophy of Religion,' pp. 249, 257, 325.

CHAPTER XVI.

THE question of 'Pantheism' becomes more difficult the more we study books written expressly to refute it. The Abbé Maret published a work some years ago in the interests of the Roman Catholic Church, in which he shows that all religions, ancient and modern, with all philosophies of religion, are Pantheistic, if not actually, yet certainly in their tendencies, excepting the Catholic religion and philosophies sanctioned by the Church, such, for instance, as the speculations of Augustine, Des Cartes, and Malebranche. Not, he says, that reason, necessarily leads to Pantheism, but this is the inevitable result of rationalism, or the denial of a divine revelation.

By a 'divine revelation,' M. Maret means an infallible church. Without this we are left to individual reason, and as all men have not the same development of reason, the same means of knowing what is truth, nor the same judgment concerning it, there cannot be for man, on the principles of reason, absolute truth and absolute error. 'Catholicism,' he says, 'starts with absolute truth. Pantheism teaches that humanity will only arrive at truth after a long history of progression.' We may object to the inference that there is no absolute truth, because it is not absolutely apprehended. As Protestants, we might say that Catholics no more than we have absolutely apprehended truth. But M. Maret's argument is that the Church has; and he proves it by reason, demonstrates it, 'gives a rigorous proof of his fundamental proposition.' 'To arrive at truth,' he says, 'we must have an idea of it.' Every method of the investigation of truth supposes the idea of that which it investigates. Now as there are but two ideas of truth, there can be but two methods of investigation, that of Catholicism and that of Pantheism. Truth is that which is; truth and being are identical. We conceive being under the two great categories of the absolute and the relative, the infinite and the finite. The infinite gives us an image of itself, or an idea of the one absolute neces-

sary and immutable truth. The finite, by its opposition to the
infinite, appears to us, in some way, as' a negation of being, a
true non-being. It only subsists by a real participation in the
infinite by the living relations which unite it to God. These
relations, these laws which harmonize and unite all beings together and the world with God, give us the idea of a mediating
truth between the infinite and the finite; the Creator and the
creature, God and the world. Now this mediating truth comes
from God; yea, it is God, and so must be like him—absolute,
eternal, and immutable.

This idea of truth leads to Catholicism, where we have a
living and infallible authority—a society which is the deposi-
tory of truth, and of the divine word. It is difficult to see the
force of M. Maret's argument from the vagueness of his definition of Pantheism. It is that belief which makes ' truth progressive and variable,' and he enumerates among Pantheists the
orthodox Guizot, the Eclectic Cousin, and the Saint-Simonian
Pierre Leroux, with all the German and French philosophers
who are not Catholics. It does not appear that all or any of
these men make truth in itself progressive and variable. It
is so only as regards man's relation to it. Man is a seeker after
truth, and as M. Maret admits, all men, even Catholics, are
' perfectible and progressive.' Even that incomprehensible
thing, the Catholic Church, according to some of the greatest
Catholic theologians, has truth only as it is developed from age
to age; new dogmas being continually added to the sum total
of the Catholic faith.

The theory of an infallible church is without doubt a happy
invention. It puts an end to all doubts, and if it permits
inquiry, it fixes its exact bounds. An infallible church is the
desired haven of every anxious and troubled mind. Had we
been the makers of revelation—that is, had it been ours to determine in what way God should reveal himself to man—we
should have caused the words of truth to be written in the
heavens, so that all men might read them, or we should have
made angels the ambassadors, so that all men might see and
hear what the immediate messengers of heaven had to say; but
if both of these were denied, the next mode of revelation would
certainly be through an infallible church. But what if this,
too, were denied? Is truth, then, impossible? Is it, there-

fore, mutable and uncertain? Whatever be the answer to this
question, we must not invent ways for God. We cannot determine beforehand how he should reveal himself; we must then
inquire how he has revealed himself. The infallible Church
has never determined what Pantheism is. It has applied the
word to certain doctrines, and to certain philosophies, with the
same indefiniteness that we find among Protestants. It has
forbidden the works of Erigena, and suffered to pass uncen-
sured the writings of the Areopagite. It has not condemned
the speculations of Des Cartes and Malebranche, the legitimate
outcome of which was the doctrine of Spinoza. It declares
itself opposed to Pantheism, but it has neither eliminated
nor explained the Pantheistic element in the fathers, whose
works it holds for orthodox, nor of the schoolmen who were
the great doctors in its medieval glory.

M. Maret's work was specially addressed to the rationalists
of France, among whom were the Eclectic philosophers, M.
Cousin and his followers, some of them, by the way, Catholic
laymen who had distinguished themselves as refuters of Pantheism. Maret found the heresy in Cousin's analysis of the
mind, which he, in some sense, identified with the divine mind,
filling up with the idea of causation the chasm between the
infinite and the finite. 'The Infinite,' says M. Cousin, 'is the
absolute cause which necessarily creates, and necessarily develops itself. We cannot conceive unity without multiplicity.
Unity taken by itself; unity indivisible; unity remaining in
the depths of its absolute existence, never developing itself into
variety, is for itself, as if it were not. It is necessary that unity
and variety co-exist, so that from their existence results reality;
and unity admits multiplicity, making up in the divine intelligence—the infinite, the finite, and the relation between them.
From this idea of the divine causation we learn what it is for
God to create. It corresponds to the effects we can produce
by the exercise of our faculties. God is an absolute and
necessary cause, he creates with himself, he passes into his
work, remaining entire in himself. The world then is created
out of the divine substance, and created necessarily. Its existence is as necessary as that of God himself, since it is only
the development of his life—the unfolding of his unity. In
human reason, Cousin says, we have found three ideas which

it did not create, but which rule and govern it. From these ideas to God, the passage is not difficult, for these ideas are God himself.' 'Again,' he says, ' the God of consciousness is not an abstract God—a solitary being, banished by creation, on a throne of a silent eternity, an absolute existence, which resembles the annihilation of existence. He is a God at once true and real, at once substance and cause, always substance and always cause, being substance only inasmuch as he is cause, and cause only inasmuch as he is substance, that is to say, being absolute cause, one and many, eternity and time, space and number, essence and life, individuality and totality ; principle, end, and middle, at the summit of being, and at its lowest degree—infinite and finite together, a triple infinite, that is to say, at once God, nature, and humanity. If God is not all, he is nothing. If he is absolutely indivisible in himself, he is inaccessible, and by consequence he is absolutely incomprehensible, and his incomprehensibility is for us his destruction. Incomprehensible as a formula, and in the schools, God is revealed in the world which manifests him, and for the soul which possesses him and feels him.' In accordance with this view of the relation between God and the world, M. Cousin propounds doctrines of psychology, of religion, and a philosophy of the progressive development of humanity. Thought is a divine inspiration, a true revelation in the soul. There is a solemn moment in which, without being sought, we are found —when without any course of our will, without any mingling of reflection, we enter into possession of life, and the three elements which constitute it ; the idea of the infinite, the finite, and their relation. This *fiat lux* of thought is a true manifestation of God in us. There are privileged men in whom the faculty of inspiration has been raised to its highest power. These men become for other men masters and revealers. Hence the origin of prophecies, priesthoods, worships.

Cousin's disciples, Jouffroy and Damiron, Michelet and Lerminier, applied their master's principles to the elucidation of the formation of dogmas ; to philosophies of history and religion ; and the last mentioned, Lerminier, to the philosophy of right. The human mind Lerminier calls ' a perpetual and necessary revelation of God.' Its progress is infinite and indefinite. In it God appears on earth, constituting law and order.

God himself is the essence of law ; and the development of this essence is the progress of society.   Maret finds the Pantheist heresy in every idea of development, as being antagonistic to his definition of revelation.   Even M. Guizot becomes a Pantheist in affirming that truth is not absolutely realised in human institutions, either political or religious.

After the Eclectics, Maret discovers the same doctrine among the Socialists of France, the followers of Saint-Simon and Charles Fourrier—but especially in the school of Pierre Leroux and the new Encyclopædists, which was developed from Saint-Simonianism.   Maret undertakes to refute them all, and to defend and exhibit the doctrines of the Catholic Church.   He has declared the certainty of revelation as man's only guide ; but he does not sacrifice reason.   He is more a philosopher than his theory would have led us to expect.   'When the spirit of man,' he says, 'in the silence of meditation, rises to the conception of eternal, necessary, and immutable ideas ; when it perceives truth ; when it sees God himself ; if it re-enters into itself after having enjoyed this magnificent light ; if it question itself, what will it think of its own nature ?   Being of a day, changeable and changing shadow of being, it will acknowledge, without doubt, that it has not been able to draw from itself the great idea of truth.   Man will acknowledge with gratitude that this idea has visited his soul, that it fell upon it like a ray of the sun on the organ of sight.   He will acknowledge that the great light has been given him, that it is revealed to him.' Independent of the Church then there is a revelation.   We might go on to ask if this revelation is fallible or infallible, if it has any correspondence to the revelation in the Church. 'We here take the word revelation,' says M. Maret, 'in its largest sense.   We believe that ideas and speech are revealed to man.   That is the revelation of which St. John speaks, which enlightens every man that cometh into the world, and which is the true source of reason.   That primitive and natural revelation, which every good psychology establishes, is in perfect harmony with the teaching which represents to us religion as born of a revelation, preserving itself and developing itself by revelation.   There is revelation in the natural order as well as in the supernatural.   There are natural truths as well as supernatural truths, which both come from God.'   It was, of course, necessary that the unity between the natural and supernatural suggested by the word revelation should be abandoned, for the class of things naturally revealed might be differently understood by different minds. They led to Pantheism. The revelation in the Church was therefore added as the ' revelation positive and supernatural.' But even this revelation runs back into the other, for Maret has to go to the dim light of Judaism and the dimmer light of the patriarchal age which possessed only the truths of natural religion, to find that Church which he reckons necessary for the preservation of the supernatural revelation. But he has maintained that there is such a thing as a revelation in the human mind. To this extent he was a philosopher; and, as such, had to accept the same conclusions that he objected against the Eclectics and Saint-Simonians. If there is a natural revelation, it is progressive; yea, and the supernatural revelation, is it not progressive too? His theory is to start with an infallible church, but in reality he begins with reason, and so must every man who does reason. The new Encyclopædists had good ground for retorting on the refuter of Pantheism that he had the leaven of it in himself; and though his ' ecclesiastical superiors gave encouragement to his feeble efforts for the defence of the faith,' his brother priest, the Abbé Peltier, who, it must be admitted, was not wanting in discernment, found in Maret's definition of God the very essence of Pantheism. Like a good orthodox priest, he said that Christians should be content with the knowledge of God given them in the catechism. He told M. Maret that his definition of God was borrowed from Hegel and Cousin; and he denounced Malebranche as a priest who substituted philosophy for the doctrines of the Church.

AMAND SAINTES.

Amand Saintes, representing the Protestant side of Christianity, says the alternative is not Pantheism or Catholicism, but Pantheism or the gospel. This is scarcely a step towards the light, for the gospel spoken of in this way is as indefinite as Pantheism. We know what the gospel is as a message of good news from God to man. We know that it is a manifestation of God's infinite compassion—a revealing of him as ' our Father in heaven,' but the theology of the gospel—the gospel as opposed to Pantheism; what is that? We have seen that the great teachers of the gospel, from St. Paul and the Alexandrian fathers, to say nothing of St. John, down through the great doctors of the middle ages, even to the Abbé Maret, have been considered more or less Pantheistic. The dogmatic teaching of the gospel is to every man what it is to his reason. The moment we have refused obedience to the authority of a church, we are cast on our own responsibility. This is the fundamental principle of Protestantism. It is useless to ignore it. Even when we give allegiance to a Church, it is only so far as that Church represents the collective wisdom of its members. The Catholic Church is a convenient refuge; for whatever a man's metaphysics may be, however much his philosophy may come in collision with the Church's dogmas, he can effect the reconciliation as Malebranche did, and indeed as every thinking Catholic does, by agreeing to submit to the decisions of the Church. But Protestantism cannot escape in this way, its boast is that reason is an essential element in all matters of religious belief.

EMILE SAISSET.

M. Saisset, representing the interests of religious philosophy, tried to show that Pantheism was not the necessary result of the exercise of reason in religion. He criticised Des Cartes, Malebranche, and Spinoza, with their disciples in France and Germany. He found the poison of Pantheism secretly lurking in the theology of Sir Isaac Newton and Samuel Clarke. The famous passage with which Newton concludes his 'Principia' we have always regarded as an expression of the purest Theism; but M. Saisset sees in it the germs of a very dangerous theology. 'God,' says Newton, 'is neither eternity nor infinity, but eternal and infinite. He is neither duration nor space, but he endures always, is present everywhere, and constitutes both duration and space.' M. Saisset interprets this as teaching that God is substance, and that infinite duration and extension are only modes of his being. 'It is true' he says, 'that Newton saw the danger of the theory, 'and tried to escape its consequences; but his qualifications are simply inconsistencies, neither explaining the first hypothesis nor expounding another.' Newton's doctrine was taken up by Clarke, who established his argument for the being of God on the fact that we have ideas of infinite time and infinite space, concluding that there must be a being to constitute these infinities —that they seem both to be but attributes of an essence incomprehensible to us. This, M. Saisset regards as but another form of the doctrine of Spinoza, who made extension or infinite space one of the attributes of God. The same objection had been made by Leibnitz to Sir Isaac Newton's definition of space as the 'sensorium' of the Deity. Clarke defended Newton, quoting his words more accurately than Leibnitz had done. 'Space is, as it were, the sensorium of the Deity.'

M. Saisset criticised all erring theologians. His work has been translated into English to check the importation of Pantheism into England, but not without a protest by the translator that M. Saisset himself has retained the very essence of the theology which he wished to refute. M. Saisset saw, as he thought, the danger of believing in infinite time and infinite space specially exemplified in the case of Newton and Clarke, yet he thought it impossible not to believe that the world is infinite and eternal. 'Away from me!' cries the philosophical refuter of Pantheism, 'away from me, vain phantoms of the imagination! God is eternally all that he is. If he is the Creator, he creates eternally. If he creates the world, it is not from chance or caprice, but for reasons worthy of himself; and these reasons are eternal. Nothing new, nothing fortuitous, can arise in the councils of eternity. The universe must express the infinity and the eternity of God. We cannot conceive of its having a beginning, nor can we anywhere set a bound to it.' M. Saisset does not forget that Giordano Bruno was led to Pantheism through this belief of the world's eternity and infinity; but, to save himself, he distinguishes between the infinity of God, and the infinity of the world—the eternity of God and the eternity of the world. The one is absolute; the other relative. The want of this distinction led Newton to confound eternity and time, immensity and space. There can be no eternal time, and no infinite space. Eternity and immensity are the unchangeable. Time and space the very conditions

of change, the Creator alone is eternal, immense, infinitely
absolute.   The creation is scattered over space and time,
subject to changes and to limits.   'Thus,' exclaims M. Saisset :
'I consider myself saved at once from Pantheism and superstition !'

CHAPTER XVII.

PHILOSOPHY.

Every philosophy of being has ended in something like Pantheism. That which IS, is permanent, stable amid all change, or, at least, a something which abides, whatever may be the changes. Even if called a becoming, it is still permanent, or abiding, as opposed to that which comes and goes. The fact of an absolute existence seems to be the most certain of all facts. The senses only reveal to us that which changes. We cannot fix on any one thing and say that it is permanent, yet it seems a certain inference, if not an axiom of the human consciousness, that the changing must have a ground on which depends the permanence of existence. Something must have always existed, and that something cannot be separated from the things which we see. If not the reality of these things, there must be the relation to them of cause and effect. But what is that which IS? We do not know. We only know our ideas about it. We find ourselves in space, and ask what it is. At first we think of it as something limited, but this conception is soon corrected, for we cannot imagine any bound being set to space. We cannot suppose, as Locke thought we could, a man at the extremity of space stretching out his hand into non-entity. We still ask for something beyond. The highest flights of imagination never reach the boundary wall of the universe. We go from world to world, and from sun to sun, and to all imaginable worlds and suns beyond, but we never reach *nowhere*. Our idea of space is infinite. We cannot give it limits. It is the opposite of finite, and as such a positive idea—that of boundless extension. This is the result of the first effort of the mind to find the attributes of being, or that which IS. Our idea of time follows the same law as that of space. We first think of time as limited; a part of time, as an hour; a day, a week; a year, a life-time. We go back to past generations—to the beginning of our own nation, to that of nations before ours—to the first nation, the first family, the first man; but there is still something before that. We cannot conceive of anything but ceaseless duration, and with that something which endures, so that absolute being is infinite as to duration and extension. That which IS, is always, has been, and will be always. These are forms in which it is conceived by the human mind. They are the first thoughts of philosophy, the clearest, the most certain, and the most universal of our ideas. But being is still something undefined. It is not any one of the finite things which we see. If these are anything beyond phenomena, they must partake of that which IS. Being, then, is some unknown universal. 'Let us call it water,' said Thales. 'Air,' said Anaximenes. 'Fire,' said Heraclitus. 'No,' said Anaximander, 'call it what it is— 'the boundless.' 'Call it the one,' said Pythagoras. 'Better still,' cried Parmenides and all the Eleatics, 'let us call it by its true name, "being," "the being," the "one being."' This was the foundation of all ancient theology. It was the first great grasp of the intellect of man in its search for God. Yet it was only the philosophical putting together of a universal truth. The Brahman had incorporated it in the legends of his gods. It was the thought which reared the vast temples of India. As the negation of the finite, it comforted the Buddhist amid the miseries of the transient life, and as the Non-being, or the above-being, it was the ground of the mystic theology of Plato's Alexandrian disciples. How it passed into the theology of the Church, and how it has leavened all theology to the present day, we have abundantly shown. It is, in fact, the ground-work of theology. A doctrine of being is implied, if not expressed, in every religious system. We are first startled when a Dionysius or an Erigena calls being nothing, and identifies that nothing with God—when a Spinoza calls it substance, a Schelling identity, or a Hegel an idea, and says that God is this substance, this identity, this idea. They transfer to the Infinite words which in our minds express only the finite. They were trying to express the Infinite, but their very words bear the stamp of the finite.

Spinoza called God substance, the idea that had been given of the universal Being under the conditions of sense knowledge; but its imperfection was manifest. Bayle, who is said to have satisfactorily refuted Spinoza, did his great work of refutation by taking advantage of this imperfection. He confounded Spinoza's substance with matter, proving that everything has its own substance, which in Bayle's sense was perfectly true ; but it had nothing to do with Spinoza.

If being be infinite as to time and space, always and everywhere, it is impossible that it can receive any addition. It is already all that is or can be. If a worm, a drop of water, or a blade of grass has any true being in itself, that is subtracted from the infinite, which thereby ceases to be infinite. It matters not whether the finite existence be a universe or an atom of dust, a deity, or an insect. The lowest conceivable existence taken for the infinite deprives it of infinity. 'God,' said the Eleatics, 'is either all or nothing, for if there be a reality beyond him, that reality is wanting to his perfection.' The finite or the infinite must go. There is either no God or no world. The Eleatics were certain of the existence of God. They were certain that being existed, and that it was infinite. They had therefore but one alternative, which was to make the world merely phenomena. How real being and created being can co-exist is the first problem of philosophy. Plato tried to solve it by means of the ideas, but he left the problem where he found it. Aristotle, notwithstanding his hypothesis of an eternal matter, and his evident leaning to a personal creative deity, fell back on abstract being, leaving the relation of God to the world undetermined, if he did not really identify the divine being with the all-life of the universe. Malebranche felt that philosophy led him inevitably to a doctrine of creation different from that of the Church, but he harmonized the two on the Cartesian principle of believing the Church's doctrine on the Church's authority ; and, therefore, though a philosopher, he believed in the existence of a material world and its creation out of nothing. M. Saisset refuted Pantheism, yet at the end of the refutation he cried, 'God creates eternally.' And this is the universal utterance of reason. 'How,' Mr. Mansel asked, 'can the relative be conceived as coming into being ? If it is a distinct reality from the Absolute, it must be conceived as passing from non-existence into existence. But to conceive an object as non-existent is again a self-contradiction, for that which is conceived exists, as an object of thought, in and by

that conception. We may abstain from thinking of an object
at all ; but, if we think of it, we can but think of it as existing.
It is possible not to think of an object at all, and at another
time to think of it as already in being; but to think of it in
the act of becoming, in the progress from not-being into being,
is to think that which in the very thought annihilates itself.
Here again the Pantheistic hypothesis seems forced upon us.
We can think of creation only as a change in the condition of
that which already exists, and thus the creature is conceivable
only as a phenomenal mode of the being of the creation. The
whole of this web of contradictions is woven from one original
warp and woof—namely, the impossibility of conceiving the
co-existence of the infinite and the finite, and the cognate impossibility of conceiving a first commencement of phenomena,
or the Absolute giving birth to the relative. The law of
thought appears to admit of no possible escape from the
meshes in which thought is entangled, save by destroying one
or other of the cords of which they are composed. Pantheism
or Atheism are thus the only alternative offered to us, according as we prefer to save the infinite by the sacrifice of the
finite, or to maintain the finite by the sacrifice of the infinite.'

Hegel, as an orthodox theologian, which he always professed
to be, maintained the doctrine of creation out of nothing. To
the denial of this he ascribed the origin of the Pantheism of
Parmenides and Spinoza. Spinoza himself thought that he
escaped Pantheism, by saying that creation, though eternal in
the sense of never ending duration, was not eternal in the
proper, philosophical, or Alexandrian sense, that eternity is
distinct from all duration, and means absolute existence or the
perfection of being. This is the sense in which it is generally
used by the more learned of the fathers, and which seems to be
sanctioned by St. John in his Gospel. Creation out of nothing
they did not understand. It was introduced, Hegel says, by the
later Christian metaphysicians. It does not mean that nothing
was the entity out of which God created, but that God called
into existence, by an act of his power, a new substance. The
Neo-Platonists called this new substance the phenomenal or
created, as distinct from the eternal and real, and probably
this was what Spinoza meant when he said there was only one
substance. There is no other conclusion consistently to be

reached, but that this substance is the reality of all phenomenal and finite existence. 'When we are aware,' says Sir William Hamilton, 'of something which begins to exist, we are by the necessity of our intelligence constrained to believe that it has a cause. But what does this expression, that it has a cause, signify? If we analyse our thought, we shall find that it simply means that as we cannot conceive any new existence to commence, therefore all that now is seen to arise under a new appearance had previously an existence under a prior form. We are utterly unable to realize in thought the possibility of the complement of existence being either increased or diminished. We are unable, on the one hand, to conceive nothing becoming something, or, on the other, something becoming nothing. When God is said to create out of nothing, we construe this to thought, by supposing that he evolves existence out of himself; we view the Creator as the cause of the universe. " Ex nihilo nihil, in nihilum nil posset reverti," expresses in its purest form the whole intellectual phenomenon of casuality.' In another place Sir William says, ' We are unable to construe in thought that there can be an atom absolutely added to, or an atom absolutely taken away from, existence in general. Make the experiment. Form to yourselves a notion of the universal; now, conceive that the quantity of existence, of which the universe is the sum, is either amplified or diminished? You can conceive the creation of the world as lightly as you can conceive the creation of an atom. But what is creation? It is not the springing of nothing into something. Far from it; it is conceived, and is by us conceivable, merely as the evolution of a new form of existence, by the fiat of the Deity. Let us suppose the very crisis of creation. Can we realise it to ourselves, in thought, that the moment after the universe came into manifested being there was a larger complement of existence in the universe and its author together, than there was the moment before in the Deity himself alone? This we cannot imagine. What I have now said of our conception of creation holds true of our conception of annihilation. We can conceive no real annihilation, no absolute sinking of something into nothing. But as creation is cogitable by us only as an exertion of divine power, so annihilation is only to be conceived by us as a withdrawal of the divine support.   All that there is now actually of existence in the universe we conceive as having virtually existed, prior to creation, in the Creator; and in imagining the universe to be annihilated by its author, we can only imagine this as the retractation of an outward energy into power.' Mr Calderwood, in a criticism of Sir William Hamilton's philosophy, denounces this view of causation and creation as essentially Pantheistic.   Mr. Mansel regretted that Mr. Calderwood should ever have charged this theory with Pantheism; for, if ever there was a philosopher whose writings from first to last are utterly antagonistic to every form of Pantheism, it is Sir William Hamilton.   But what in all the world is Pantheism if it is not that God evolves the universe out of himself?   Mr. Stuart Mill denies the statement that we cannot conceive a beginning or an end of physical existence.   Its inconceivableness belongs only to philosophers and men of science, not to the ignorant, who easily conceive that water is dried up by the sun, or that wood and coals are destroyed by the fire.   But surely a metaphysician like Mr. Stuart Mill knew that the phenomenon of thought is not to be taken from what the fool thinks, but from what the philosopher thinks.   The true phenomenology of mind is not that of the ignorant unthinking mind, but of the mind which thinks.

CHAPTER XVIII.

NATURE.

THE poetical interpretation of nature has generally been Pantheistic. In the words of Cowper,

> 'There lives and works
> A soul in all things, and that soul is God.'

There is a soul in nature—a soul which in some way is God himself. A dim conception of this was the foundation of the ancient mythologies, which peopled all nature with living spirits, connected a deity with every field and forest, every road and river. This conception placed Jupiter in Olympus, Apollo in the sun, Neptune in the sea, Bacchus in the vintage, and Ceres among the yellow corn. It filled the fountains with Naiades, the woods with Dryades, and made the sea to teem with the children of Nereus. At last, advancing reason became dissatisfied with the multitude of divinities, and poets and philosophers treated them as the creations of fancy, yet as embodying the higher truth, that 'all things are full of God.'

That the soul which lives and works in nature is God, is the partial truth of all the theories of progressive development. These theories were the inevitable result of the study of nature. There, all is progress. Everything unfolds. The highest organism has its beginning in the smallest form of life. The visible starts from the invisible. The things which are seen are made from things which are not seen.

The oldest cosmogonies recognized the law of progress in nature. The ancient Brahman looked upon creation as the outbeaming of the Deity—the going forth of Brahmă. It was not a work, but an unfolding; a manifestation of mind in matter; a development of the one into the many. The spiritual shone out in the material. The real was visible in the phenomenal. It was a strange dream, but it has been the dream of poetry, and the romance of science. The Egyptian did not materially differ from the Brahman. Nature was the

emanation of Osiris and Isis ; the gushing forth of Nilus ; the
one deity, whatever was his name, for he was called by all
names, passing into the manifold.   The Greeks, who may have
got their knowledge from Egypt's priests, had the same
thoughts of nature.   The old Ionics were on this track when
they sought for the first element out of which the all was
formed.   The Atomic philosophers, whom Plato describes as
'sick of the Atheistic disease,' Democritus and Epicurus, and in
later times Lucretius, were all, after a fashion, inquirers concerning the progress of nature.   Atoms wandering in the
vacuum of infinite space, like motes dancing in the sunbeam,
they supposed to be the first matter.   These atoms, in the
lapse of ages, gathered into a solid mass, and became suns and
moons, stars and worlds.   Through the blending of all things
with all things, the waters brought forth vegetables and
animals.   These took their form and character from the
climate in which they lived, and the conditions on which life
was permitted them.   Special organs and particular members
of the body took their origin from the same conditions.   By
long practice they learned to fulfil their offices with a measure
of perfection.   Birds learned to fly, and fishes to swim.   Eyes
became skilful in seeing, tongues in talking, ears quick to hear,
and noses to smell.   Plato, indeed, in the Timæus, confounds
this development with creation.   After describing how Oceanus
and Tethys sprang from heaven and earth, and from them
Phorcys, Kronos, and Rhea, from whom sprang Zeus and Hera,
he says, ' The Artificer of the universe commanded them to
create mortal natures as he had created them.'   Ovid, too, gives
an account of creation which resembles that of Moses, but
Horace represents the general belief of antiquity, where he thus
describes the origin of men.   ' When animals first crept forth
from the newly-formed earth, a dumb and filthy herd, they
fought for acorns and lurking places with their nails and fists,
then with clubs, and at last with arms, which, taught by experience, they had forged.   Then they invented names for things,
and words to express their thoughts, after which they began
to desist from war, to fortify cities, and to enact laws.'   All the
old philosophers were agreed that the working of nature was a
process of advancing development, but Democritus and his disciples left the evolution to chance, while the wiser philosophers

regarded it as the working of God, but of God as the soul of nature.

DE MAILLET.

The development doctrine was revived in the beginning of the last century by De Maillet, an eccentric Frenchman. It is scarcely evident that De Maillet believed all he said, for what he calls his facts are, some of them, fictions wild enough; and his analogies and correspondences in nature are often not only fanciful, but merely verbal. With Homer, Thales the Milesian, and the Nile worshippers of Egypt, he traced the origin of all things to the element of water. He quotes Moses as teaching the same thing, where he speaks of the Spirit brooding over the face of the deep. He argues from geology that the ocean must once have swept over the entire globe, and nourished nature in its cool embrace. It treasured up the seeds of plants and flowers. It watered the undeveloped monads of fishes and foxes, mammoths and men. All things rejoiced in the rolling wave and 'the busy tribes of flesh and blood' slept as softly on beds of seaweed as dolphins and mermaids on the bosom of Galatea. The ocean, said De Maillet, still witnesses to its universal fatherhood. Its kingdoms, animal and vegetable, are closely analogous to those on dry land. We have the same unity of type, and in many cases the species correspond. The sea has flower-beds as rich and varied as those on land and corresponding to them, as the very names show. We have sea-roses, sea-lilies, sea-violets, and sea-vines. When the water receded from the land, the plants and flowers remained. What changes they have since undergone are due to the influences of the sun and fresh water, being nourished by the rain and the rivulets that water the earth. Similar conformations are visible in animals. Varieties of plumage and form in birds have their analogies in the shape, colour, and disposition of the scales of fishes. The fins of a fish are arranged like the feathers in its analogous bird. If we attend to the flight of birds, we shall discover a likeness to the mode in which the corresponding fishes swim in the water. The same analogies De Maillet finds between land animals and sea animals. When the waters left the land, the marine animals had no alternative but to become land animals, and should the ocean again overflow the world, what could they do but again betake themselves to the sea ? In the struggle for life many would doubtless perish, but some would eat the herb of Glaucus, and when used to the new element, would find a congenial home with their ancient marine relatives, the children of Nereus and Doris.

ROBINET.

De Maillet's doctrine was never regarded in any other light but that of a wild theory, of which the object was amusement rather than serious inquiry. But the development doctrine was soon after taken up by a Frenchman of a very different character. This was Jean Baptiste Robinet, the able author of ' De la Nature '—a work which Lord Brougham pronounces to have greater merit than the famous ' System of Nature,' which bears the name of Mirabaud. Brougham says that both these works have the same tendency, but this is entirely a mistake. Mirabaud's, or rather D'Holbach's ' System of Nature,' was avowedly Atheistic ; Robinet's was avowedly Theistic. D'Holbach was the leader of the French Atheists ; Robinet claimed to be a religious philosopher all his life. In his latter years he became a Catholic, and died in the faith of the Roman Catholic Church.

Nature, Robinet said, is not God, nor any part of God, yet it results, necessarily, from his divine essence. It never had a moment which was not preceded by another, and it never will have a moment to which another will not equally succeed. In other words, it never had a beginning, and it will never have an end. Moses says that creation took place in ' the beginning ' —that is, out of time, in that abyssal eternity, which is not constituted by duration. It will never have an end. ' New heavens ' and ' new earth ' mean only that the heavens and the earth will be changed. The matter is the same ; they are new as contrasted with previous forms.

Nature thus co-existing, necessarily and eternally with the divine essence, develops unceasingly its types and forms, according to its own eternal laws. This development is progressive. The first axiom in natural philosophy is this—' Nature makes no leaps.' Everything begins to exist under a very little form—the smallest possible. It passes, necessarily, from the state of seed to that of species. The more complete the organisation, the longer the time required for development. An insect reaches its perfection in a day. A man requires many years; an oak centuries. The difference between the acorn and the oak, the germ cell and the full-grown man, is vast, but vaster still between the seed of the world and ' the world formed.' How immense, then, the length of time required by the law of development to bring the universe to the point of increase which it had reached, when our earth was formed.

Robinet could see in nature no mode of operation but this of progressive development. He could find no trace in the past of a working different from what he saw going on in the world now. This unceasing law forms the universal all. This all is infinitely graduated. It is without bounds, and its divisions are only apparent. Nature has individuals, but no kingdoms, no classes, kinds, or species. These are artificial—the work of man; but having no existence in nature. Originally there is but one being—the prototype of all beings—and of this one all are variations, multiplied and diversified in all possible ways. This seemed so obviously true that Robinet wondered any naturalist should dispute it. But he complained chiefly of those who did not acknowledge any absolute difference between animals and vegetables, and who yet made a bridgeless chasm between the lower animals and man. Why, he asked, this great stride ? Why should the law suffer an exception ? Why be deranged here ? Have we not the links of the chain to complete the continuity of the gradation of being ? Robinet, indeed, was not convinced of the consanguinity of apes and men, but there were *mer*men and *mer*maids whom De Maillet had described. There was, moreover, the ' ourang,' which Robinet supposed to be more nearly allied to men than to apes, but its existence had not yet been satisfactorily proved to the naturalists of France. The links of the complete chain, he thought, could not be far off; if not actually discovered, science must soon discover them.

Nature has had her eye upon man from her first essays at creation. We see all beings conceived and formed after a single pattern. They are the never-ending graduated variations of the prototype—each one exhibiting so much progress towards the most excellent form of being, that is, the human form.   Man is the result of all the combinations which the prototype has undergone in its progress through all the stages of progression.   All were types of man to come.   As a cave, a grotto, a wigwam, a shepherd's cabin, a house, a palace, may all be regarded as variations of the same plan of architecture, which was executed first on a simple and then on a grander scale, so in nature.   The cave, the grotto, the wigwam, the cabin, and the house are not the 'Escurial' nor the 'Louvre,' yet we may look upon them as types; so a stone, a vegetable, a fish, a dog, a monkey, may be regarded as variations of the prototype, or ideal man.

Robinet's theory was vastly comprehensive, uniting all kingdoms, classes, and species.   He believed that he had found the key of the universe, and that he laid the foundation of all true science, in being able to say, 'Nature is one.'   He had fewer fictions than De Maillet, but his analogies were not altogether free from fancy.   Beginning with minerals, he found stones that in shape resembled members of the human body—the head, the heart, the eye, the ear, the feet.   Among vegetables, he found plants resembling men and women; these, however, were not, he admitted, normal growths.   Among zoophytes, he found many points of resemblance to the human form, as the names indicated; such are the sea-hand, sea-chest, and the sea-kidney.   Among fishes, he found some of human shape; but these were in distant seas.   The fish of St. Pierre, which is caught on the coasts of America, engenders in its body a stone which has the shape of a man.   The 'Pece Muger,' as the Spaniards call it, has a woman's face.   Some sea-monsters are two-handed, as the whale, the sea-fox, and the sea-lion. Coming to land animals, Robinet traced the same gradation from the lowest form of life to the highest, to the topstone of nature's efforts—the being nobler than all others, with an erect look and lofty countenance, the lord of creation—man.

LAMARCK.

Robinet's principles were taken up and illustrated by another Frenchman—the famous naturalist, Lamarck.   He was more scientific than Robinet, and mingled with his inquiries less theology and metaphysics—less of Plato and interpretations of Moses, yet he recognized the same relation between nature and the divine Being that had been set forth by Robinet. Nature, he said, is a work, and its great Author is the ever-present worker. It can do nothing of itself; it is limited and blind. But, though nature is a work, it is yet in a sense a laboratory. In this laboratory the Author of nature works incessantly. He never leaves his creation. We say that he gave it laws; but he is himself ever present, the immediate executor of all law, the doer of all nature's works.

Lamarck discarded all the divisions and sub-divisions of plants and animals, which other naturalists had made. Like Robinet, he regarded them as having no real existence in nature, being only the arbitrary arrangements of man. Nature is one and undivided. It knows of no orders but the order of progression. Nature makes nothing great at once. Unnumbered ages are required to bring to perfection the workmanship of her laboratory. The fluid which impregnates an egg, and gives vitality to the embryo of a chick, is a principle analogous to that by which life presses into the world. A seminal fluid pervades all nature, and impregnates matter when placed in circumstances favourable to life. Nature begins with the humblest forms. It produces ' rough draughts ' —infusoria, polypi, and other similarly simple forms. When life is once produced, it tends to increase the body that clothes it, and to extend the dimensions of every part. Variations are the result of circumstances. A plain proof of this is seen in the production of new species. Dogs, fowls, ducks, pigeons, and other domesticated animals have superinduced qualities which did not belong to them in their wild state. These have arisen entirely from the circumstances and conditions of their existence as domesticated animals. The same law prevails in the vegetable kingdom. The wheat from which we make bread is originally a wild grass. It is due to cultivation that it has become wheat.

The characteristic part of Lamarck's doctrine is the way in which he endeavours to account for the possession of senses and special bodily organs. They were acquired by what he calls ' an internal sentiment.' By this ' sentiment,' animals have

z

desires; and, by frequent endeavours to gratify these desires, the organ or sense necessary for their gratification was produced. The duck and the beaver, for instance, had an 'internal sentiment' to swim; and, after long and persevering efforts, webs grew on their feet, and ducks and beavers learned to swim. The antelope and the gazelle were naturally timid, and, being often pursued by beasts of prey, they had an 'internal sentiment' to run fast, and much practice in running, the result of which was that suppleness of limb which is their only resource in times of danger. The neck of the camel-leopard became elongated through stretching its head to the high branches of the trees on which its food is found. The dumb race of men had an 'internal sentiment' to speak. They exercised their tongues till they could articulate sounds. These sounds became signs of thoughts, and thus arose the race of articulate-speaking men. The senses, capacities, and organs thus acquired by the efforts of many successive generations were transmitted to their offspring, and in this way arose those differences and resemblances on which naturalists ground the idea of species.

ST. HILAIRE.

The doctrine of development, even with Lamarck, is still in the region of romance. His illustrious contemporary and fellow-labourer, Geoffroy St. Hilaire, first gave it a really scientific form. Lamarck's studies were chiefly in botany. St. Hilaire applied himself to zoology. In this he was joined by Cuvier. Hitherto there had been no serious effort at a scientific classification of the animal kingdom. The old writers on natural history were content with a general division of animals into wild and tame, or animals living on land and animals living in water. Until Linnæus, no naturalist had got beyond the divisions of beasts, birds, fishes, and reptiles. And Linnæus himself could find no better principle for the classification of mammals than a purely artificial arrangement, grounded on the number and shape of the teeth. Cuvier and St. Hilaire endeavoured to discover the natural classification that they might classify the animal kingdom as they found it in nature. They co-operated harmoniously for many years, scarcely conscious that they were each pursuing widely different principles, and when they did find out how and where they differed, neither of them seemed conscious of the magnitude or importance of the difference. They were seeking the natural classification, but that classification eluded their search. St. Hilaire doubted its existence. Cuvier confessed that he could not find it, but he believed it was to be found. St. Hilaire was at last convinced that the search for it was as vain as the search for the philosopher's stone—that the lines supposed to separate between genera and species are as imaginary as the lines of latitude and longitude which divide the globe. This was the first manifestation of difference between Cuvier and St. Hilaire, but the difference had roots as yet unseen, and branches undeveloped. Cuvier said that the business of a naturalist was simply to observe nature and try to discover nature's classification. St. Hilaire said it was more than this. The naturalist must also reason from his facts. He must draw inferences from his observations. There must be room for the noble faculty of judgment. When the facts are established, scientific results follow, as stones that have been quarried and dressed are carried to their places in the building.

St. Hilaire was well-known as a naturalist before his doctrines were formally announced to the world, but the careful reader of his early essays may find it there without any formal declaration of its presence. St. Hilaire waited, it is said, for the publication of Cuvier's 'Animal Kingdom' that the world might be in possession of the facts necessary to secure for his doctrine an impartial hearing. This may be true, but in one of his earliest compositions, that 'On the Frontal Prolongation of Ruminants,' he compares the neck of the giraffe with that of the stag, explaining the difference by the inequalities of development—a prophetic intimation of what was afterwards known as 'the theory of arrests.' In another piece of the same date he clearly evinces his belief in the essential unity of organic composition. Nature, he says, has formed all living beings on a unique plan, essentially the same in principle but varied after a thousand ways in all its necessary parts. In the same class of animals the different forms under which nature is pleased to give existence to each species, are all derived from each other. When she wishes to give new functions, she requires to make no other change but in the proportion of the organs—to extend or restrain the use of these suffices for her object. The osseous pouch of the allouat, the organ by means of which it makes its strange howl, is but an enlargement of the hyoid bone; the purse of the female opossum is but a deep fold of the skin; the trunk of the elephant, an excessive prolongation of the nostrils; and the horn of the rhinoceros, a mass of adherent hairs. In this way, in every class of animals, the forms, however varied, result from a common organism. Nature refuses to make use of novelties. The most essential differences which affect any one family come solely from another arrangement, complication, or modification of the same organs. The doctrine thus early announced is distinctly avowed in St. Hilaire's later compositions. By it he accounted for the existence of vestiges and rudiments of organs. The ostrich, for instance, though it does not fly, has rudimentary wings, because this organ played an important part in other branches of the same family. Similar rudiments, unseen by ordinary observers, are yet seen by all careful anatomists. In some quadrupeds, and in most birds, there is a membrane which covers the eye in sleep. Anatomists find a rudiment of this membrane at the internal angle of the human eye. 'So numerous,' said St. Hilaire, 'are the examples of this kind disclosed by comparative anatomy, that I am convinced the germs of all organs which we see, exist at once in all species, and that the existence of so many organs half-effaced or totally obliterated is due to the greater development of others—a development always made at the expense of the neighbouring organs.'

In 1830, Cuvier and St. Hilaire had their famous discussion before the French Academy. The chief subject was the mutability of species—Cuvier maintaining that the same forms had been perpetuated since the origin of things; and St. Hilaire, that all species are the result of development. Never were disputants more equally matched. Never was evidence more equally balanced. Never did a controversy find a wiser Palæmon. 'I do not judge,' said Goethe, 'I only record.' So great was the interest in this discussion that it pre-occupied the public mind, though France was on the very eve of a great political revolution. 'The same year—almost the same month,' says Isidore St. Hilaire, in the biography of his father, 'took away Goethe and Cuvier. Unity of organic composition—admitted by the one, denied by the other, had the last thoughts of both. The last words of Cuvier answer to the last pages of Goethe.'

Forty years before the discussion between Cuvier and St. Hilaire, Goethe had announced the doctrine of development as the law of the vegetable kingdom. In his 'Metamorphoses of Plants,' he supposes nature to have ever had before her an ideal plant—an idea corresponding to Robinet's more general conception of an ideal man. To realize the ideal plant was the great object of nature. Every individual plant is a partial fulfilment of the ideal—every stage of progress an advancement of the concrete to the abstract. Not only are all plants formed after one type, but the appendages of every individual plant are repetitions of each other. The flowers are metamorphosed leaves. Goethe's doctrine was afterwards taken up by Schleiden, but in a modified form. He supposed every plant to have two representative organs, the stem as well as the leaf. The leaf is attached to the ascending stem, and, besides its common form, it takes other forms, as scales, bracts, sepals, petals, stamens, and pistils. What seemed at first but the fancy of a poet is now the scientific doctrine of vegetable morphology.

SCHELLING.

The French naturalists reached the doctrine of development through the study of external nature. But, with the Germans, it followed upon their transcendental philosophy. Spinoza's theology recognized a bond between God and nature, unknown both to the theologians and the naturalists of that day. In his theology, creation was the emanations of the Deity as well as his work. This had been the dream of the Brahman; and though the dream might not be true, the transcendentalists thought that there was truth in the dream. 'Nature produced' was the mirror of 'nature producing.' The One who was working in nature, produced in nature the image of himself. In Schelling's philosophy, nature was the counterpart or the correspondent of mind. 'The final cause' said Schelling, 'of all our contemplation of nature is to know that absolute Unity which comprehends the whole, and which suffers only one side of itself to be known in nature. Nature is, as it were, the instrument of the absolute Unity, through which it eternally executes and actualizes that which is prefigured in the absolute understanding. The whole absolute is therefore cognizable in nature, though phenomenal nature only exhibits it in succession, and produces in an endless development that which the true and real eternally possesses.' Lorenz Oken, a disciple of Schelling's, found in actual nature what his master found in ideal. Nature was a divine incarnation—the progress of Deity in 'his other being'—from imperfection to perfection. Deity reaches its full manifestation in man, who is the sum total of all animals, and consequently the highest incarnation of the Divine.

The Vestiges.

The doctrine of development was first made popular in England by the 'Vestiges of a Natural History of Creation.' The author of the 'Vestiges' rejected, as vicious, Lamarck's notion of an 'internal sentiment.' But even St. Hilaire had seen that the function followed the organ, and not the organ the function. He adopted Robinet's principle, that the phenomenon of reproduction was the key to the genesis of species. This, to some extent, had been accepted by Lamarck, but more fully by Robinet, who, like the author of the 'Vestiges' in showing the progress of the development of men from animalcules, illustrated it by the changes which the tadpole undergoes in its progress towards being a perfect and complete member of the Batrachian order. Oken, too, had adopted the same principle, illustrating the stages of development from vesicles to men by corresponding stages in intro-uterine life.

To make earth, according to this analogy, the mother of the human race, it was necessary to suppose that the earth had existed long before man appeared. That such had been the case was now evident from geology. The earth had travailed in birth, from the earliest of the geologic ages till the close of the Tertiary, when divine man, her noblest child, was born. La Place had shown, in his nebular theory, how the earth and other planets were first formed by the separating and condensing of nebular matter. Supposing his theory to be true, it was only necessary to show the continuation of the same progressive movement, and the same working of natural laws. La Place may have thought it unnecessary to suppose that the divine mind was directing this natural law in its operations. But the author of the ' Vestiges ' saw in this progressive working the mode of operation most becoming the divine Being, and most analogous to all that we know of his ordinary working. In nature, there are no traces of ' divine fiats,' nor of ' direct inter-ferences.' All beginnings are simple, and through these simples nature advances to the more complex. The same agencies of nature which we now see at work are sufficient to account for the whole series of operations displayed in organic geology. We still see the volcano upheaving mountains, and new beds of detritus forming rocks at the bottom of the sea. ' A common furnace exemplifies the operation of the forces concerned in the Giant's Causeway, and the sloping ploughed field after rain showing at the end of the furrows, a handful of washed and neatly composed mud and sand, illustrates how nature made the Deltas of the Ganges and the Nile. On the ripple bank or sandy beaches of the present day we see nature's exact repeti-tion of the operation by which she impressed similar features on the sandstones of the carboniferous era. Even such marks as wind slanted rain would in our day produce on tide deserted sands have been read on the tablets of the ancient strata. It is the same nature—that is to say, God, through or in the manner of nature, working everywhere and in all time, caus-ing the wind to blow, and the rain to fall, and the tide to ebb and flow, immutable ages before the birth of our race, the same as now.'

The author appeals to the astronomical discoveries of Newton and La Place ; and to the facts in geology attested by Murchi-son and Lyell, as affording ample ground for the conclusion that the Creator formed the earth by a complicated series of changes similar to those which we see going on in the present day. As he works now, so has he wrought in the ages that are past. The organic, indeed, is mixed up with the physical, but it is not, therefore, necessary to suppose that because there are two classes of phenomena, there must be two distinct modes of the exercise of divine power. Life pressed in as soon as there were suitable conditions. Organic beings did not come at once on the earth by some special act of the Deity. The order was progressive. There was an evolution of being, corresponding to what we now see in the production of an individual. That life has its origin from inorganic bodies is shown by the very constitution of the organic, these being simply a selection of the elementary substances which form the inorganic or non-vitalized.

DARWIN.

The development doctrine found a rigidly scientific advocate in Charles Darwin. He was not content with general principles and theories, but collected a multitude of observations or facts which tend to show not only that all complex organisms have undergone changes, but how the changes were effected. Any naturalist, he says, reflecting on the natural affinities of organic beings, their embryological relations, geographical distribution, and geological succession, might reasonably come to the conclusion that each species had not been independently created, but had descended, like varieties from other species. But the conclusion would not be satisfactory till it could be shown how the different species were modified so as to acquire that perfection of structure and co-adaptation which excite our admiration. Darwin admitted that external conditions, such as climate and food, may have had some influence, but he thought them insufficient to account for all the changes, and so he added what he called the principle of 'natural selection.' Among the multitude of beings that come into existence, the strong live and the weak fail in the struggle for life. As the struggle is continually recurring, every individual of a species which has a variation, in the way of a quality superior to the others, has the better chance of surviving the others. And as individuals transmit to their descendants their acquired variations, they give rise to favoured races, which are nature's 'selections.' The neck of the giraffe has not been elongated by having made efforts to reach the branches of the lofty trees, but in a time of scarcity a longer-necked variety being able to obtain food where others could not obtain it, it survived the other varieties and thus become a species.

Darwin's doctrine of natural selection was suggested by the varieties produced in domesticated animals through man's selections. But the deeper principle is the great tendency to variation, which is found in all plants and animals. Variations determine the selection. The early progenitor of the ostrich, for example, may have had habits like the bustard, and as natural selection increased in successive generations the size and weight of the body, its legs were used more and its wings less, until they became incapable of flight. In Madeira there are two species of one kind of insect. The one has short wings, and feeds on the ground; the other has long wings, and finds its food on trees and bushes. The wings of each have been determined by the conditions on which they could live in the island. Those which were able to battle with the winds continued to fly, and their wings grew larger; those that were unable to battle with the winds found their food on the ground, and rarely or ever attempted to fly. Animal life will adapt itself to any climate, and become adapted to any conditions of existence, provided the changes are not effected suddenly. The elephant and the rhinoceros, though now tropical or sub-tropical in their habits, were once capable of enduring a colder region; species have been found in glacial climates. This capacity for variation is not denied by any naturalists. Some suppose it to have limits beyond which nature never passes, but these limits cannot be defined. Darwin could see no trace of them, and for the facts which he noticed he could find no explanation but in the doctrine he advocates, that nature forms varieties, and these in time, through natural selection, become new species.

The development doctrine has received but little additional illustration since Darwin's work. From a more extensive study of the mode of nature's working connected with researches in geology, Sir Charles Lyell was led to adopt the doctrine of the mutability of species; and Professor Huxley has endeavoured to find the missing and most missed link in the development chain—that which connects man with the brute creation. This intermediary was the great want of De Maillet and Robinet. The sea-man was legendary, the ourang was little known, and M. Du Chaillu had not yet invaded the territory of the gorilla. Professor Huxley finds most humanity in the chimpanzee. He has, perhaps, demonstrated that monkeys, as well as men, have the 'posterior lobe' of the brain, and the 'hippo-campus minor'—that they are no longer to be classed as 'four-handed' animals, but as having two feet and two hands; the feet consisting, like a human foot, of an *os calcis*, an astralagus, and a scaphoid bone, with the usual tarsals and metatarsals.

ALL ONE IN NATURE.

The doctrine of development may be denied, but the facts which have led to a belief in it remain the same, and require to be explained. These facts are an obvious unity in the plan of nature's works, which is now acknowledged by all scientific men. Professor Owen says that he withstood it long, but he was finally compelled to yield. The remarkable conformity to type in the bones of the head of the vertebrate animals led him to a re-consideration of the conclusions to which he, as a disciple of Cuvier, had previously come. On reviewing the researches of anatomists into the special homologies of the cranial bones, he was surprised to find that they all agreed as to the existence of the determinable bones in the skull of every animal down to the lowest osseous fish. That these bones had, in every case, similar functions to perform was a supposition beset with too many difficulties to be entertained for a moment. There are marked sutures in all skulls, but these sutures cannot serve the same end in marsupials, crocodiles, and young birds, which they are supposed to serve in the head of a child. According to Professor Owen, more than ninety per cent. of the bones in the human skeleton have their homologies recognised by common consent in the skeletons of all vertebrata. The same uniformity recognised in the animal structure is acknowledged by botanists to prevail in the vegetable world. Even the duality of Schleiden has been rejected, and scientific botanists have adopted the unity of Goethe. 'Every flower,' says Professor Lindley, 'with its peduncle and bracteolæ, being the development of a flower bud, and flower buds being altogether analogous to leaf buds, it follows as a corollary that every flower, with its peduncle and bracteolæ, is a metamorphosed branch. And, further, the flowers being abortive branches, whatever the laws are of the arrangement of branches with respect to each other, the same will be the laws of the flowers with respect to each other. In consequence of a flower and its peduncle being a branch in a particular state, the rudimentary or metamorphosed leaves which constitute bracteolæ, floral envelopes, and sexes, are subject to exactly the same laws of arrangement as regularly shaped leaves.' The recognition of typology and morphology would not have been so tardy but for the belief that it came in collision with the obvious fact that nature is working for an end. The disciples of Cuvier have been compelled to acknowledge the principle of archetypal order, so precious in the eyes of St. Hilaire—a principle originally connected with the mental philosophy of Plato, and the mystical dreams of the later Platonists, but now established by observations on external nature. And the lesson which Cuvier's disciples have learned is, not that the doctrine of special ends or 'final causes' is lost or obscured, but that it receives new illustrations and a new form. They have learned, that, though the works of God, in some aspects, resemble the works of man, there is a point where the resemblance ceases, and the working of the divine is no longer analogous to that of the human worker.

The unity of nature does not cease with that of animal or vegetable structures. Matter, as a substantial existence independent of the forms and qualities it assumes, has been banished from the world by all genuine metaphysicians since the days of Plato. It has a supposed existence in the laboratory of the chemist, but it ever eludes his grasp, like the sunbeam through the window or the phantasmagorian images on the canvas. It is the supposed something which is beyond all analysis. A mind at work is the most obvious fact in nature alike to the metaphysician and the natural philosopher. 'The attentive study,' says Robert Hunt, 'of the fine abstractions of science lifts the mind from the grossness of matter, step by step, to the refinements of immateriality, and there appear shadowed out, beyond the physical forces which man can test and try, other powers still ascending until they reach the source of every good and every perfect gift.'

Even the forces of nature lose themselves in each other, and are reduced to one force, its nature and essence escaping observation. Heat, light, electricity, magnetism, chemical affinity, motion, are all correlative or have some reciprocal dependence. No one of them by itself can be the essential cause of the other, and yet it may produce, or be convertible into, any of the other. Heat may produce electricity; electricity may produce heat. Chemical affinity may produce motion, and motion chemical affinity, each force as it produces merging itself as the other is developed. 'Neither matter nor force,' says Dr. Grove, 'can be created or annihilated—an essential cause is unattainable—causation is the will, creation the act of God.' Life itself is supposed to be but a higher degree of the same power which constitutes what we call inanimate objects —'an exalted condition of the power which occasions the accretion of particles in the crystalline mass,' the quickening force of nature through every form of existence being the same. When we say life is present or absent, we only mean the presence or absence of a particular manifestation of life. The all-life of the universe is the Deity energising in nature— this is the theology of science. The conception of the universe is incomplete if it is not conceived as a constant and continuous work of the eternally-creating Spirit. 'External nature,' says Ruskin, 'has a body and soul like man, but the soul is the Deity.' Though nature be not God, the thoughts of nature are God's thoughts. Religion, poetry, and science all demand that, however much God may transcend his creation, he must in some way be immanent therein.

CHAPTER XIX.

CHRISTIAN THEOLOGY.

THERE is no systematic theology in the Scriptures. We do not therefore expect to find more than occasional passages which may have a Pantheistic meaning. There is doubtless in the New Testament idea of God more of the Hellenic element than in the Jewish conception of the absolute Unity. The Pantheism of the Scriptures is rather future than present. The world is not only in separation from God, but is alienated from him. It is indeed said that of him and through him and to him are all things. Again, it is said that in him we live and move and have our being. But this is an ideal unity—something in the background which we may believe, though it is not now evident. The gospel announces its realization. Redemption is the reconciling of all things whether in heaven or earth or under the earth. Jesus prayed that his disciples might be one with him as he was one with the Father, and that they all might be one with the Father and with himself. But the great Pantheistic text is the words of St. Paul, where he describes the consummation of the work of Christ when the kingdom shall be given up to the Father, and then God shall be all in all. The Greek words mean, literally, that God shall be all things in all things or in all men. 'God,' said Dean Stanley, 'shall be the pervading principle of the universe. Christ is the representative to our dull senses of him who is above all and beyond all. The distinction shall cease, and God will fill the universe and be himself present in the hearts of men.' St. Paul's words etymologically form the combination which makes Pantheism. But God is not yet all. That is something to come. He is to be all things when creation is restored to the bosom of its Creator.

PERSONALITY.

It is sometimes said that the real essence of Pantheism is the denial of the divine personality. The Theist believes in a personal God; the Pantheist in an impersonal. But these words fail to mark the distinction intended. God is never called a person in the New Testament. The only place that can be alleged is Hebrews ii. 3, where the Greek means simply that Christ was the representative of God, 'the figure of his substance,' as the Vulgate renders it. The word 'person' carries with it the idea of a body. We do not apply it to a mere body. We do not call any of the lower animals persons. A person is a body in union with a soul. It is, in fact, a man. We only call God, angels, or any heavenly intelligences, persons, because we picture them as like ourselves in shape and form. Corporeity was originally so associated with personality, that in the third century the monks of Egypt made a riot because Theophilus the bishop said that God had not a body. This was to them the denial of God. The idea of corporeity can only be eliminated from personality by an effort of the mind, and after it is eliminated it continues to do service. There is still something in the word 'person' which implies a limit. Mr. Gladstone, criticising this remark, once wrote, that of the proposition that personality implies limitation he had never yet seen a proof.* Professor Lotze, Dr. Christlieb, and some others, have also maintained that limitation is no necessary attribute of personality. But they give the word 'person' a meaning different from the ordinary one, and then contend for its use on the ground that if God is not personal he must be a mere force or unconscious law. Personality seems to them the only mode of consciousness, or rather the word is taken as if it were identical with consciousness. Lotze, in this following Hegel, made personality the opposite of individuality. 'It was,' he said, 'to be found only in God, while in all finite spirits there exists only a weak imitation of personality, the finiteness of the finite is not a productive condition of personality, but rather a hindering barrier to its perfecting development.† Lotze's mean-

* 'Contemporary Review,' June, 1876, p. 25, note.
† 'Mikrokosmos,' Vol. III., p. 570.

ing may not be different from ours, but we know nothing of this use of the word. He has deprived it of the idea of limitation to make it applicable to God. Personal being is the highest conception of being which we can reach from the anthropomorphic side. But God may be impersonal in the sense that there is being above personality, which, according to our definition of person, God must be. Mr. Herbert Spencer says : 'It is an erroneous assumption to suppose that the choice is between personality and something lower than personality, whereas the choice is rather between personality and something higher.' He asks, 'Is it not just possible that there is a mode of being as much transcending intelligence and will as these transcend mechanical motion ?'* Mr. Matthew Arnold in some sense denies to God thought and love. To make God personal appears to him like making God only a magnified man. But God is something higher. That 'not ourselves which makes for righteousness' is most reverently spoken of when least defined, or when we least attribute to him human attributes. God is impersonal in the sense of superpersonal, or as not adequately represented by the idea of personality.

We receive the doctrine of the Trinity as one of the fundamental doctrines of the New Testament. It is in fact preeminently the New Testament doctrine of God. But the Trinity is substantially a denial that God is a person. The old Unitarians fought hard for the divine personality, and to save it denied the Trinity. But the Christian Church in all its great branches has been steadfast in the faith that God 'is not one only person, but three persons in one substance.'† Gregory of Nyssa, and other theologians of his school, made Deity above the Trinity, which means that God was more than the hypostases, or the forms under which the Godhead is conceived by man. Dr. Newman says, 'It is the doctrine of the fathers that though we use words expressive of a Trinity, yet that God is beyond number, that Father, Son, and Holy Ghost, though eternally distinct from each other, can scarcely be viewed together in common except as one substance, as if they could not be generalized into three *any* whatever, and as if it were strictly speaking incorrect to speak of a person as otherwise than of *the* person, whether as of Father, or of Son, or of Spirit. The

* 'First Principles,' p. 109.   † Pref. Com. Office, Trinity Sunday.

question has almost been admitted by St. Augustine, whether
it is not possible to say that God is one—*one person.'* *   Archer
Butler, in a Sermon on the Trinity, says, that there is no more
difficulty in supposing a thousand persons in the Godhead than
in supposing a single person.

The philosophy of the Trinity is the superpersonality of
God.   Its practical use is to represent the Godhead under forms
of personality suited to the capacity of the human mind.   It
acknowledges the mystery of God without saying that it is
impossible to know him, that is, without denying the truth of
the human conception of him.   Every religion and every system
of religious philosophy, with but few exceptions, has been in
some form Trinitarian.   They have all set forth a being, a mind
and a relation ; a subject, an object, and a bond between them.
The expressions are often widely different; but the idea is
generally the same.   In the Christian religion we acknowledge
a Father, a Son, and a Holy Ghost—three persons, yet one
God.   The Father is God, the Son is God, and the Holy Ghost
is God ; 'and yet,' adds the orthodox creed, 'there are not three
Gods, but one God.'   The Arian objected that this was a manifest contradiction.   Looking only to the finite side, and over-
looking the conditions on which a knowledge of God is possible
to man, he said—'The Son must be inferior to the Father;' but
the Nicene fathers were guarded against 'dividing the substance.'   The Sabellian tried in another way to escape the
Trinitarian contradiction by saying that the three persons
meant three manifestations of the divine Being—'That the
monad develops itself into a triad in the Son and in the Spirit,
and yet there is only one essence in three different relations.'
But the orthodox fathers were guarded against 'confounding
the persons.'   The heresy of Arius was as much a heresy against
the Alexandrian philosophy as against the doctrine of the
Church.   He interpreted eternity by his idea of time, supposing
that in eternity there was temporal priority.   He said that the
Father must have been before the Son.   'There was, when the
Son was not.'   But in the Neo-Platonic philosophy, eternity
and time were entirely different in kind.   The process of development or manifestation which Plotinus and his disciples
placed in the Godhead was an eternal process.   'The Being'
was always generating the 'mind' or divine reason, and the

* 'Select Treatises of St. Athanasius,' p. 155.

Spirit was eternally proceeding from the ' Being ' through the ' mind.' When Arius assailed the doctrine of the Nicene fathers, St. Athanasius equipped himself with the Neo-Platonic arguments that the eternal Light could never have been without its radiance, that if ' there was when the Son was not, then God was once wordless and wisdomless.' Or, to use another of his illustrations, ' if the fountain did not beget wisdom from itself, but acquired it from without, there is no longer a fountain, but a sort of pool.' The ' mind,' Logos, or God in his personality must have been eternally with and in God in his impersonality, otherwise God would not be God.

Of all the heresies on the Trinity, that of Sabellius was nearest to the doctrine of the Church. It differed from it only in this, that though Sabellius called all the three ' hypostases ' persons, yet he explained that they were only three modes or manifestations of the divine nature. In this way he secured the uni-personality of God. But the right faith is that God is tri-personal. Implicitly, then, in the orthodox doctrine of the Trinity, personality as applied to God is not the same as personality applied to man. Trinitarian apologists have rarely failed to show their Unitarian antagonists that ' person ' in the Godhead does not mean a distinct individual existence, but an indefinite hypostasis, so that the Trinitarian holds the doctrine of the divine unity as firmly as the Arian, the Sabellian, or the Unitarian. If Trinitarianism neglected the unity and held only to the tri-personality, it would be simply tri-theism; but the creed declares, that though the three persons are each ' uncreate, incomprehensible, and eternal,' yet there are not ' three uncreated,' ' three incomprehensibles,' or ' three eternals;' which implies that the personality of God was something transcendent; to us an impersonality, not less but more than the personality of man. Each of the three persons has distinct operations; but, even in the Scriptures, the work of the one is ascribed to the other, so that every idea of personal plurality is distinctly removed. The doctrine of the Trinity is not the irrational contradiction which the Church of Rome makes the doctrine of the Eucharist. St. Athanasius was right in calling the Arians ' insensate.' They were not the rational party. The orthodox doctrine was the last word of reason concerning God. It was

the recognition of him in his transcendency as personal and yet
above personality.

Though God transcends personality, we must still think of
him as personal. If we are to speak of God at all we can only
speak of him in human language, and that being imperfect, our
meaning must often be expressed by a verbal contradiction.
The thoughts thus expressed may be imperfect and yet true.
Archdeacon Hare says, 'The ladder of our human conceptions must rest on the earth, we cannot hook it into the
sky. Even in speaking of himself God has clothed himself in
the attributes of humanity, nor can we conceive what these
attributes are in their heavenly exaltation, except by considering in the first instance what they mean in their earthly debasement.' * Mr. Maurice says, 'Those who are flesh and
blood and not speculators and philosophers must have an
actual object to believe in, or they must give up belief altogether. They can be theists or atheists, but they cannot float
in a cloudland between the two, confessing God and making
him nothing under pretence of making him everything.'† This
is said truly but timidly, and not with sufficient justice to
those who are called Pantheists, for into that 'cloudland' the
human intellect is ever drifting as if by a necessity of its
nature. Athanasius said wisely, that 'all human expressions
of God are symbols, that even creation is not to be thought
of as the human mode of forming.' ‡ Tertullian arguing
against Praxeas for the incarnation of the Word in summing
up the Old Testament representations of God, recognised him
as invisible and yet visible, not like man and yet in condescen-
tion to man clothed in human form. His words are 'God is
that being whom no eye hath seen, nor can see, who dwelleth
in light inapproachable, who dwelleth not in temples made with
hands, before whose sight the earth trembles, in whom is every
place, but who is in no place, who is the utmost bound of the
universe, and yet who walked in paradise at the cool of the day,
shut up the ark after Noah, and refreshed himself at Abraham's
tent, called Moses out of the bush, and appeared as one like
the Son of man in the burning fiery furnace.' A God who is

* 'Victory of Faith,' pp. 35, 36.
† 'Patriarchs and Lawgivers of O. T.,' p. 34.
‡ Neander, vol. II., p. 32.

in no place and yet is the utmost bound of the universe is very like the 'cloudland' which Mr. Maurice dreaded. To some men God must come under the forms of human personality, otherwise he is no God. Augustus de Morgan bluntly manifested himself as belonging to this class when he expressed a hope that the college with which he was connected would 'rise into prosperity under the protection, not of the Infinite, not of the Absolute, not of the Unconditioned, but of God, the Creator and Father of all mankind.' *

It seems a necessity of the human mind that God be conceived under the forms of humanity. We rise through the human to the divine. By anthropomorphic conceptions of God we reach higher conceptions. Our first thought of God is that he is a person as we are persons, only greater and wiser. The manifested intelligence of nature speaks an intellect in some way resembling ours. Then comes a sense of the dissimilarities which must be between an infinite and a finite mind, but the process by which we come to this sense is and must be anthropomorphic. This is the meaning of the fact that in all religions the divine wisdom is personified as the agent of the divine activity. But the idea of God as super-personal is ever in the background. It may be God as the unknown, the absolute, the unconditioned, but it is God known as the unknown, the absolute, the unconditioned. We cannot dismiss this idea and suppose that God is nothing beyond the human conception by which he is supposed to be fully known as simply a person.

The Bible may be regarded as a revelation of God on the human side. But no doctrine of the Bible will be properly understood till we have looked beyond the anthropomorphisms. The Bible indicates what reason confirms—that every doctrine which concerns God must be thought of first as if God were a man, and then as if he were not a man. To begin with

CREATION.

The book of Genesis gives an account of the creation of the world in six days. God appears as a man—a great artificer—at whose command all things spring suddenly into being. He

* Memoirs by his Wife, p. 345.

is a man, but very mighty. After his work he rests. Whatever may be the partial or provisional truth in this record, it
cannot be received as a full or exhaustive account of creation.
The history of the earth has no trace of plants and animals
coming into existence in the mode recorded in Genesis. As
nature works to-day, so apparently has it always worked.
There is no sudden creation, no leap in the succession, but everywhere a graduated chain of existence, as if all things had
grown out of each other, the continuity and essential unity of
the whole being inviolably preserved. Neither Moses nor
modern science has revealed the secret of creation. What is
evident is that God does not work as man works, and that his
thoughts are not as our thoughts. Our line is cast into
an ocean which we cannot fathom. We are everywhere
surrounded by the mystery of God. Athanasius has been
quoted, saying that we must not think of creation as we do of
man's working. When God is represented as labouring and
resting, these are mere figures. The word which we translate
created is admitted by the best Hebrew scholars not necessarily to mean more than formed, so that even the Mosaic
record does not profess to give an account of the origin of the
world. Milton called the matter of the universe ' an efflux of
God,' and maintained that this was the doctrine, not only of
the old fathers, but of the New Testament. ' It is clear,' he
says, ' that the world was framed out of matter of some kind
or other. For since action and passion are relative terms, and
since, consequently, no agent can act externally unless there be
some patient such as matter, it appears impossible that God
could have created this world out of nothing, not from any
defect of power on his part, but because it was necessary that
something should have previously existed capable of receiving
passively the exertion of the divine agency. Since, therefore,
both Scripture and reason concur in pronouncing that all these
things were made, not out of nothing, but out of matter, it
necessarily follows that matter must either have always existed
independently of God, or have originated from God at some
particular time; that matter should have been always independent of God (seeing that is only a passive principle
dependent on Deity and subservient to him; and seeing,
moreover, that as in number, considered abstractly, so also in

time or eternity there is no inherent force or efficacy)—that matter, I say, should have existed of itself from all eternity is inconceivable. If, on the contrary, it did not exist from all eternity, it is difficult to understand whence it derives its origin. There remains, therefore, but one solution of the difficulty, for which, moreover, we have the authority of Scripture—namely, that all things are of God.' But if matter thus emanates from God, if the matter of the universe proceeds immediately from the universal mind, there must still remain some bond or ground of union between mind and matter in their limited or finite forms. Milton is not afraid to carry this out, perhaps as far as Schelling did. He says that 'man is a living being intrinsically and properly one, and individual, not compound or separable, not according to the common opinion made up and framed of two distinct different natures as of soul and body ; but the whole man is soul, and the soul man—that is to say, a body, a substance individual, animated, sensitive, and rational.' This will explain the doctrine of the following lines from ' Paradise Lost : ' —

> ' O Adam ! one Almighty is, from whom
> All things proceed, and up to him return,
> If not depraved from good, created all
> Such to perfection. One first matter all,
> Indued with various forms, various degrees
> Of substance. And, in things that live, of life,
> But more refined, more spirituous and pure,
> As nearer to him placed or nearer tending,
> Each in their several active spheres assigned,
> Till body up to spirit work, in bounds
> Proportioned to its kind. So from the root
> Springs lighter the green stalk, from thence the leaves,
> More aery, last the bright consummate flower
> Spirits odorous breathes, flowers and their fruit,
> Man's nourishment, by gradual scale sublimed.'

ORIGIN OF EVIL.

In the Bible narrative sin is the result of disobedience. God made a covenant with Adam like what one man would make with another. There was a tree of which he was not to eat. He disobeyed. In the cool of the day God, as a man, walked in the garden, and charged Adam with his transgression. The story in its literal form is open to the objection that if God were a wise and good being he would have foreseen the event, and like any good and thoughtful parent would have anticipated and prevented injury to an inexperienced child. The objection becomes stronger when it is added that the whole human race was involved in the consequences of the sin of the first man. The narrative is purely anthropomorphic, as if God did not know what was to happen, but had to learn by experience and then devise a remedy. But these objections are the same in kind as are involved in all that concerns God when conceived in the form of man. The story has probably a basis in history, and the idea which it gives of sin corresponds to human experience and to the conception which generally pervades the Scriptures. It shows prominently the connection between sin and suffering, but it leaves unexplained a background which probably, with our present faculties, is to us necessarily a mystery. Evil did not begin with man. There was an outward tempter. The serpent is not directly identified with Satan, but the whole story assumes that there is an enemy of good already in existence. The origin of evil is thus moved back to an undefined period in past eternity, or, to speak philosophically, evil was in eternity. But this is to suppose with the Parsees and the Manichæans that an eternal— which, in this sense, means a substantial—principle of evil exists in conflict with the good. This again supposes that God is not an absolutely perfect Being since he is opposed by another almost as mighty as himself. The answer is that of St. Augustine, that evil is no actual being, but only the deprivation of good. To the same conclusion came Anselm, Spinoza, Malebranche, Leibnitz, and other ontological theologians. Evil thus became a step in the procession to higher good. Some of the old Gnostics said that if man had not eaten of the tree of knowledge he would never have been man, but would have remained a mere sensuous animal. Something like this is found in Erigena. It is directly defended by Schiller, who says that the fall, in an intellectual and moral view, might be called an advance. Even in the Scriptures the fall of Adam results in a greater good, though the good is effected by God overruling the evil that had been accidentally introduced. By redemption man rises to a higher state than that in which he was created. Through the first Adam he had the animal or natural life ; through the second the higher and spiritual life. But a second plan, after the first failed, is too like man. In the divine proceeding there can be no contingency. All is foreseen. God is out of time. He is in eternity. To him past and present are the same. Evil, then, in the abstract must have some inseparable connection with things finite. It has been thought of as existing only in the eyes of man—a part of a whole not comprehended by him, but which if comprehended the evil would be seen to be only apparent. This has been expressed by Pope in the lines—

> ' Discord is harmony not understood ;
> All partial evil universal good : '

and again—

> ' Whatever wrong we call,
> May, must be, right as relative to all.'

It may also be conceived that sin in the abstract is not simply a relative, but a real imperfection. A fault inseparable from creation which must always lack the perfection of that which has independent existence, or really is. It follows then, that so long as created things exist, evil must also exist. It can only end by the creature ceasing to be a creature and becoming God.

REDEMPTION.

As man fell in Adam, so he rises in Christ. This is the general truth of redemption. It is set forth in the Bible as a plan devised by one person and executed by another. It is described in Jewish language and illustrated by Jewish customs. The very word means buying back, and is taken from the redemption of captives. Christ's death was the price paid for sinners. His blood made atonement or propitiation. It satisfied the demands of justice, and, like the blood shed in Jewish sacrifices, it had the power of purification. The blood of Jesus Christ cleanseth from all sin. It may not be said in so many words that Christ's death appeased God, but it is evidently implied. The Jewish sacrifices appeased God, and Christ made peace through the blood of the cross. All this language and these illustrations regard God as a person—in

other words, a man. He is angry, jealous, and though merciful,
yet inexorably just. When the representation is taken literally, God does not always appear as even one of the best of
men. Many efforts have been made to give atonement a milder
form. It has been said that the Jewish sacrifice was the in-
version of the heathen. In the one case, God manifested his
love, while the other was intended to turn away wrath. Some
have said that Christ reconciled man to God, but that God was
already reconciled to man; while others have denied all
necessity of atonement, and explained the New Testament
language as merely Jewish figures. But those who suppose
redemption was merely the divine mercy, regard God as a man
quite as much as those who take literally the sacrificial language
of the atonement. Those who denied propitiation merely
substituted for the terrible God a benevolent Father. But the
incompatibility of the representations with each other, might
have taught all parties that while each of them explained the
truth in part, none of them set forth the whole truth. Christ
was the propitiation for our sins, and yet God so loved the
world that he gave his Son. Christ died for the elect only, and
yet he died for all men. Under the aspect of a price, the
atonement could belong only to them that were finally saved;
but under the aspect of a manifestation of love, it was for all
men. Christ is both the victim slain and the priest who
offers the oblation. He is the Advocate who undertakes our
defence, the Intercessor who pleads for us, and yet the Judge
who acquits or condemns. These figures merely represent the
human side of redemption. When we reflect that God must
be thought of as a man and then as more than a man, we see
their imperfection, and, at the same time, the justification of
their use. The Son who accomplished this work of redemption is as much God as the Father, who is satisfied with
the work. Theologians who have clung tenaciously to the
literal meaning of the Bible words have often dimly intimated that they had a sense of something in redemption
more than was expressed by the mere literal words. It
used to be argued by the Calvinists or Agustinians, and
with some ground of truth, that though man could be unjust on the side of mercy, yet God could not. The meaning
of this is that if God were merely a man, he could have

forgiven without regard to his justice, but justice enters into his very being, and, as St. Augustine said, is identical with that being. The theory of St. Anselm, which is the very backbone of the ecclesiastical doctrine of the atonement, that sin being an offence against an infinite God required an infinite satisfaction, is the outcome of Anselm's conception of God as abstract Being. The eternal order of the universe required to be vindicated. While a personal being could forgive, an impersonal or superpersonal was bound to observe even in forgiveness the order of justice. This may be the deeper meaning of atonement and propitiation. We go back, then, to the vindication of the strongest Scripture language. We justify the old theologians who spoke of the Son appeasing the Father, and the devout souls who delight in the mercy of God under the image of the blood of Christ. What is imperfect in the language is eliminated, but the thought is as near the truth as human imperfection can come. We must rest in the apparent antinomy, which runs through all theology and which comes out with a manifest consciousness in our Church Articles. In the first, God is defined as a Being ' without body, parts, or *passions*,' and yet in the second, it is said that the Son died ' to reconcile his Father to us.' If he was really without passions, there could be no need of reconciliation. It is only those who are angry that require to be appeased. Christ's blood was shed in time, yet he was the Lamb slain from the foundation of the world. As God transcends human personality, so may redemption in its true aspect transcend all human representation.

REGENERATION.

To be regenerate is to be born again, to have a new life different from the animal life, and yet as real. Jesus told Nicodemus that a man must be born again before he could enter into the kingdom of God. This birth was as necessary for a man to realize the kingdom of righteousness as the natural birth to know what was the life of the natural world. The ruler of the Pharisees was confounded. He was a teacher of Israel, but this was all strange to him. He could understand obedience to the laws of the Jewish religion, and he could understand what it was to have good desires, for he had such

in himself; but that anything good should require a new birth
was marvellous to him. He thought the words were mis-
applied, and the multitude of Christian theologians have
thought regeneration to mean less than Jesus meant by it.
Even those who speak of the converted, the changed, the renewed, will explain that it is only by a figure, or in a very
secondary sense, that men can be sons of God. Sonship is
reserved for Christ, and this in a sense transcending the human
sense. We may be like God conceived as a person, but we
cannot in any proper sense be sons of God. The Arians denied
the sonship of man, but the Alexandrian fathers made it a
reality, though they strove to distinguish between men as
children of God and Christ as the only begotten. Basil said
that we are sons 'properly' and 'primarily,' in opposition to
figuratively. Cyril said that we are sons 'naturally,' as well
as 'by grace.' Athanasius was anxious to maintain the reality
of our sonship, and yet, if possible, not to identify it with that
of Christ, who was 'truly and naturally' the Son of God, while
we were sons, but not as he was 'by nature and grace.' The
Word being consubstantial with the Father we become sons in
the Word, having a perfect union with the Father through
union with him. Dr. Newman says, 'St. Basil and St. Gregory
Nyssa consider son to be a term of relationship according to
nature.' The actual presence of the Holy Spirit in the regenerate in *substance* constitutes this relationship of nature,
and hence St. Cyril says that we are sons naturally, because
we are in him and in him alone. So also, Nyssa lays down
as a received truth that to none does the term properly apply
but to one in whom the name responds in truth to the nature.
And he also implies the intimate association of our sonship
with Christ, when he connects together regeneration with our
Lord's generation, neither being of the will of the flesh. St.
Augustine said, he called men gods as being deified of his grace,
not as born of his substance, Bellarmine said that the saints
were gods by participation of the divine. A theory has recently been put forth by some English divines that, in the
Eucharist, the incarnation of Christ is extended to the com-
municants. The divine Word, so to speak, incarnates himself in
the Church. The process is mechanical, but the idea is that of
man becoming divine. The words of the Bible are stronger

than the words of the fathers. St. John says, expressly, 'Now are we the sons of God,' and as if this relationship was far beyond what mortal man could understand: he added, 'It doth not yet appear what we shall be, we shall be like him, for we shall see him as he is.' The words of Jesus also point to something beyond the reach of our present conceptions. He prayed for his disciples that they might be one with him, as he was one with the Father, that they might be in him as he was in the Father. This is no mere figure, but implies a mysterious union by which man may be consubstantial with the Father and the Son. What else could St. Paul have meant when he spoke of the saints, knowing that which passeth knowledge, and being filled with all the fulness of God?

PROVIDENCE.

If God's government of the world is not personal, it seems to us to be no government. Religion always represents the divine care as extending to the minutest affairs both in nature and in human life. Among the Pagans some god presided over every element and ruled in every region of nature. In the Old Testament God presides over the nations, and rules them as King of kings and Lord of lords. With Israel he dealt specially as their ruler, giving them fruitful seasons and filling their hearts with joy and gladness. All suffering also came direct from him. Affliction was his hand. If there was evil in the city it was the Lord who did it. Jewish history is the record of God's personal dealings with men, families and nations. The same divine care of men is taught in the New Testament. The very hairs of our heads are numbered. A sparrow does not fall to the ground without the heavenly Father, and we are of more value than many sparrows. This is the lesson of religion but not of our common experience. If it be true, it is true in a way unknown to us. The race is not to the swift nor the battle to the strong, but time and chance happen to all men. We are at the mercy every hour of blind forces, or liable to suffering from the unconscious transgression of irresponsible laws. While we trust to providence, the observer of the order of nature tauntingly asks,

' When the rude mountain trembles from on high,
    Shall gravitation cease if you go by ? '

Nature may seem to care for the species, for the preservation of the race, or at least for the continuance of life, but she casts the individual to the winds or the waves when her purpose is served. In the mere natural world the good as such have no advantage over the wicked. This has been noticed from the earliest time of man's history. Job marked the prosperity of the wicked, and how the tabernacles of the robbers prospered while the righteous were often in adversity. David had complained of the same thing, but when he went into the temple of God he seemed to have a glimpse into the order of the universe, and saw that in spite of outward appearance justice reigned supreme. Jesus spoke of the impartiality of God in the present life, making his sun to shine on the just and the unjust and being good, even to the unthankful and the evil. Though providence is special, yet even in the Bible there are intimations of general laws to which all men are subject. The two things seem incompatible, and the reconciliation of them impossible, but as we must think of God as personal, we may believe the one, and as God is more than man, we may also believe the other. The laws of nature are the expression of God immanent in the world.

MIRACLES.

The Bible begins with a miracle. God conceived as man makes the world, or rather, as a mighty monarch, commands it to exist. There is an interference, real or apparent, with the order established before creation. A new order begins. With this order God has interfered at different times. Jesus Christ as the Son of God wrought many miracles. His apostles had this power conferred on them as a divine gift. On the supposition of a personal God miracles are probable. We might expect them as the revelation of what is behind nature, or of something not to be learned from nature. The world is conceived as a machine which God superintends. Its very existence may be the best proof of the being of God, and of his care for all that lives. But in reality the multitude of men connect the divine existence more with interference in the order of nature than with that order itself.   Men crave miracles.   The only thing against them is that they are out of the range of our experience.   They depend on history, and are only credible because of the objects they are intended to serve.   But all our knowledge of nature declares that the order is inviolable.   If we are to believe the miracles, we must suppose that in some way unkown to us they are not out of the order of nature, or that they are according to an order unknown to us.   That God became man is no miracle, if it be that God is daily incarnating himself in the world and in man.   The resurrection of Christ is no miracle if men are to rise from the dead by an order similar to that by which they live and die.   The ascension was no miracle, if men's natural bodies are to become spiritual and be freed from all the grossness of matter.   'A miracle,' says Bishop Butler, 'is something different from the course of nature as known.'   It may be in harmony with that course as unknown to us.   'The difference,' says Mr. Rogers, 'between the natural and the supernatural is relative, not absolute—it is not essential.   These miracles, so we on earth must call them, and which we are accustomed to speak of as inroads upon the course of nature, are, if truly considered, so many fragmentary instances of the eternal order of an upper world.'   Thomas Carlyle, with a deeper view of the divine impersonality than was possessed either by Bishop Butler or Mr. Rogers, teaches the same doctrine concerning miracles. In 'Sartor Resartus' the question is asked, 'Is not a miracle simply a violation of the laws of nature?'   'I answer,' says Teufelsdroeck, 'by this new question what are the laws of nature?   To me, perhaps, the rising of one from the dead were no violation of these laws, but a confirmation, were some far deeper law now first penetrated into, and by spiritual force even as the rest have all been, brought to bear on us with its material force.   They (the laws) stand written in our works of science, say you, in the accumulated records of man's experience?   Was man with his experience present at the creation, then, to see how it all went on?   Have any deepest scientific individuals yet dived down to the foundations of the universe and gauged everything there?   Did the Maker take them into his council ; that they read his ground-plan of the incomprehensible all, and can say—This stands marked therein and no more than this ? Alas ! not in any wise.   These scientific individuals have been nowhere but where we also are, have seen some handbreadths deeper than we see into the deep that is infinite without bottom and without shore.'

We conceive of all that God does as done after the manner of man. Miracles and God as man go together. But it is only as thus conceived that difficulties arise about the agreement of miracles with the order of nature. The more we can think of God as present in nature, the more the distinction between order and interference will disappear.

PRAYER.

It is recorded that in the days of Seth men began to call upon the name of the Lord. The meaning seems to be, that after an age of wickedness men became more devout. They called upon God, that is, they prayed to him. Prayer was an important part of Jewish worship, as, indeed, it is of all worship. It follows naturally on the belief, that there is a God in whose hands we are for good or for evil. We ask that we may receive good, and that evil may not come upon us. On the supposition that God is perfect, he would freely bestow what is good without the necessity of our asking. But the weakness is on our side, not on God's. We build a house of prayer as if God dwelt in temples made with hands, and yet of the noblest buildings and erections of human hands we have to say as Solomon did that the heaven of heavens cannot contain him much less any house that man can build. We ask things of God though he knows our necessities before we ask and our ignorance in asking. Jesus taught his disciples to pray, and also not to be over-anxious about temporal things, for their heavenly Father knew that they had need of these things. Shelley said of the ' spirit of nature,' that 'unlike the God of human error, it required no prayers nor praises.' If all is inviolably fixed it seems idle to pray. If God has put within our own reach all which he intended that we should have, why ask him for more ? Can our petitions change his order ? Will he be moved by our importunity ? Reason tells us that he cannot. Yet we pray. Religion teaches men to pray. Those who try to explain it say that it is God's will that we should pray—his will to give us things on condition that we ask them, as a father gives his children gifts, yet requires that they ask him for them. Thus prayer becomes a religious exercise, profitable to ourselves by raising and cherishing in us good dispositions. And so rational men fall back on the worship of God in his impersonality. Prayer becomes lost in praise. It is a life, a love, a longing, a feeling of the divine within us. 'The best of all prayers,' says Fenelon, 'is to act with a pure intention, and with a continual reference to the will of God. It is not by a miracle, but by a movement of the heart that we are benefited, by a submissive spirit.' Hence petitions to God are not like petitions to men. The same words are repeated in liturgies. We repeat them for centuries. They are never old. They never change God. They are not meant to change God, but they produce good dispositions in the sincere worshipper. And thus we sometimes sing our prayers as well as our praises, for rational prayer cannot be other than praise. Is not this the reconciliation of Wordsworth's Pantheism with his High Churchism? The cathedral is not the dwelling-place of God, but it helps us to realise the presence of the Ever-Near. The very stones are made to sing psalms to God. We project the divine within us, and that externally realised, speaks to the divine in others. From God as personal we expect direct answers but the highest prayer is a simple spirit of submission.

PREDESTINATION.

It has been a great controversy if there is such a thing as predestination in the Bible. There is so much that is like it, that many who had no love for the doctrine have confessed that they were bound to believe it, and those who believe it, as well as those who do not, have felt that it was impossible to reconcile it with the attributes of either justice or mercy. The compilers of the Church Articles, while receiving the doctrine as taught in Scripture, yet added a warning against the danger of dwelling too much upon it, especially by curious and carnal persons. John Wesley, on the other hand, said that no Scripture could prove predestination. He would rather give up Christianity than believe that God had ordained men to eternal death before they had done good or evil. But in all churches, and in all centuries of the Christian era, there have been

devout men who not only believed that predestination was in
the Bible, but necessary to the very thought of the divine
perfection. Bishop Heber once wrote that Calvin and his
master, St. Augustine, were 'miserable theologians.' But this
is not the judgment of the universal church. There is no
phenomenon more remarkable in the history of theology than
the persistency with which predestinarianism has asserted
itself in all churches and in all sects. Pantheism alone com-
petes with it for catholicity, and both carry with them corresponding contradictories, which must be reconcilable in some
deeper ground. When God is regarded as the counterpart of
man, only greater than man, predestination in all its forms is
open to many objections. By an act of will he is supposed
to have decreed whatever comes to pass, whether good or evil.
The actions of all creatures, even the meanest, are supposed to
be predetermined. Bishop Hopkins interpreted God's special
care of sparrows as extending to the determination of all their
movements. 'Though the price of a sparrow,' he says, 'is but
mean and contemptible, yet God has appointed what bough it
shall pitch on, what grains it shall pick up, where it shall lodge,
and where it shall build, on what it shall live, and when it
shall die.' The popular theological form of predestination is
that of an eternal decree, by which a portion of mankind are
to be saved, and an accompanying decree by which the rest
were to be left unsaved. These doctrines, when pushed to
their direct logical issues, take away freewill from man,
destroy human responsibility, and deprive God of some of the
attributes necessary to perfection. The predestinarian in his
defence falls back on the impersonality or superpersonality of
God. With St. Augustine, he resolves all the divine attributes
into that of being, or with Archbishop King, in his ' Sermon on
Predestination,' he maintains that these attributes are ' of a
nature alogether different from ours, and that we have no direct
or proper notion or conception of them. We know them only
by analogy, or as a blind man knows colours, and therefore cannot say what is consistent or not consistent with them.' God,
' as he is in himself, is as different from God, as we conceive him,
as China is from a map of China.' Here we return to Spinoza,
whose dog in the heavens and the dog that barks were used
for the same contrast.

The ancient philosophers were strong predestinarians. Predestination entered into their conception of God. It was God's
providence considered absolutely. They did not always distinguish between the divine will and necessity. And yet each
is distinctly acknowledged. The union of them, if in any way
they can be harmonized, would correspond to the 'free necessity' of Spinoza. The recognition of a divine will is the
recognition of a personal Deity. Fate is the silent impersonal
power through which the purposes and designs of God are
accomplished. This fate is often identified with the being of
God, as in Seneca, where he says, ' Will you call him fate ?
You will call him rightly, for all things depend on him. He is
the cause of causes.' It is sometimes called law. Seneca again
says, ' All things go on for ever according to a certain rule,
ordained for ever.' To this agree the words of Cicero, ' All
things come to pass according to the sovereignty of the eternal
law ; ' and those of Pindar, where he calls law ' the ruler of
mortals and immortals.' But this fate or law was yet in some
way the expression of a mind. ' Nothing is more wonderful in
the whole world,' said Manilius, ' than reason, and that all
things obey fixed laws.' The reason manifest in the world is
so inseparably connected with the laws, that the one seems to
be always assumed when the other is mentioned. ' I am firmly
of opinion,' says Sophocles, in the Ajax, ' that all these things,
and whatever befals us, are in consequence of the divine purpose. Whoso thinks otherwise is at liberty to follow his own
judgment, but this will ever be mine.' Chyrsippus, the Stoic,
defined fate as ' that natural order and constitution of things
from everlasting, whereby they naturally followed upon each
other in consequence of an immutable and perpetual complication.' The Stoics, more than all the philosophers of antiquity,
connected the divine Being with the universe. He was the
active principle in nature, or the first nature, corresponding to
the ' nature-producing' of Spinoza, while created things were
' nature produced.' Laertius says that they defined fate as
' the Logos whereby the world is governed and directed.' God
himself is subject to fate, yet he is the maker of that fate to
which he is subject. ' The same necessity,' says Seneca, ' binds
the gods themselves. The framer and ruler of all things made
the fates indeed, yet he follows. He always obeys. He com-

manded once.' And Lucan to the same effect : ' He eternally
formed the causes whereby he controls all things, subjecting
himself likewise to law.' This interpretation of the fate of the
Stoics has the sanction of St. Augustine, who says, ' we acquiesce
in their manner of expression, because they carefully ascribe
this fixed succession of things, and this mutual concentration
of causes and effects to the will of God.' Nothing could be
nearer Spinoza's necessity than that of the Stoics. The very
words of Seneca enter into his definitions of freedom and necessity. ' A thing is free,' said Spinoza, ' when it exists by the
sole necessity of its nature, and is determined to action only by
itself.' ' Outward things cannot compel the gods,' said Seneca,
' but their own eternal will is a law to themselves.' ' God acts
by a free necessity,' said Spinoza ; and Seneca, to the same
effect, said, ' God is not hereby less free, or less powerful, for
he himself is his own necessity.'

We return to the same antinomy between what God is conceived as a person and God as impersonal. When Wesley said
that predestination made God the author of sin, Toplady
answered almost in the words of Spinoza, that the wicked
must be punished because they are wicked, just as men destroy
vipers because they are hurtful. ' Zeno, the founder of the
Stoics,' Toplady said ' one day thrashed his servant for pilfer-
ing. The fellow, knowing his master was a fatalist, thought
to bring himself off by alleging that he was destined to steal,
and therefore ought not to be beaten for it. The philosopher
answered : ' You are destined to steal, are you ? Then you are
destined to be thrashed for it.' ' Christ,' Spinoza said, ' was
goodly necessity, but he did not therefore cease to be good.
Judas was predestined to betray Jesus, but he was not therefore less Judas, or less culpable.' Predestination may be true ;
that God has no attributes like those of man may also be true ;
but the region of such predestination is beyond the reach of the
finite intellect of man. We must come back to what Bishop
Butler said : ' And, therefore, though it were admitted that
this opinion of necessity were speculatively true, yet, with
regard to practice, it is as if it were false, so far as our experience reaches ; that is, to the whole of our present life. For
the constitution of the present world, and the condition in
which we are placed, is as if we were free.'

Rational theologians, like Erigena, Spinoza, and Schleier-macher, who have been predestinarians, have believed in the final predestination of all men to eternal life. This is the only form of the doctrine satisfactory to reason, as it supposes the final triumph of good over evil.

RESURRECTION.

We think of resurrection as a miracle, a sudden work effected by the will of God. Some suppose that the body as it now is will be restored, that the identical particles will again be brought together. This is the impression given by the words of Scripture in many places. They that are in the dust of the earth shall awake. At the sound of the archangel's trumpet the dead in Christ shall rise. The sea shall give up its dead. This is the resurrection according to man's conception. It is the truth as set forth by images, the truth as man would think of it at that stage when he thinks of God as like himself. But the Scriptures give intimations of something deeper than the idea conveyed by the mere images. To know God is eternal life. Jesus told the sisters of Bethany that he was the resurrection and the life. While they were thinking of a last day resurrection, he spoke of those who believed in him as those who would never die. The bodily resurrection might apply to Lazarus and his return to this life, but the greater resurrection was something more than that, something which included, or perhaps superseded, the bodily resurrection. When St. Paul argued for the resurrection of the body, it was not the body as flesh, but as spirit. 'Thou fool,' he exclaimed, 'thou sowest not that body which shall be but bare grain, and God giveth it a body as it pleaseth him, and to every seed its own body.' The stalk of wheat is in reality the wheat seed which was sown. They are to appearance altogether different, but the substance of the seed has passed into the plant, and they are in an important sense the same. Such may be the identity and difference between the present body and the resurrection body. It is sown a natural body. It is raised a spiritual body. It is no more carnal. St. Jerome wished that the words in the creed might be the resurrection of the flesh, but St. Paul's arguments and illustrations put the flesh out of sight and rise

to a better resurrection.   Every idea of materialism is removed
by the words 'spiritual body.'   The material dies and is cast
into the ground, as the seed sown dies and decays, giving its
life a sacrifice to the new life.   But in the natural body there is
a seed which will grow up a spiritual body.   Reason tells us that
the same carnal or material body cannot rise again.   The substance of our bodies has changed several times.   It has constituted other bodies, and may yet constitute others for generations to come.   On the supposition of a carnal resurrection,
we might ask where shall the bones be, the particles of which
have formed the bones of many different persons?   What
Toland wrote in his epitaph was well said : 'He would rise from
the dead, but he would never again be the same Toland.'   We
may believe in the resurrection, but according to our idea of
person, it will not be a personal resurrection.

FINAL JUDGMENT.

In the book of Daniel it is said of the dead that some shall
rise to everlasting life and some to shame and everlasting
contempt.   This reads as if each on rising would know his
doom without the utterance of any words or the presence of
any judge.   But the final judgment is set forth in the New
Testament under the figures and with the pomp of an earthly
assize.   The Son of Man is to come in the clouds of heaven.
All nations are to be gathered before him.   He is to divide the
righteous from the wicked, as a shepherd divides the sheep
from the goats.   To the one he will say, ' Come, ye blessed ;'
to the other, ' Depart, ye cursed ;' and both will be equally
astonished to hear their sentence.   Similar to this is the
picture in the Revelation of St. John, where a great white
throne is set.   The Judge descends, and the dead are judged
out of the books according to what they have done.   Here God
is a person clothed like an earthly judge with the terrors of
judgment.   But other Scriptures speak as if sin produced its
results by an inevitable law, as certain and as unmerciful as
the laws of nature.   Whatsoever a man soweth, that shall
he also reap.   They that have sown to the flesh shall of the flesh
reap corruption.   They that have sown to the spirit shall reap
ife everlasting.   The good tree brings forth good fruit ; the

corrupt, evil fruit. The destiny of the good is life; of the evil, destruction. The kingdom of heaven is constituted by righteous men. Wisdom is a tree of life. There is an eternal order by which the wise are protected, and the unwise perish. There is no need of a fixed day for judgment nor of the sentence of the judge. It is already determined. Every action stereotypes its results. What a man does is done for ever. What he has written is written, and cannot be effaced. All this seems impersonal, yet both Scripture and reason seem to determine that it is God's mode of judgment, and a mode which corresponds to the higher conception of God.

It is here that we may come nearest to the solution of the question of eternal punishment. All that is said of it in Scripture is set forth under images taken from things earthly and temporal. The never-dying worm and the unquenchable fire are figures from Isaiah, who applies them in a temporal sense, referring probably to the valley of Hinnom. As heaven is portrayed as a golden city with all that man desires from the point of view of his earthly misery, so hell is pictured as the consummation of all which he dreads. But no ideas borrowed from things temporal can be construed literally when applied to things eternal. Time implies duration. Eternity is the opposite of that which is constituted by duration. Punishment may be in eternity, may be eternal, and yet not be never-ending. The temporal images decide nothing. They only tell how terrible the consequences of sin are and must be. This subject is not one for dogmatism. There may be a probation in the future, but we do not know what may be the extent of the inevitable consequences of sin. There is enough said to check presumption and to make the unrighteous tremble. But there is also ground for eternal hope, for faith in the final triumph of good over evil, for St. Paul's Pantheism that God may yet be all in all.

IMMORTALITY.

In the Bible the future life is represented as fulness of joy in the presence and with the open vision of God. He is sometimes represented as a person, a Father with his children, a King with his loyal subjects, or as a King among kings who reign with him. In the magnificent imagery of the Revelation of St. John, the Lamb that was slain or the glorified Jesus takes the place of the Eternal, who disappears as if no human thought was an adequate conception of him. The picture represents man as with God, but there is a deeper intimation that as God appears as man, so man appears as God. Schleiermacher connected our individuality with our imperfection. It was the darkness which obscured the unity of God and man. In the future life evil shall be removed and the blessed shall realise their immortality, not as individuals, but as they exist in God. Spinoza said that now we were modes of the Eternal. As he believed in immortality, it may be inferred that he thought men should exist in the future life as higher modes. St. John, taking a passing glance at the mystery, exclaimed, ' It doth not yet appear what we shall be.' The created may participate of the uncreated. As Christ, according to St. Athanasius, became man without losing his divinity, so man may become God without losing his humanity.

Conclusion.

Dean Mansel, in his famous Bampton Lectures, which were written to check all speculations concerning the Infinite, and to confine religious thought within the bounds of ecclesiastical dogmas, yet made the following remarkable confession: ' There is a sense in which we may not think of God as if he were man, as there is a sense in which we cannot help so thinking of him. When we read in the same narrative, and almost in two consecutive verses of Scripture—The strength of Israel will not lie nor repent, for he is not a man that he should repent ; and again, The Lord repented that he had made Saul king over Israel—we are imperfectly conscious of an appeal to two different representations involving opposite sides of the same truth ; we feel that there is a true foundation for the system which denies human attributes to God.' It is this denial which is the root of what is called Pantheism. It is the theology of reason, of reason it may be in its impotence, but still of such reason as man is gifted with in this present life. It is the goal of Rationalism, of Protestantism, and of Catholicism, because it is the goal of thought. There is no resting-place but by ceasing to think on reason, on God, and things that concern God. Individuals may stop at the symbol ; churches and sects may strive to make resting-places on the way by appealing to the authority of a church, to the letter of the Scriptures, or by try-ing to fix the limits of religious thought. But the reason of man, in its inevitable development and its divinely appointed love of freedom, breaks all such bonds and casts away all such cords. They are but the inventions of men which the human soul in its onward progress holds in derision. It knows that God is infinite, and only as the Infinite will it acknowledge him to be God.

What has generally been called Pantheism is but the effort of the human mind to know God as Being, infinite and absolute. It is ontological Theism, a necessary and an im-plied form of all rational Theism. It need not exclude the others. The argument from teleology gives God with some likeness to man, that from ontology God infinite. We cannot take the one without the other, whatever may be the diffi-culties of the reconciliation or the conclusions to which each leads us. The difficulties arise from the vastness of the subject ; but though we do not see further than we do see, that is no reason for shutting our eyes to what is manifest.

And is not this the reconciliation of the supposed contra-diction in Plato's theology ? Who was more decidedly Pan-theistic than Plato ? Is he not the great ancestor of all rational or Pantheistic theologians ? And yet who is clearer on teleology than Plato ? In the ' Timæus' God is a Creator distinct and separate from creation, and apparently, too, from the ideas, after which creation was modelled. From nature and its regulation according to laws, Plato derives his principal reasons for belief in the Divine existence, and from the con-stant mobility of nature he concludes the necessity of an originating, moving principle. Every doubt as to Plato's belief in a personal Deity who works in nature for special ends must be removed by the following passage from the ' Sophistes : '—

' *Guest of Elea.* But with respect to all living animals and plants which are produced in the earth from seeds and roots, together with such inanimate bodies as subsist on the earth, able to be liquified or not, can we say that, not existing pre-viously, they were subsequently produced by any other than some fabricating God; or making use of the opinion and the assertion of the many?

'*Theœtetus*. What is that?

'*Guest*. That nature generates these from some self-acting fortuitous cause and without a generating mind, or (is it) with reason and a Divine science originating from God?

'*Theœtetus*. I, perhaps through my age, am often changing my opinion to both sides. But, at present, looking to you and apprehending that you think those things are produced according to (the will of) a Deity, I think so too.

'*Guest*. It is well, Theætetus; and if we thought that you would be one of those who, at a future time, would think differently, we should now endeavour to make you acknowledge this by the force of reason, in conjunction with the persuasion of necessity. But, since I know your nature to be such, that without any arguments from us it will of itself arrive at that conclusion to which you say you are now drawn, I will leave the subject, for the time would be superfluous. But I will lay this down, that the things which are said to be made by nature are (made) by divine art, but the things which are composed from those of men, are produced from human (art); and that, according to this assertion, there are two kinds of the making art—one human and the other divine.'

Plato's teleology exposed him to the reproach of anthropomorphism as much as his ontology to the reproach of Pantheism. Plutarch says, 'Even Plato, that magnificent reasoner, when he says that God made the world in his own mould and pattern, savours of the rust and moss of antiquity. . . . . He represents the Divine architect as a miserable bricklayer, or a mason, toiling and sweating at the fabric and government of the world.'

But the elements which Plato inherited form Parmenides were never renounced. God was still 'the Being'—existence itself. He was without passions, incapable of repentance, anger, or hatred. He was best worshipped by pious feeling and upright conduct. Ceremonies, prayers, sacrifices were no honour to him. They did not secure his favour; they did not change God. Not only was God 'the Being,' but he was 'the Good'—absolute goodness. Plato's modern disciples have been perplexed by the identification of God with 'the Good,' and have tried to explain that this was not his meaning; but all his ancient followers, Platonists and Neo-Platonists alike, so understood him. 'This opinion,' says Dr. Thompson, 'is evidently difficult to reconcile with the personality of the divine Essence, and with those passages in the "Timæus" and elsewhere, in which that personality seems to be clearly asserted. Are we to suppose that such passages are to be taken in an exclusively mythical sense, and that we are to look to the "Republic" and "Philebus" as conveying Plato's interior meaning?' But what need for all this criticism and these suppositions, if the Theism of ontology is a necessary part of all rational Theism? That which reconciles Plato with himself, reconciles Schleiermacher, the modern Plato, with himself. His short-sighted critics talk piteously of the Pantheism of his youth, and express rejoicing that in his later years he saw more distinctly the personality of God. But that great spirit who had a genius for theology, such as is rarely to be found in the course of ages, saw clearly that the theology of the 'Discourses on Religion,' was the same as the theology of his 'Sermons.'

Man is made in God's image, and the qualities of love, goodness, justice, with many others which are in man, are also in some way in God. Every philosophy and every religion has returned to acknowledge this, however much they may have denied it. What but this is the meaning of all Polytheism, and the incarnations of the gods? In all religions there is a human deity corresponding to the wisdom of God; a Brahmā, a Buddha incarnate, a Hermes, a Honover or a Logos. In the Hebrew religion, though God was the impersonal 'I Am,' he was yet a personal God, appearing to the patriarchs in a human form, leading forth the people out of Egypt, abiding in the cloud by day and the pillar of fire by night. All religions, even those which have speculated most on the Infinite, have yet conceived God under a human form and as possessing human attributes. Nor is this wonderful when we consider that man is the highest being of whom the mind can form a distinct image. He is to himself the representative of all that is great; the examplar of mind; the highest manifestation of spirit. Provisional, the conception of God as personal may be, corrected by the other it must be, yet it is necessary to a true knowledge of God. 'The pious soul craves a personal Deity.' We crave to worship man.

It is equally true that God is infinite and that he can be represented under the form of the finite. So has he been represented in him who is the visible 'image of the invisible God'—him we can worship without idolatry, for in him the Divine was clothed in human form. Man is made in the likeness of God, and the converse is fully true that God is in the likeness of man. He wills and designs. He has passions—anger, jealousy, love, and hatred—but he has them without the limitations and infirmities which they imply when predicated of men. So long as we hold fast by this we are free to indulge in the widest and fullest speculations concerning the being of the infinite God. He invites us to such inquiries. They are natural to the human mind. They are connected with the highest theologies and the deepest and most devout feelings of men. We could not believe in a Logos, did we not believe in a 'Being,' or a 'Bythos' beyond ; or to use more Christian language, we could not believe in Christ who is the Son, but for our belief in God who is the Father. We could not believe in a personal God who creates the world and rules it as a king or judge, but for our belief in a Spirit which is everywhere, and yet nowhere. The argument from final causes proves the existence of a world-maker. It demonstrates that there is a mind working in the world. It is a clear and satisfactory proof to the ordinary understanding of man, but it proves nothing more than a finite God. We must supplement it by the argument from ontology. The one gives a mind, the other gives being, the two together give the infinite God, impersonal and yet personal—to be called by all names, or, if that is irreverent, to be called by no name. Our thoughts concerning God reach a stage where silence is the sublimest speech. Like the little child that at even-time lifts its eyes to the great blue vault of heaven, and says of the ten thousand stars that are twinkling there, these are God's eyes, he is the silent witness and watcher of my deeds ; so must we say of the great world that God is everywhere, in all things he sees us, in all things we may see him. The profoundest philosopher, the man most deeply learned in science, returns to the creed of the world's infancy, and hears in the roar of the thunder that voice which is full of majesty, sees in the lightning the flashes of the divine presence, and in all the operations of nature's manifold laws the working of an ever-present God.

Pantheism is a question of the right of reason to be heard in matters pertaining to religion. We have seen the conclusion to which reason inevitably comes. Is it anything so fearful that to avoid it we must renounce reason ? To trace the history of theology from its first dawning among the Greeks, down to the present day, and to describe the whole as opposed to Christianity, is surely to place Christianity in antagonism with the Catholic reason of mankind. To describe all the greatest minds that have been engaged in the study of theology as Pantheists, and to mean by this term, men irreligious, un-Christian, or atheistic, is surely to say that religion, Christianity, and Theism have but little agreement with reason. Are we seriously prepared to make this admission ? Not only to give up Plato and Plotinus, Origen and Erigena, Spinoza and Schleiermacher, but St. Paul and St. John, St. Augustine and St. Athanasius ? It may be said that the philosophy of the Greeks and Alexandrians corrupted the simplicity of the Gospel of Christ, and that an apostle says ' the world by wisdom knew not God.' It might be enough to answer with St. Augustine that by wisdom St. Paul here means the philosophy of such as Democritus and Epicurus, not that of Socrates and Plato. The first teachers of Christianity—those who had their commission immediately from Christ—appealed to the truths of natural religion, and incorporated as their own all that was true in the teaching of the heathen world. St. Paul quoted and sanctioned the Pantheism of one of the most Pantheistic of the Greek poets. He did not stop to explain in what sense we are the offspring of God. He took the words of Aratus as they stood. He did not explain the Monotheism of the Greeks as a spurious Theism, nor did he say that the God whom the Greeks worshipped was not the same God whom Jesus revealed. He quoted the words of the philosophical poet without qualification or explanation. He made use of heathen wisdom to refute heathen folly. Christianity, indeed, clothed itself in Greek forms of speech. It adopted, corrected, or modified the great truths of natural religion that were known to the heathen world. Even the Logos, which in St. John is the designation of the Son of God, previous to his incarnation, was in familiar use in the theology of the schools. Throughout St. Paul's Epistles, and the Epistle to the Hebrews, close parallelisms may be traced both in thought and language, between them and the writings of the Alexandrian philosophers, and especially those of Philo, the Jew, who preceded the apostles in translating Hebrew thoughts into Greek forms. ' Alexandrianism,' says Professor Jowett, ' was not the seed of the great tree which was to cover the earth, but the soil in which it grew up. It was not the body of which Christianity was the soul, but the vesture in which it folded itself—the old bottle into which the new wine was poured. When with stammering lips and other tongues the first preachers passed beyond the borders of the sacred land, Alexandrianism was the language which they spoke, not the faith they taught. It was mystical and dialectical, not moral and spiritual; for the few, not for the many ; for the Jewish therapeute, not for all mankind. It spoke of a Holy Ghost, of a Word, of a divine man, of a first and second Adam, of the faith of Abraham, of bread which came down from heaven; but knew nothing of the God who had made of one blood all nations of the earth, of the victory over sin and death, of the cross of Christ. It was a picture, a shadow, a surface, a cloud above, catching the rising light ere he appeared.' Christianity recommended itself by its reasonableness to the philosophers of Alexandria. These passed into the Church and became its first great teachers after the days of the Apostles. Their deep longing for yet higher and clearer truth was satisfied in Christianity. The Gospel became to them the true Gnosis, the knowledge which Plato had taught men to see after as the highest good.

The province of reason is twofold—to inquire and to formulate. Inquiry is necessary for its self-protection, and formulating is its legitimate occupation. At the present time much is said against scepticism on the one hand, and dogmatism on the other, but it is by reason itself that both dogmatism and scepticism are to be corrected. The human mind must have some evidence or satisfaction that what is to be believed is true. It is the spirit of doubt, not the duty of inquiry, which constitutes scepticism. On the other hand it is not making dogmas, that is, formulating beliefs, but resistance to inquiry which constitutes dogmatism. Reason is free, but not free to bind itself in fetters. We must receive light as we can receive it, and under the conditions on which it can be received. If we have not the abundance for which the mind craves, we must not therefore invent a theory of truth which will check reason in its free exercise. The relations of reason and revelation are reflex. As reason becomes more perfect, revelation becomes clearer, and as revelation developes, reason advances to perfection. Bishop Butler spoke of the Scriptures as a field of discovery corresponding to the natural world. The whole scheme of Christianity, he said, ' was not yet understood, and if ever it should be, the means would be the same as in natural knowledge.' Under this aspect, revealed truth will be further revealed by the development of man's reason and his progress in knowledge. The speculations which have been called Pantheistic are legitimate exercises of the human intellect. They are efforts to think and speak of God under the aspects in which God has appeared to different minds, or has been viewed under different relations. To call God Being, Non-Being, Substance, Becoming, Nature, the Absolute, the infinite I, the Thought of the Universe, or the ' not ourselves ' which works for righteousness, is to speak of God with the imperfections of human thought and language, and yet such names are as legitimate as Creator, vast Designer, eternal Geometrician, or to those who can receive it, even as Lord, supreme Ruler or Father of men. ' The most precious truth,' said Richard Baxter, ' not apprehended doth seem to be but error and fantastic novelty.' But for all this seeming, it is not less ' precious truth.' Reason has had many wanderings and many guesses. She has often been right when she seemed to be wrong, and wrong when she seemed to be right. The Catholic Baronius wished to expel ' the Hagar ' with ' her profane Ishmael ; ' but, with all her conjectures, her dreams, her air castles, that is true which was said by One wiser than Baronius even by him who was the incarnation of the divine reason—wisdom is justified of all her children.